OPERATION IRAQI FREEDOM

OPERATION IRAQI FREEDOM

WHAT WENT RIGHT, WHAT WENT WRONG, AND WHY

Walter J. Boyne,
Colonel, USAF (Ret.)

Foreword by General Ronald R. Fogleman,
USAF (Ret.), former Chief of Staff, USAF

A Tom Doherty Associates Book
New York

This book is dedicated with heartfelt gratitude to the men and women of the military services of the United States and its coalition partners.

CONTENTS

ACKNOWLEDGMENTS

It would have been impossible to do this book without the assistance of many people, all of whom were already overloaded with their own work, but who responded readily and completely to an urgent request not just for help, but for "swiftly responding help."

No words can convey the gratitude I feel for the monumental assistance provided by Major General Donald Shepperd, USAF (Ret.). Don is the former commander of the Air National Guard and is now widely recognized as perhaps the best military commentator on television today, working primarily with CNN. Don was able to put me into immediate contact with a host of truly knowledgeable people who provided the book an authenticity and an authority that would not have been possible otherwise. He also took time from his insanely busy schedule to offer good advice on subject matter, format, and presentation.

It was gratifying in the extreme to discover, through Don's intercession, that I was going to be able to interview so many top military and civilian figures. They included the present Chief of Staff of the United States Air Force, General John P. Jumper, and four former Chiefs of Staff, including Generals Merrill A. McPeak, Ronald R. Fogleman, Michael E. Ryan, and Larry D. Welch. General Michael Loh, once the Acting Chief of Staff and first commander of Air Combat Command, was kind enough not only to grant an extensive interview, but to review the manuscript. General Fogleman broke into his busy schedule to write the excellent foreword. Retired Lieutenant General Bernard Trainor, USMC, an outstanding military analyst, provided an excellent interview as did Vice Admiral Timothy Keating, who was Commander, Coalition Forces Maritime Component in OIF. USAF General Charles "Chuck" Horner, who had been Combined Forces Air Component Commander in Operation Desert Storm, supplemented his interview with a series of first-rate, thought-provoking papers.

Acknowledgments

Major General David Deptula, USAF, also added to his interview with some important papers, as did retired Colonel John Warden. Both officers are quoted extensively in this book. Rear Admiral Stephen Baker, Major General Perry Smith (also a distinguished military commentator), and Brigadier General David Grange, an expert on special forces, were most helpful, as was Colonel Timothy Hyde of the Air Force's famed "Checkmate" office. Lieutenant General Paul V. Hester, commander of Air Force Special Operations Command, gave a lengthy interview and put me in touch with Colonels Frank Kisner, Thomas "Randy" O'Boyle, and Bryan Greenshields, who conducted SOF action on the Al Faw peninsula. Colonel Darrel Whitcomb provided insight on Combat Search and Rescue operations. A fine scholar, Joseph Copalman gave insight into F-18 procurement. Steve Llanso prepared the gargantuan appendix 1, which lists all major coalition weapon systems. Major General James Dubik and Lieutenant Colonel John Koenig helped me with insight into Army operations.

There were, in addition, several civilians, many of them retired military personnel, who provided invaluable insight, and they include, in alphabetical order (it would be impossible to rank them by the importance of what they gave me, as all of it was so valuable): Warren Bodie, Bruce Callandar, Ralph R. Echtinaw, Fred Frostic, Chris Gartner, William Blair Haworth, Frank Hoffman, Jo Jones, Dennis Jenkins, Tom Lapuzza, Robert Leonhard, Alvin Lloyd, Terri Maddox, Brent Marler, Richard C. May, Ron Maynard, Wally Meeks, George Mellinger, Robert Mullins, Lon Nordeen, Brian Perry, Nick Schirripa, Robert Wachter, George Watson, and Robert Work. Dr. Shannon Brown responded swiftly with a whole series of valuable bibliographies and other leads. The incredibly knowledgeable David Isby reviewed the work, made excellent comments, and bore up well under my nomenclature problems.

A whole host of people facilitated the interviews, making them happen despite the fact that there was clearly no time in the principals' busy schedules for them. They include my old friend Joe Arena, Jonna Beveridge, Ali Donahue, Debby Germuns, Major Karen Finn, Judy Herrman, Lieutenant Colonel Terrance "Doc" Holliday, Captain Thomas Knowles, and Tonya Pitrof.

In preparing the manuscript, I had the always welcome, most perceptive, and extremely thorough advice of Philip and Mary Handleman, whose quick turnaround of chapters was remarkable. At Tekno-Books, Marty Greenberg, John Helfers, and Larry Segriff were, as always, very helpful. At Forge, my editor, Bob Gleason, was encouraging and provided great suggestions; he was assisted by Brian Callaghan. David Moench, Eric Raab, and Joe Rinaldi were, again, as always, most helpful. Guy Aceto of *Air Force Magazine* was generous with photos. My two daughters, Molly Boyne and Peggy Coleman, were of great assistance.

I am sure that there were many others who helped me in the mad rush to research, write, and publish, and if I have forgotten your name momentarily, please forgive me, for I do appreciate all that you did.

FOREWORD

by
General Ronald R. Fogleman, USAF (Ret.),
former Chief of Staff, USAF

In this book, Walter Boyne uses narrative, timeline, and theme to tell an amazing chapter in the history of warfare, Operation Iraqi Freedom. Based on the information available to the public and to the insight of operation leaders, he has done an excellent job of researching and documenting the story and distilling the lessons learned from this operation. He was able to do this as a result of his credibility and standing as a writer of contemporary history. This credibility gave him access to the key players in a timely manner. A quick check of the footnotes will indicate the broad spectrum of informed people who provided the author with their insight into the events in Iraq. Further, the manuscript was reviewed by a number of respected authorities to insure that it was as factual as possible.

Some might argue that it is too early to produce a definitive and accurate work on a military campaign that concluded less than ninety days ago. I would argue the opposite. The best time to capture the unvarnished truth is to do it as close to the event as possible. That certainly proved to be true for the official account of the 1991 war, Operation Desert Shield/Desert Storm. In the late spring of 1991, the Department of Defense published a preliminary account of the war. Based on my knowledge of the facts and conversations with the leadership of the coalition, this preliminary history was more factual and accurate than the final official history produced months later. Unfortunately, the official history was influenced by those who recognized that allowing the unvarnished truth to become part of the record might threaten the U.S. military establishment in ways that would lead to real change in resource allocation and thinking about how future wars should be fought.

Using the correct resources—and checking the facts—was important not only for covering the swiftly unfolding events in Iraq, but to establish the truth about many of the weapon systems that were employed there. One of the striking features of Operation Iraqi Freedom was that forty-year-old weapon systems, such as the B-52 and the KC-135, could be employed in combat with the newest weapons in the American arsenal. Perhaps even more surprising—at least to an airman such as myself—was that "legacy" equipment in the Army, Navy, and Marine Corps were also employed with such great effect in concert with brand-new equipment.

This melding of resources is a tribute to both the armed services and to the defense industry that spawns the technological advances to meet military need. And just as the services are demonstrating "jointness" in the exercise of combat operations, so are the defense contractors teaming together to provide modern weapons. And the parallel extends beyond jointness to "combined" operations for both the military and industry. The U.S. services (Army, Navy, Marines, Air Force, and Coast Guard) worked hand in glove with forces from the United Kingdom, Australia, and Poland. In a similar way, industrial concerns now operate on an international basis, as demonstrated by the Litening II targeting pod, which was developed by the Rafael Corporation's Missiles Division in Haifa, Israel, and Northrop Grumman Corporation's Electronics and Systems Integration Division of Hawthorne, California.

Operation Iraqi Freedom represents a validation for those who have long pushed for a true transformation in the thinking and fielding of U.S. military forces. To be sure not everything was perfectly planned and executed, but in the main, this campaign gave the world a glimpse of what is possible when a commander plans and executes an operation that combines information dominance with integrated precision strike and maneuver. OIF also exposed those whose thinking is frozen in the past. The nature of warfare has been transformed forever by the advances in intelligence, surveillance, reconnaissance, and precision location and strike capabilities. The interdependence of these capabilities enabled by a command and control system that gives all the players the required operational picture was demonstrated for all to see.

Some will try to make Operation Iraqi Freedom a testament for airpower, armor, special operations, space warfare, and any number of parochial advocacies. Walt Boyne does not fall into that trap. He tells the story in such a way that the reader can see the contributions of all the elements of the coalition. More important, this book leads the reader to the conclusion that it was the raising of the interoperability and interdependence of the forces to previously unheard of levels that resulted in a swift and total victory over a well-entrenched enemy determined to defend its homeland. However, that defense was not possible because of the new American way of war unveiled in OIF.

Perhaps the most distinctive element of Operation Iraqi Freedom was the difference in the leadership and personnel of the opposing forces. Iraq was completely dominated by Saddam Hussein, who dictated strategy and tactics. Hussein refused to delegate meaningful authority to his military staff, in part because he feared that doing so might provide someone with the strength to act against him. His methods deprived the Iraqi military of all initiative, all desire to innovate, and in the greatest measure, any wish to resist the overwhelming might of the coalition.

In contrast, once he had set the defining goals for the war, President George W. Bush delegated both authority and responsibility to his military commanders. They, in turn, delegated both authority and responsibility down to the lowest possible levels of command. The result was a fighting force with enormous initiative, ready and willing to innovate, and totally confident in its own prowess.

The results speak for themselves. The combat in Operation Iraqi Freedom was sudden, sharp, and successful. There still remains the inevitable settling of postwar problems, establishing a democracy in Iraq, and helping the Iraqi people realize their own best interest lies in rebuilding the economy.

The United States and its coalition partners can be proud of their work in Operation Iraqi Freedom, and this book offers the first best look at how well they did their job.

PREFACE

Nothing could be riskier for a historian than to begin writing a history of a war on the day it begins, rather than many years after it ends. Yet, when asked to do so, I gladly agreed, because it was evident that this was to be a new and exciting type of warfare, one fought with the latest weapons and the finest people against a truly evil regime.

One of the difficulties in writing about a war as it is waged is that things change. Stories that were incontrovertibly true at one time are later altered or perhaps even disproved as new information is acquired. A case in point: In the first chapter I address the capture of Private Jessica Lynch, based on the information known at the time. Now, six weeks later, I am all too aware of the growing controversy. The same danger applies to every element of the narrative.

Yet I accept this difficulty readily, for the vast bulk of the material herein is absolutely accurate and will remain so, as it is based upon impeccable sources. As my acknowledgments section (and the endnotes) will reveal, I was assisted by the very top civilian and military thinkers in the nation, who generously gave of their time and ideas to help me determine the essential questions that the book asks: What Went Right, What Went Wrong, and Why, and What Were the Lessons Learned?

From the very first, I intended to prove a concept I have espoused, i.e., that the military planners in the United States had, in a time of declining budgets, done a remarkable job in predicting the best way to fight a future war. Further, after predicting the best way, they made literally millions of decisions about budgetary requirements, weapons procurement, force structure, maintenance considerations, logistics, research and development, personnel requirements, and all of the other elements that make up a fielded force. Their decisions, which reach back more than twenty years, provided the incredible equipment that enabled the coalition forces to have complete air and information dominance. Possession of these two factors made it possible to fight an entirely new kind of warfare, one in which ground forces were willing to be totally dependent upon tactical aircraft and consequently were able to move without taking heavy artillery with them. This enabled them to move with a speed and agility that completely confused and disoriented the opposing forces.

Former USAF Chief of Staff General Larry D. Welch has accurately described this technique as "distributed operations," in which forces do not sweep out to seize and occupy every bit of enemy territory. Instead, working with reliable networks, the distributed units form "lily pads" that control critical areas and key intersections, and are willingly dependent upon outside sources for knowledge of what is going on, fire support, reinforcement, and logistics.[1]

Such distributed operations would have been impossible if the leaders of this operation, from President George W. Bush down to squad level, had not been willing to conduct seamless joint (Army/Navy/Marine/Air Force) and combined (U.S./coalition forces) operations. Doing so permitted airpower to be truly integrated for the first time in history.

I wished also to emphasize a second point, and that is the incredibly high caliber of U.S. and coalition forces personnel, for our allies in this venture sent their very best people. The military has rarely been treated kindly by film, television, or other fictional or documentary treatments. Beetle Bailey's General Halftrack and Marlon Brando's Colonel Kurtz in *Apocalypse Now* are the traditional starting points for these treatments, and nothing could be further from the truth. The modern U.S. military, an all-volunteer force, has more capable people at every level—enlisted, noncommissioned, and officer—than any business counterpart you can name. This may be difficult to accept at face value, but the proof may be found in the brilliant execution of Operation Iraqi Freedom and in the opinions of the embedded reporters who witnessed the action firsthand.

Operation Iraqi Freedom was unusual in the way that innovation was exploited at every level and in the manner in which traditional doctrine was jettisoned to be replaced by new concepts such as focused logistics, distributed operations, and integrated capabilities. It will be the task of the next generation of war fighters to incorporate these manifold new concepts into new doctrine for the future—and to be equally willing to jettison that doctrine when further innovative efforts are known to be better.

July 2, 2003

OPERATION IRAQI FREEDOM

1

A Contrast in Values

The conduct of the coalition forces led by the United States in the brilliant campaign against Saddam Hussein's regime in Iraq has been unique in history. Never before has there been a war waged in which the difference between an evil regime and its captive population was so clearly defined and in which hostile actions were aimed solely at the regime. Never before has an enemy been assaulted with such precise force and firepower. Iraq was buried in a technological avalanche that decapitated leadership, disrupted communications, and devastated forces in the field yet permitted civil life to go on relatively untrammeled.

Coalition forces moved swiftly while taking care to avoid collateral damage, which confused not only the enemy but also much of the media reporting the conflict. Within days of the war's start there was intense clamoring about Operation Iraqi Freedom (OIF) being "bogged down" and of the certain prospect of Baghdad turning into a Stalingrad-like graveyard for coalition forces. Experts of gloom and doom cited dozens of possibilities about what could go wrong, but even as they speculated, the fingers of coalition forces closed around the enemy's windpipe.*

The reportorial situation simmered in the ironic contrast between the often-carping questions at the daily CENTCOM (central command) briefings at the in-theater headquarters and the obvious front-line excitement reflected by the embedded reporters who saw firsthand how well the war was executed.

The luster of the campaign is all the more striking as a portent for the future. For the past decade, concerns have been raised about "asymmetric

---

* The author humbly admits to being one of the minor "armchair" experts, having called early on for less concern about collateral damage and more concern about troop safety. As events developed, new procedures reduced the risk, but I still adhere to the concept of "our troops first."

21

warfare" being waged against the United States, offsetting the immense advantages in technology, mobility, and firepower it possesses. The coalition forces reversed the process in Iraq, using its advantages to fight an asymmetric war against a continually confused, out-maneuvered, and out-anticipated opponent. Some airpower theorists have searched since World War I for the means to strategically paralyze the enemy. The search was derailed by the advent of nuclear weapons so terrible in their destructive capacity that they became means of deterrence rather than of warfare. But today's technology has advanced to the point that the concepts of later theorists, including John Warden and David A. Deptula, can work to a degree beyond the dreams of Giulio Douhet, Billy Mitchell, and even Curtis E. LeMay. It can be said that ideas similar to those of another airpower theorist, John Boyd, worked equally well in land warfare.*

WHAT THIS BOOK IS AND WHAT IT ISN'T.

Operation Iraqi Freedom: What Went Right, What Went Wrong, and Why is an analysis of the military actions taken by the armed forces of the United States and its coalition allies against the regime of Saddam Hussein. Its purpose is to examine the efficacy of U.S. and coalition strategy, tactics, operational methods, weapon systems, and personnel during the period of armed conflict. It is not intended to investigate stability and control (the so-called peacekeeping) operations, except in passing. It will not cover counterinsurgency actions, nor will it speculate on the prospects of extended guerrilla warfare.

In terms of time, this book, *Operation Iraqi Freedom*, is confined to the period from March 19, 2003, through May 1, 2003. It is primarily focused on the actions that took place up through, and shortly after, April 9, 2003.

The problems of peacekeeping and counterinsurgency will be extended and lend themselves to an entirely new operational name—and an entirely new book.

Perhaps even more important than the actual combat was the black-and-white contrast of the ethics and the humanity with which the war

---

* Many dispute the originality and the pertinence of John Boyd's contributions, which will be discussed later. The dispute is really immaterial, for the theory of conflict attributed by many to him was employed in the Iraqi war and will be discussed in depth.

was waged. While coalition air strikes and artillery fire conscientiously sought to avoid damage to civilian institutions, particularly schools, mosques, and cultural centers, the hard-core members of Saddam's regime used those very places to store ammunition, act as communication centers, and occasionally serve as impromptu fortresses. When hostile gunfire erupted from these locales, the withering return fire of coalition forces was featured prominently on Al-Jazeera television and in other Arab media.

The most instructive demonstration of the difference between the two opposing forces' view of human life and the worth of an individual soldier came two weeks into the war.

On April 1/2, 2003, the United States put together a joint (combined services) special operations team on a daring rescue mission that went into enemy-held territory to rescue a badly injured American soldier, young Private First Class (PFC) Jessica Lynch. The twenty-year-old Army supply clerk was one of twelve members of the 507th Ordnance Maintenance Company who were captured on March 23 after making a wrong turn in An Nasiriyah. Ambushed, the unit fought fiercely but was captured by overwhelming forces.

Lynch was placed in an Iraqi hospital.* A sympathetic Iraqi informed coalition forces of her situation, even as a Marine unit moving up for an attack on Tikrit was made aware of the proximity of American prisoners of war being held by the enemy.

The United States used a full panoply of weapons and techniques for the rescue, including the use of an unmanned Predator aircraft, patrolling over her location, viewing the activities in real time.† But this was only the beginning; an Air Force Special Operations Lockheed Martin AC-130 gunship, perhaps the most formidable close-air support (CAS) weapon in existence, was on hand for fire support. Beneath the AC-130 was a flight of USMC Bell AH-1W Cobras, in concert with Army Special Operations Boeing MH-6 Little Bird helicopters. Backing up this already-formidable combination were two Marine AV-8B Harriers. The action began when the two vertical takeoff fighters from VMA-214 created a diversion by striking a Ba'ath Party headquarters. Two other Harriers then took up position to provide additional firepower, staying in the area for almost forty minutes and not departing until after the rescue party

---

* At the time this is written, there are rumors that the Lynch story had been given some propaganda spin. If so it is regrettable but irrelevant; for the fact is that the operation took place at great cost and risk to the participants. Brigadier General Howard Bromberg, commander of the 32d Army Air and Missile Defense Command at Fort Bliss, Texas, has ordered a probe of the entire situation, described as "extremely complex."
† The specifications of all weapon systems may be found in appendix 1.

had left. The Harriers were equipped with the Northrop Grumman-Rafael (Israeli) Litening-II targeting pods, one of which was an advanced model with a video downlink to provide real-time imagery. Both carried Laser Guided Bombs (LGBs).

The Harriers worked in concert with a Lockheed Martin EP-3 Orion aircraft that was monitoring Iraqi communications. Ten Marine helicopters, five Sikorsky CH-53E Super Stallions, and five Boeing CH-46 Sea Knights landed near the hospital to deliver the Kevlar-clad rescue force.[1]

PFC Lynch was rescued by the integrated team of special operation forces; which, in the heat of battle, behind enemy lines, and against the press of time, exhumed and brought out the bodies of nine American soldiers.

In a parallel development, Marines encountered seven missing prisoners of war walking near the biblical town of Samarra. The seven were flown by helicopter to an airfield in southern Iraq, transferred to a C-130 transport, and taken to Kuwait for further medical evaluation and treatment.

The national jubilation when PFC Lynch was brought home was soon matched by a similar outpouring of joy when five other members of her unit and two Apache attack helicopter crew members were returned to freedom on April 14.*

In sharp and bitter contrast, on April 3 the Iraqi military forced a pregnant and obviously unwilling woman to undertake a suicide bombing mission against a coalition-manned checkpoint about seven kilometers from the Haditha Dam. The dam is northwest of Baghdad and about fifty kilometers from the Syrian border. Screaming hysterically with fear, knowing that she and her baby were doomed, the woman stumbled out of a civilian vehicle in a desperate attempt to escape to the sympathetic coalition troops moving forward to help her. The Iraqis detonated the car bomb, killing her, her unborn child, the driver of the car, and three coalition soldiers. Two other coalition soldiers were wounded. Only a week previously, another suicide bomber in a car killed four American soldiers at a checkpoint in An Najaf.

This ghastly sacrifice of a woman and her unborn baby occurred even as Saddam Hussein's forces, including the special Elite Republican Guard, the Fedayeen Saddam, and the supposedly effective regular Republican

---

* The five soldiers from the 507th are Sergeant James J. Riley, 31, of Pennsauken, New Jersey; Specialist Shoshana N. Johnson, 30, of El Paso, Texas; Specialist Edgar A. Hernandez, 21, of Mission, Texas; Specialist Joseph N. Hudson, 23, of Alamogordo, New Mexico; and PFC Patrick W. Miller, 23, of Walter, Kansas. The two Apache pilots, Chief Warrant Officers David S. Williams and Ronald D. Young, are members of the 1st Battalion, 227th Aviation, at Fort Hood, Texas. The pilots had been captured near Karbala on March 23.

Guard, disappeared from the battlefield, retreating from the savage pounding by coalition airpower. Rarely in the history of warfare has an enemy used more cowardly, unwarlike tactics than those of the Iraqi armed forces, who increased their threats of homicide bombings even as they cast off their uniforms and scurried from the battlefield.

The contrast in behavior was accentuated in the respective ways that prisoners of war were treated—humanely and in accordance with the Geneva Convention by the United States and coalition partners and inhumanely and in violation of that convention by the Iraqis.

Saddam Hussein's colossal disregard for the well-being of his people was expressed in his disastrous planning. Seldom has an enemy force been so badly led as Iraq's, and never has an enemy government been so obviously willing to sacrifice its civilian population, for not even Adolf Hitler called upon Germany's women and children to march as hostages in front of his troops. As will be seen in the later day-by-day description of the conflict, the dispositions and the decisions made by Saddam Hussein ran counter to all military logic and played directly into the hands of the coalition forces.

The banality of Saddam's orders can only be understood in the light of his complete misreading of the United States and its leadership. He held a mythic vision that he could wage a traditional war of attrition, inflicting unacceptably heavy casualties on the U.S. and coalition forces. He believed that American popular opinion would revert back three decades to the era of the Vietnam War and that an outraged public would demand an end to the conflict. Saddam expected to survive as he had done after the war with Iran and again after his 1991 debacle in Kuwait. He apparently was realist enough not to expect military victory but counted on his backers—a majority of the Arab world and, somewhat less officially, France, Germany, and Russia—to help him secure a second negotiated peace from a suddenly war-weary United States.

It was an intoxicating perspective. In his own mind (and in the minds of many Arabs) he had won the 1991 Gulf War merely by surviving it. Surviving again would be another victory and he would have thus "won" two wars against the Americans. Doing so would raise his standing in the Muslim world to the level of his Tikrit hometown hero, Saladin, who defeated the Christian Crusaders and captured Jerusalem in 1187. It was a policy of unimaginable hubris, possible only for a murderous dictator whose followers never dared give him advice contrary to his whims. To Saddam, the willing sacrifice of the lives of thousands of his followers was a mere bagatelle for his opportunity to gain the highest place in Muslim mythology.

The following chapters will demonstrate the depth and degree to which Saddam was out-thought as much as he was out-fought. Many of the weapon systems used by the coalition forces were excoriated as "billion-dollar blunders" by opponents, from the earliest talk of their existence to their deployment and beyond. Some, such as the Northrop Grumman B-2A Spirit, were derided as too expensive, unworkable, and prone to failure. Others, such as the Predator, were considered totally impractical and vulnerable to air defenses, human error, and weather during wartime conditions. A few (e.g., the Global Hawk) were forced upon the military against its wishes but were proven in combat. Almost every weapon system deployed in the war, from the venerable Bradley Fighting Vehicle through the Tomahawk cruise missiles and the Joint Direct Attack Munition (JDAM) had vehement detractors. Fortunately, almost all of the weapon systems performed superbly in action. (There were exceptions, and they will be noted.)

The proper functioning of these weapon systems into an integrated war-making capability was important to the coalition leaders. Failure to perform as required would have been intolerable, for the United States, under the leadership of President George W. Bush's choice for Secretary of defense, Donald H. Rumsfeld, and his deputy, Paul Wolfowitz, was demonstrating a true Revolution in Military Affairs (RMA). RMAs are often talked about but rarely seen; in the case of Operation Iraqi Freedom, the entire world watched, first in confusion, then in disbelief, as the advancing coalition forces secured an impressive victory in a matter of days.

What was less obvious and will be covered in some depth later is the fact that there was not only an RMA but also an RDA—a Revolution in Diplomatic Affairs. The swift, sure actions of the coalition forces have swept the cards off all the diplomatic tables in the world, and for the foreseeable future the United States will not only select the diplomatic game to be played but also deal the cards. To implement this RDA will require a transformation of the Department of State on the scale and to the radical degree that the Department of Defense is starting to be transformed.

This new high tide of military proficiency was demonstrated on a far greater scale than anyone except those in the tightest inner circle of planners could imagine and was of a degree completely unanticipated by Saddam, the United Nations, or anyone else.

The standard truism that "the next war is always fought like the last one" was totally disproved in the brilliant display of American transformational strategy and tactics that disregarded the past even as they painted bold new strokes for the future. These radically new methods, only superficially similar to those employed in the 1991 Gulf War, and far more sophisticated and daring, were implicitly riskier from a political viewpoint than a military one.

The new methods were less militarily risky because the revolutionary techniques had been tested in Kosovo and Afghanistan and there was tremendous confidence in the Pentagon, particularly in the Checkmate* planning office. A less confident set of leaders might have experimented on a smaller scale to validate them. The new methods were much more politically risky because if they didn't work, the effect on the war on terror, on international world opinion—and on the chances of President Bush's reelection—would have been disastrous.

The gamble (and neither Bush nor Rumsfield would have characterized the operation as such) to use the available array of modern weapon systems in the revolutionary manner in which they were employed paid off handsomely and clearly charts the future of military operations. Another factor illustrating the imagination of the Bush team was that while they learned from the lessons of the 1991 Gulf War, they elected not to mimic the highly successful strategy used there.

The 1991 Gulf War came about abruptly when, desiring to recoup the billions he had spent in the Iraq/Iran war, Saddam seized the rich oil reserves of Kuwait by overrunning that small emirate in August 1990.

At that moment, the Iraqi dictator, Hussein, possessed the sixth-largest air force and the fourth-largest army in the world, both well seasoned in the bitter eight-year war against Iran. His army was equipped with 5,530 main battle tanks, 7,500 armored vehicles, 3,500 pieces of artillery, and 1,800 surface-to-surface missiles, including both static and mobile ballistic missiles.† His air-defense system was formidable, with as many as 17,000 surface-to-air missiles (SAMs) and about 10,000 antiaircraft guns connected with redundant links to a vast radar network. His 1,000-plane air force included 550 combat aircraft, including MiG-29s, one of the finest fighters in the world.[2]

---

* Checkmate is the unofficial name for AF/OOOX, a USAF special planning department that will be covered in detail in chapter 3. It distinguished itself in the Gulf War.

† The Scud was a primitive missile, reminiscent of the German V-2, designed and built in the Soviet Union and widely exported. About 33 feet long and 33.5 inches in diameter, the 14,000-pound Scud had a range of about 175 miles and carried a warhead of 2,205 pounds. Inertially guided, it had an accuracy of about 1.5 miles from the center of any intended target. The greatest danger of the Scud was that its indiscriminate employment against Israel might have brought that nation into the war, an event that would immediately have shattered the U.N. coalition by antagonizing the critical Arab members. Operation Iraqi Freedom was in similar danger, and every effort was made to suppress the Scud (and other missile) threat from the start.

SADDAM'S STRATEGY:
STUPID OR UNBELIEVABLY CUNNING?

In the 1991 Gulf War, Saddam Hussein believed that the United States would not have a stomach for fighting and would, after encountering heavy losses, quit the war. Even after the extremely effective aerial bombardment, he continued to dispose of his forces in a way that showed he anticipated a grueling land battle. When that did not materialize, he sought the cease-fire, which returned independence to Kuwait—but maintained his power within Iraq. He later interpreted this as a victory, and it was widely seen as such in the Muslim world.

In 2003, Saddam Hussein hoped that the United States, faced by opposition from France, Germany, Russia, and most of the United Nations, would back down and not go to war. If this happened, he would have become an even bigger hero to the radical Muslims in the world and to the people who backed him in his own country.

Saddam certainly knew that he could not defeat the United States in battle; his second hope, however, was, as stated elsewhere in this book, to inflict so many casualties on the U.S. and coalition forces that popular sentiment in America would turn against the war, as it had done during the Vietnam War. In that case, a negotiated settlement in which he retained power would still be widely interpreted as a victory.

A third, and far less likely case, is that Saddam Hussein was so wonderfully cunning that he *planned* to lose the wars and turn it, as it has, into a guerrilla conflict. It is difficult to believe that even a canny clansman from Tikrit would sacrifice his army, his infrastructure, his nation, and most of all, the oil revenues that he was so assiduously skimming to become a resistance leader. First of all, he had to reckon with being killed—as he so nearly was on two occasions at least; and second of all, he had to reckon with all the people who have scores to settle with him. Without his elaborate security procedures, he is more likely to be killed by an aggrieved Iraqi than by an American patrol.

The fourth, and more likely case, is that he (a) expected the U.S. not to fight, or to quit if it fought and suffered casualties and (b) that having lost, he turned to the only thing he has left, guerrilla warfare—a term that does not fit because there is no popular sentiment involved.

Saddam's advance forces stood on the border of Saudi Arabia and could have covered the 200-mile distance from Kuwait to Dhahran in little more than a day. To deter him, the United States dispatched forty-eight McDonnell Douglas (now Boeing) F-15 Eagles from the 1st Tactical Fighter Wing at Langley Air Force Base, Virginia. After as many as seven in-flight refuelings for the roughly sixteen-hour flight, the Eagles landed directly in Saudi Arabia. The F-15s, with their implicit promise of American involvement, were, with the partly effective Royal Saudi Arabian Air Force, all that stood between Saddam Hussein and the conquest of Saudi Arabia. (There was also a brigade of Saudi National Guard ground forces.)

The President, Secretary of Defense Richard Cheney, and the Chairman of the Joint Chiefs of Staff, General Colin Powell, began a double-track process involving intense diplomatic action at the United Nations and reinforcing Kuwait.

General Powell, who recalled the bitterly disappointing way the United States had waged war in Vietnam, had enunciated a doctrine stating that military action should be used only as a last resort but when used should be applied with overwhelming force.

To apply overwhelming force against Saddam's huge military meant building up a mammoth array of power during a holding operation called Operation Desert Shield. An enormous ground, sea, and air buildup followed, and it was revealed that both military air- and sea lift were inadequate. The airlift was partially alleviated by the first-ever use of the Civil Reserve Air Fleet (CRAF). By the January 17, 1991, start of Operation Desert Storm, more than 125,000 personnel and 400 tons of cargo had been flown in. The peak rate of 17 million ton-miles per day was exactly ten times the rate of the famous Berlin Airlift. Nonetheless, the war revealed the serious inadequacy of both air and sea-lift capability, and these shortfalls were only partially remedied in the years that followed.

While the buildup proceeded, President George Herbert Walker Bush used the unprecedented effect of a U.N. Security Council Resolution to conduct the war. An intensive air campaign was designed to exploit the coalition's strengths when all alternatives to war had been exhausted. This occurred on January 15, 1991, the deadline set by the United Nations for Saddam's withdrawal. On January 16, the day before Operation Desert Storm began, the coalition had an air force of 2,790 aircraft ready to take to the skies, with 600,000 ground troops, 4,000 tanks, and a formidable naval force with more than 150 warships on hand.

The coalition forces' superior command and control network was ready to direct the activities of its superbly trained aircrews. The United States planned to employ special operation forces, stealth aircraft equipped with precision-guided munitions (PGMs), and very accurate cruise missiles that would suppress enemy air defenses and eliminate the enemy's integrated air defense and command and control systems. Initial strikes were intended to destroy or degrade Iraq's weapons of mass destruction and the reputedly effective Republican Guard divisions.

Three phases, intended to last from eighteen days to thirty days, were planned for the air campaign. They included a general strategic air campaign, the elimination of Iraqi capability in Kuwait, and direct attacks on Iraqi army units. The fourth phase was the ground campaign to liberate Kuwait, amply supported by airpower. The fourth phase was expected to be short—but no one expected it to be as swift as it turned out to be, a mere 100 hours, or just over four days. (Extraordinarily bad flying weather forced an extension of the air campaign from the planned thirty to thirty-nine days.)

In addition to the initial objectives, the air campaign was intended to establish complete air supremacy, destroy key military production facilities, knock out Scud missiles and launchers along with their production and storage facilities, and bring about the collapse of the Iraqi Army by destroying its mechanized equipment.

The plan was initiated when a flight of seven Boeing B-52Gs made the first takeoff for the campaign, lifting off from Barksdale Air Force Base, Louisiana, at 6:36 A.M. on January 16, 1991, for what would become the longest air combat mission in history at that time. The next morning, the B-52s (the prototype of which first flew in 1952) launched their Boeing AGM-86C conventionally armed air-launched cruise missiles (CALCMs)* at key Iraqi communications, power generation, and transmission facilities.[3]

The CALCMs were joined by the General Dynamics (now Raytheon) Tomahawk land attack missiles (TLAMs) launched from naval warships, and they were followed by a host of special mission U.N. aircraft that filled the Gulf skies.

While the TLAMs were still in flight, Air Force Sikorsky MH-53J Pave Low led Army McDonnell Douglas (now Boeing) AH-64 Apache helicopters to attack Iraqi radar sites, destroying them with withering blasts of Hellfire missiles and cannon fire. The combination of helicopter, stealth, and cruise missile operations peeled Iraqi defenses apart, permitting nonstealth aircraft a less hazardous approach to Baghdad and other targets in Iraq.

This was the beginning of a forty-three-day air campaign in which the coalition achieved almost immediate air supremacy and fulfilled all of the assignments it received—with two exceptions. The Iraqi mobile ballistic

---

* The original ALCMs were armed with nuclear warheads and were navigated by a terrain matching system. The CALCM had a conventional 1,000-pound high-explosive warhead and was navigated by multiple systems including Global Positioning System equipment—one of the first uses of space-linked weapons in the war.

missiles were difficult to find and destroy, and a lack of information made it impossible to destroy all of the elements of the Iraqi nuclear industry.[4]

The air campaign was such an overwhelming success that it made the ground campaign painless. The coalition flew 109,876 sorties, of which the U.S. Air Force flew 59 percent.[5] Precision weapons were used with great effect but constituted just less than 9 percent (7,400 tons) of the total of 84,200 tons of munitions dropped during the war. (As a matter of comparison, 1,613,000 tons were dropped on Germany and 537,000 tons on Japan during World War II.)

The results were so spectacular that they caused a complete reexamination of strategy by the Soviet military, who in August 1991 had tried to seize power. The ill-fated coup was put down, and the commanders did not receive the summary executions that would have been standard in Stalin's time. Instead, there was a recognition that they could no longer compete with the United States, and the Soviet Union dissolved with a whimper—and not a nuclear bang—on December 25, 1991. Even the allies in the coalition were startled at the comparative advances made by the U.S. forces, and many were forced to recognize that they were in fact so far behind that they were, to a greater or less degree, "noninteroperable" with U.S. forces.

Such overpowering success might have led to hubris, but the U.S. military faced a ten-year-long period of budget reductions, so it became imperative to learn as much as possible about what went right and what went wrong in the Gulf War.

First and foremost, the training of the U.S. and coalition forces had brought them to a level of efficiency that made difficult operations seem easy. The integration of air and space technology, as costly as it was, also worked very well, with some exceptions. The expensive (and much criticized) space and satellite systems that provided intelligence, communications, navigation, and meteorological information were indispensable. The Northrop Grumman E-8A Joint STARS (Surveillance Target Acquisition Radar System) prototypes were rushed into action some five years in advance of their intended operational debut. Perhaps the most amazing discovery was that stealth actually worked. No one had really known for sure that the Lockheed Martin F-117A Nighthawk would be able to perform as intended. In practice it did better than expected, attacking 31 percent of Iraqi strategic targets on the first day, although constituting less than 2.5 percent of the allied force.[6] And it did this with impunity, flying through the flak-filled skies of Baghdad without ever taking a hit.

Some things did not work, and the most costly of these were the low-level tactics employed by the Royal Air Force, which lost three Panavia

Tornado GR.Mk 1 aircraft in delivering airfield-denial bomblets at a 200-foot altitude. The Royal Air Force then switched to using LGBs from a medium altitude.

There was also a severe shortage of PGMs. Had they been available in greater quantities, many fewer missions with conventional bombs would have had to be flown, and results would have been greater.

The intelligence systems, particularly those involving Bomb Damage Assessment (BDA), did not operate as efficiently as they should have because of a lack of a high-resolution system to analyze mission results.

When the weather was poor, the accuracy of LGBs was impaired. After the war, the Air Force Chief of Staff, General Merrill A. "Tony" McPeak, and Secretary of the Air Force Donald B. Rice assigned themselves the task of solving this problem. On a single sheet of memorandum paper they wrote their requirements. The new PGM was to be in the form of a kit that could be strapped onto a conventional "dumb bomb." It was to have its guidance system continuously updated by GPS (Global Positioning System) until it struck its target, with a Circular Error of Probability (CEP) of thirteen meters. Its cost was not to exceed $20,000.

After much work in development, they got the JDAM, which has a better CEP than specified and cost less than $20,000.[7]

Another problem existed with communications. While the Air Force's Computer Aided Management System (CAMS) could distribute the daily air tasking order (ATO) to most units electronically, the lack of an interface with the Navy's computer system required that a floppy disk containing the information be *hand*-delivered each day.[8]

A problem that was more political and psychological than military was the difficulty encountered trying to find and destroy the mobile missile launchers, and a disproportionate number of sorties were devoted to the task. Postwar analysis revealed that not even one ballistic missile was successfully attacked.

All of these problems were addressed in the years after 1991, not all with equal success. As serious as some of them were, it was obvious that more had gone right than had gone wrong in the Gulf War. So, when it was apparent that the United States intended to use military force if Saddam Hussein did not comply with the requirements of U.N. Resolution 1441,* it was widely assumed that the general 1991 pattern of combat would be repeated. One aspect that was not only repeated but also improved upon was the minimization of collateral damage. The leaders of the Coalition of the Willing made it absolutely clear to the public but, more important, to their military leaders that collateral damage was to be

---

* See appendix 2 for the full text of U.N. Resolution 1441.

kept to an absolute minimum, that the Iraqi infrastructure was to be preserved to the greatest extent possible, and that Iraqi civilian casualties were to be avoided at almost any cost. This became an open invitation to the hard-core Baa'thist leaders to use civilians as hostages and shields and to seize upon every casualty as a propaganda triumph. They were ardently supported in this by the Arab media and, to a somewhat lesser degree, by many of its coalition counterparts. Nonetheless, the concept was adhered to with gratifying results.

Instead of repeating 1991's strategy and tactics, the newly "transformed" forces of the coalition employed asymmetric, network-centric warfare* in an exhilarating demonstration of both joint operations (Army, Air Force, Navy, Marine, and Coast Guard) and combined operations (U.S., U.K., and other forces). Two additional factors added to the drama and to the success of the concept. The first of these was the effective integration of space-based technology with every aspect of military operations. The second was the unique demonstration of the capabilities (and perhaps the ultimate limits) of the Total Force concept, in which reservists and National Guard members are woven into extended combat operations.† And while the numbers of personnel and equipment employed were far fewer than in 1991, they still represented overwhelming force in the manner in which they were applied. Colin Powell's doctrine was not abandoned, just improved upon.

The war (or in current terminology, the Battle of Iraq in the War against Terrorism) was won by an unprecedented confluence of political and military forces. The coalition intelligence organizations, so fiercely and perhaps appropriately castigated after the September 11, 2001, terrorist attacks, were extremely effective (with the perhaps glaring exception of being unable to bring first Osama bin Laden and then Saddam Hussein to justice and to find weapons of mass destruction). One vital use of the intelligence gathered was enabling a very large number of special operation forces to wreak havoc upon Iraqi civil and military organizations, operating alone or in concert with coalition military units. The exact techniques and the true achievements of the special operation forces will not

---

* According to a definition in the June 5, 2003, Congressional Research Service Report *Iraq: War Defense Program Implications for Congress*, network-centric warfare refers to using networking technology—computers, data links, and networking software—to link U.S. military personnel, ground vehicles, aircraft, and ships into a series of highly integrated local- and wide-area networks capable of sharing critical tactical information on a rapid and continuous basis (CRS-46).

† At the time of the Iraq war, about 220,000 reservists were on active duty. By April 25, 2003, 286,000 reservists were activated for federal service, while another 47,000 were tasked for other situations, e.g., to serve as members of the National Guard. Since World War II, only the Korean War mobilization of 858,000 reservists was larger (CRS-46: *Iraq War: Defense Program Implications for Congress*).

be known for years, if ever, for reasons of security. These SOF actions, combined with brilliant target selection and expert bombing execution, provided an entirely new method of battlefield preparation. Instead of days of bombings to prepare a battlefield for a massive advance of huge numbers of ground forces, the aerial attacks were conducted with a rapierlike precision, enabling relatively small numbers of highly trained ground forces to seize critical points before the Iraqis were even aware that they were in danger. Much experience had been gained in Afghanistan, and it was put to good use in Iraq. It is difficult to find a civil analogy to the degree of change in the military from 1991 to 2003; in medical terms, it might be the movement from the use of traumatic invasive procedures to microsurgery.

There has been speculation that among the achievements of the special operation forces was the systematic payoff to critical leaders.* While this purchase of a monumental bug-out is not impossible, it is more realistic to attribute the rapid dissolution of Saddam's forces to the relentless application of integrated air and ground power. (The opposing view might be that the "bug-out" was not paid for but was, instead, part of Saddam's diabolical plot to create a huge underground movement.) From the surprisingly few opening bombs of the war to the last surgical strike against irregular forces, the air war was conducted with a precision and scientific discipline that makes the highly successful conduct of air operations in the Gulf War seem primitive in comparison.

Ironically, the Olympian success of the air war has gone largely unappreciated and under-reported. (General Charles "Chuck" Horner, the Joint Force Air Commander during the Gulf War, believes that reporters should have been embedded on air operations in the two-seat Lockheed Martin F-16s and Boeing F-15Ds, despite the attendant risks. He feels that the airmen deserved to have their story told as well and if the reporters "puked on the camera and the cockpit, just give them some Handi-Wipes," for it would be a great story to tell.)[9]

The air war was conducted on two levels, one of which was the precisely executed bombing of carefully selected targets in Baghdad. The other level was the relentlessly savage hammering of Iraqi ground forces wherever they were found, far away from any television camera. In the April 27 briefing at the U.S. Air Operations Center (AOC), Air Force Lieutenant General T. Michael "Buzz" Moseley, of the Coalition Forces Air

---

* If the fix was in and key members of the Iraqi military were promised money and future careers to tell their armies not to fight but to simply disappear into the Iraqi desert, then the conduct of Iraqi Freedom goes beyond brilliant into a stellar achievement that makes the best campaigns of Napoléon, Wellington, Rommel, and Giap seem like futile excursions into the macabre. If the war was fought this way, it should be the pattern for all future wars.

Component (CFAC), said, "We're killing the Republican Guard, but I want you to kill them faster."[10] A veteran F-15 pilot with 2,800 hours' flying time, Moseley is the Commander of U.S. Central Command Air Forces and Ninth Air Force and the architect of the successful air plan. Said with a deceptively mild homespun demeanor, Moseley's words did not mean that he enjoyed killing but that he recognized the duty of his air forces to eliminate ground opposition to advancing coalition forces.

Air- and ground power worked with an alternating synergistic effect. Airpower sought out and destroyed enemy forces, but they were sometimes difficult to find when in static positions. The amazingly rapid movement of coalition ground forces forced the Iraqi military to try to move its own crack divisions to new defensive positions. When they moved, airpower found and destroyed them, day or night in any weather.

The effect of this combination of attacks was to sap the strength of the Iraqi divisions, destroying their communications and effectively neutering them. The air attacks on Iraqi combat units did not just take them far below the 50 percent level that is usually regarded as adequate for their elimination as a coherent fighting force; it utterly destroyed them. Yet, as devastating as they were, these strikes went largely unreported in the media, and were given only minor emphasis in CENTCOM briefings, usually in the form of two or three video presentations showing PGMs eradicating a tank or a parked aircraft. (Reporters, like the public, quickly become blasé. These presentations, which in 1991 aroused vicarious video-game excitement, were regarded with ho-hum indifference this time. Just as with man and dog biting stories, if a precision-guided bomb missed a mosque, there was no interest, but if a mosque was accidentally hit, that was news.)

The air attacks, conducted far behind the front lines, lacked the excitement of "embedded" reporting and thus allowed the shift in the public's attention away from the heart of the air-war action to ground operations. Reporters riding in Bradley armored vehicles, bonding with the troops, provided a correct and very agreeable image of coalition armored forces. They permitted the world to see the massive firepower wielded by pleasantly mannered young American soldiers who could blast an enemy target into submission and then ten minutes later risk their lives to save Iraqi civilians. There was no room to carry reporters on aerial combat missions, so live television coverage was limited almost exclusively to shots of naval aircraft taking off or landing on the massive aircraft carriers that lingered in harm's way. These were impressive of themselves, but they did not carry the cachet of an unbathed, bewhiskered, obviously fatigued reporter viewed by a night-vision camera, surrounded by soldiers who have just brought him another quick thirty klicks into enemy territory.

The degree of the success of air operations was further obscured by the fact that individual sorties were no longer the measurement used to gauge the intensity of the conflict. The reason for this was the fact that individual bomber and fighter aircraft had such a vastly increased capability to take out targets. As an example, the Northrop Grumman B-2A Spirit, the beautiful flying wing stealth bomber that flew from its home at Whiteman Air Force Base in Missouri, as well as from new island facilities at Diego Garcia, could strike as many as sixteen different targets with PGMs in a single raid. The long-derided Boeing B-1B and the veteran Boeing B-52 did even more spectacular work, and just as so many right-thinking officers have demanded since Vietnam, results were measured in the number of targets destroyed, not in the number of missions flown.

In the following chapters, the efficacy of all of the services will be depicted on a day-by-day basis, with emphasis given to the background of the successes but also with full acknowledgment of defects.

MILITARY VERSUS POLITICAL CONSIDERATIONS

The road to the hell of the Iraq war was paved with good diplomatic intentions. The United States, surprised and sandbagged by its erstwhile friends France, Germany, and Russia, was unable to obtain the U.N. sanction that it sought. Instead of the desired U.N. support for a coalition, the United States and Great Britain announced that they were joined by a "Coalition of the Willing," nations that supported the idea that Saddam's repeated violations of U.N. Resolution 1441 had to be addressed, by force if necessary.

Political and economic factors, combined with a complete misreading of President Bush's firm resolve to combat terrorism and its sponsors, seemed to induce France, Germany, Russia, and much of the U.N. leadership to attempt to delay an American-led military intervention in Iraq to a time when it would no longer be politically practical. Many volumes will be written about the personal connections between France's President Jacques Chirac and Saddam Hussein as well as the long-standing business, scientific, and military collaboration between the two countries—a collaboration that led to the creation of the Osirak nuclear facility that Israel fortunately bombed out of existence in 1981.

There are obvious parallels between the Israeli decision to bomb Osirak and the U.S.-led invasion of Iraq more than twenty years later. Israel had come to a political decision that Iraqi possession of nuclear weapons would be fatal to Israel as a state. The raid took place on the afternoon of June 7, 1981. American-built McDonnell Douglas (now Boeing) F-15s and General Dynamics (now Lockheed Martin) F-16s flew a long low-level route that evaded enemy radar. The F-16s then popped up and, using accurate dive-bombing techniques, demolished their target. The raid itself lasted one minute and twenty seconds. The destruction of the reactor had tremendous implications for the Middle East.

In 2003, the United States faced the same dilemma, the certainty that Iraq had possessed and used weapons of mass destruction in the past. Their future use, either locally or by provision to al Qaeda or other terrorists, was potentially fatal to the United States. The President decided that it was not a question that could be left to chance or to the hope that the Iraqis had in fact gotten rid of all weapons of mass destruction as they had claimed.

Russia seemed to join France in opposing the United States in a less contentious manner. For his part, President Vladimir Putin had to consider the long relationship that the Soviet Union had maintained with Iraq, as well as the huge Iraqi debt owed to Russia, estimated to be between $7 and $12 billion. (Yet to be fair, we have to acknowledge that the United States has both a national and a personal interest in Iraqi oil. Firms such as Carlyle, Halliburton, and Chevron-Texaco made enormous sums over the years from trade with Iraq, and many members of the administration—Condoleeza Rice, Vice President Richard Cheney, and others—were formerly involved with those very firms.) Russia, now potentially the most oil-rich nation in history, had grave concerns about the conduct of the Iraqi oil operations. But more important, Russia had legitimate worries about the possibility of an Arab–Kurdish conflict breaking out, one that might result in Islamic fundamentalists assuming power in what had formerly been a secular state. Both Russia and France have large and growing Muslim minorities and regard them as political factors that must be catered to. The prospect of Islamic fundamentalists in control of both Iran and Iraq was frightening.

In Germany, Chancellor Gerhard Schroeder had only recently eked out a narrow electoral victory on the basis of his anti-American fulminations and had virtually no choice but to oppose American actions in the United Nations. (In fairness, Germany helped guard American facilities and provided almost unlimited overflight privilege).

The Chirac-Schroeder-Putin combination scored initial successes in the U.N. arena, which was generally biased against the United States. The three nations pleaded for more time for small and obviously ineffective teams of U.N. inspectors to be led to Iraq's weapons of mass destruction even as Saddam's followers hid them well. France, Germany, and Russia had all voted for U.N. Resolution 1441, and Iraqi violations of that resolution had already provided adequate justification for military intervention. Yet they joined forces to succeed in discouraging the United States in its ill-advised attempt to obtain another resolution that would provide for actions already sanctioned in 1441. This success, won in part by the expected results of Chirac's ardent lobbying of former French colonies in Africa, may have led them to overestimate their joint capabilities. They apparently came to see their three countries as a potential "New European" counterbalance to U.S. economic and political influence. Contributing to this international hubris was their private and disparaging assessment of President Bush, who they believed could be finessed into a long delay in attacking Iraq and perhaps, in the face of their joint intractability, might ultimately be persuaded not to attack at all. (They overlooked the fact that France undertook military action in Africa without requesting U.N. sanction.)

Ironically, it is entirely possible that the delays encountered at the United Nations may have been not only welcome but also necessary to implement the daring plan of attack envisioned by Bush, Vice President Richard Cheney, Secretary of Defense Rumsfeld, and their military leaders. This time they did not have the luxury of creating a counterpart to Operation Desert Shield, in which defenses were slowly gathered over several months to defend Saudi Arabia from meeting Kuwait's fate in 1991. But they did need time to prepare for the hard-hitting Operation Iraqi Freedom, which would out-storm Operation Desert Storm and use the lessons learned from it. The result would be unique in history, an amazing combination of an RMA that dazzled the soldiers of the world and an RDA that rocked diplomats in embassies all over the globe.

It is interesting now to see how combat action in Operation Iraqi Freedom compares with what was expected and what was planned. As previously noted, one of the most extraordinary aspects of Operation Iraqi Freedom was the degree to which collateral damage was minimized. Ironclad procedures and protocols defined exactly how operations would be conducted, and, in short, it is no surprise that the coalition was successful in reducing the casualties in a savagely fought war to a minimum.

For almost ten years, the United States had been developing Operations Plan (OPLAN) 1003, Major Theater War–East, to defend Kuwait and Saudi Arabia from Iraq. The OPLAN also provided for the security of U.S. interests, including its military and civilian personnel and equipment.

The original OPLAN 1003 relied on deterrence first; if that failed, U.S. forces were to be rapidly deployed using prepositioned stocks to establish a defense that could hold until sufficient forces arrived to undertake an offensive. The phases overlapped, with the deployment to establish a defense lasting for 90 days, while the defensive phase was to last from Day 45 until the conflict was concluded.

The second Bush administration insisted that a counteroffensive element be added to the plan, one that foresaw the elimination of the Iraqi regime. A counteroffensive was to begin as soon as sufficient forces were available to fix and destroy Iraqi forces, with attacks coming from the north, the south, and the west; it was expected to last twenty days. The battle was expected to be one of attrition, in which American ground forces would engage Iraqi forces depleted from air attack and destroy them.

When war seemed inevitable in Iraq, a series of revisions were made by the Joint Chiefs of Staff to OPLAN 1003, ultimately resulting in OPLAN 1003V, which greatly reduced the number of troops involved and increased the tempo of operations. In the U.S. Air Force, for example, the Checkmate office worked with others to plan a series of alternatives that included the prospect of Turkey refusing to allow troops to cross her borders. It was conceded that all plans change with the first contact of the enemy, but OPLAN 1003V would be at least a baseline from which deviations could be charted.

It is important to note that while some have said that there was no "softening-up" air campaign as there had been in Desert Storm, this was not the case. The Air Force Chief of Staff, General John P. Jumper, is emphatic about the advantage that studying the enemy on a daily basis during the twelve years of air operations over the Iraqi "no-fly zones" gave the United States. And after the Commander in Chief of Central Command, General Tommy R. Franks, allowed full implementation of the applicable rules of engagement (ROE), no fewer than 8,600 sorties were flown from July 2002 to March 19, 2003. These significantly reduced Iraqi SAM capability as well as their command and control networks.[11]

OPLAN 1003V was put to the test on March 20, Baghdad time.

2

The Forces Compared

IMMEDIATE BACKGROUND TO THE WAR

On March 17, 2003, Secretary of State Colin Powell announced that the United States, the United Kingdom, and Spain had decided not to ask for a vote on another U.N. resolution requiring Iraq to take the opportunities afforded by Resolution 1441.* This facing up to diplomatic reality cleared the way for a speech at 8:00 that evening by President George W. Bush. The President addressed the nation and the world as he delivered a unique ultimatum, a demand from one head of state to another, calling for the latter to step down. The President told Saddam Hussein, quietly but unequivocally, "All the decades of deceit and cruelty have now reached an end. Saddam Hussein and his sons must leave Iraq within forty-eight hours. Their refusal to do so will result in military conflict, commenced at a time of our choosing. For their own safety, all foreign nationals—including journalists and inspectors—should leave Iraq immediately."

The U.N. Secretary General, Kofi Annan, made his first accommodating gesture in weeks by ordering all U.N. personnel, including the blue-capped inspectors who had hoped to be led to Iraqi weapons of mass destruction, to leave. Many embassies were closed, and thousands of foreign workers left. The United States took precautions against possible further acts of terrorism or even the employment of Iraqi missiles by ordering all government dependents and nonessential staff out of Israel, Kuwait, Syria, the West Bank, and the Gaza Strip.

Not surprisingly, Iraq rejected Bush's ultimatum but did issue a somewhat conciliatory statement that quoted Saddam Hussein as denying that

---

* See appendix 2 for full text of U.N. Resolution 1441.

Iraq possessed weapons of mass destruction. The conciliatory note was muted, as Saddam also threatened retaliatory action all over the world. Iraqi diplomats charged that war was a mistake and implicitly threatened that an attack by the United States on Iraq would have a destabilizing influence on the Muslim world.

The intervening forty-eight hours ticked away, filled with drama and anticipation fueled by a concept that proved to be more buzzword than buzz saw: "Shock and Awe." The U.S. military helped heighten the speculation that the initial air attacks on Iraq would be of such a cataclysmic nature that those of Desert Storm would seem gentle in comparison. Other currents of opinion saw many ominous signs ahead. Although the number of coalition troops being readied for the war was not known with actuarial accuracy, it was obvious to most that they amounted only to about half the number that were on hand to start the ground war in 1991. The clamor for "more boots on the ground" became a drumroll. The specters of the Vietnam War and of the Soviet Union's Afghanistan disaster were continuously raised, as was the wholly irrelevant claim that the war might invite retaliation from al Qaeda—as if an invitation were required.

The March 2 decision of the Turkish Parliament to refuse access to U.S. troops was yet another in what seemed an infernally long series of diplomatic rebuffs and was not alleviated when the new Turkish Prime Minister, Abdullah Gul, declined to attempt to reverse the decision. There was little to be done except to withdraw the huge multibillion-dollar aid package that had been the deal sweetener and ultimately move the 4th Infantry (Mechanized) Division around to Kuwait and seek alternatives to a "northern front." Turkey was a strong friend of the United States, and U.S. fighters had patrolled the Iraqi no-fly zones from Incirlik Air Base for more than a decade. In addition, the Turks had allowed use of Diyarbakir and Batman Air Bases to support combat rescue and special operations during the first Gulf War. The refusal was inexplicable to Americans but perfectly logical to the Turkish public, which was almost unanimous in its opposition to the idea. The Turks strongly opposed helping Americans against another Muslim state, no matter how troublesome Iraq had been in the past. The Turks had waged a guerrilla war against Kurdish dissidents for many years and were extremely concerned that the war might foster the establishment of an independent Kurdish state, one that would have visceral implications for Turkey as a nation. Many military commentators thought that the Turkish refusal jeopardized the entire war plan, for they deemed the insertion of as many as 60,000 troops into Iraq from the north absolutely crucial. Hopes lingered for weeks that a change in the Turkish government might bring a change of heart. In Washington, statements were released that the Turkish refusal was not really a setback and that alternative options were available. There were, but they were far less desirable and entailed considerably more risk and expense to employ.

Before getting into a detailed day-by-day account of the war itself, it is instructive to compare what was known of the two opposing forces before the war began.

THE IRAQI MILITARY SITUATION

The tribal beat of Iraqi national politics was heard on March 15 when Saddam Hussein instructed the Iraqi Revolutionary Command Council (RCC) to announce the division of Iraq into four military command regions.

Saddam selected his younger son, Qusay Hussein, to command the vital "Central Region," which included what the Iraqis termed the *governates* of Al-Anbar, Babil, Baghdad, Salah Al-Din, Tikrit (Saddam's hometown), and Wasit. Qusay was undoubtedly overwhelmed, for he already commanded the Republican Guard and also had the responsibility for the Special Security Organization Troops, who controlled chemical and biological weapons. His equally notorious elder brother, Uday, had authority over internal security forces and was to act as the general coordinator with the other regions if communications with the central command were disrupted. (Both of Saddam's sons were killed in a July 22, 2003 firefight.)

In the north, the Kurdish area, a top Ba'athist, General Izzat Ibrahim, the Deputy Commander in Chief of the armed forces, was given control of the oil-rich areas that included as-Sulaymaniyah, Al-Ta'mim, Arbil, Da-huk, and Ninawa.

Saddam's cousin General Ali Hasan al-Majid was given control of the southern provinces of Basra, Dhi Qar, and Maysan. Hasan, the ill-famed "Chemical Ali," was the general who was responsible for the actions that killed at least five thousand Kurds in a chemical weapons attack on Halabjah on March 15, 1988. In 1991 he ruthlessly suppressed a U.S.-encouraged uprising south of Iraq. (He and some of his deputies were thought to be found dead on April 7, 2003, but after combat ended it was rumored that he had survived.)

Deputy Prime Minister and Finance Minister Mizban Khadar Hadi (later known as the Eight of Diamonds in that stroke of PR genius, the deck of cards with its wanted members of the regime) was named commander of the provinces of Al-Muthanna, An Najaf, and al-Qadisiyah and the key area of Karbala.

All four men were to report directly to Commander in Chief Saddam.

Saddam retained under his personal control the operation of the Iraqi Air Force and the strategic employment of missiles. Saddam's apparent decision to excuse his Iraqi Air Force from the war was perhaps the first time in history that such a potentially capable force was ordered to stand down rather than risk a fight. The Iraqi Air Force was worn down during the twelve years in which the 1st Wing and others enforced the northern and southern no-fly zones.

Lieutenant General Bernard E. Trainor has speculated that the Iraqi Minister of Defense and Armed Forces Commander, Staff General Sultan Hashim Ahmad, had to execute a thankless task. He and his staff of virtual Saddam Hussein look-alikes knew that there was no way to win the war and, in Trainor's scenario, had to give this potentially fatal advice to Saddam himself.[1]

Saddam's two-track campaign plan was not attractive, but there seemed to be no alternative. Most hope was placed on the diplomatic effort being led by France, Germany, and Russia on Iraq's behalf. The second track was the traditional one of trying to slow a coalition advance through attrition warfare, where heavy casualties would alienate the American public.

A general agreement would have been reached that the defense of the middle of Iraq, with Baghdad being considered critical. All six Republican Guard divisions were concentrated on the southern approaches to Baghdad in two broad bands. In Baghdad itself, some fifteen thousand special Republican Guard forces would assume the principal defense duties.

Saddam, who at one time had more than 1 million men in his armed forces, must have faced the war with trepidation, despite the bravado of his statements. On the eve of Operation Iraqi Freedom, he had a total of about four hundred thousand soldiers in units of varying quality. Iraqi infantry divisions have a nominal strength of about fourteen thousand men and less than 100 tanks, while armored divisions are supposed to have twelve thousand men and 245 tanks. In practice, the units rarely approach their table of organization strengths.

Most of the soldiers were conscripts, parceled out to seventeen regular army divisions that were routinely used for internal security and tacitly conceded to be not only untrustworthy but also a threat to the regime. Eleven of the seventeen divisions were deployed in the north facing Turkey and Iraqi Kurdistan, tasked to defend Mosul, Kirkuk, and the adjacent oil fields.

It speaks volumes to note that units of both the regular army and the Republican Guard were carefully and ruthlessly monitored by special security units loyal to Saddam.[2]

In this hypothetical briefing to his officers, General Sultan would have emphasized the need to slow down the American advance by destroying bridges, mining the river crossing points, and setting up artillery fields of fire to exact the greatest cost. The oil fields were to be burned and every weapon capable of delivering chemical weapons—artillery, missiles, and aircraft—was to be used. If the Kurds caused any problems in the north, they were to be suppressed, once again with chemical weapons. Not surprisingly, the staff was stunned by the prospect of facing the known quantity of American airpower with the unknown quantity of chemical warfare. They knew that chemical weapons could hurt their own forces more than those of the Americans. Sultan would have attempted to rouse their enthusiasm, pointing out that the Americans were not invincible, that they depended too much on technology to fight their wars, and that the Iraqis could be as clever as the Serbs had been in Kosovo.[3]

Yet for the most part, the regular forces of the Iraqi army had known only defeat. Their equipment was outdated, and their training was inadequate. Saddam's real hope lay in the approximately seventy thousand men of his iron-core Republican Guard.

Like Hitler's feared SS, the Republican Guard began as bodyguards, a special force of trusted tribesmen to protect Saddam. As it grew, it took over the defense of Baghdad, and when it had reached the size of six divisions, three armored and three motorized infantry, each with three brigades, it assumed responsibility for the defense of key areas of the country. The men and officers of the Republican Guard were all volunteers and received far better training and equipment than regular soldiers. They also received personal benefits such as increased pay, furnished housing, automobiles, and more, depending upon their devoted service. Yet Saddam had his doubts even about these troops and began inserting clansmen from Tikrit into positions of authority, a process that pushed the already-depressed morale even lower. He affronted his senior military officers by appointing his son to lead the Republican Guard, despite Qusay's utter lack of military experience. The officers did not protest, however, valuing their lives and those of their families. Underlying all their concerns was the realization that despite official Iraqi claims to the contrary, the Iraqi air defense system had not been rebuilt since 1991. (Some effort had been made to upgrade the system with a fiber-optic network, but the U.S. and British no-fly patrols kept the system from materially advancing.)

The most potentially useful group remaining to Saddam were about fifteen thousand men in special Republican Guard units that were trained in urban warfare. If properly motivated and well led, they had the capability to turn Baghdad into a mini-Stalingrad. There was also a "Popular Army," essentially an Iraqi *Volkstrum* that did not eventuate, and the far more dangerous *Fedayeen* Saddam (Saddam's Martyrs), fanatics devoted for whatever reason to Saddam and his cause.

In terms of equipment, the Iraqi Army still possessed as many as 2,000 tanks, including perhaps 700 T-72 tanks. The T-72s are clearly not in the Abrams category but are nonetheless formidable enough with their 125mm smoothbore main cannon. In addition, the Iraqis operated nearly 4,000 light tanks and armored personnel carriers (APCs) and half that number of heavy self-propelled artillery pieces. The Iraqi inventory of SAMs was greatly reduced from 1991, with about one thousand of the smaller, man-portable SA-7/14/16s and 400 of the larger SA-2, SA-3, SA-6, SA-8, and Roland varieties. The 6,000 antiaircraft guns Saddam possessed were as effective at low altitudes as ever. Saddam Hussein had an air force that consisted of about 300 modern fighters ranging from MiG-21s to MiG-29s, but many of these were not in combat-ready condition. He elected to hide them on the ground.

HOW NATIONS GO TO WAR

Nations go to war in a variety or ways and in a variety of means. Adolf Hitler thought it was bizarre to declare war upon a country when it was so much easier just to invade. In contrast, Great Britain, in both World War I and World War II, made very deliberate attempts to avoid war by delaying formal declarations of war.

In contrast, nations actually go to war for one reason: to further their perceived national interests. In the case of the United States and Iraq, no formal declaration of war was made; instead, the United States acted under the umbrella of the U.N. Resolution 1441.

Clearly, President George W. Bush, and his advisers, considered that it was in the interest of the United States to defeat Iraq in combat, end Saddam Hussein's regime, and prevent his use or distribution of weapons of mass destruction.

There may have been larger interests. Oil is an obvious possibility. And Iraq may have been seen as the keystone in the larger, longer, ongoing war against terror, and that it was merely in the interest of the United States to remove a threat and gain an overarching geographic, political, and military position in the Middle East—the heart of terrorist organizations and their support systems.

The advisability of going to war really boils down to a computation of expected values. Was the expected value of allowing Saddam Hussein to continue to lead his country, to support terrorism, and to (possibly) manufacture and use weapons of mass destruction equal to or less than the expected value of going to war, sustaining casualties, suffering the ill will of many countries, and becoming engaged in a protracted occupation?

It is the author's belief that the administration decided that the expected value of going to war was far greater than the expected value of Saddam Hussein's continuing to lead his country. In other words, the possible threat to U.S. security was so great that it warranted military action. Further, I believe that Operation Iraqi Freedom was intended as a warning, an object lesson in just how powerful the United States is, to Saudi Arabia, Syria, Iran, and other countries supporting terrorism.

Yet, the question of the moral right to go to war will in many people's minds be whether Iraq had weapons of mass destruction AT THE TIME THE UNITED STATES ACTUALLY WENT TO WAR. If so, the following questions immediately arise: Where are those weapons of mass destruction? If those weapons of mass destruction actually existed, why were they not used? Have those weapons of mass destruction been hidden or transferred to other countries?

These questions may be answered before this book is published. But it is the author's present belief that the weapons of mass destruction existed and were transferred to either/or Syria and Iran prior to March 19, 2003, and that Saddam did not use them because he felt doing so would lose the support he had gained with Russia, Germany, and France.

Larger issues immediately emerge. What about North Korean nuclear weapons and nuclear facilities in North Korea, China, Russia, and many of the former Soviet republics? Each one will have to be dealt with separately over the next few years. In the case of Russia and the former Soviet republics, the concept of Mutual Assured Destruction (MAD) still holds sway, along with a fragile hope for democracy and consumerism.

China is a different question, for in Chairman Mao's simple mathematics, China should be willing to accept massive losses of its own population in exchange for total destruction of an enemy population. China is also vulnerable to a growing nationalism, one that might encourage the rise of a young Napoleon in the ranks of its new and young leaders, a Bonaparte who may want war for war's sake. The great danger of China, of course, is its massive energy, intellect, and quest for advancement. Using ever-newer and more powerful generations of computers, Chinese science will surge forward and threaten technologies such as stealth and GPS that we are now dependent upon. We must maintain our present military advantage or simply be forced to submit at some point perhaps twenty years in the future.

Finally, North Korea is impossible to fathom. It is run by a dictator who willingly lets his people starve to death while threatening the world with nuclear weapons. Mutually assured deterrence turns into mutually assured destruction in his hands. The range of threats is terrifyingly great.

Yet people of all nations understand power, and they can comprehend the tremendous advantage the United States holds today. I believe that the victory in Iraq, done in so convincing a fashion, will serve as a lesson to the world, even to North Korea, and may well be the best purchase of peace that the price of war has ever achieved.

Traditional warfare calls for a three-to-one superiority of offensive over defensive forces, but this was not going to be a traditional war. In 1991, the ratio had been roughly three offensive troops for five defensive. Initially, General Tommy Franks, Central Command Commander, had about 230,000 men. Of these, the United States contributed about 190,000 Marine, infantry, airborne, and special forces, while the United Kingdom provided 42,000 troops, including Royal Marines and paratroopers. These were joined by 2,000 Australians, including special forces troops, and a very small but welcome number of Polish forces. This force would grow to 340,000 in the crucial next three weeks.

The great distinguishing characteristic of this coalition army was the fact that up to 8 percent of its strength was invested in special operation forces, operating clandestinely from well before the outbreak of the war and ranging all over the country. They achieved political, military, economic, and psychological successes of great importance, so much so that the composition of U.S. and perhaps British forces will be altered in the future to include many more SOF personnel. This extremely high percentage of SOF forces characterizes the newness, the daring, and the ingeniousness of the war plan and strategy as a whole.

Not all of Franks' forces were used immediately. A new buzzword was created to explain the smaller number of troops in place and offset the continuing cries for more boots on the ground. In the new terminology, forces were "flowed" into action as required. Much of the initial whirlwind success of the attack would come from about 130,000 troops.

In equipment, there was no contest, from the intensively used satellites down to the meals supplied the troops on the march. The coalition forces had total air and space supremacy, and the more than 1,800 aircraft employed worked in symphonic concert through new, responsive command and control systems. On the ground, it was much the same, with the 900 Abrams M1A1 tanks joined by the British Challenger main battle tank, which, while not so swift and mounting a different fire control system, is much more heavily armored. The weapons, body armor, uniforms, and especially night-vision equipment of the coalition forces were infinitely superior not only to the Iraqis' but also to the coalition forces of 1991.

Backing up all of this coalition might were 150 ships, including four U.S. aircraft carrier battle groups (to start, a fifth was added), amphibious assault ships (intended to be used this time, unlike 1991, when they were used as a tactical deception feint to hold Iraqi forces in place in southern Kuwait), and a host of supporting vessels. The striking power of this fleet was immensely greater than that of the Gulf War. (See appendix 7: "US Navy Order of Battle—Operation Iraqi Freedom.")

OPERATION IRAQI FREEDOM:
March 19, 20, and 21

Just as SOF operations had hunted down missiles and other important Iraqi weapons, many important initial air attacks came one day before "G" Day, March 20, the launch of ground operations. These included intensified action by Operation Southern Watch aircraft using PGMs against military targets in both southern and western Iraq. The targets included communications sites, mobile early-warning radar, an air-defense command center, SAM systems, long-range artillery positions, and an air traffic control facility at Basra. The air traffic control facility's wartime mission was to direct antiaircraft fire against coalition aircraft.[4]

At 5:43 A.M.on March 20, Baghdad time, four bombs came whistling out of the dark, followed almost immediately by forty missiles, their lethal contents guided by laser and by the GPS. Signals from space took them unerringly to their surprise destinations. The first attack came not with shock and awe but with a blinding series of concussions that saw picked targets in Baghdad collapse into a heap of smoking rubble. The targets reportedly included the residence of Qusay Hussein, where Saddam was supposed to be holding a meeting. Intended by President Bush as a decapitation strike, beheading the Iraqi government, the raid was two days in advance of the intended avalanche of no fewer than 3,000 weapons intended to bring Baghdad to its psychological knees. It had been hoped that the raid might have effectively ended the war before it began; in the end, it cast questions upon the intelligence reports that selected the target.

Also targeted were communications and storage facilities, all to the south and east of Baghdad.

The first four bombs were EGBU-27s dropped from two stealthy Lockheed Martin F-117A Nighthawks. This was the first combat use of the EGBU-27, which is built by Raytheon.[5] The EGBU-27 is an air-to-ground penetrating weapon equipped with an advanced guidance kit using a semiactive laser system and an inertial guidance/GPS system. It weighs 2,170 pounds and can glide for eleven miles. Some reports indicate that the Nighthawks were operating brazenly, without electronic support; others indicate that Northrop Grumman E-A6B Prowlers provided electronic countermeasures coverage. Others indicate that Boeing F-15E Strike Eagles also participated.

The forty BGM-109 TLAMs were fired from four ships and two submarines. The ships included the USS *Bunker Hill* (CG 52) and USS *Milius* (DDG 69) in the Arabian Gulf and the USS *Donald Cook* (DDG 75) and USS *Cowpens* (CG 63) in the Red Sea. The two submarines were the USS *Cheyenne* (SSN 773) and the USS *Montpelier* (SSN 765).

Thirty more TLAMS were fired later. Ten were fired against three Republican Guard targets near Kirkuk in the north, while twenty were fired against eight Baghdad targets, most of which were Special Security Organization sites. This organization is charged with protection of the senior Iraqi leaders. (In the course of the war only about 1 percent of cruise missiles failed, compared to the 5 percent failure rate expected. Those that crashed in Saudi Arabia and Turkey caused minor diplomatic problems.)

Captured on film by the ever-present media cameras, the battle was totally different from that of January 17, 1991, when the skies of Baghdad were brilliantly illuminated with intense SAM and antiaircraft fire. The 2003 defenses were desultory and erratic, the antiaircraft artillery (AAA) being barrage-fired rather than fired by radar control. In addition, SAMs appeared to be fired unguided. Television caught the image of rolling roseate clouds illuminating the buildings of Baghdad, most of them unshaken, their lights still burning.

In the south, the 3rd Marine Aircraft Wing (3rd MAW) was discountenanced when ground operations proceeded toward Basra before a major air attack had taken place. This was contrary to doctrine and planning, and the Marine pilots felt that the ground troops were placed in jeopardy because of it. Fifty thousand Marines of the 1st Marine Expeditionary

Force (MEF) were sent directly from Kuwait into Iraq. The LAV-25 light armored vehicles clashed with Iraqi APC, destroying two of them.

The principal opposition was not from the neutered Iraqi Air Force but from Iraqi oil fires whose smoke was designed to impair the U.S. targeting systems. The Iraqis did put up heavy antiaircraft fire and prudently fired only unguided SAMs, thus avoiding being hammered by Marine air-defense suppression weapons.

True to their doctrine, the Marines were provided shipboard logistic support from five amphibious warfare ships, all of which were prepared to move directly into Iraq as enemy forces were driven farther north.

Late on the twentieth, a combined operation successfully occupied the gas and oil platforms of the Al Faw oil-refining and shipping facility, thwarting Iraqi plans to flood the Gulf with crude oil.

On March 21, the United Kingdom's Royal Marines from the 3rd Commando Brigade (a joint service unit) made a successful amphibious assault on the Al Faw peninsula, while elements of the United Kingdom's 1st Armored Division marched toward Basra. (See appendix 8.)

Coalition ships stopped and boarded Iraqi tugboats in the Khor Abdullah waterway, finding weapons and more than 130 mines destined to be employed in the Shatt al Arab waterway and the Gulf. These could have been a real hazard to operations.[6]

The 3rd U.S. Infantry (Mechanized) Division continued its surprise thrust toward Baghdad, moving faster than anyone could have planned—particularly the Iraqis—and raising concerns about its outrunning its supply lines. Included in the attack were more than 10,000 vehicles, from huge trucks to Abrams tanks.

Iraq struck back around noon, firing three (Kuwaiti accounts say four) tactical ballistic missiles against targets in Kuwait. The Patriot PAC-3 missile system intercepted a missile. (No Scuds can be confirmed as fired in 2003.) Another, either a Frog or an al Simoud, landed near the Camp Commando complex,[7] and a similar missile impacted near troops of A Company, 3rd Battalion, 7th Infantry Regiment. The major result was forcing troops into MOPP (Mission Oriented Protective Posture) gear, Level 4, putting on their masks, protective suits, and butyl gloves in anticipation of chemical attack. The attack emphasized the well-publicized shortage of Patriot PAC-3 missiles, causing concern about future Iraqi attacks. Older Patriot missiles are useful against aircraft and missiles, but the proximity of Iraqi missile sites meant there were only a few minutes from launch to impact, and the PAC-3 offered superior performance.

Later on March 21, the U.S. 3rd Infantry, using Paladin M109A6 self-propelled 155mm howitzers and the Multiple Launch Rocket System, engaged enemy forces. By the end of the day, the 3rd had seized a bridge near the Talil Air Base and was almost one-third of the way to Baghdad. (Although this has not been absolutely confirmed, it appears that special operations forces paved the way for this event.) Meanwhile, tanks of a 7th Cavalry divisional reconnaissance unit also headed to Iraq's capital, crossing the dusty desert in soaring summer temperatures.

There were brilliant operational coups in the west and the south of Iraq. British, Australian, and U.S. special operation forces seized two critically important airfields in western Iraq, H-2 and H-3, and immediately put them to use. During the first Gulf War the extensive hardened facilities at H-2 and H-3 were used by the Iraqis to store, hide, and launch Scuds into Israel, Kuwait, and Saudi Arabia. The area around H-2 and H-3 was called "the Scud box."

Here credit must be given to the significant and heroic actions of the 410th Air Expeditionary Wing (AEW) and the 120th Expeditionary Fighter Squadron (EFS) of the Air National Guard. Equipped with Lockheed Martin F-16C/Litening II SADL aircraft, with both laser-guided and JDAM weapons, a "rainbow" squadron (cf. the "Fighting 69th" Division of World War I) of Colorado, Alabama, and D.C. Air Guard F-16 units that were activated in early February flew hundreds of night and day missions. The 410AEW/120EFS was responsible for missions in western Iraq, preventing the firing of missiles on Israel, fostering the capture of the H-1, H-2, and H-3 airfields, and conducting the air battle of the Haditha Dam. In the process they dropped hundreds of PGMs and destroyed the largest number of time-critical targets in the war.

More important, the Air National Guard unit pioneered the combat tactics, techniques, and procedures for integrating Army special forces in western Iraq. This was the best example of not just Total Force integration but also Air National Guard Joint Integration ever.

With the airfields captured, their most important function was to suppress ballistic missiles, for it was absolutely vital that Iraq be prevented from firing missiles into other countries, particularly Israel. Israel had vowed that it would retaliate if Iraq repeated the Scud attacks of 1991, and had it done so, Arab host nation support for the Coalition of the Willing might have been jeopardized. The two fields also immediately became a landing site for tactical transports bringing in supplies.

In the south, the strategic oil fields west of Basra were seized by Royal Marines of the 3rd Commando Brigade and U.S. Marines of the 1st MEF. Although extensive mining operations had taken place, the retreating Iraqis were able to set only a few wells on fire, in contrast to the widespread devastation of Kuwait's oil fields in 1991. More than 1,000 aircraft have flown sorties in Operation Iraqi Freedom, including Northrop Grumman

F-14 Tomcats, which dropped PGMs on missile sites in southern Iraq.*

In one incident, foreshadowing the degree of interservice cooperation, a Navy Lockheed Martin P-3C Orion sent infrared images of an Iraqi patrol boat to an AFSOC (Air Force Special Operations Command) Lockheed Martin AC-130 gunship, which used the data to destroy the patrol boat before it could damage the oil platforms it was threatening.

The first aircraft loss occurred on the twenty-first, when a Marine Corps CH-46E Sea Knight from HHM-268 (Camp Pendleton, California) crashed near Highway 801 in Kuwait, south of Umm Qasar. Four U.S. and eight U.K. men died in the crash that was almost certainly due to a mechanical malfunction.

In a DOD briefing, Secretary of Defense Donald H. Rumsfeld outlined the military objectives of Operation Iraqi Freedom. They were:

First, end the regime of Saddam Hussein.
Second, identify, isolate, and eliminate Iraq's weapons of mass destruction.
Third, search for, capture, and drive out terrorists from that country.
Fourth, collect such intelligence as we can relate to terrorists networks.
Fifth, collect such intelligence as we can relate to the global network of illicit weapons of mass destruction.
Sixth, end sanctions and immediately deliver humanitarian support to the displaced and to many needy Iraqi citizens.
Seventh, secure Iraq's oil fields and resources, which belong to the Iraqi people.
Eighth, help the Iraqi people create conditions for a transition to a representative self-government.

On March 21, more than 1,000 sorties were flown against several hundred targets in all parts of Iraq. More than 400 Tomahawks were fired from U.S. and U.K. ships and submarines, and 100 air-launched cruise missiles (ALCMs) were fired from USAF bombers.

THE "VIEW" FROM THE OTHER SIDE

The pro-Iraqi media, both in the Muslim world and in those countries that opposed U.S. policy, conducted an extensive campaign to interpret

---

* The rapid conversion of the F-14 from fleet defense work to close air support with PGMs is a strong indication of the increasing ability of the military services to adapt to changing circumstances.

and sometimes invent news that appeared favorable to Saddam Hussein's regime. This news was collected by Russian intelligence agencies, as well as by using the Russian Internet system. Often it was based on morsels of fact, but many times it was simply fabricated. It nonetheless provides insight into the minds of these opponents and into their methods of psychological operations (Psyops). On March 20, reports played up a disagreement between British Prime Minister Tony Blair and President George Bush over the early air operations, putting the word *unfriendly* into Blair's mouth. The reports portrayed the lack of Iraqi air defenses as a clever ploy designed to lure coalition forces in closer before Iraq made a counterstroke.*

WHAT WENT RIGHT AND WHY

At the command level, the brilliance and the resolution that would characterize Operation Iraqi Freedom were vividly illustrated on March 19 when, in the space of three hours, the President and his advisers, acting on intelligence presented by George Tenet, Director of Central Intelligence, made a decision to launch a limited precision air strike designed to kill Saddam Hussein and leading members of his government.

This attempted decapitation strike "went right" because the President had the courage to take a radical decision, almost certainly against the advice of some of his senior military advisers. It "went wrong" only in the sense that it did not succeed in killing Saddam. This strike took place before G Day and before air supremacy was established. Had it been possible, as it was later in the war, to have a Boeing B-1B or Northrop Spirit B-2A orbiting in the area, the time delay between decision and bomb drop (approximately two hours) could have been reduced to perhaps fifteen minutes and the strike may have succeeded in its aim. Known as "compressing the kill chain" or "reducing the sensor to shooter time," this technique was used later on April 7, as will be noted, but its results were apparently similar and for the same reason: the not-so-paranoid security precautions routinely employed by Saddam and his family.

Instigated by some earlier and perhaps ill-advised military pronouncements, the world waited for the "Shock and Awe" bombing campaign to begin. The world was disappointed, for while the bombing was severe, it did not reach the thunderous proportions that had been predicted. In part,

---

* IRAQWAR.RU, based on Russian Military Intelligence (GRU) Reports, provided to the author by George Mellinger.

it did not because that was unnecessary. The campaign had been preceded by years of "Bleed and Weed,"* an attrition campaign via air operations over the Iraqi no-fly zones. In those operations, U.S. aircraft
would respond to Iraqi provocations with attacks. During Operation
Southern Watch, these responses had totaled 63 in 1999, 32 in 2000, 34 in
2001, and 78 in 2002, 34 of which came in the last two months. Then in
the first three months of 2003, the responses leaped to 92, meaning that
a significant number of Iraqi radar and missile sites had been discovered
and attacked.

By March 21, it was evident that far from "Shock and Awe" the war
was going to be fought as an Effects Based Operation (EBO), an idea
strongly advocated by then Lieutenant Colonel David A. Deptula in the
Gulf War. EBO calls for focusing on certain desired objectives and determining how to employ weaponry to achieve those objectives rather than
simply employing weapons to destroy targets. An EBO campaign is congruent with a campaign designed to minimize collateral damage. It en-
sures that the desired goal (destruction of the integrated enemy
air-defense system, elimination of missiles, etc.) is achieved not by oblit-
erating all of the elements in a carpet bombing campaign but instead by
taking out the key components without which the system will not function. The result of EBO is more effective and less costly bombing, less
collateral damage, and fewer aircraft losses.

The advantage in command, control, communications, computers, intelligence, surveillance, and reconnaissance (termed C⁴ISR) information
that the coalition possessed was the result of years of creating two sets
of very expensive instruments. The first of these allow space-based assets,
command and control aircraft, combat aircraft—the "shooters"—ground
control centers, armored units, and even individual soldiers to operate
with a free flow of real-time information and intelligence. This has never
been possible before in warfare, and it provides the basic underpinning
for the transformation that is under way. The second of these works in
information warfare to deny the enemy the capability to have any communications at all short of messages carried by runners. In Operation Iraqi
Freedom, both instruments worked superbly, and their elements will be
discussed at length later.

From the end of the 1991 Gulf War to G Day of Operation Iraqi Freedom, Iraq had been under a degree of surveillance that would have made
George Orwell shake his head at his own lack of imagination. The country
was watched constantly by satellites, reconnaissance aircraft, and intelligence aircraft gathering data on communications, radar systems, and

* The phrase originates with my colleague Steve Llanso.

antiaircraft and missile systems. Human intelligence, obtained by the CIA, special operation forces, friendly nations, or from dissident Iraqis flowed continually, to be melded with the other information-gathering methods. As the war seemed inevitable, there were months of clandestine operations by the CIA and special operation forces within Iraq, using deception, bribery, and, where necessary, force.

In the United States, all the military services carefully reviewed the lessons of Bosnia, Kosovo, and Afghanistan. In the USAF planning for Iraq, a battle roster of all the commanders who would be deployed was prepared and all of the commanders were brought together at a briefing at Langley Air Force Base. There they "chair-flew," in General Jumper's words, the whole war, going through each phase of the plan as it existed at the time, deciding what was strong and what needed help, then applying the talent and resources as needed. Knowing that hunting for missiles was crucial, they analyzed all the available intelligence and made predictive analysis on how the missiles could be located and destroyed.[8] The other services made similar studies.

Given this level of preparation, the timing and makeup of the coalition forces were well thought out. There was a natural reticence on the part of some of the Arab states that assisted. There was effective support from Jordan, Kuwait, Oman, and Qatar, and despite earlier disclaimers, Saudi Arabia provided valuable assistance, permitting overflights and the use of certain airfields. The Saudis also allowed, to the surprise of some, the use of the new, modernized Combined Air Operations Center (CAOC) at Prince Sultan Air Base for air operations. Israel, for its part, honored its agreement not to intervene, which was vitally important.

Although there was pressure for an earlier attack for many reasons (the prospective increase in daily temperatures, catching Saddam off-guard, concerns about problems with North Korea), the buildup for the attack was thorough. The deliberate manner in which forces were mustered was laudable, especially after the contretemps with Turkey.

General Franks' decision to strike with the relatively small number of forces in the theater and to strike prior to a heavy air attack was both brave and correct. Given that everyone was expecting Shock and Awe, launching the ground war first was the best way to obtain surprise. The surprise was sustained throughout the ground operations, as the Third Army moved swiftly toward Baghdad in a process that approximated John Boyd's theory of the OODA (Observe, Orient, Decide, Act) loop.*

---

* Boyd described a decision-making cycle as an OODA loop, in which an observation is made, orientation is achieved, a decision is made, and action is taken in a process that involves the continuous feedback of information to modify and shape each of the steps. The person who exercises his OODA loop activities faster than an opponent will win; the goal

As events developed, the attack "went right" because of an imaginative and audacious strategy and plan, air and space dominance, overwhelming C⁴ISR capabilities, tactical surprise, speed, the high quality of coalition troops, including their equipment and training, the manner in which U.S. and coalition assets were used, and the inferior troops, leadership, and planning of the Iraqis.

The actions of the special operation forces were and continue to be incredible, and the degree to which things "went right" due to them is remarkable. It is difficult to believe that even a nation as large and wealthy as the United States could field so large a force of capable, fit, intelligent warriors, able to operate in a Ninja style that transcends any of Eric Van Lustbader's fiction. This force of more than 9,000 to 10,000 personnel from the Army, Navy, and Air Force, the United Kingdom, Australia, and Poland was larger than the 6,000 or so reportedly used in Afghanistan and much larger than the number used in the 1991 Gulf War.[9]

These special operation forces were part of both the RMA and the RDA, and their diplomatic efforts may have transcended their military triumphs. Surprisingly, the brilliant and ever dangerous SOF campaign resulted in light casualties. You will not find a more complete true story of SOF operations than is in this book for years to come, for their clandestine efforts are highly classified. It is a shame, for many a decoration, perhaps including the Medal of Honor, has been well earned.

In a secondary development that is still not confirmed, the President is said to have been persuaded not to unleash the full "Shock and Awe" air attack that had been both planned and touted, on the grounds that it was not necessary and that it might shock the world more than it would awe Iraqi opposition. This decision was consistent with the general desire to avoid collateral damage and ensure a minimum of Iraqi civilian injuries.

Almost any military officer not required to toe the official line would have disagreed with this decision in the early days of Operation Iraqi Freedom. It simply defies traditional doctrine and military logic to have overwhelming airpower and not apply it with the intense ferocity demonstrated in Operation Desert Storm. There are "unknown unknowns" on the battlefield as well, and it was possible that failure to employ overwhelming airpower might have allowed some elements of the Iraqi forces to resist in a more effective manner.

Yet in the end, the decision was not only sound but also brilliant, for

---

is to get "inside" the enemy OODA loop and stay there. For an excellent discussion of Boyd's theory see "John Boyd and John Warden: Airpower's Quest for Strategic Paralysis" in *The Paths to Heaven, The Evolution of Airpower Theory*, edited by Philip Meilinger. Maxwell AFB, AL, Air University Press, 1997.

it allowed the full employment of EBO while at the same time at least attempting to assuage Arab hatred of the United States for its invasion of an Arab country.*

From a maritime perspective, everything went right, both in combat terms and logistically.

In combat terms, the Navy had shrunk in size from 569 combatant ships at the time of the Gulf War to 305 today. In the 569-ship Navy, almost all long-range striking power was resident in the aircraft carriers, which were defended by all of the other ships in the group. The new 305-ship fleet has grown vastly in power, due in great part to an unheralded transformation brought about by the introduction of the MK 41 Vertical Launch System (VLS) for firing a wide variety of armament. The ships that used to be only defenders now have the capacity to strike themselves. In the 569-ship Navy, there were fifteen striking units, the carrier task forces. In the smaller Navy, there are still twelve carrier task forces, but there are also 116 surface combatants, thanks to the wider employment of the TLAM, which dates to the 1970s.

Earlier missile launchers had above-deck "rail" missile launchers loaded from below-deck rotary magazines and a fire control system that required that the target be continuously illuminated.

Intended initially to confront the threat of saturation antishipping missile launches from Soviet Backfire bombers, the VLS and the AEGIS combat system introduce a radically new shipboard missile capability.

The VLS is a canister launching system that provides rapid-fixed launch capability against multiple threat. Each missile launcher consists of a single eight-cell missile module, capable of launching a variety of missiles up to twenty-five inches in diameter. Smaller-diameter missiles, like the evolved Sea Sparrow, can be "quad-packed" in a single cell. Because VLS cells serve as both magazine and launcher, they are space-efficient and allow more missiles to be carried. As an example of the VLS ability to increase firepower, the cruiser USS *Ticonderoga* carried 88 missiles in its original configuration. Its sister ships were rebuilt with the VLS and now carry 128 missiles, with a higher rate of fire.

The submarine fleet has received a similar boost; the last thirty-three *Los Angeles*–class nuclear submarines had twelve TLAM cells built into the hull.

The advent of the sophisticated AEGIS Weapon System Mark 7, com-

* This is to the extent that Arab opinion of the United States and its policies can be affected positively by short-term actions. It is the author's belief that the decision to pursue the policy of minimizing collateral damage does not secure the "hearts and minds" of the Arab world but certainly must have an effect upon other nations. Securing genuine and widespread Arab friendship will not occur for many decades, if ever.

bined with the VLS, greatly increased Navy firepower. The AEGIS is the most capable surface-launched missile system in the Navy. It can train its weapons on aircraft or missile targets over a wide variety of altitudes from wave-top to directly overhead, at all speeds, and in all environments. It can search, track, and provide missile guidance for up to 100 targets simultaneously and needs only to illuminate its target in the terminal homing phase of the engagement. The combination of AEGIS/VLS allows much higher rates of fire than previous systems.

The improvement in Navy logistics was perhaps even greater, if less dramatic. Shortfalls in sea lift during the 1991 Gulf War were overcome by improvements to the Maritime Sealift Command throughout the 1990s. At a time when the combatant arm of the Navy shrank from 569 ships to around 300 ships, the logistics component increased to 115 sea-lift ships and 40 prepositioning ships, along with 33 ships of the naval auxiliary force and 25 special mission ships.

During the 1991 Gulf War, the entire sea-lift fleet had an average speed of advance of thirteen knots; this was increased to twenty knots during Operation Iraqi Freedom. Among the stars of the fleet were the nineteen Large Medium Speed Roll-on/Roll-off Ships* (LMSRs), each one 950 feet long or larger, capable of twenty-four knots, and able to carry some three-hundred-thousand square feet of equipment, the equivalent of 1,000 Bradley Fighting Vehicles.

The LMSRs were key, for they can be off-loaded in twenty-four to thirty-six hours, vital because Kuwait lacked the huge ports of Saudi Arabia.[10] At the peak of the Iraqi war, no less than 62 percent of the Military Sealift Command's prepositioning and surge sea-lift ships were directly supporting the war. The three Maritime Prepositioning Ship (MPS) squadrons used for prepositioning of Marine Corps equipment had been beefed up with additional vessels. Two of the squadrons were used during Operation Iraqi Freedom, delivering the equipment and supplies for two Marine Regimental Combat Teams.

During the Gulf War, the Pentagon chartered 215 foreign ships to carry cargo. For Operation Iraqi Freedom, 43 extra ships were charted, many after the Turkish Parliament's decision to deny U.S. troops passage through their country.[11]

---

* A roll-on/roll-off ship is equipped with ramps and one or more large vehicle decks (as in a ferry) for the swift movement of wheeled vehicles.

WHAT WENT WRONG AND WHY

At a macro level it must be said that Operation Iraqi Freedom was an astounding military victory and from a "big picture" and strategy standpoint almost nothing went wrong; however, it may be instructive to closely examine "what could have gone wrong" that would have turned Operation Iraqi Freedom into a disaster rather than an astounding success.

For example, the decision to strike with the relatively small number of forces may also have been a force-fed effort to prove the concept of transformation. If this is the case, then the administration, and particularly Secretary Rumsfield, was at fault. Something totally unexpected— Rumsfield's own "unknown unknowns"—could have occurred, and a larger number of the proverbial boots on the ground would have been not only welcome but also essential. Here are a few of the things that could have gone wrong and made many more troops not only desirable but also critically necessary:

1. The most obvious: effective deployment of chemical or biological weapons that killed or incapacitated a large number of coalition troops.
2. Armed intervention by another Arab state or a defection by an Arab state quietly backing the United States, e.g., Saudi Arabia or even Turkey. Suddenly bereft of bases and ports to flow in reinforcements and supplies, the troops on the ground might have had a much more difficult fight. Further, any such event would have slowed the coalition OODA cycle and given Iraq time to recover.
3. A natural (i.e., not caused by the enemy) outbreak of the SARS epidemic among the troops. As improbable as this might seem, given the high health standards and the physical shape of the troops, one must remember the infamous "Spanish flu" of World War I, which swept around the world in months.
4. Effective use of Silkworm-type antishipping missiles by the Iraqis, taking out shipping in the narrow littoral waters in which the U.S. Navy was deployed. This would include later use of Silkworms as the 4th Infantry Division equipment and personnel were moved on the long journey to Kuwait.

Things could have gone very wrong indeed—but they did not.

KEY WEAPON SYSTEMS

In this and subsequent chapters, key weapon systems will be examined to determine how they affected events in Operation Iraqi Freedom. The examination will cover the original requirements and the weapon systems' development and employment and include an evaluation of their success or failure. In the course of these several examinations, certain things will become evident. These include the following:

1. Deciding which weapon systems will be required ten to twenty years in the future is a demanding process, one that only really dedicated individuals in the military, industry, and government, working for the best interests of the nation, can determine after years of deliberation. Once a decision is made, producing those weapon systems requires even greater effort, for there are many ever-present threats, ranging from technological problems to budget cuts.

2. There are inherent flaws in the weapons acquisition system that makes successful weapons acquisition ever more difficult. It is an advocacy system that depends upon the integrity, connections, motivations, and good judgment of its backers. It is propelled by human beings, most of whom are patriots seeking the best for their country but a few of whom are looking out for their own careers, both in the military and in business. Inevitably, there will in some instances be human errors and/or human weaknesses involved.

3. The decisions on weapon systems are made in an ever-changing environment and in the light of countermeasures that are being created by possible opponents. As an example from the past, the Rockwell XB-70 might have been a splendid bomber had it not been for the Soviet development of sophisticated SAMs that rendered it obsolete. As an example from recent years, the September 11, 2001, terror attacks changed weapon system requirements in an instant. There was suddenly a massive expansion in the requirement for defensive equipment and creation of the requirement for entirely new and specialized offensive equipment.

4. Funds for defense spending are limited and must be divided among the five services. Then they must be apportioned within those services among vitally needed weapon systems competing with one another. The current state of the USAF tanker fleet is a case in point, despite its utter centrality to all air operations. The average age of a U.S. tanker is forty years, yet new tanker procurement has continually been put aside for other systems deemed more urgent. A

dozen other examples could be cited from each of the services, with aging helicopters being a common problem.

5. Things change. Few of the people forecasting weapon system requirements in 1981 could have anticipated the utter collapse of the principal enemy of the Cold War, the Soviet Union, in 1991. Fortunately, some of the top leaders of the U.S. Air Force clearly saw that the Soviet Union was faltering and began planning for a critical downsizing and reorganization that took effect in 1992. Other elements of the Department of Defense conducted similar reductions in force.

6. The congressional and media environment for weapon systems is utterly ruthless. Congresspeople—and in particular, their staffs—wire-brush every procurement at every stage, not always looking out for the best interests of the country but for the best interests of their political constituency. As a result there are procurement anomalies such as the General Dynamics F-111, which was maintained at a low production rate (twelve per year) for years against the express wishes of the U.S. Air Force. The reason was jobs in Texas, and it did not matter that such a low rate of production forced unit prices up dramatically and allowed companies supplying components to make huge profits on small production runs. There was no choice—if you only require twelve special valves of an aircraft hydraulic system a year and there is only one source, you have to pay what the company demands, or it will simply stop manufacturing that component.

7. The more sophisticated and advanced weapon systems become, the more expensive they are, and the more open to scrutiny. Further, failure is no longer tolerated. If a weapon system does not meet all of its milestones, on time and on budget, it becomes a highly visible target for cancellation. If a weapon system does not meet all its tests on the first trials, its enemies begin to clamor for cancellation in an ever-louder chorus. In contrast, the single most important intelligence-gathering system in our history (until that time), the CORONA Spy Satellites, failed miserably twelve times, flew a successful thirteenth test mission, but did not accomplish its goal of photographing the Soviet Union until the fourteenth attempt. In today's environment, CORONA would have been laughed off the stage of military testing by its fourth failure—and we might have lost the Cold War (or worse, been involved in a hot nuclear war) as a result.

8. The sheer technical demands being placed on today's weapon systems is an order of magnitude greater than twenty years ago, when real-time targeting, PGMs, and airborne lasers were just beginning

to be considered. Greater technical demands mean greater expense and a far greater chance of failure.

9. A variety of other factors influence weapons procurement, including the very artificial but huge expense of doing business with the federal government, whose specifications, regulations, record keeping, reporting requirements, and investigative teams would bankrupt a General Motors or a Ford.

10. The weapon systems fielded in Operation Iraqi Freedom come after a period when defense spending as a percentage of Gross Domestic Product (GDP) declined steadily, from 5.4 percent in 1992 to 3.0 percent in 2001. (In 2002, it crept back up to 3.4 percent.) During the same period, the demands placed on the military for military operations, humanitarian and compassionate relief missions, homeland defense, and other requirements increased on the order of 300 percent. This increase was met in the only way possible, by getting more out of the people and the equipment through increasing the tempo of operations to an unprecedented degree. (A current comment to illustrate how intensively people are used by all the military services is the saying "there are no rock painters out there," a reference to the long-bygone days of the draft when idle soldiers were assigned the task of whitewashing anything that didn't move and saluting anything that did.)

    When defense spending declines in this manner, at a time when military operations expand so dramatically, the military leaders have to balance force structure, personnel considerations, recapitalization (adding new equipment), and research and development in a Solomon-like manner.

Given all of these hazards in the weapon systems process, it is good to contemplate the overwhelming success of the weapon systems employed in Operation Iraqi Freedom, which were immensely superior to those so brilliantly displayed in the 1991 Gulf War. Put simply, despite all of the criticisms in the media and in Congress, someone in the acquisition community was doing a superb job of matching operational requirements to available assets and making the right choices. This is not to say the process was perfect, but it does definitely state that compared to other armed forces in the world and compared to other huge organizations, from the United Nations, to the Ford Motor Company, to the Catholic Church—you name it—the U.S. military has made an astounding series of correct decisions that raised the nation even above superpower status. A new term is coming into vogue to express the U.S. ascendancy: *hyper-*

power. With few exceptions, it appears the American military buys the right things and what it buys works.

Perhaps even more astounding, this massive accretion of selective power puts the United States in the position to do what it has done best in all its history, doing good for the world. No other nation in history has done so much "good" so unselfishly for so many as the United States. The United States never went to war for conquest or treasure. To paraphrase Secretary of State Colin Powell, the only land we ever sought from others was enough to bury our dead.

One facet of this emerging capacity to do good may well be a badly needed economic revolution for the Islamic states that are currently mired in economic squalor. The absolute military superiority of the United States really means that traditional arms races are not only obsolete but also irrelevant. If nations need only see to their internal security, that means that global spending on armaments can decline. (It peaked in 1985 at $1.3 trillion and is currently down to about $840 billion in 2002.[12])

Given the incredible difficulties in the procurement process and the heady prospects resulting from it, that process needs to be examined in the light of the great successes, and sometimes failures, against the background of critics who, if listened to, would without exception have stopped almost every single one of these procurements, including those that proved most successful.

A close analysis of the weapon system acquisition process demonstrated in Operation Iraqi Freedom leads to the conclusion that while things can always be improved and while savings can always be increased, the irrefutable fact of life is that the United States' weapon system procurement system has resulted in the most effective military force in history, one that truly is fitting for the sole superpower to exercise. Further, this is usable power. In the past, when there were two superpowers, the United States and the Soviet Union, each side possessed enormous nuclear power—but was unable to use it effectively because of the catastrophic consequences. Both nations still possess great nuclear power, but the United States alone possesses a flexible, highly trained, well-equipped, well-motivated array of armed forces that can project conventional power globally on an almost instantaneous basis.

So transcendent is the effective military power of the United States that no other nation in the world can change its methods, equipment, and defense expenditures to reach a similar status. Further, the United States is at the beginning of a rising curve of military power and efficiency. It is perhaps only 10 percent of the way along the curve where current technology and research will take it in the next twenty years. For instance, plans are already under way to achieve by 2010, a Space-Based Radar system that will become the focal point for the integration of manned and unmanned vehicles and space platforms, as directed by General John Jumper, USAF Chief of Staff.[13] Space operations hold the potential to eventually put the United States centuries ahead of other nations, as opposed to decades.

The success in Operation Iraqi Freedom also points to the fact that for the future single-mission fighter and bombers are out, while flexible fighters like the F-22A/B and JSF are in, along with concepts such as the "smart tankers" equipped with "ride-along" sensors and collectors.

EXAMPLES OF SUCCESSFUL (IF OFTEN CRITICIZED) PROGRAMS

Given the overwhelming importance of the coalition advantage in information, individual elements of the systems that gather information, collate, transmit, and use it will be treated throughout the rest of this book. Following will be a very broad-brush characterization of the many elements that make up the principal C⁴ISR systems that provide command, control, computing, communications, surveillance, intelligence, and reconnaissance capability and which conferred an inestimable advantage upon coalition forces. The system senses vital information (targets, friendly forces, enemy communications) and provides the information to the decision maker who then commands and controls the "shooter" (which could be a fighter, bomber, unmanned combat aerial vehicle, or cruise missile) to attack with a specific weapon at a specific time and place. The specificity of time and place has improved immeasurably over the years. Where once as much as twenty-four hours might have been required to establish the mission and execute it, that is now done within minutes. And where the target once might have been designated with somewhat questionable accuracy, it is now precisely defined by laser designation and/or the use of the GPS. Accuracy has been improved to the point that exact bull's-eyes seem customary and hits more than a dozen feet from the center of the target are regarded almost as balefully as a miss might be. Equally important, all services and appropriate command levels share the same "common operational picture," a gift from C⁴ISR systems to the command structure.

It is difficult for the scientist, much less the layperson, to grasp the enormity of the aggregate of satellite systems that are routinely employed, and this enormity applies to their orbital dimensions, their number, and their cost, for everything about a satellite is expensive, from its design through its manufacture and launch into orbit. There, to be useful, it requires a very costly system of ground stations to receive, collate, interpret, and retransmit the information provided. (In the future, microsatellites may be launched from rockets mounted under the wing of a jet aircraft, and costs may be thus reduced.)

The best way to visualize the vast utility of this complex information-gathering system is to view it at one of its central terminals, the huge wall display at the CAOC at Prince Sultan Air Base in Saudi Arabia. There depicted in real time are all the targets and locations of all the airborne coalition assets and even the ground troops. From hundreds of sources information flows in to be digitally converted into a map that allows commanders to see a common operational picture to know how to fight the war. If a new target appears, an attack can be launched against it in a matter of minutes. Smaller, and sometimes less capable, terminals are also found on aircraft, ships, and even SAM batteries. Never in history has so much information been available to a fighting force, nor has there ever been a greater difference in capabilities, for the Iraqi forces had scant information-gathering equipment, and most of this was jammed or destroyed. While the coalition command structure knew almost everything about the locations of Iraqi combat troops, the Iraqis operated blind.

The information is provided from a profusion of sources, and the system is intended to remove friction among tactical, theater, and national assets so that they will work together hand-in-glove.

Air Force Space Command is part of U.S. Space Command, which is a unified DOD command that includes the Navy Space Command and U.S. Army Space Command. Air Force Space Command is headquartered at Peterson Air Force Base, Colorado, and commanded by General Lance W. Lord. It is responsible for critical U.S. military space satellite systems. These systems include the GPS, Defense Support Program, Defense Meteorological Satellite Program, Defense Satellite Communication System, Milstar Satellite Communication System, and Polar Milsatcom System. (For a discussion of some of the other satellite systems, see appendix 3.)

According to Lieutenant General T. Michael Moseley (CENTCOM Joint Forces Air Component Commander), there were more than fifty satellites (Air Force, Navy, and National Reconnaissance Office) that directly supported operations in Iraq.[14]

Other systems used to gather information include the Lockheed Martin U-2, Boeing E-3 Airborne Warning and Control System (AWACS), Northrop Grumman E-8 Joint Surveillance and Target Attack Radar (Joint STARS), Boeing RC-135 Rivet Joint, Cobra Ball, Cobra Judy (deployed for its first operational use) and Combat Sent, Northrop Grumman E-2 Hawkeye and EA-6B Prowler, Lockheed Martin EP-3 and P-3C, and Beech Raytheon RC-12 Guardrails. The unmanned aerial vehicles included the

Predator, the Global Hawk, and a classified version of the Lockheed Skunkworks' former Dark Star.

To illustrate the scrutiny, the criticism, and the outright opposition that all weapon systems face, it is instructive to examine the case of the Boeing E-3 Sentry, an early "C-Cubed" (C^3 or Command, Communication, and Control) aircraft, the AWACS. Essentially a modified Boeing 707 with a thirty-foot rotating dome, it, like many other weapon systems, had difficulty in convincing critics that it would do the job it was built to do.

The April 13, 1974, issue of *New Republic* called the mission of the latest USAF aircraft, the AWACS, a complete phony. It was described as yet another ploy designed to keep hard-earned taxpayer dollars flowing to bloated defense contractors who were offering a shimmering idea that could not be achieved. The title of the article was "AWACS: The Plane That Would Not Die."[15] The aircraft itself (which was in fact quite beautiful) was sneered at as "a mushroom with elephantiasis."

The *New Republic* article was, like so many of its kind, not based on an understanding of the mission, the technology, or the requirement for the aircraft. It was instead a knee-jerk reaction against military spending on big-ticket items, particularly those where security requirements do not allow immediate explanation of the rationale for the acquisition.

The first AWACS aircraft was delivered on March 24, 1977. The small AWACS fleet (there are currently thirty-two in the inventory) is termed a "high-demand, low-density platform" and has done yeoman work all around the world. Hidden in the burden of the AWACS's research, development, and production costs was its role as a force multiplier, an aircraft that could make a handful of aircraft do the work of hundreds. In effect the AWACS was infinitely more capable than the Chain Home system that defended Great Britain in 1940 or the DEW Line (Distance Early Warning Line) upon which U.S. defenses depended, for it provided early warning against any incoming Soviet aircraft.

Then Secretary of Defense James R. Schlesinger realized that the AWACS could be enhanced so that it could serve not only as an early-warning aircraft but also as an airborne command-and-control center for use in tactical-air operations. This was a revolutionary step forward, one that provided radar with a positive offensive capability by making it a force multiplier.

The product that the *New Republic* scoffed at had been under way since 1965; it had developed its own streamlined management system that became a model for later programs; it conducted an extensive airframe fly-off competition that saw the Boeing 707 win over the McDonnell Douglas DC-8 and the Lockheed EC-121. It held an even more intensive radar system competition in which Westinghouse was selected over Hughes.

But Schlesinger's suggestion for expanded use of the AWACS was attacked as meaning that the aircraft had no mission and that a phony mission was being created to justify its expense. The idea sped to opponents in Congress, particularly Colorado Representative Patricia A. Schroeder in the House and Missouri Senator Thomas F. Eagleton. Fortunately, Congress created a special review committee that came to the conclusion that the system would work and was necessary.

The rest of the world soon saw that AWACS fulfilled its mission, and members of the NATO alliance, France, Saudi Arabia, and the United Kingdom, bought sufficient aircraft to swell the worldwide fleet to sixty-six aircraft. Japan more recently purchased four Boeing 767–based versions.

Since its debut, the AWACS has performed brilliantly domestically and in conflicts around the world, including those in Panama, Grenada, Haiti, Kuwait, Kosovo, Serbia, Afghanistan, and Iraq. In the 1991 Gulf War, the all-seeing eye of the AWACS completely encompassed not only the country of Kuwait but the entire area of responsibility (AOR) as well, detecting and noting where every aircraft flew every moment of the day. The AWACS provided information to guide more than 120,000 sorties by coalition forces, flying more than 5,000 hours on 400 missions to do so. It took part in thirty-eight of the forty aerial victories gained by the coalition air forces.[16] Perhaps most important for the average American, the AWACS became so absolutely indispensable to homeland defense after 9/11 that five NATO E-3 aircraft and crews were deployed to the United States to monitor commercial traffic—a mission clearly never foreseen by any planner.

In Operation Iraqi Freedom, all of the satellites, manned aircraft, and Unmanned Aerial Vehicles (UAVs) work in concert with still other information sources to provide commanders with real-time information in visual formats. The information comes in a continuous stream that requires computers and able, well-trained personnel to translate it into meaningful combat action. That translation was done adeptly in Operation Iraqi Freedom and was a significant factor in the rapid "inside the enemy's decision loop" advance of the coalition forces to Baghdad and beyond.

3

"G" Day Before "A" Day: Saddam's
World Turned Upside Down

OPERATION IRAQI FREEDOM:
March 22, 23, and 24

"A" Day, the first air attacks, had followed "G" Day, the first ground attacks, in a brilliant move that confounded the Iraqis while still providing grist for the doubting mills of commentators. General Franks' forces demonstrated an amazing flexibility. The heavy 3rd Infantry Division (Mechanized) moved with extraordinary speed, racing more than 200 miles in a short period of time. It was aided by the air assault capability of the 101st Airborne Division (Airborne Assault), which provided the reach and the striking power of a large number of Apache helicopters. The Army elements were complemented by the 1st Marine Expeditionary Force (MEF), engaged in proving that it was as formidable launched deep into the desert as it was on the beaches and by U.K. forces, operating primarily in the south.

On the diplomatic scene, the United States gave up any last hope of Turkey allowing troop transit and began to send elements of the 4th Infantry Division (Mechanized), the most technically advanced armored infantry unit in the U.S. Army, to Kuwait through the Suez Canal, vulnerable en route to any sort of ragtag missile attack and even to the vagaries of Egyptian politics. Turkey was not so confused that it could not slip almost 1,500 of its own tough soldiers over the Iraqi border into Kurdish territory, where their ostensible purpose was to "maintain order" but their real mission was to be the thin edge of a Turkish military wedge. The Turks were concerned about a Kurdish demand for an independent state that would include Turkey's Kurdish population—and Turkish territory.

The Turks did at last allow the use of Turkish airspace, permitting strikes from the USS *Harry S. Truman* and USS *Theodore Roosevelt*, but no combat fighter missions were allowed to be flown from Incirlik Air Base, which had been the bastion of Operation Northern Watch for over ten years.

Under the command of Lieutenant General William A. Wallace, V Corps romped forward, out-Rommeling Rommel, avoiding cities where possible, and using airpower to sap the strength of enemy forces. In boxing terms, the coalition forces danced like a butterfly but stung like a bee, the long arms of its airpower and its vastly superior armor and artillery crushing Iraqi resistance at a distance. The 4,500 soldiers in each of the individual brigades of the 3rd Infantry Division (Mechanized), commanded by Major General Buford Blount, leapfrogged one another, one moving ahead to seize a position[1] while another stopped, refueled, rearmed, and "rested," a term that falls far short of describing the well-deep slumber of the adrenaline-drained Kevlar-clad soldiers as they flopped into foxholes scooped out of the desert floor.

The swift advance of the American units posed all sorts of genuine problems: defense of the flanks; supply of water, ammunition, and fuel; and the administration of prisoners of war. A delay of almost twelve hours occurred because of routine mechanical breakdowns and the inevitable difficulties of launching a division-sized attack. Fortunately, it was the media and the military commentators who leaped on these difficulties and exploited the breakdowns rather than the Iraqis, who were relieved to have a breathing spell for whatever reason. The United States was already inside the Iraqi decision cycle, spreading confusion and anticipating reactions.

The armed forces of the United States have a long history of using airpower to cover their flanks. Elwood Quesada's Ninth Air Force did it for George Patton in Europe, and Charles Horner's coalition air forces did it for Norman Schwartzkopf in Desert Storm. It worked again in Iraq, and backed by the crushing firepower of aircraft and its own 11th Aviation Battalion AH-64 Apache helicopters and bolstered by vastly superior intelligence, surveillance, reconnaissance (ISR) assets, the 3rd peeled off individual battalions to protect its flanks and stop Iraqi forces from intervening. This was in every sense both an air and ground occupation of Iraq. So great was the difference in firepower that the Iraqi 11th Infantry Division, defending Talil airfield, surrendered to the 1st Battalion, 15th Infantry Regiment after the briefest exchange. Nonetheless, a decision was made to delay entrance to the city of An Nasiriya, as the 3rd was determined not to bog down in urban warfare.

Tradition was reversed when the 3rd Brigade of the 3rd Infantry Division seized a bridge crossing the fabled Euphrates River outside of An Nasiriya, holding it until a Marine unit arrived to take over and allow the

brigade to resume its march up Highway 28, west of the river.[2] The Marines moved primarily in their Assault Amphibious Vehicle P7-A1
(AAV/LTVD-7) series thirty-two-ton amphibious armored vehicles
(familiarly, the "amtrack"), which hold 171 gallons of diesel fuel—and get
about one mile per gallon. Stops are required every thirty to sixty miles
to be sure there is adequate fuel on board for any combat that might
occur.

In southern Iraq, Basra remained an elusive goal as both the 1st Marine
Division and U.K. forces moved to encircle it. In the days to come the
long delay in taking Basra would be endlessly misinterpreted. While the
city remained controlled by Ba'athist Party officials, a small element of
the Iraqi 51st Mechanized Division did what all of Saddam's forces had
been expected to do: dug their tanks into defensive positions and put up
a stiff but losing fight.

The Marines took on ten T-55s that were defending oil fields and
ripped them to shreds with antitank missiles, including the new Raytheon/
Lockheed Martin Javelin "fire and forget" shoulder-launched weapon that
launches a $75,000 missile with a 2,000-meter range, and the Hughes BGM-
71 TOW (Tube-launched, Optically tracked, Wire guided). TOWs were
mounted on the famous HMMWV, while the Javelins were shoulder-fired.

Built in a bewildering number of versions, by American Motors General, the HMMWV (High Mobility Multipurpose Wheeled Vehicle—
Hummer or Humvee in the civilian world) is a direct descendant of the
famed Willys Jeep and is the daydream vehicle of anyone trapped in highway traffic. The difference between it and its Iraqi counterpart, the "technical" (Somali slang, usually a commercial light truck with machine guns
on an improvised mounting), was a metaphor for the war in general. The
"technical" falls short in every way when compared to the diesel-powered
HMMWV with which the coalition forces roamed deserts and towns like
a well-mannered—but easily offended—Hell's Angels motorcycle gang.
The Marines purchased more than 20,000 of the HMWVs at a bargain
$50,000 each.

Unlike his T-55 tank unit, the Iraqi Commanding General of the 51st
Mechanized Division was not disposed to fight and surrendered to the
Marines. Almost 8,000 men of the Iraqi 51st Infantry Division, reportedly
equipped with 200 tanks, surrendered to U.S. troops with virtually no
fighting. The 51st was designated to defend Basra and, oddly enough, was
praised in a rambling speech by Saddam a few days later. Later analysis
showed that the 51st had done the smart thing, as it was poorly trained
and poorly equipped. Among its training instructions was found advice
on reconnaissance (climb a palm tree) and the salutary effect on one's

soul of suicide attacks. Most of the 8,000 men of the 51st were not imprisoned but simply disappeared from the battlefield.

Farther to the south, the most dangerous Iraqi resistance to date, that of the fanatical *Fedayeen* Saddam, fought to delay the coalition seizure of Umm Qasr. Members of the *Fedayeen* Saddam apparently believed that they had nothing to lose and might as well die fighting. While not a tactical threat, they presented a danger that would persist for months to come and, like suicide bombers, inflicted pointless but unavoidable casualties. Outside of Umm Qasr, extensive mine-sweeping operations were conducted to remove mines and allow compassionate supplies to reach the port and be unloaded for distribution. This was one of the first times in the history of warfare that compassionate relief for enemy populations arrived concurrently with ongoing military operations, sometimes to the detriment of military resupply operations. It sent a signal to the Arab and Muslim worlds that apparently has not yet been recognized.

The RMA was advanced another notch with a General Atomics Aeronautical Systems Corporation MQ-1 Predator firing an AGM-114K "Hellfire II" missile against an Iraqi Shilka, a ZSU-23-4 tracked, self-propelled antiaircraft gun located near Al Amarah. The Soviet-built ZSU-23 fires four 23mm AZP cannons and was used with effect against the Israeli Air Force during the 1973 Yom Kippur War. The Lockheed Martin Hellfire II comprises a whole family of missiles for antiarmor, antishipping, and so on, but the real advance in warfare is the use of the UAV to take out an enemy vehicle on its first sortie in Operation Iraqi Freedom. (The Predator had scored previous successes in Afghanistan.)

(Later in the campaign, the Iraqis would move a satellite television antenna next to the Grand Mosque in Baghdad, believing it would be safe there from air attack. A Predator with a Hellfire destroyed it without damaging the mosque.)

Because "G" Day had preceded "A" Day, aerial activity had seemed to get off to a slow start. Even the real-time video presentation of the bombing of key targets in Baghdad did not capture the extent and intensity of air operations, which had reached more than 1,000 sorties on the second day of the war and were sustained at or above that level.

On Day 4 of the war, March 23, twelve troops of the 507th Ordnance Maintenance Company were reported missing at An Nasiriyah, where fighting was sustained and heavy. Some fifty Marines of Task Force Tarawa were wounded after entering the city and engaging in street fighting. Two bridges were secured east of the city.

The Iraqis introduced a new and despicable tactic, illegal under the Laws of Armed Conflict, by signaling their intent to surrender, then opening fire on American forces as they approached. Such ambushes killed nine Marines. The American reaction was close air support (CAS) with Boeing F/A-18 Hornets, Boeing AV-8B Harrier II vertical takeoff and landing fighters, and Boeing (Fairchild Republic) A-10s Warthogs coming in to hammer the Iraqis.

The 3rd Infantry Division sprinted to within 100 miles of Baghdad, with one unit, the 2nd Brigade, thrusting forward for 230 miles in the previous forty hours. During that advance, the 2nd Brigade had engaged Ba'ath Party militiamen near the city of An Najaf, on the western banks of the Euphrates.[4] Once again it was a long-range sparring process, with the greater reach of American weapons killing more than 100 of the enemy.

In the south, the deliberate movement of British forces and the continued fighting around Basra continued to spur speculations of imminent disaster in the media. Brigadier Maurie McNarn, the National Commander of Operation Falconer (the Australian code name for the war), sent Australian boarding parties composed of both men and women aboard Iraqi ships. Three enemy vessels carrying a total of eighty-six mines plus a large assortment of other weaponry were seized. This operation was a crucial step forward to permit the port of Umm Qasr to open and receive the humanitarian aid supplies that were on board ships just outside the harbor. In other action, HMAS *Anzac* supported British commandos operating on the Al Faw peninsula with naval gunfire. Australian special forces, as tough and skilled as any in the world and bearing the heritage of the World War II commando teams, continued to operate deep within Iraq in the strategic reconnaissance role.

In the air, coalition forces continued to decimate Iraqi ground forces in the field while making pinpoint attacks against the headquarters location of the Iraqi Intelligence Service and the Special Security Service. The attacks were not without incident. An RAF Panavia GR4 Tornado was shot down by a PATRIOT missile when returning from a combat mission. Flight Lieutenant Kevin Main (Pilot) and Flight Lieutenant Dave Williams (Weapon System Officer) were killed. The disturbing aspects of this friendly fire incident were compounded thirty miles south of An Najaf the next day when, in self-defense, a U.S. Lockheed Martin F-16CJ attacked with a HARM (High-Speed Anti-Radiation Missile) the U.S. PATRIOT battery that had locked on to it. There were no deaths or injuries, and the full results of the subsequent investigation have not yet been released.

Earlier in the day, two Royal Navy Sea King helicopters collided, killing all seven aboard.

On March 24, the fifth day of the war, bombing operations were extended 210 miles north of Baghdad at Mosul, heralding increased coalition activity in northern Iraq. More than 1,500 sorties were flown on the twenty-fourth, and a new pattern of air warfare began to emerge. Where in the past the targets had almost all been carefully identified prior to the mission, on the twenty-fourth only 200 of the 800 strike sorties were flown against preplanned targets (i.e., listed in the ATO). The remaining 600 were flown against "emerging" targets, meaning targets that had been identified by ISR elements as targets of opportunity. It was in this capability that the full coalition information domination became apparent.

Among these 600 were the sorties flown by elements of the 332nd AEW. Lockheed Martin F-16s and Fairchild-Republic (Boeing) A-10s also provided CAS to the Marines. For the F-16s, it was a change in tactics, operating at lower altitudes in a high-threat environment provided by antiaircraft guns and shoulder-fired SAMs, the Man Portable Air Defense Systems (MANPADs).

CENTCOM noted that more than 2,000 PGMs had been dropped since the start of operations.

The Iraqi response was feeble; at 1:00 A.M., a tactical ballistic missile was fired against Kuwait. It was intercepted and destroyed by a PATRIOT missile, ending the PATRIOT's day on a brighter note than it had begun.

Many Boeing AH-64 Apache helicopters of the 11th Aviation Regiment sustained severe damage in a predawn attack on an entrenched brigade of the Republican Guard Medina Division stationed between Karbala and Al Hillah. One Apache was shot down and its two crew members captured.* The Iraqis had apparently used cell phones to relay warning of the Apache's attack.

At sea, the USS *Theodore Roosevelt* launched its first strikes, attacking one of Saddam Hussein's palace complexes and an AM radio broadcasting station in central Iraq. The mission, flown by Carrier Air Wing 8, lasted for several hours and took multiple refuelings. The combat strike was noteworthy, as "The Big Stick," as the carrier is known, had completed its initial training only four months earlier.

In general, March 24 was assessed as a bad day for the coalition by some of the media. The downing of the RAF Tornado on the previous day, the loss of the Apache, and the display of American prisoners of war on Al-Jazeera and Iraqi television, the problem posed by Turkish troops entering northern Iraq, and the inability to get compassionate aid flowing into Umm Qasr were all regarded as downticks in reporting the war's progress.

---

* Chief Warrant Officer David S. Williams, 31, of Orlando, Fla., and Chief Warrant Officer Ronald D. Young, 26, of Atlanta, Ga., were freed on April 12, 2003.

THE VIEW FROM THE OTHER SIDE

Enemy supporters continued to spin dross rumor into gold propaganda in the face of the looming disaster. On March 22, General Franks was quoted as saying, "We've just spent three days trying to capture one small town, so we can only guess what awaits us in Baghdad!" The general tenor of the anti-American reports was to exaggerate both the severity of coalition air attacks and the number of coalition losses. On the same day, the reports indicated that the 51st Iraqi Division was fighting strongly and that the 3rd Infantry Division and 1st Marine Infantry Divisions were in an "exceptionally difficult situation" thanks to a decisive attack by eighty Iraqi tanks that put the coalition forces in danger of being surrounded. On March 23, the GRU reports indicated "up to twenty" Iraqi tanks lost, with one hundred troops killed, while the coalition lost ten tanks, several APCs, and fifteen troops killed.

Interestingly enough, the reports indicated that Jordan's "top leadership" had a secret agreement with the United States to allow coalition use of its air bases and permitted up to 400 SOF personnel to operate from Jordan. The success of the SOF personnel was ensured by the extraordinarily effective operations of the 410 Air Expeditionary Force (AEF) and the 120 EFS, whose brilliant precision bombing confounded the Iraqis.

By March 24, the GRU reports indicated that coalition forces were exhausted and that a huge battle between the U.S. 3rd Infantry Division and the Iraqi 3rd Army Corps had no significant results. Iraqi special forces units were singled out for praise in action against the British.[5]

WHAT WENT RIGHT AND WHY

Despite the rumbling of media discontent at any sign of the advance slowing down, and in the face of continual warnings of a pending trap to be sprung by Saddam's elite forces near Baghdad, the coalition forces played two totally different games at one time and did very well with both.

American forces moved with the swiftness and the motion of a sidewinder* as they relayed themselves up the western desert areas of Iraq and the Tigris-Euphrates river valleys, moving ever closer to Baghdad.

---

* Not to be confused with the later Operation Sidewinder to round up dissident Iraqi militants.

There were some inevitable problems getting sufficient fuel and water supplies, but these were overcome. Security requirements veiled the exact positions of the 3rd Infantry Division, the 1st Marine Division, and the 101st Airborne Assault Division. In the south, British forces played python to the 3rd's sidewinder, slowly contracting its grip upon Basra and undertaking the steps that would (1) isolate and destroy the Ba'athist Party officials and (2) provide a means of getting humanitarian supplies to the Iraqi people.

The American movements were facilitated by airpower reducing enemy opposition to fire and smoke. The ground forces were protected by the inherent power of its often-criticized General Dynamics Land Systems M1A1/M1A2 Abrams tank and the United Defense M2/M3 Bradley Mechanized Infantry/Cavalry Fighting Vehicle.

True, the Abrams gulped fuel at the rate of two gallons for every mile it traveled, but its digitized, direct fire capability and its 120-mm M256 smoothbore cannon dominated the battlefield. Both the Bradley and the Abrams rank with the Lockheed C-5 in terms of the length and bitter degree of the controversy generated. Yet the Bradley worked well with the Abrams in Desert Storm and even better in Operation Iraqi Freedom.

In Basra, schooled by decades of experience in Northern Ireland, the British employed every trick in their repertoire in slowly but inexorably taking possession of Basra. There was a curious interface between the British and the Iraqi people, who were threatening when watched by the Ba'athist Party members who stayed behind but encouraging when they felt they were not watched. Instead of charging in to destroy the relatively few still loyal to Saddam, the British flushed them out, cutting off and searching one area of the town at a time. At a time when their American opposite numbers were speeding northward at a record pace, the British were doing their assigned job just as well, but without the dramatic speed.

Perhaps the thing that went best was the smooth cooperation among the coalition components, which operated from the start with a greater, smoother degree of "jointness" (willing and active cooperation among the various armed services) than had ever been seen before, including the recent wars in Bosnia, Kosovo, the Gulf, and Afghanistan. The goal of jointness had been sought without much luck since the Revolutionary War. It received a big boost with the Goldwater-Nichols Defense Reorganization Act of 1986, which greatly increased the powers of the Chairman of the Joint Chiefs of Staff and had been in part intended to force jointness upon the services.

In the military, as in business or academia, smooth relations ultimately depend upon personalities, and the American forces were fortunate to have leaders who had served, trained, and exercised together and knew how to get along. The success in Iraq was so dependent upon these personalities and upon the degree of sophistication and training that the modern military requires of its officers that they deserve individual recognition as representatives of the general high level of quality of leadership engaged in OIF.

In every organization, the people in charge have to take the blame when things go wrong; unfortunately, when things go right, they seldom get the credit. Things went right for General Tommy R. Franks, who projected a levelheaded (if not charismatic), basically friendly personality both in his television interviews and in private with his staff. Franks avoided publicity, declining all but three invitations to do the briefing at CENTCOM. Far easier to get along with than General Schwarzkopf had been during the 1991 Gulf War, Franks set the tone for cooperation among all the services. Commissioned from Officer's Candidate School in 1967, Franks' background was in Field Artillery. He served as Assistant Division Commander, First Cavalry Division, during Operation Desert Shield/ Desert Storm. As Commander in Chief, U.S. Central Command, he had full responsibility for operations for the war in Afghanistan, where he established targets for jointness that matured in Iraq.

Franks has two senior officers upon whom he relies implicitly. The first is his CENTCOM Deputy Commander, Lieutenant General Michael P. DeLong. A Naval Academy graduate who flew helicopters in Vietnam, DeLong has more than 5,600 hours' flying time, of which 800 hours were in combat. Serving as Franks' Deputy Commander (Forward) is Lieutenant General John Abiziad, whom some consider to be a "polar opposite" to General Franks. Noted for his quick decision making and fluent in Arabic, he earned the nickname "the Mad Arab" at West Point, from which he graduated in 1973. He started his career with the 504th Parachute Infantry Regiment and commanded a Ranger company during the invasion of Grenada in 1983. It was there that Abiziad pulled a trick straight from John Wayne's repertoire when faced with an entrenched body of Cuban troops. Jumping from a C-130 at less than 600 feet, Abiziad ordered one of his officers to hot-wire a bulldozer and drive it toward the enemy, while Abiziad and his men advanced behind the improvised armor, firing as they came. Abiziad exemplifies the Army's post-Vietnam breed of officer, according to Loren Thompson, head of the Lexington Institute.[6]

There are four component commanders who report to Franks, and they are all praised for the smooth, cooperative manner in which they get along. Their cooperation allowed Franks to devote all of his energies to running the war, without worrying about jurisdictional disputes. A brief review of those component commanders will illustrate the generally high intellectual standards found in the armed services today.

The U.S. Navy, for some very good reasons (including an overwhelming concern about fleet defense), was in the past generally regarded as the service least inclined to sacrifice much to the concept of joint operations. The Chief of Naval Operations, Admiral Vern Clark, made a decided effort to change his service's point of view, as a story about him illustrates. During the war in Kosovo in 1999, President William J. Clinton had wished to avoid the use of ground forces. Airpower had been used sparingly, and the war was going slowly. An Air Force colonel, Kevin Kennedy, pointed out to Admiral Clark, who was director of the Joint Chiefs of Staff at the time, that if the war was not won soon, there could be as many as 1 million refugees who would have to be taken care of when winter came. Clark understood, and advocated the Air Force recommendation, an intensive air campaign, to the Joint Chiefs of Staff. As a result, NATO cranked up the air war, and the Kosovo conflict was brought to a conclusion on June 9.[7] It was a portent of things to come in the jointness arena.

Clark's leadership style has created many followers who emulate him, and one of these is the Commander, Coalition Forces Maritime Component, Vice Admiral Timothy J. Keating. A native of Dayton, Ohio, Keating graduated from the U.S. Naval Academy in 1971. A pilot with more than 5,000 hours and 1,100 "traps" (carrier landings), he was formerly Commander of the Naval Strike Warfare Center at Naval Air Station, Fallon, Nevada—a key job for his current position.

"Tim" Keating oversees no less than 140 ships, including five carrier battle groups, the most powerful naval forces ever to be concentrated in the Middle East. In the course of Operation Iraqi Freedom over 70 percent of the Navy's ships and 50 percent of its submarines were at sea, including seven carrier strike groups (CSG), three amphibious ready groups (ARG), and two amphibious task forces (ATF), for a total of more than 77,000 sailors and embarked Marines. The extensive naval presence in the Gulf, including Headquarters U.S. Fifth Fleet and the two secure ports in Kuwait, enabled efficient, swift off-loading.[8] Many of the coalition nations provide ships to his fleet. Admiral Keating was affable, able to conduct a press briefing with both humor and discipline, even when the media touched on sensitive subjects such as the use of carbon filament warheads on Tomahawk missiles or the shortage of aerial tankers for in-flight refueling.

Keating's Marine counterpart is Lieutenant General Earl B. Hailston, a muddy-boot Marine who enlisted in 1967 and was commissioned in 1968 in the Enlisted Commission Program. This is perhaps the most demanding route to flag officer rank, and only a very focused individual, with all the right leadership traits, can follow it. Hailston won his wings in 1973 and subsequently flew the McDonnell Douglas F-4 Phantom fighter. He attended the U.S. Army War College in 1985, followed by a tour with the U.S. Eighth Army in Korea, further polishing his skills in joint operations.

It was a significant, even revolutionary, step that the MEF would operate under the command of the third element of the four-service cooperation package, Lieutenant General David D. McKiernan, the Coalitions Forces Land Component (CFLC) Commander. A 1972 ROTC graduate from the College of William and Mary, McKiernan has been involved with armor for almost his entire career. During the Gulf War, he ran the Corps Tactical Command Post. He joined the Allied Command European Rapid Reaction Force in 1996, operating in Bosnia-Herzegovina. In 1999, he conducted operations with the Seventh Army in Bosnia, Albania, and Kosovo. His leadership skills and his aptitude for joint operations have been demonstrated in Iraq, where he had soldiers, sailors, airmen, and Marines, along with representatives of eleven other coalition nations, under his command. It was McKiernan, with his operational knowledge, daring, and intuitive leadership style, who accepted the risk of the Third Army's continuous high tempo of operations while extending his lines of communication and thinning his logistics train.[9]

But McKiernan was confident that his flanks and lines of communication would be covered by coalition airpower, under the command of Lieutenant General T. Michael "Buzz" Moseley. Moseley, the Coalition's Joint Force Air Component Commander (JFACC), is an ebullient sixth-generation Texan, quick with a quip, some of them salty. A graduate of Texas A&M, a veteran Boeing F-15C Command Pilot, Moseley commands operations of more than 2,000 aircraft based at thirty different locations, as well as from bases in Europe, aboard five U.S. Navy carrier battle groups and four Marine amphibious readiness groups. This is his sixth joint assignment.

A taste of Moseley's style came in an April 5 briefing, with Moseley talking by phone from Prince Sultan Air Base in Saudi Arabia for the Coalition Forces Air Component Command Brief. Bob Burns of the Associated Press asked, "Could you tell us what your airborne sensors are showing about where some of the Republican Guard units have gone since American ground forces approached Baghdad?" Moseley replied, "That's a good question. I'll tell you up front that our sensors show that the preponderance of the Republican Guard divisions that were outside of Baghdad are now dead. We've laid on these people. I find it interesting when folks say we are softening them up. We're not softening them up; we're killing them."

These four officers—Keating, Hailston, McKiernan, and Moseley—trained and schooled in "jointness," would be remarkable in the armed forces of any nation. What distinguishes them, however, is that they represent the upper levels of a pyramid of intellectual quality that has as its foundation the best-trained, best-equipped, all-volunteer enlisted force in the world. There are currently calls for the reinstitution of the draft as a means of "leveling the social playing field." If the playing field has to be leveled, let it be by a draft that provides opportunities for social service, perhaps like the Depression's Civilian Conservation Corps, but the draft must not be used as social engineering to provide the armed services with personnel. Only a volunteer organization can achieve the level of proficiency and training that the U.S. armed forces currently possess.

One of the unrecognized strengths of the U.S. armed forces is the noncommissioned officer corps. The enlisted men and women of the military services are led by extremely competent noncommissioned officers, who represent an element of strength in U.S. armed forces that is matched only in the United Kingdom and Australia. These noncommissioned officers are the backbone of their respective services, and one need only ask any officer if this is the case. Without them, all of the armed services would collapse. They get responsibility and authority at a level never dreamed of in the past, and they are provided a degree of education previously unheard of for noncommissioned ranks. The services' internal education programs turn out thinking, skilled warriors able to operate sophisticated equipment.

When relations began to thaw between the United States and the Soviet Union, each country hosted visits by the military leaders of the other. The Soviet leaders were blasé about the superb U.S. equipment, its well-kept bases, and the amenities available to service families. However they were thunderstruck at the quality of the U.S. noncommissioned officers, for whom there was no Soviet counterpart. The fact that a high percentage of the noncommissioned officers were women utterly astounded the Soviets.

The services are led by professional officers, also volunteers, well schooled, well motivated, and a vital part of the civilian community. There are many dimensions of the intellectual quality of the armed services that had an effect in Operation Iraqi Freedom, but two deserve examination here. The first of these is the extraordinary level of training that is provided at all levels. This includes the basic training given soldiers, sailors, and airmen as they begin their career as enlisted personnel. It applies to officers who graduate from the service academies, as well as those who come in by other routes to a commission. It also includes the various specialty schools and the service staff colleges that are conscientiously designed to be true "centers of excellence" and that provide additional degrees of training as officers progress through the ranks. A relatively new example of these highly refined institutions is the School of Advanced Aerospace Studies, at Maxwell Air Force Base, Alabama. It compares in course difficulty, quality of students, and prestige within the service with the Harvard School of Business.

One thing that distinguishes this training and the applicable schools is the extraordinary rigor and frequency of the testing process. There are few occupations in civilian life where a participant is tested more often than a serviceperson. And for the most part, there is no "Gentleman's C": you are required to do well on the tests or repeat the course work. In the practical tests—such as in Air Force Operational Readiness Inspections (ORIs), in the many competitions, or in advanced training such as Red Flag or Top Gun—the testing is so close to the real wartime environment that veterans of the schools sometimes find actual combat a comedown.

The other dimension of intellectual quality to be discussed here is the rare combination of academic and practical philosophy that has found expression in the U.S. Air Force in the work of such officers as Colonels David S. Fadok and John Warden and Major General David Deptula. These three men represent a host of others in the Air Force and in other services who are warrior/philosophers, combat veterans at the operational level. They study the art of war in a deep and consistent manner and write about it regularly in service journals. The standards of these journals are quite high, and the articles in them generate a great deal of debate. Further, they equal or eclipse any corresponding publications of preceding generations in terms of their scope and rigor. And it is fair to say that it is the work of these warrior/philosophers that has helped bring American warfare to its current high state.

The U.S. Air Force has a central planning office that epitomizes this new breed of warrior/philosophers. Known officially in the Pentagon as AF/XOOC but more familiarly as "Checkmate," it was established in 1976 by then Chief of Staff General David C. Jones. He wanted a cadre of experts on NATO and the Warsaw Pact, formed into "Red and Blue teams" to test alternative strategies and war plan scenarios.

By 1991, the diminishing threat of the Soviet Union allowed Checkmate to transform into an air operations planning unit. Its first efforts, for Desert Shield/Desert Storm, received mixed reviews initially, but when JFACC brought Checkmate officers into the area, they played a major role.

Since that time Checkmate has transformed again, with a new charter to become the principal air and space planners of war at the operational level. Checkmate is designed to build bridging mechanisms from the strategic level to the operational level and from the operational level to the tactical level. Directed currently by Colonel Timothy H. Hyde, Checkmate is staffed by some of the ablest officers in the Air Force.

Members of the 379th Expeditionary Maintenance Squadron roll out an AGM-130. The squadron built up more than 5,000 weapons during the four weeks before air operations began over Iraq. The AGM-130 is an air-to-surface guided and powered bomb that has a weight of almost 3,000 pounds. It uses either a television or an infrared guidance system and has a range of about thirty-four miles. The warhead is a standard Mark 84 bomb. The AGM-130 can hit within ten feet of its target. *(Courtesy: U.S. Air Force)*

The beautiful Boeing B-1B with its wings extended for lower-speed flight. At higher speeds, the wings sweep back. The B-1B became the backbone of the bomber force during Operation Iraqi Freedom. *(Courtesy: U.S. Air Force)*

The ancient Boeing B-52 was mated with the ultramodern Litening II pod to give it an unprecedented capability at night and an unprecedented accuracy. *(Courtesy: U.S. Air Force)*

The entries that this young crew chief makes in the Boeing B-1B maintenance log are absolutely crucial; an error or omission could mean the crash of the aircraft. *(Courtesy: U.S. Air Force)*

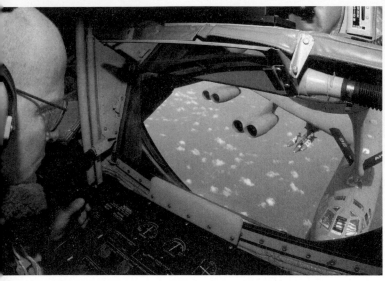

In-flight refueling is the magic wand that extends the range of our bombers, fighters, and transports. Here a JDAM-equipped B-52 prepares to hook up, confident in the skills of the "boomer." *(Courtesy: U.S. Air Force)*

Master Sergeants Tom Rutt (foreground) and Scott Nybakken work in unison to get a C-130 Hercules ready for takeoff. Both airmen are assigned to the Delaware Air National Guard's 166th Airwing. *(Courtesy: U.S. Air Force)*

The most reliable, most versatile turboprop transport ever built, the Lockheed Martin C-130 served in a wide range of roles in Iraq. These aircraft are from the West Virginia Air National Guard's 130th Airlift Wing at Charleston. *(Courtesy: U.S. Air Force)*

The Lockheed Martin C-5B is a reliable old workhorse. *(Courtesy: U.S. Air Force)*

A Lockheed Martin HC-130 off-loads fuel to a Sikorsky HH-60G Pave Hawk on May 5, 2003, in support of Operation Iraqi Freedom. Both aircraft belong to the Air Force Reserve Command's 920th Rescue Wing at Patrick Air Force Base, Florida. *(Courtesy: U.S. Air Force)*

A Boeing E-3A AWACS banks away after refueling from a Boeing KC-10 Extender on March 22, 2003. About 15 percent of the total missions flown during Operation Iraqi Freedom were aerial refueling missions, and they made 90 percent of the remaining missions possible. *(Courtesy: U.S. Air Force)*

The Sikorsky HH-60 Pave Hawk is invaluable in rescue operations. Training exercises like this one ensure that patients are well treated when the actual rescue attempt takes place. *(Courtesy: U.S. Air Force)*

The angular lines of the Lockheed Martin F-117A do not contribute much to its beauty but contribute greatly to its stealth capability. *(Courtesy: U.S. Air Force)*

The sheer intensity of the effort to place modern munitions on a Boeing Hornet aircraft is reflected in the focused determination of the armament personnel. *(Courtesy: U.S. Navy)*

A 494th Fighter Squadron Boeing F-15E Strike Eagle in full afterburner as it takes off en route to Operation Iraqi Freedom *(Courtesy: U.S. Air Force)*

From left to right, Captains Tally Parham and Mary Melfi and 1st Lt. Julie Ayres walk down the flight line at a forward-deployed air base in the Middle East on May 3, 2003. All three officers are assigned to the 379th Air Expeditionary Wing and flew combat missions during Operation Iraqi Freedom. Ayres and Melfi are F-15E Strike Eagle weapon-systems officers deployed from the 366th Air Expeditionary Wing at Seymour Johnson Air Force Base, North Carolina. Parham is an F-16 pilot from the 157th Expeditionary Fighter Squadron from the South Carolina National Guard Base. *(Courtesy: U.S. Air Force)*

The Boeing F/A Hornets did a brilliant job in Operation Iraqi Freedom. *(Courtesy: U.S. Navy)*

A veteran Boeing KC-135R tanker (forty or more years old) leads a flock of seven fighters. *(Courtesy: U.S. Air Force)*

General Richard B. Meyers visits troops of the 67th Air Expeditionary Wing in the field; his grin shows how much happier he is doing this than facing a room full of reporters. *(Courtesy: U.S. Air Force)*

The unusual-looking Global Hawk unmanned aerial vehicle was a tremendous success in Operation Iraqi Freedom, and calls for its use have expanded greatly. *(Courtesy: U.S. Air Force)*

The U.S.M.C. made excellent use of the Boeing AV-8B Harrier, keeping maintenance rates high and flying many missions. *(Courtesy: U.S. Navy)*

The Lockheed Martin EC-130E Commando Solo aircraft is used in psychological warfare but has a secondary electronic-jamming capability. *(Courtesy: U.S. Air Force)*

Sikorsky helicopters are used for the swift insertion of special operations forces into dangerous areas. *(Courtesy: U.S. Air Force)*

From the left, Tech Sgt. Chris Hickman, Master Sgt. Greg Lewis, and Senior Airman Gerald Brown, all with the 379th Expeditionary Maintenance Squadron's ammo flight, move a GBU-31 Joint Direct Attack Munitions into position for disassembly and shipment at a forward-deployed location. The pace of work of the munitions people is swift and never-ending. *(Courtesy: U.S. Air Force)*

With their wings folded to save space, Hornets line the side of a carrier flight deck. *(Courtesy: U.S. Navy)*

The Boeing KC-135R is absolutely invaluable to the fighters, bombers, and transports of Operation Iraqi Freedom. *(Courtesy: U.S. Air Force)*

The Northrop Grumman E-8A Joint STARS (or JSTARS) aircraft is filled with electronic equipment to scan the sky and earth, but the pilots still need to be able to see clearly out of the front windshield. *(Courtesy: U.S. Air Force)*

Torpedoman's Mate 1st Class Leverette Harper from Tuscaloosa, Alabama, salutes the color guard aboard the USS *Kitty Hawk* in honor of Lt. Nathan "O.J." White, an F/A 18 Hornet pilot of VFA 195 who was killed in action on April 2, 2003. *(Courtesy: U.S. Navy)*

The slender wings of the Predator give it the look of a huge, prehistoric flying animal, a true predator of the skies. The UAV's long range and loiter time make it perfect for surveillance. The Predator's great success has set the stage for further UAVs and UCAVs in the future. *(Courtesy: U.S. Air Force)*

A Sikorsky MH-53 Pave Low helicopter is about to insert its boom into the "basket" of the refueler. Aerial refueling permitted helicopters to range all over Iraq. *(Courtesy: U.S. Air Force)*

War is not all combat, and guard duty in Iraq can be as hazardous as a night firefight. Staff Sgt. Brett Duncan keeps watch over a lineup of Lockheed Martin C-130s at a forward-deployed location. Duncan is assigned to the 379th Expeditionary Security Forces Squadron. *(Courtesy: U.S. Air Force)*

In Iraq, good water is more precious than fuel or food, and Tech Sgt. Ken Joy stands guard as firefighters pump water from a stream near Bashur Airfield in northern Iraq. Joy belongs to the 86th Expeditionary Contingency Response Group, which patrols the base perimeter, provides airfield protection, and escorts all airmen who leave the camp. *(Courtesy: U.S. Air Force)*

An A-10 pilot pats the Lockheed Martin (formerly Fairchild Republic) Thunderbolt II, more familiarly known as the "Warthog." The cannon is a 30mm seven-barrel GAU-8 Gatling gun. *(Courtesy:* Air Force Magazine*)*

The heat inside the aircraft is often greater than the heat outside, but the essential paperwork still must be completed before the maintenance is considered finished. *(Courtesy: U.S. Air Force)*

Perhaps the most successful combination of weapons of Operation Iraqi Freedom: a Boeing B-1B bomber and a JDAM *(Courtesy:* Air Force Magazine*)*

A Northrop Grumman B-2A Spirit taxiing out for a mission *(Courtesy:* Air Force Magazine*)*

In Operation Iraqi Freedom, General Moseley used Checkmate to provide alternative scenarios for force structures, bed-down locations, logistic problems, and possible reactions of the Iraqis. The result was a series of war plans that contemplated a host of alternatives that included things that happened, including adverse weather and the refusal of Turkey to allow the passage of troops.

Hyde is quick to point out two of the most important factors in the war going well, one generally acknowledged and the other generally overlooked. He places a great deal of importance on President Bush and Secretary Rumsfeld having given clear objectives and then not deviating from the objective. Unlike almost every past war, this time there was no "mission creep" in which additional demands were placed on the forces without adding additional resources.

The second factor, one that almost never gets the proper credit, is the logistics triumph. It was shared by all the services, but Hyde uses the Air Force as a typical example, noting that the embedded reporters were with the combat tip of the spear, but the logistics shaft of that spear went largely unnoticed.

Hyde credits Lieutenant General Michel Zettler, who as chief of the Air Force Installations and Logistics Division saw to it that sufficient arms, food, spare parts, and all of the impedimenta of war were prepositioned correctly and that there was a constant stream of ships and aircraft departing at exactly the right time to maintain the required level of support. This is "just-in-time" logistics on a scale never dreamed of by the most expert Japanese manufacturer.[10] It was matched by having the right military technicians on the spot primed to do critical high-volume work such as assembling the PGMs that were used so intensively.

WHAT WENT WRONG AND WHY

Not everything went perfectly. In hindsight, at least an initial increment of the 4th Infantry Division's equipment should have been sent south to Kuwait on the very day that the Turkish Parliament voted against permitting U. S. troops to cross through Turkey. A corresponding number of 4th Infantry Division troops could have been airlifted from the United States to arrive coincident with the equipment. They would then have been in a position to either assist in the action around Basra or serve as a cleanup unit for the advancing 3rd Infantry Division. Further, they would also have been a potent signal to Turkey that we were prepared to adjust and fight the war without their help. The 4th Infantry Division was not moved for two reasons. The first was because there remained a slender hope that Turkey would somehow conform to the wishes of the United States. The second was that the 4th Infantry Division might still invade northern Iraq. The simple threat of the 4th Infantry Division "fixed" many Iraqi regular army divisions in place in northern Iraq, thus preserving an element of tactical surprise for General Franks' war plan.

Again adjusting hindsight for a twenty-twenty view of the past, there should have been a high-level headquarters specializing in the postvictory stability operations. Far more Military Police should have been on hand for immediate insertion into the cities, relieving the 3rd Infantry Division of such tasks and introducing a more rigorous control earlier on. This might have avoided the spurious flap over museum and hospital looting that dominated the headlines for a few days later in the campaign. They were not on hand because in the planning for the assault they had less relative importance; it was not perceived that if the assault went as planned, Military Police would be as important as another heavy division.

Coalition intelligence failed to register the relative importance of the *Fedayeen* Saddam, who, though small in numbers, multiplied their effect by terrorizing their Iraqi countrymen into carrying out their orders in support of Saddam's rule. The *Fedayeen* Saddam were established by Uday Hussein in 1995 but subsequently placed under Qusay Hussein's control. The force reputedly totals as many as 25,000 to 40,000, depending upon the source, and is spread throughout Iraq. The soldiers are usually young (some preadolescent) and recruited from the Tikrit clan area. Not especially well trained, they are nonetheless vicious street fighters, terrorists using guerrilla-style tactics, able to throw up a barrage of AK-47 fire, then disappear into the crowd and reappear at a different point later. Their strategy was simple: they were to operate independently, without any central command and control system. Huge quantities of weapons and ammunition were stocked in schools and mosques for their use. Retired Marine Lieutenant General Bernard E. Trainor noted that the Iraqis applied a "citadel strategy." The mission of the citadels was to maintain an iron grip on the local Shias, whom the United States had assumed would welcome coalition forces with open arms. The citadel forces were also intended to wreak havoc with coalition supply lines. If possible, they were to slow the advance on Baghdad by causing injuries not only to the coalition forces but also to Iraqi civilians. In the process, they were to see that sacrosanct edifices and institutions were destroyed, to inflame the Arab world further against the United States.[11] Perhaps their most important influence, however, was to be a "stiffener" to the Iraqi civilian populace, to whom they are known. They will continue to be a baleful force long after the war is over, for the future is grim for them, inside or outside of Iraq. Look for them to support and then seek control of any organization that presents a strong united front against the U.S. presence and to intimidate and assassinate those who cooperate with the United States.

The failure to estimate the value of the *Fedayeen* Saddam to Iraqi resistance stems from a generic American and a particular military problem. The nation and its armed forces have not received the training necessary to understand the Arab/Islamic mentality at almost any level, and most particularly at the level of the radical Muslim. The means to conduct this training are still not available, and there is an apparent antipathy to the subject that will make such training difficult. In the continuing war on terrorism, one of the United States' greatest weaknesses will continue to be this fundamental blindness to the mind-set of a dedicated enemy.

General Trainor also raised some doubts about the wisdom of the air strikes on Baghdad. His point is that no one of value would be in the targets inside the city limits, as they were obvious strike points, and the bombing destroyed important files while it gave the United States a bad name for bombing a civilian area.[12]

At a far more practical level, the talcum powder fine dust of the Iraqi desert was hard on optical equipment and on the machinery of the tanks and trucks, and improvised methods had to be used to lessen the effect. But this was minor compared to the two major areas where things went wrong during this three-day period: the PATRIOT missile system and friendly fire—now inevitably called blue on blue—casualties and the downed Apache Longbow helicopter.

The PATRIOT System

Development of the PATRIOT missile system began in the 1960s as part of both the Field Army Ballistic Missile Defense System and Army Air Defense System (AADS-70), as a means of combating the increasing capabilities of the Soviet Union in both aircraft and tactical ballistic missiles. The two programs merged in 1965 as the "SAM-D" program, and first flight tests commenced in 1970. Testing proved to be difficult, and full-scale development was delayed until 1974. By 1976, Army public relations had devised a name that would lend a striking acronym, the Phased-Array Tracking to Intercept of Target—or PATRIOT.

Initial production was slow, and the first deliveries did not take place until 1982—almost twenty years after the program's inception. The program received a boost when Japan purchased twenty-six batteries, 130 launchers, and 1,300 missiles in 1985. This was followed in 1988 by Italy's purchase of twenty missile batteries (soon canceled), with 160 launchers and 1,000 missiles. Other nations, including Germany, Israel, and Kuwait, also purchased PATRIOTS.

The first wartime test of the PATRIOT came in reaction to Saddam Hussein's occupation of Kuwait in August 1990. PATRIOT missile batteries were sent to Saudi Arabia, and Israel received batteries in early January 1991, as Desert Storm overtook Desert Shield. The first Israeli missiles were fired against incoming Iraqi ballistic missiles on January 22 of that year.

During Desert Storm the Iraqis rained a total of eighty-six ballistic missiles (mostly Al-Husayns, not Scuds) down against targets in Kuwait, Saudi Arabia, and Israel. Not all of them were aimed at areas within the PATRIOT protection envelope. Some 158 PATRIOTS were fired from ninety launchers. It was originally claimed that 80 percent of the Iraqi missiles that entered the zone covered by the PATRIOT in Saudi Arabia were destroyed, but later analysis reduced this estimate dramatically. A General Accounting Office report said that there were only four hits on Scuds in forty-seven firings. It blamed the apparent failures on proximity fuse limitations and a software problem in the weapons control computer, which led to an inaccurate tracking calculation. The problem worsened over time, so that by the time a battery had operated for 100 hours, its accuracy was so degraded that it would search the wrong areas for an incoming Scud. On February 25, 1991, one of the systems, operating at Dhahran, Saudi Arabia, failed to track an incoming Al-Husayn, which struck a warehouse and killed twenty-eight Americans.[13]

The PATRIOT was originally intended primarily as an antiaircraft system but evolved into a stopgap antimissile system. The system was modified and improved immediately after the Gulf War as the PATRIOT Advanced Capability (PAC)-1, Raytheon PAC-2, and Lockheed Martin PAC-3. A few of the PAC-3 systems were available in the Iraqi War. Raytheon and Lockheed Martin Vought Systems are the prime contractors for the PAC-3. Final configuration includes additional software improvements for battle management, improved radar, and a remote launch capability.

As previously noted, the PATRIOT had some significant initial successes in destroying nine of fourteen Iraqi missiles fired into Kuwait. The five that it did not fire upon were on paths that led them to land in an unpopulated area. Six of the nine PATRIOT missiles fired during a thirteen-day period beginning March 20 were of an improved type introduced into service in 1996 and known as the PAC-2 Guidance Enhanced Missile (GEM). The number seven missile was a GEM-plus with an improved fuse and the ability to "see" smaller targets. Only two of the latest model, the PAC-3 type, were used to shoot down Iraqi missiles. The GEM-plus (like all PAC-2s) is an interceptor missile, designed to detonate by a proximity fuse. The PAC-3 is a "hit-to-kill" missile without an explosive warhead. Pure kinetic energy makes explosives unnecessary. The standard technique for firing PATRIOTs is to shoot at least two missiles for every one incoming; doing so establishes a 90 percent probability of a kill.

According to Brigadier General Howard Bromberg, Commanding General of the 32nd Army Air and Missile Defense Command, the Iraqis were bringing their missiles into position, firing, and then departing the area immediately to elude counterfire. (This was absolutely essential to avoid the devastating counterbattery fire of U.S. precision artillery, which uses massive computers to detect the ballistic trajectory of an incoming missile [or shell], then defines its source as a target. With its proud boast that it can hit a fifty-gallon drum from fifteen miles away, American precision artillery proved deadly to the Iraqis.)

One problem that the PATRIOT and most weapons systems face is the bewildering barrage of electronic information saturating the battlefield. According to Bromberg, the Tornado did not appear on the radar as a typical airplane, which led the operator to misidentify it as an incoming missile. The decision to fire or not fire has to be made in split seconds

Another argument has it that a software flaw in the PATRIOT fire control system was the cause of the system ignoring the IFF (Identification Friend or Foe) on the Tornado and the Hornet. (IFF is a problem of long standing.) Lieutenant General David McKiernan, the well-liked veteran of Army armored units, refused to accept the idea that the PATRIOT's problems might be technological. According to McKiernan, the risk of fratricide, or "blue on blue," is not so much in the technology as in tactical discipline and rules of engagement (ROE). There are both ground and air ROE. Both the PATRIOT batteries and coalition airmen have to be aware of the hazards and comply exactly with procedures. The difficulty with imposing too many exacting rules of engagement is that it slows the decision process and permits the enemy "seams" through which to employ his weapons.

Unfortunately, there were two instances in which a PATRIOT destroyed a coalition force aircraft. The first was the RAF Tornado incident on March 23, in which both crew members were killed. Two days later, a PATRIOT battery locked its radar onto a Lockheed Martin F-16, which responded in textbook fashion by firing HARM missiles that knocked out the PATRIOT radar system before it could fire. Then on April 2, a PATRIOT shot down a Boeing F/A-18, near Karbala, south of Baghdad. The aircraft was operating from the USS *Kitty Hawk* in a very active battlefield area in which there was heavy artillery and missile fire from both sides.[14] Thirty-year-old Lieutenant Nathan White was killed. The impact of the PATRIOT (and possibly of two missiles) apparently caused his ejection seat to operate, throwing him out of the aircraft. His parachute was found floating in Lake Karbala, and after ten days the Navy initiated Operation Dogwood to use sophisticated teams to recover his body.

White, who had graduated at the top of his flying class, was well aware of the hazards of operating in the PATRIOT's environment and had discussed the hazard the missile batteries presented in his last E-mail message home before his death. En route home from a mission over Karbala, White radioed that he had seen two missiles launched. Six seconds later, both missiles struck his aircraft, blowing it apart.

The possibility was raised that the missile battery actually had locked onto an incoming missile but "transferred" the lock to the F/A-18 as it crossed the missile's path. This certainly can happen, but it has not been proven to be the case in this instance.

There are several ways that a PATRIOT missile battery can detect whether an incoming object is friendly or hostile. Some of these are subjective, by identifying the aircraft visually or via radio transmissions. Others can be identified by passive electronic queries that indicate the type of aircraft. Some objects can be identified as friendly by the geographic routes they are flying—a known predesignated track.

But the most important system is active, the transponder, the IFF that was used in World War II. The IFF is not fool proof—it can fail or be turned off or the operator can enter the wrong code—but it is the most positive means of identification, and why it did not intervene in both the Tornado and the Hornet shoot-downs has not been determined.

There was immediate speculation on the PATRIOT's difficulties. All weapon systems, from a private's rifle to a nuclear weapon, have precise rules established for their use. In the case of missile batteries, there are three general conditions. In the most stringent "Weapons Hold," the weapon can be fired only in self-defense or upon a direct order to fire. In the second case, "Weapons Tight," the weapon can be fired only when the incoming system is identified positively as hostile. This was a major problem during the Vietnam War, because the requirement for positive visual identification of North Vietnamese MiGs prior to firing usually put American fighters at a disadvantage in terms of their ability to use their missile systems, placing the target inside the minimum range of the AIM-7 Sparrow, for example. This was eventually partially overcome by the installation of an internal cannon and the installation of TISEO, an extended-range telescopic system.) The third case is "Weapons Loose," in which missile crews can fire at any target not positively identified as friendly.

Some attributed the Hornet loss to the fact that the PATRIOTs were not held in the "Weapons Tight" mode or might even have been in an automatic firing mode.[15] The danger of the effect of a chemical or biological weapon "leaking" through PATRIOT defenses was very great. A counterargument was made that maintaining a "Weapons Tight" status would render the PATRIOTs vulnerable to enemy cruise missile fire. (The PATRIOT was not designed to engage cruise missiles.) And the counter-counter argument was that the likelihood of enemy cruise missiles having the accuracy to seek out a PATRIOT battery was so low that it was an acceptable risk.

Others were inclined to look to the saturation of the battlefield with electronic signals, making it imperative to create new and more discriminating software to permit individual or missile identification instantaneously.

Yet the general consensus was that in the heat of battle, errors were made in procedure that allowed the accidents to happen. As the services move to more and more automated systems, it is possible that human errors will be diminished, but there is some haunting probability that they will be banished from the firing line only to emerge in the lines of code in the automatic systems.

Apache Down

Analyzing why something went wrong with the employment of the Apache helicopter requires some background and the knowledge that this was not the first but rather the third incident in which this fantastically capable (and remarkably expensive) weapon has been accused of failing. In fact, the Apache as a weapon system has not failed, but Army doctrine in its employment has.

To understand the nature of the problem, it is necessary first to understand the sophistication and complexity of the weapon itself. The Boeing (formerly McDonnell Douglas, formerly Hughes) AH-64 Apache is a formidable attack helicopter, designed originally to be an efficient tank killer to help redress the numerical advantage in armor possessed by the Warsaw Pact nations. It entered service in 1984, and the U.S. Army has more than 800 in service, and about 1,000 have been sold to Egypt, Greece, Israel, the Netherlands, Saudi Arabia, the United Arab Emirates, and the United Kingdom.

The Apache illustrates how closely integrated rival defense companies now have to be to survive during a period of reduced military spending; Boeing, General Electric, Lockheed Martin, and Northrop Grumman are just a few of the major manufacturers that teamed up to help create the Apache.

Heavily armored and cleverly designed for survivability, the Apache was dramatically improved in the AH-64D Longbow version. About half of the 501 Apaches scheduled to receive the Longbow upgrade are already in service. (Many foreign countries are also requiring Longbow upgrades.)

The AH-64D, with a crew of two, features the Northrop Grumman millimeter-wave (MMW) Longbow radar fire control system and the Longbow MMW Hellfire missiles, up to four of which it carries under each stub wing. These MMW missiles can acquire and attack a target in less than thirty seconds and perform in the "fire and forget" mode, meaning once the pilot has punched off the missile, he doesn't have to painstakingly guide it to the target. The Hellfire has a range of almost five miles. The Apache also carries the devastating punch of the 30mm Boeing M230 Area Weapons Systems (AWS), the "chain gun" located in a chin turret under the fuselage.

The Longbow fire control system incorporates an integrated radar frequency interferometer for passive location and identification of radar-emitting threats, making it invaluable for the suppression of enemy air defenses. The Target Acquisition Designation Sight (TADS) works in concert with the Pilot Night Vision Sensor (PNVS), both developed by Lockheed Martin. The image from the PNVS is displayed in a monocular eyepiece mounted on the Honeywell Integrated Helmet and Display Sighting System (IHADDS). These helmets look clumsy, but pilots who have once flown with night-vision equipment never want to fly at night again without it.

Two General Electric T700-GE-701 turboshaft engines provided 1,890 shaft horsepower each, allowing a cruise speed of 147 knots and (with additional tanks) an endurance of three hours.

Given this crushing combination of speed, agility, firepower, and survivability, how and where did the Apache fail?

The first instance was in Kosovo. The AH-64s deployed to Albania, but neither its pilots nor its mechanics were fully trained and ready. There were two crashes, and the AH-64 was never used in combat, a fact that caused a swell of indignation to roll through the media.

The second failure came in Afghanistan, in Operation Anaconda. (See appendix 4 for details.) In this instance, the Army attempted to "go it alone" with Apaches in Paktia Province and was severely mauled. Five Apaches out of six were put out of commission. As appendix 4 shows, fixed-wing air support was apparently not coordinated in the operation. This led to a complaint by Major General Franklin L. Hagenback about an alleged lack of Air Force CAS. In fact, eventual joint operations salvaged the situation, but not before the Apaches received an unnecessary bloody nose.

The third experience occurred on March 24 in Iraq, when 11th Aviation Regiment Apaches attempted to shoot up an entrenched brigade of the Medina Division but came back badly shot up, with one shot down and its pilots taken prisoner. (The Iraqis made the propaganda claim that the Apache had been shot down by a farmer with a shotgun. This story made for good television in the Arab world, but the Iraqis would have served themselves better by telling the truth: it was concentrated ground fire from dug-in troops firing everything from AK-47s to rocket-propelled grenades [RPGs] that won the victory.) The Apaches did demonstrate a remarkable ability to take punishment in this action.

In the second and third failures, the Apaches were placed in jeopardy because the Army was attempting to use them as deep interdiction aircraft without proper preparation of the battlefield. The Apaches (and other attack helicopters) are designed from the beginning to be employed with artillery, rockets, and, where required, fixed-wing aircraft in an engagement. In short, this was not a failure of the Apache but of the Army chain of command who violated their own doctrine by trying to make the Apache do more than it is capable of doing.

One of the basic issues here that must be resolved before the next conflict is the hot argument over CAS, the Fire Support Coordination Line, and the Forward Edge Battle Area. Each of these relate basically to the trust (or lack of same) that the Army places in firepower that it does not control and represent missing pieces in the quest for jointness.[16]

Former Air Force Chief of Staff General Merrill McPeak subscribes to this view, but with greater reservations on the role and utility of the Apache. McPeak questions whether or not the Apache can actually do CAS at all, as it is a "big, fat, slow target with no way to get operationally meaningful stealth." At one point in his career, McPeak made an offer to trade CAS (the Fairchild Republic A-10) to the Army in exchange for the Hawk and PATRIOT missile systems. His goal was to integrate CAS into the Army (à la the Marines) while integrating theater air defense into the Air Force mission. The offer was declined on the basis that A-10s were "too expensive."[17]

The war in Iraq ended without further Apache combat losses, but to get things to "go right" in the next war there will have to be changes made in Army doctrine on their employment.

4

Bad News (for Saddam) Blowing in the Sandy Wind

OPERATION IRAQI FREEDOM:
March 25, 26, and 27

Blowing worse than the bad news of the twenty-fourth, sandstorms of 100-mile-per-hour intensity obscured the battlefield, bogging down operations for both land vehicles and helicopters. Fortunately, the combination of aerial sensors and PGMs made it possible for air activity to continue almost unabated. Boeing B-1B bombers of the 405th AEW continued their operations, which saw the "Bone," as it is called by crew members, drop as many as twenty-four of their GPS/inertially guided JDAMs on a single mission. Like most organizations in the war, the 405th operates on a twelve-hour shift, around-the-clock, with commission rates (79.4 percent) staying higher than the peacetime average.

Fourteen hundred strike missions were flown, with the major targets remaining the same: Republican Guard divisions, key command and control facilities, and surface-to-surface missile facilities. The venerable Boeing B-52 continued in operations from its deployed base, where operators and maintainers of the 457th Air Expeditionary Squadron had an inventory of $81 million in spare parts to keep the forty-one-year-old aircraft flying.

U.S.-led forces approached to within less than fifty miles of Baghdad, despite Iraqi radio and television broadcasts that the coalition forces were contained or in retreat.

The 7th Cavalry of the 3rd Division crossed the Euphrates. In a continued demonstration of the effects of swift, unexpected movements, the 3rd was able to make a surprise flanking movement near al Summalah, where the Iraqis failed to blow up bridges as expected.

Some coalition casualties were incurred in the last two days near An

Nasiriyah, while inflicting heavy losses on enemy personnel and armor. Marines of Task Force Tarawa captured a hospital that had been used as a staging area for Iraqi paramilitary troops. The troops, dressed in civilian clothing, apparently were driven to and from the hospital in buses to obtain weapons and ammunition for the fight in the city. A disturbing element was the discovery of 3,000 chemical suits and masks.

In the south, *Fedayeen* elements of the civilian Ba'ath Party continued to cause unrest in Basra, including firing on their own civilian populace. North of the city, a mixed Iraqi attack took place. The initial attack was by several tanks, which were joined by civilian buses and other civilian vehicles, all carrying *Fedayeen* Saddam forces. The attack was repelled, with heavy losses inflicted on the Iraqis.

U.K. forces made rapid progress in establishing security in the town of Umm Qasr and the southern oil fields. Work on clearing the port also advanced.

One clear sign of General Franks' wisdom was assigning the British to undertake the task at which they were best, the encirclement and reduction of Basra, while giving the V Corps, the 3rd Infantry Division, and the Marines the task of racing toward Baghdad, for which they were best suited. Near Basra, the British 1st Armored Division's AS-90 self-propelled artillery destroyed Iraqi artillery and tanks.

In the growing trend from preplanned targeting to time-sensitive strikes, the USS *Constellation* (CV 64) Battle Group destroyed significant Iraqi targets near Basra. Two Boeing F/A-18 Hornets from Strike Fighter Squadron VFA 151, "The Vigilantes," participated, along with a Lockheed Martin S-3B Viking from Sea Control Squadron (VS) 38, "The Red Griffins." In a precedent-breaking incident, an F/A-18 "painted" an Iraqi target with a laser designator, while the S-3B fired an AGM-65E Maverick guided missile. The versatile S-3B, though getting long in the tooth (its first flight was in 1972), serves as tanker and antisubmarine aircraft and in the electronic countermeasures role.[1] Fans of the Viking, now scheduled to be retired, hope it may get a new lease on life, as the A-10 did during operations in Desert Storm.

Reports of electrooptical and GPS jammers supplied by Russia to Iraq continued to surface. GPS-jamming attempts from six jammers were recorded in Baghdad, and JDAM bombs, using GPS/INS guidance, were used to destroy them, in a move Air Force Major General Victor "Gene" Neuart described as "ironic."

Two unsettling sets of numbers were discussed at various briefings. Instead of floods of refugees crossing Iraq's borders into neighboring countries, there were almost none. The initial interpretation of this was that people were afraid to flee, for if Saddam Hussein somehow remained in power they would be branded as traitors and killed. The second number was that of the estimated 4,000 Iraqi prisoners of war, which was far fewer than anticipated. It is presumed that under the pressure of constant aerial bombardment, Iraqi soldiers were electing to leave their units and return to their homes rather than be killed or forced to surrender.

Since the beginning of the war there has been one conflict in which both sides have done well, and that is in psychological operations. The coalition forces dropped millions of leaflets and broadcast on five different frequencies twenty-four hours a day to explain the coalition goals to the Iraqi people. The leaflets also cautioned against using or supporting weapons of mass destruction. The Iraqi forces concentrated their psychological operations on the Arab world, showing videos of captured Americans, the downed Apache, and, in wearisome repetition, photos of dead or wounded Iraqi civilians. Both campaigns gave evidence of success, with the edge perhaps going to that of the Iraqis. Saddam's psychological operation (terror) continued to work well against his people.

March 26, Day 7 of the campaign, saw the adverse weather continue, with naval flight operations limited to 160 launches by poor visibility.

An Najaf, on the Euphrates, was encircled by the 3rd ID, after bridges to the north and to the south were captured. RPGs antitank missiles damaged two Abrams tanks, and one Bradley Fighting Vehicle of the 3rd Squadron, 7th Cavalry Regiment. One tank crewman was killed. Iraqi casualties were in excess of 1,000. Advocates of the Abrams and Bradley quickly pointed out that lighter vehicles, fitted with less armor, could not have survived either the RPGs or the antitank missiles.

Reports circulated that Iraqi Republican Guard reinforcements were moving south from both Baghdad and Karbala. These reports were difficult to confirm at first, as the movement was exactly what coalition forces wanted. When the Iraqi forces revealed themselves, they were instantly acquired by the system of sensors overhead, their location fixed by GPS, and they were destroyed by PGMs, including the Wind-Corrected Munitions Dispenser (WCMD). Even in a sandstorm, the exercise was easier than shooting fish in a barrel, thanks to the vastly improved ISR cueing, targeting mechanisms, and PGMs of coalition aircraft.

Units of the 101st Airborne Division (Air Assault) continued to move north into Iraq by road, supplementing the advance of the Army and Marine ground forces. The normal helicopter gunship support was absent because of the continued severe weather.

Late in the evening of March 26, approximately one thousand paratroops of the 173rd Airborne Brigade, stationed in Vincenza, Italy, seized Harir, a strategic airfield in Kurdish-controlled territory, near Bashur, another strategic airfield in Kurdish-controlled territory. The airfield, with its single runway, had already been under coalition control, thanks to about 160 members of special operation forces, who used the field as a base from which to direct air strikes against Iraqi targets.[2] The troops were dropped from USAF Boeing C-17As and supported by AFSOC AC-130 gunships. This was the first time the Globemaster III had made such a drop. The transports were flown by crews from the 437th and 62nd Airlift Wings.

At CENTCOM, the brilliant spokesman and West Pointer Brigadier General Vincent Brooks conducted a briefing that provided insight into the accuracy of the air war, showing before and after video clips of attacks on multiple rocket launchers, aircraft, a tank, and a military headquarters. While the films vividly depict the accuracy and ferocity of the air attacks, they were simply "views through a soda straw" and unable to give a view of the vast scope of the operation that extends in a perimeter hundreds of miles around Iraq and goes from beneath the surface of the sea to land locations all over the world, through the atmosphere, and finally to great galaxies of satellites in space. The jaded reporters, familiar with the presentation technique, seemed increasingly unimpressed, lending validity to General Horner's wish that reporters be embedded in combat aircraft, despite the cost of HandiWipes.

Coalition aircraft struck again at Baghdad's main television facility. The decision—or the inability—to remove Iraqi television and radio broadcasting completely from the air was found to be a major aggravating factor diluting the effects of coalition Psyops (psychological warfare). The coalition aircraft also destroyed nine SAM sites.

The weather improved on March 27, to the great relief of the unwashed soldier in the field and to the airmen striking Iraq. The weather and some mild concerns about logistics had put the 1st MEF three or four days behind the planned advance. For the first time CENTCOM announced the relative whereabouts of the 3rd Infantry Division and the 1st MEF. The greater part of the 3rd was approaching the key junction of Karbala and the Karbala Gap, between the town and Lake Razazah, where heavy resistance by Iraqi Republican Guard forces was expected, while part of it continued to pound the Iraqi forces inside a surrounded Najaf. Iraqi strength near Karbala was estimated at between three and six thousand, including paramilitary forces. The 1st MEF was identified as being to the east of Karbala and, by inference, farther to the south.

In the south, the UK forces continued with a wide array of goals. In the extreme south, the 3rd Commando Brigade, operating with the U.S. 15th MEU, mopped up residual resistance on the Al Faw peninsula. The 7th Armored Brigade continued its perimeter watch on Basra, a city of 1.3 million, detaching some units to join with the 16th Air Assault Brigade as it finished up securing the Rumaila oil complex. There were nine oil-head fires, three of which were quickly extinguished.

A column of fourteen Iraqi T-55 tanks attacked a squadron of the Royal Scots Dragoon Guards, which was equipped with fourteen Challenger 2 tanks. The battle was no contest, with all of the T-55s being destroyed and the Challengers suffering no damage.

The Royal Air Force continued to operate at around one hundred sorties per day, with the offensive sorties by Tornado GR4s and Harrier GR7s being supported by tankers and AWACS aircraft. The Tornado GR3 fighter maintained combat air patrols and did SEAD (Suppression of Enemy Air Defenses) work with the ALARM (Air Launched Anti-Radiation Missile).

Some humanitarian supplies began to trickle through, but the Royal Fleet Auxiliary (RFA) ship *Sir Galahad* was still delayed because of potential mines. The *Sir Galahad* carried 200 tons of food and medical supplies.

In the north, the Kurds, supplemented by coalition forces, occupied Iraqi positions near Kirkuk. Three MH-53M SOF helicopters landed at Harir airfield near Bashur. When the airfield was finally secured, C-17As began airlifting in M1A1 Abrams tanks and Bradley Fighting Vehicles.[3]

THE VIEW FROM THE OTHER SIDE

Interestingly, Russian internal Internet reports on the activity asserted that "coalition forces are clearly insufficient to continue the attack." They also stated that because thirty armored vehicles had been lost to guerrilla attacks General Franks "ordered the 22nd SAS Regiment, aided by the U.S. 1st, 5th and 10th Special Operations Groups to carry out this operation. Each of these groups has up to 12 units numbering 12–15 troops each. All of these units have some Asiatics or Arabic-Americans [sic]." The reports also announced the destruction of five armored vehicles and fifty troops killed by friendly fire from A-10s on a coalition convoy. The same bulletin also noted the loss of seven armored vehicles and forty casualties to an attack by Grad multiple rocket launchers on a coalition position. While recognized as demonstrably false in the West, the propaganda was read with pleasure by Arab and other anti-American groups.[4]

WHAT WENT RIGHT AND WHY

Satellites could detect the approach and progress of the disheartening sandstorms that slowed the coalition advance, but no power on earth could divert or prevent the path of the swirling sand—it simply had to be endured. For many weapon systems, including heavy armor, the weather shut down operations. The delay was seen as a double boon for the Iraqis. Their forces could move, hidden by the sand from prying coalition eyes, and the delay in the desert would afford Saddam Hussein more time in working toward his goal of survival.

Unfortunately for Iraqi planning and for the hundreds of Iraqis killed in the process, the sandstorm did not inhibit the ability of satellites, Joint STARS, or UAVs to operate successfully. When any Iraqi unit—from a technical vehicle to an armored column—began to move, it was immediately identified by the Joint STARS Moving Target Indicator (MTI) systems and its geographic coordinates determined by GPS. Once identified and located, it was killed by PGMs from a coalition aircraft. Joint STARS was able to focus on destroying enemy troops on the move, rather than blowing up bridges to impede their movement, a brilliant example of "EBO." In many ways this capability was the very heart of Operation Iraqi Freedom, and it was also the clear precursor of future warfare—and diplomacy. The Chief of Staff of the U.S. Air Force, General John P. Jumper, has stated that later analysis will prove that the capability of the U.S. Air Force to operate through the sandstorm and destroy the Medina Division as it moved forward may well have been the turning point in the war.[5]

The scope of this effort is so extraordinary that to even to begin to depict "what went right and why," it must be placed in context over a two-decade period.

The United States had a contingency plan for operations in Iraq for many years, and for the last ten years it has been updated continuously. Part of that planning included the thoughtful prepositioning of equipment and stores in vast quantities at a number of locations. Doing so is fraught with political and military risk, for a sudden change in international politics can not only put a supply base off-limits to the United States; it can also provide a bonanza in arms to a new political enemy. It is also expensive, continually threatening operations and readiness at home when essential supplies are designated for overseas prepositioning—and the budget often doesn't provide enough to cover the shortfall. Yet these risks paid off in Iraq.

F^2T^2EA: Find, Fix, Track, Target, Engage, Assess

In the course of the years of planning, Iraq became one of the most "digitized" countries in the world. The Iraq database of targets, routes, altitudes, defense areas, and so on was constantly updated. As a single example, the potential routes and targets for Tomahawks and CALCMs were revised on an almost weekly basis. This is mind-numbingly dull work that suddenly comes alive when needed. To take advantage of additional information, the cruise missiles were appropriately updated with new GPS coordinates. The platforms (aircraft, ships, and submarines) from which the cruise missiles were fired were similarly modernized.

These and many other similar weapon system improvements all took place coincident with the development of a target cycle concept General Jumper has termed "Find, Fix, Track, Target, Engage, Assess (F^2T^2EA)," which is more colorfully known as the "kill chain." Essentially, Jumper believes that the armed services of the United States should have, in the aggregate, the ability to find targets anywhere in the world, fix them in a database, track them as necessary, designate them as a target, engage them with the appropriate weapon at the appropriate time, then assess the damage done to the target—all in a very compressed period of time. The armed services should also have a similar (if even swifter capacity) to do the same to targets that emerge suddenly from hiding.

The Iraqi military and other enemies of the United States have carefully monitored its actions in Bosnia, Kosovo, and Afghanistan. They know how vulnerable fixed targets are and attempt to keep them hidden, use decoys, or keep them moving. Therefore, there is an urgent requirement to compress the kill chain, to reduce it, if possible, to fewer than ten minutes. Doing so involves the actions and reactions of air-, ground-, and space-based assets, working in concert and possessing the same understanding of the situation.

The concept is not difficult to understand but required extraordinary long-term investment in research, development, production, training, and employment to bring to fruition. Most of this effort was done in an atmosphere of uncertainty, for there was no assurance that all of the elements could be brought together to operate as planned.

Three elements of the equation, F^2 and T (Find, Fix, and Track), have been operational for years. They are provided by any of the following systems or any combination thereof:

Boeing E-3C Airborne Warning and Control System (AWACS): A modified 707 that tracks hundreds of aircraft over an enormous area.

Northrop Grumman E-8C Joint Surveillance Target Attack Radar System (Joint STARS): A modified 707 used by a joint Air Force/Army program that provides detection of moving (and stationary targets) on the ground in an area as large as southern Iraq; it also targets slow-moving aircraft, along with theater missile defense targets.

Lockheed Martin EP-3: A Navy modified version of the Orion used to collect electronic intelligence, which became famous as a result of a collision with a Chinese fighter aircraft in 2002. Originally an anti-submarine aircraft, the EP-3 performed well in the ISR role.

Beech RC-12 Guardrail: An Army twin-turboprop aircraft, heavily laden with antennae and electronic equipment for providing Signal Intelligence via the Guardrail Common Sensor system.

Boeing RC-135 Rivet Joint: A Boeing C-135 modified to collect electronic intelligence on radars, communications, and other systems.

General Atomics Aeronautical Systems RQ-1A Predator: A USAF-and-CIA-operated UAV, remotely piloted at medium altitudes and low speeds to obtain detailed video imagery of enemy vehicles. Some have been modified to serve as laser designators, and some deliver Hellfire missiles on target. (The Predator is relatively slow, and jokes are made that it takes off, cruises, and lands, all at seventy miles per hour.) Some Predators take off and land from bases close to Iraq but, once airborne, are remotely operated through "reachback" by pilots in Nevada and the information from their video cameras analyzed at either Langley Air Force Base, Virginia, or Beale Air Force Base in California.[6] The remote analysis is termed *reachback*, an expression widely used to convey going further up the technological chain to obtain additional information. In Iraq, members of the 46th Expeditionary Reconnaissance Squadrons maintain the aircraft on a twenty-fourth-hour basis.

Northrop Grumman RQ-4A Global Hawk: A large UAV able to fly at high speeds and altitudes and loiter over a designated area for many hours to collect images of interest.

Lockheed Martin U-2: Famous for its role in the Cold War, the U-2 remains a valuable high-flying reconnaissance aircraft that collects digital imagery in several wavelengths. During operations in Kosovo, the U-2 would collect information, send it back, via satellite, to its home at Beale Air Force Base, California, where it would be analyzed and forwarded to the CAOC in Vincenza, Italy, where a decision could be made about striking the newly found target. All of this transpired within as little as twelve minutes.[7]

These and other air, ground, and space assets are orchestrated in the ATO. The ATO is a very detailed preplanning document governing the integrated flow of aircraft operations each day. Typically, the ATO looks seventy-two hours into the future and refines the orders in forty-eight hours and then again twenty-four hours before execution. It provides for immediate on-call air support as well. The ATO defines what aircraft will be involved in which strike packages, where refueling will take place, what electronic countermeasures aircraft will fly and where, the ROE, and so on, to include every detail of each day's air operations.[8]

Once found, the target has to be "fixed"; that is, its location must be determined with precision. The location can be determined by comparing it with the precise position of previously defined locations or by use of the GPS satellites. If the target is mobile, it is monitored in what some have called the "Wolfpack ISR" mode, in which a number of sensors combine to keep track of the target until the kill is made.

The word *target* means more than the bull's-eye of an enemy asset. It also covers the concept of "time-critical targeting," meaning the interval of time it takes to decide whether or not to strike a target that had been found, fixed, and tracked. This is crucial in dealing with pop-up targets such as mobile Scud launchers or mobile SAM batteries. All of the targeting considerations have to be folded in, including assurance that it is a legitimate target, concern for collateral damage, the selection of the most appropriate weapon, the ROE, and so on. While this was done quite rapidly in Operation Iraqi Freedom, the goal is to reduce the time as much as possible in the future.

It is important to remember that the process of engaging can be as useful in delivering food supplies to a group of refugees as delivering a missile on a tank.

When the targeting information has been confirmed, it becomes the basis for determining where the bomb will strike. The effects of the GPS system are familiar to many ordinary civilians in many guises, including automobile or private aircraft navigation systems, handheld systems for hunters and campers, and systems for use by surveyors, land developers, and so on. But the mechanics of the system are less well known.

General John Michael Loh credits Brad Parkinson, an Air Force officer who taught astrophysics at the test pilot school, as the designer and father of GPS.[9] The late professor Gerard O'Neill of Princeton was one of the early proponents of a GPS. Preliminary work on a worldwide navigation system began in the early 1960s in NASA, the Department of Defense, and the Department of Transportation. The first attempt, Transit, became operational in 1964 but was limited to slow transportation platforms such as ships. In 1969, the Secretary of Defense established a single joint-use system, NAVSTAR GPS.

The first GPS–Block I satellite was boosted into orbit on February 22,

1978. By December of that year, four satellites were in place, allowing the very first three-dimensional positioning capability from space.[10] The GPS system was vital in the 1991 Gulf War but was incomplete, not reaching full operational capability until April 27, 1995.

Today the GPS consists of nominally twenty-four satellites that orbit the Earth, a comprehensive ground system to control operations, and the various users of the system. There are three series of satellites, Block II, IIA, and IIR; they orbit above the Earth at 12,636 miles (II/IIA) and 12,532 miles, respectively. The II and IIAs have solar arrays that generate 70 watts, while the IIR generates 1,136 watts.[11]

The GPS satellites orbit the Earth every twelve hours, emitting continuous navigation signals so accurate that time can be figured within a fraction of a mile per hour and altitude and location to within a few feet. With this capability, precision bombing, combat search and rescue, and navigation can take place on a global scale.

So important was GPS in Operation Iraqi Freedom that a special space tasking order (STO) was established to detail how spaced-based constellations were to be set up, just as ATOs have been used in the past. This was part of the process that enabled the military forces to leverage their space capability to gain a decisive edge in combat. Colonel (Brigadier General–select) Larry D. James, Commander of the 50th Space Wing at Schriever Air Force Base, Colorado, describes Operation Iraqi Freedom as the "first real space war" in which space capabilities were integrated through the entire spectrum of combat.

Lieutenant General Moseley, the CFACC, was also charged with the responsibility for integrating DOD space activities for all services and also all intelligence agencies.[12] (In this regard, Moseley's counterpart in the first Gulf War, General Charles Horner, feels that this was a halfway measure and that there should have been a Combined Forces Space Component Commander [CFSCC] appointed as the individual to whom all services look for space products and services. The CFSCC should also, in Horner's opinion, be designated the Information Operations Manager to avoid areas of conflict.[13])

It is probable that the Navy would dispute General Horner's point of view.

The flow of information was complicated. The ATO/STO was forwarded to the CAOC, which forwarded it on to Air Force Space Command and Fourteenth Air Force. The latter then directed GPS, communications satellites, missile warnings, and others to do whatever was required to meet the needs of the ATO/STO.

The personnel at the 50th Space Wing were able to "tweak" the twenty-eight-satellite GPS constellation so that it provided an accuracy of 10 feet throughout the campaign and, at times, improved this to an accuracy of 6.7 feet. The satellites were provided navigation corrections on each orbit.[14]

In short, the skill and accuracy of personnel operating thousands of miles from the scene of combat were as essential as the skill and accuracy of pilots sitting in the strike aircraft. They worked together so well that the length of the communication channels and the number of organizations that took part did not diminish the powers of the GPS system.

Once a decision is made to strike the target—to "engage"—the tactical proficiency of U.S. airpower (USAF, Navy, and Marine) in delivering bombs is unmatched. General Jumper states that "the engagement piece has always been our strong suit . . . If we know where the target is, we have things that will get that target."[15]

Attempts to develop PGMs began as early as 1917. PGMs saw limited but often dramatic success in World War II, when the Germans, in desperation, fielded several promising designs. One, the Fritz-X, a free-fall bomb steered by radio control, sank the Italian battleship *Roma*, on September 8, 1943. It sank or damaged eighty other vessels, including the veteran battleship HMS *Warspite*, in the course of the war.

The United States experimented with a variety of PGMs but achieved its first genuine combat successes in Vietnam in 1972, when LGBs and Electro-optically Guided Bombs (EOGBs) were used to destroy the previously indestructible Paul Doumer Bridge outside of Hanoi.

PGMs reached a higher level of capability in the first Gulf War, when they were used by the Lockheed Martin F-117A Nighthawk stealth fighter to take out 95 percent of the key targets attacked by manned aircraft in Baghdad. The General Dynamics F-111F Aardvark reached greater effectiveness with PGMs, destroying 2,203 targets in just 2,500 sorties.[16]

In Operation Iraqi Freedom, the use of PGMs became almost standard, for in the ten years after Desert Storm a tremendous effort was made by all the services to adapt PGMs to all of their aircraft. Even the Northrop Grumman F-14 Tomcat, long kept sacrosanct as the fleet defender, was given a new mission as the F-14D (the "Bombcat"), using PGMs.

While a wide variety of PGMs were available, including such standards as the Maverick, HARM, and several varieties of LGB, increased reliance was placed on the JDAM, which was not only accurate but also relatively inexpensive. Other precision munitions used included the AGM-154 Joint Standoff Weapon (JSOW) and the WCMD.

Once PGMs have destroyed the target, the next step in the "kill chain" is "assessment," and this requires diligent assessment. UAVs orbiting near the target make this possible in real time, but if they are not available, it is more difficult for another reconnaissance asset to pick out the exact point where a target was struck and evaluate the damage that was done. Sometimes on-site visits are required to make a final determination; this was the case in Serbia, where decoy assets were widely used as a means of deception. Improved cruise missiles and even precision-guided bombs may have on board cameras transmitting real-time imagery as they fly to the target, providing real-time Battle Damage Assessment (BDA).

Assessment is doubly vital; if the target was not hit, then it had to be engaged again; if it was hit, a second strike must not be wasted upon it. One of the common threads in the various assessments of "lessons learned" in Operation Iraqi Freedom was that BDA is still not being performed with the desired speed and accuracy, and there will certainly be a heavy investment in improving this capability in the future. General Jumper states that there is a confusion of definitions and processes in BDA that keeps it from being timely. Understanding the strategic aspects of BDA is often a long and cumbersome process, one that prevents a tactical commander from getting the BDA information he needs to decide whether or not to restrike the target.[17]

The concept of F²T²EA raised some concerns that the volume of available information might lead to command decisions being increasingly centralized, leading to a situation such as the Vietnam War, when targeting decisions were made in the White House. This did not occur in Operation Iraqi Freedom, where the battle plan was executed at the direction of General Franks, who further decentralized the decision-making process. He was able to do so in large part because not only his component commanders but leaders at every level down to those in the columns advancing on Baghdad had exactly the same "common operational picture." It was one of the first instances in wartime when most of the people engaged in an operation shared the same degree of situational awareness, and it paid off handsomely. Had it not existed, the rapid movement of the Army and Marine troops would not have been possible. Most important, Franks did not use the common operational picture to "micromanage." He maintained it as a situational awareness tool for decision makers.

Getting to Joint STARS

When service leaders like General Jumper or his predecessors as Chief of Staff, Generals Michael E. Ryan and Ronald R. Fogleman, or their Army, Navy, and Marine counterparts conceive of a new plan of operations, they do not implement it by snapping their fingers at some poor colonel or by throwing a few quick billions at a contractor. The role of these service leaders is double-tracked. To establish techniques useful in the here-and-now, they must seize upon ideas that they inherited. Many of these (if not most) were initiated as much twenty years before they arrived at their leadership position. They must mold them together into an operational concept, while at the same time dealing with real-world events—barracks bombings, assaults in Somalia, 9/11 terror attacks, the eradication of terrorism. Despite the urgency of this work, their more important task is to look to the future and determine what research and development needs to begin now, to provide their successors, one, two, or more decades later, with the tools they will need. It is a never-ending research relay race, in which the baton of research capability is passed every two to four years from one generation of leaders to the next.

In the case of Joint STARS, the program began more than twenty years ago in two separate programs of the Army and the Air Force. Both aimed at developing MTI, i.e., radars, that could pick up and track moving targets on the ground. General Loh, first Commander of Air Combat Command, was an early advocate in the 1980s of a DARPA program known as Pave Mover.[18] The Army developed its Stand Off Target Acquisitions System (SOTAS), a helicopter-based program that ran into severe engineering problems.

In 1982, the Undersecretary of Defense for Research and Engineering wisely decided to combine the two programs into what was later designated Joint STARS. The Air Force's Electronic Systems Division (ESD) at Hanscom Air Force Base, Massachusetts, was designated as the lead organization for the program.

At this point there was not widespread backing for Joint STARS. It was such a highly classified program that not much was known about it; even its strongest advocates could not say all they wished to say, yet it had to compete for funds with every other weapons program in every budget exercise. The hazard in this is multiplied when two services are involved in a single program, for either service might encounter a situation in which a "pet" program of some powerful advocate (e.g., the Chief of Staff) would gobble up available funds.

The Joint STARS program proceeded at a reduced pace for almost four years before an agreement was reached by the Chiefs of Staff of the Army and the Air Force in May 1984. Joint STARS would use the Boeing 707 as a platform and combine both MTI and Synthetic Aperture Radar (SAR) with weapon guidance capabilities. It would operate in conjunction with Army Mobile Ground Station Modules (MGSMs), which were also a considerable technological challenge.

The Grumman Aerospace Company won a contract in September 1985 for Full Scale Development and subcontracted the development of the radar to Norden Systems. The phased-array radar was to be carried in a twenty-six-foot-long canoe-shaped radome under the forward fuselage.

The primary mode of the radar was a Wide Area Surveillance (with a range of 155 miles) MTI. The MTI is so sophisticated that Joint STARS can tell the difference between wheeled and tracked vehicles. The SAR/Fixed Target Indicator allows a photographic-like image or map of geographic regions. Such data maps can give the exact location of non-moving targets such as bridges, airports, and even stopped vehicles. The contract called for two test and as many as seventeen production aircraft to be built. This was later increased to a total of twenty-two, but some were deleted by budget requirements. As many as thirty or forty Joint STARS could be used effectively, but the fleet will probably be limited to just seventeen.

The intent of Joint STARS was to create a platform that could operate in any weather, on-line, in real time, twenty-four hours a day, anywhere in the world.

There followed over the next two years an endless series of Preliminary and Critical Design Reviews involving equipment design, selection, installation, and operation. It is difficult for an outsider to understand the tons of paperwork, hundreds of thousands of hours of computer time, arguments that destroyed long-standing friendships, and career paths made and ruined that go into these initial, formative efforts and which continue through the life of a system. What is particularly difficult to grasp is the interweaving of the intricate fabric of a new program such as Joint STARS with old programs, existing programs, and future programs.

It was not until April 1988 that Grumman was able to have a twenty-year-old commercial 707 rebuilt and outfitted with prototype equipment. Radar was fitted later, with a full test flight made in December 1988. (The original plans called for new Boeing airframes to be built for production aircraft, but cost considerations demanded that used 707 airframes be employed for the production run. The unit cost of a production E-8C is $225 million; this represents only a part of the total cost of all the programs involved.)

In 1991, as Commander of Tactical Air Command, General Loh fought for a force of forty Joint STARS, including five per Army corps, to give continuous support to each corps in Europe. Unfortunately, only fifteen were procured, meaning that the Joint STARS crews will be deployed up to 240 days a year.[19]

Northrop and Grumman merged in 1994, and two prototype Northrop Grumman E-8As deployed in 1991 to participate in Operation Desert Storm, where they flew forty-nine combat sorties. Joint STARS proved particularly important in the Battle of Khafji, where a column of eighty Iraqi vehicles, intending to move to the town of Khafji, was detected and then stopped by tactical airpower.

Joint STARS aircraft and their crews had proved effective, but the U.S. Air Force wanted to solve some development problems that had surfaced and resisted congressional pressure to accelerate production. Instead, production of E-8C models was begun in 1993, along with production of a dozen of the Mobile Ground System Modules (see below).

Training the aircrew of the Joint STARS did not pose a significant challenge, but training the eighteen specialized operators who man the consoles and maintaining the sophisticated equipment were far more demanding. Equipment had to be developed, training schools created, simulators established, and instruction provided—all as the real aircraft-installed equipment was being developed, meaning that all of the inevitable changes had to be tracked and compensated for.

This is but a brief—and very sanitized—portrayal of the hurdles involved in getting the weapon system developed and into combat. It is not easy to comprehend that every element of this complex system faces exactly the same hazards of design competition, procurement decisions, design reviews, testing, installation, and integration. Each and every system has to face the vagaries of the budget cycle, where unexpected cost overruns of a totally different weapon system may force cuts and even determine the life or death of the program. (As an example from the past, the very promising Martin P-6M Seamaster, a jet-powered sea-based bomber and reconnaissance aircraft, had its program funding eliminated in 1955 by then Naval Chief of Operations Arleigh "Thirty-Knot" Burke when the more important Polaris submarine program required additional funds.[20])

Further, so rapid is the pace of development that improvement programs have to begin concurrently with the development of original equipment, and these must all be kept compatible with the platform (the aircraft) and the related systems. This is not just the fit and finish compatibility of a completed aircraft; it is also software compatibility, with all the ramifications that come with interoperable open architecture software in a rapidly changing digital environment over an extended period of time.

As an example of the difficulties inherent in this process, the Radar Technology Insertion Program (RTIP) requires the contractor to design, develop, install, test, and integrate advanced radar systems into the Joint STARS system. Similar programs were required for the sensor subsystems. An Improved Data Modem (IDM) was required to provide an interoperable, full duplex, direct targeting support data link to the U.S. Army's Aviation Command and Control System and to Apache attack helicopters.

Additional Joint STARS systems (Enhanced SAR, Link 16 Upgrade, and Automatic Target Recognition, to name but a few) all had to go through the demanding process indicated earlier, and all had to do it in concert, for changes in one might require changes in all. Each one of the subprograms called for the vision, the dedication, the competitiveness, and the endurance that the Joint STARS program as a whole demanded.

One facet of the system that was praised for its work in both providing and protecting intelligence was the Common Ground Station (CGS), used by the Army, Marines, and Air Force. It was supplied real-time intelligence from Joint STARS, U-2, Predator, and the Hunter UAV and other intelligence-gathering equipment. In a single example, information from a CGS was used to alert a unit of the 3rd Infantry Division about a convoy of more than 200 Iraqi vehicles moving toward it. The unit was guarding a bridge. Specialist Jacob Mayer, a CGS operator for the B Company, 103 Military Intelligence Battalion, 2nd Brigade of the 3rd Infantry Division, said that the system worked very well, enabling them to destroy the vehicles when they were still more than ten minutes away from the bridge. Without Joint STARS and the CGS, the unit might have been overrun.[21]

The CGS showed exactly where the Iraqi vehicles were and gave the Marines a picture of the battlefield unavailable anywhere else. The CGS can be mounted on a Humvee and has equipment designed to process data from the real-time sensors.

The CGS is another reminder that Joint STARS is just one element in the spectacular array of weaponry—other aircraft, satellites, UAVs, cruise missiles, and PGMs—and that each of these is being continually updated and improved. Slightly later in the campaign, for example, a Northrop Grumman RQ-4A Global Hawk was used for the first time to pass data to a Boeing F/A-18 for an attack on an Iraqi missile system.[22]

The information went to the fighter cockpit via a ground control center. The Global Hawk had used its Raytheon SAR to signal the AAQ-16 electrooptical/infrared (EO/IR) sensor that there was a missile launcher in view, although it was partially obscured by being hidden under a bridge. This information was correlated with the onboard LR 100 electronic surveillance system and then relayed to the ground for analysis before being passed to an F/A-18 that was on station. The Hornet processed the information and attacked the missile launcher, destroying it without destroying the bridge. The total lapsed time from the SAR pickup to the missile's destruction was about twenty minutes.[23]

Each individual element in the information-gathering array has a long heritage, some reaching much further back into history than Joint STARS, each facing the same hurdles, and each coming together in the symphony of warfare that was Operation Iraqi Freedom.

So the short answer to "What went right and why?" in this case is the U.S. Army and Air Force, in selecting, creating, producing, and using a sophisticated Joint STARS system that could interact with satellites as with its mobile ground stations and be translatable through GPS to guide PGMs (an admittedly difficult technological task).

Thus it was that the Republican Guard tanks that moved southward to defend Baghdad, hoping that the sandstorm would conceal them, were attacked by forty-year-old B-52Hs. They were found and fixed by a program that had originated more than twenty years earlier. They were destroyed by systems that were proposed over ten years ago (WCMD), and the results of the attack on them were assessed by UAV assets pressed into service in just the last few years.

WHAT ELSE WENT RIGHT AND WHY

In the west, the twenty-four F-16s, with advanced Litening II targeting pods and GBU-27 LGBS, continued to distinguish themselves as the "rainbow" 120th EFS of the 410th AEW.

Flying from an "undisclosed location" in the Middle East (read: "Jordan"), the 120th EFS took part in operations that secured three airfields and in the battles of Al Qaim and Baghdad. Al Qaim, near the Syrian border, was being defended rigorously by hold-out Iraqi troops.[24]

In the north, paratroopers from the 173rd Airborne Brigade signaled an important addition to the rather thinly spread special operation forces who had been stiffening Kurdish national forces in the area. The seizure of Bashur airfield meant that Lockheed Martin C-130s could begin bringing in personnel, supplies, and equipment at an increasing rate. This operation would have almost certainly have been considered too hazardous to undertake in any previous war. Yet it went well because of the circumstances that prevailed: complete information and airpower dominance. But underlying those circumstances, invisible, but all-important was the smoothly efficient logistical system that not only saw that supplies were moved from factory to depot to ship to airplane to Bashur but also had previously established the accounting, inventory, and procurement systems that made the supplies, in all their manifold variety, available, on time, and in place years before.

WHAT WENT WRONG AND WHY

Two areas, helicopters and tankers, stand out as the major examples of "what went wrong," and the same "why" applies to both.

The helicopter fleets of all of the armed services have been neglected. The fleets are filled with aircraft that have served for twenty or more years, many of which should have been replaced long ago. The average age of the Air Force's Sikorsky H-53 type helicopter is thirty-two; Navy and Marine helicopters are, for the most part, of similar vintage. The Apache AH-64 entered service in 1984, and many were converted to the AH-64D Longbow configuration about ten years ago, making them the youngsters in the fleet.

Two things have hindered the procurement of new helicopters. The first is budget considerations. In the annual process the services always opt for the production of new combat aircraft—fighters or bombers—over what are considered "service" aircraft, despite their continual insertion into combat situations. All of the services recognize the higher cost of maintaining an older fleet; all are faced with the problems of parts shortages, "cannibalization" (using parts from one helicopter to repair another), and increased downtime. Yet the depots and the maintenance workers do a fantastic job of keeping the older helicopters flying, and year after year their replacement needs are deferred in the face of other pressures.

There is a secondary factor with helicopters, and that is that some of the intended replacements (including the Boeing/Bell V 22 Osprey) have run into development problems that delayed their procurement even as they consumed large fractions of the available budget.

The result of this neglect manifested itself in accidents and in an increased workload for maintenance personnel to keep helicopters flying. There is no immediate solution to this situation, but a congressionally mandated reequipment, with the funds to do so, would be the best start. However, concerns about the vulnerability of the Apache in Operation Iraqi Freedom may very well cause reexamination of such action.

The shortage of tankers manifested itself early on, and preliminary analysis indicates that perhaps thousands of missions that would have otherwise been flown were not, because of the tanker shortage. In Operation Iraqi Freedom, this was acceptable; in another conflict, against a more capable enemy, the tanker shortage might have proved fatal.

Although tankers receive far less media coverage than most combat aircraft, they have become the single most critical element of airpower. Without them, the fighters, bombers, transports, and even many helicopter types would be absolutely useless as combat units. The tankers are in effect huge force multipliers, able to convert a relative handful of bombers and fighters into a far larger force by enabling them to fly farther and many more missions in a given interval. In addition, future UAVs will likely require midair refueling.

The average Air Force Boeing KC-135 tanker is forty-three years old. The demands for in-flight refueling are continually increasing; in 2002 the tankers flew about 50 percent more sorties than they flew in 2001, and the rate increased dramatically in 2003. The utility of tanker aircraft is also governed by the basing available. The Turkish government's refusal to allow U.S. aircraft to operate against Iraq from Turkish bases caused an immediate crisis. Because tankers could not sortie from Turkish bases to refuel Navy aircraft, the latter were unable to produce the planned volume of sorties. Because Navy aircraft use probe and drogue ("basket") while the Air Force uses boom ("receptacle") refueling, the positioning of tankers with compatible equipment becomes important.

The tanker shortage forced the Navy to do some improvisation. Carrier Wing 11, of the USS *Nimitz*, "lent" four F/A-18E/F Super Hornets to Carrier Wing 14, aboard USS *Abraham Lincoln*, to fly in the buddy tanking role. The Super Hornets had to make an initial flight of 1,700 miles, using drop tanks and refueling from tankers from the *Nimitz* (tankers refueling tankers is almost always a sign of a significant shortage of tankers) and landing at Diego Garcia. The second leg of the flight was 2,300 miles and involved another in-flight refueling, this time by KC-135s, before the aircraft could touch down on the *Abraham Lincoln*. The pilots took turns flying Super Hornet tanker missions, so that all would get a chance to go into combat.

About two hundred Air Force tankers were stationed at fifteen different bases in the area, in addition to RAF, Royal Australian Air Force, and Marine tankers. This placed a demanding task on those planning the refuelings. Serial refueling—a method enabling planners to keep aircraft airborne for longer periods of time so that they can respond instantly to any emerging target, was used, and tankers were positioned far forward over the battlefield. This could have been dangerous, particularly if the Iraqis had been the beneficiary of any one of a number of new, longer-range SAMs.

The timing for each refueling was carefully controlled to reduce the number of aircraft in a given area. Nonetheless, there were a flood of complaints from both Navy and Air Force pilots who felt they were short-changed on air refueling.

The entire refueling situation is implicitly fraught with hazard but is done so often under the most appalling conditions that it is accepted as routine. Everything, from planning to execution, is demanding. The tankers are placed on certain specified tracks, at specified altitudes and places. Aircraft returning from combat have specific tankers assigned to them, but if short on fuel, they refuel where they must, no matter how it complicates schedules.

A typical tanker mission lasts between four and six hours, and as many as six coalition aircraft are serviced on each mission. The 340th Expeditionary Air Refueling Squadron reported that it had flown 116 missions and refueled 491 aircraft in the first six days of the war. As with other refueling squadrons, about one-third to one-half of the unit's aircraft are in the air at all times.[25]

The number of available tankers was somewhat reduced because of ongoing operations in Central Asia and because an "air bridge" of tankers was created across the Atlantic to speed tactical aircraft and transports to bases in the area.

In a related situation, only twenty-four Lockheed Martin KC-130 tankers were assigned to the region, at a time when the Marines were in a "surge" mode, launching as many of their F/A-18s and Boeing AV-8Bs in as short an interval as possible. The situation was detrimental to both of the fighters, which are relatively short-ranged without refueling. Harriers from VMA-214 had little time to spend in their assigned "kill box" around Baghdad.

The Marines attempted to alleviate the situation by establishing forward operating bases for the fighter aircraft. It also built Forward Areas Refueling Points (FARPs) for its helicopters, sometimes bringing fuel in by a tanker.

Why did a shortage occur? For many of the same reasons affecting the helicopters. Even beginning the replacement of the tanker fleet has been deferred from year to year, despite the fact that its use has increased dramatically, as has its fundamental importance. There is at present a controversy going on over a lease arrangement that will begin to phase tankers based on the Boeing 767 commercial aircraft into the fleet. These aircraft will have a substantial operating advantage over the existing fleet in terms of range and operating costs.

In the case of both the helicopters and the tankers, the real onus of responsibility lies upon the services themselves first, the Congress of the United States second, and the people of United States third. The tanker fleet, especially, is essential to the global power and global reach of America. Both helicopter and tanker fleets are known to be required and are known to be old. The public should have demanded their replacement, the Congress should have funded the demand, and the services should have done their best to see that the public and the Congress were so sufficiently informed and motivated that adverse budget cuts would not have occurred. Both fleets (and many other problems) could have been addressed over the years by increasing the defense budget by about 1 percent of the GDP in each of the years from 1991 through 2003. Instead, as the Cold War came to a close, the percentage of GDP declined through ten of those years and the military is faced with replacing many essential fleets all at once, a steep hill to climb.

Compared to the multibillion-dollar issue of helicopters and tankers, the problem of a pistol magazine seems minor—but not to the Marine who requires it for combat. Under the conditions in Iraq, the ubiquitous M9 pistol magazines did not work properly. The springs were weak, and the follower did not move forward when rounds were removed. The result is a malfunctioning weapon. The result was that many elected to carry an M16 rifle instead, despite the fact that many felt the pistol was a better weapon for room-to-room fighting in buildings.

For similar reasons, the troops preferred a smaller weapon than the 40.3-inch-long M16. Some picked up captured AK-47s, only 34.5 inches long, for city fighting. Many M4s (a shorter version of the M16), only 33.3 inches long overall, were used and were better suited for many of the engagements.

There were other problems with infantry weapons. The M249 squad machine guns were reported to be wearing out, some literally falling apart in combat. The newer 7.62mm M240 machine guns were well liked. The 5.56 round was criticized as being too light unless it hit the enemy in the head or the chest.

Despite these and other minor problems, the overall execution of the war in the next fifteen days demonstrated conclusively that much more was going right than was going wrong.

5

Combined Operations at Their Best

OPERATION IRAQI FREEDOM:
March 28, 29, 30, and 31

The ninth day of the war saw coalition aircraft fly more than 1,500 sorties, with Baghdad getting hit harder than any time since A Day. In one of the increasingly frequent "emerging target" responses, two Boeing F-15E Strike Eagles used information from a special forces team to place bombs on a building in Basra where more than 200 Ba'ath Party members had assembled to meet. In preplanned attacks, Boeing F/A-18Cs used PGMs to strike targets near Basra and also Baghdad. Some six thousand PGMs had been dropped to that date in the war.

The Navy fired their Tomahawk inventory to supplement the air offensive, and a total of 675 cruise missiles (at about eight hundred thousand dollars per missile) had been launched to date. A temporary halt in firing the Tomahawk missile over certain routes was required when several missiles went off-course to land in Saudi Arabia, Iran, and Turkey, causing some diplomatic flurries.

The ubiquitous workhorse Lockheed Martin C-130s starred in their traditional role when the 320th AW flew tactical resupply flights into Talil, nicknamed "Bush International Airport" by members of the 82nd Airborne Division, just four miles from Al Nasiriyah.[1] The C-130s brought badly needed supplies right to the front lines in the role for which Willis Hawkins had designed them some fifty years before. (Within five days, personnel from Air Mobility Command headquarters at Scott Air Force Base, Illinois, had cleared the Talil runway and restored it to operation.)

MC-130s of the 352nd Special Operations Group performed a similar role at two airfields in northern Iraq, Harir, near Bashur, and an improvised airstrip west of as-Sulaymaniah.[2]

While Iraqi air opposition continued to be nil, tactical ballistic missiles continued to be fired at the rate of about one per day. Most were of the Frog, Ababil-100, or Al Samoud type, and all were launched from Iraq into Kuwait.

Helicopters of the 101st Airborne (Air Assault) Division conducted deep attack operations against the Republican Guard Medina Division in the vicinity of Karbala.[3] In the longest helicopter assault operation ever undertaken, the 101st Aviation Brigade flew more than 200 helicopters, including Bell OH-58Ds, Boeing CH-47Ds, Boeing AH-64Ds, and Sikorsky UH-60s, to forward operating bases south of Karbala.[4] Blowing sand obscured visibility during landing situations, causing two AH-64Ds of the 101st Aviation Regiment to crash and two OH-58Ds of the 17th Cavalry Squadron to make hard landings.

A USAF Fairchild-Republic A-10 was involved in a friendly fire incident, attacking two British APCs and killing one soldier. The field of battle is crowded with APC-like vehicles, making fratricide in the heat of battle ever more likely.

Special forces continued to operate almost with impunity throughout Iraq. Raids and the use of laser designators to direct air strikes proved particularly effective.

At Umm Qasr, the RFA *Sir Galahad*, with 200 tons of relief supplies, was finally able to dock after mines had been cleared from the shipping channel.

At the daily CENTCOM briefing, two major issues were raised, the first of which was the remarks of Lieutenant General William Wallace to the effect that the enemy he was facing was "a bit different" from the one he war-gamed against. Wallace was referring to the training the Army troops had received versus the enemy tactics actually encountered, but much more was read into the statement. Brigadier General Vincent Brooks, the CENTCOM Deputy Director of Operations, parried the question, as he would do to the second difficult one, which concerned the widespread reports that supply lines were being stretched too thin and this was becoming a real problem in the field. Some reporters inquired if this did not indicate that the war in Iraq would have the duration of the war in Vietnam.

On the tenth day of the war, 2,300 Marines from the 24th Marine Expeditionary Unit (MEU) landed in Kuwait, prior to taking up positions in southern Iraq.

The U.S. Air Forces Air Combat Command made history when it launched a mission against Baghdad combining three major bombers in the inventory. Boeing B-1Bs of the 405th Aerial Expeditionary Wing (AEW), Boeing B-52Hs from the 40th AEW and the 457th Air Expeditionary Group, and Northrop Grumman B-2As from the 40th AEW. Taking off from widely separated bases, they rendezvoused over Baghdad to make simultaneous preplanned strikes on regime and command and control targets.[5]

U.S. supply convoys continued to be attacked by guerrilla forces around the city of An Nasiriyah, which has a population of about half a million. Saddam's *Fedayeen* units made hit-and-run attacks and are now the focus of intense counterinsurgency efforts.

The 3rd Infantry Division paused between An Najaf and Karbala, preparing to assault the Medina Republican Guard Division prior to continuing on to Baghdad. The delay made the questions concerning overstretched supply lines more pertinent but was used to advantage by coalition aircraft. USAF-10s and F-16s, Army AH-64s, RAF Harrier GR.7s, and U.S. Navy F/A-18s attacked the reported 200 T-72 tanks of the Medina Division, destroying many of them, along with their supporting APCs, AAA systems, and radars.[6]

The intensity of air attacks fell off somewhat, with 1,000 flown on March 29. At one point, over 300 coalition aircraft were in the air at one time, taxing the capability to control them.

A casualty report indicated that twenty-eight Americans were dead, sixteen missing in action, and 107 wounded to date. Baghdad continued to protest civilian casualties, which they blamed exclusively on coalition bombing. At least fifty-eight Iraqi civilians were killed in an explosion of yet undetermined origin in a marketplace in northwest Baghdad.[7]

On March 30, the eleventh day of the war, extensive ground operations were under way. Three Republican Guard divisions were assigned to defend Baghdad. The Medina Armored Division, probably the most capable of the three, was placed to the south of the city. The Al Nida Armored Division was positioned to the east of Baghdad, while the Baghdad Motorized Infantry Division was posted near the city of Kut, farther east still and on the Tigris River.

Preparing for the battle, the 3rd Infantry Division reached Al Hillah, just southeast of Karbala. The Karbala Gap, a key pass between the city of Karbala and Lake Razazah on the route to Baghdad, lay ahead. Continuous air strikes decimated three Iraqi mechanized units that were guarding Karbala. The militiamen were more aggressive than the beaten-down Iraqi army troops, attacking with assault rifles and the ever-present RPGs. The militiamen were brushed aside by concentrated fire from both precision tube artillery and multiple rocket launchers.

Concern about guerilla attacks on supply lines persisted, and the 1st Brigade of the 101st Airborne (Air Assault) Division attacked militiamen responsible for the hit-and-run attacks near An Najaf, on the Euphrates

River. Apache helicopters were called in but once again had to abandon their attack because of heavy enemy fire.

Fifty miles farther south at Samawah, still on the Euphrates, two battalions from the 82nd Airborne Division engaged a force of over 1,000 militiamen. The battle was a further confirmation of the pressure placed on coalition supply lines and the Iraqi hope that such attacks would delay the advance on Baghdad by a few days. Even farther south, 100 miles from the 3rd Infantry Division's advance position, in the previously mentioned trouble spot of An Nasiriyah, a Marine force seized a warehouse of the Iraqi 11th Infantry Division and found more than 300 chemical suits with the attendant masks, antidote injectors, and other materials necessary for chemical warfare. This fanned the hopes of the imminent discovery of weapons of mass destruction.

In Basra, the British forces continued their tactics of cordoning off a section of a city, then raiding it to target Iraqi military officers and Ba'ath Party leaders. The work is slow and dangerous, but seemed to be agreeable enough to the Iraqi population, where individuals could take a quiet pleasure in seeing their erstwhile tormentors taken into custody. There was no widespread open expression of joy until the Ba'athists had been substantially cleared out.

General Franks gave one of his rare press briefings on March 30 providing a nine-point review of how his plan of operations had proceeded on track in terms of operational objectives. The following transcript is made with some additional commentary:

> First, the coalition has secured the oil fields in the south from regime destruction, which was attempted, and this vital resource has been preserved for Iraq's future. [This loomed so large in General Franks' mind that he made the decision for ground operations to precede air operations.]
>
> Second, we have air and ground freedom of action in western Iraq, working to protect Iraq's neighbors from potential regime use of weapons of mass destruction [almost equally as important as the oil fields, for the repercussions of a missile attack on Israel were unfathomable].
>
> Third, our air forces work 24 hours a day across every square foot of Iraq. And every day, the regime loses more of its military capability. [This is almost a throwaway line, for it does not begin to hint at the methodical disembowelment of Iraqi forces by the relentless attacks of the air component.]
>
> Fourth, we are now staging and conducting air operations from a number of Iraqi airfields now under coalition control.
>
> Fifth, coalition forces have attacked and destroyed a massive terror-

ist facility in the last 48 hours in northern Iraq, and ground forces, as we speak, are exploiting the results of that strike. [This comment would be severely cross-questioned by reporters.]

Sixth, the entire coastline of Iraq has been secured and her ports stand today as a gateway for humanitarian assistance to the Iraqi people. As you know, the first humanitarian shipments have arrived in convoys, and additional shipments are on the way.

Seventh, the coalition has in fact introduced a very capable ground force into northern Iraq. These forces, along with large numbers of special operations troops, have prevented the rekindling of historic feuding that we've seen in past years between the Turks and the Kurds, and these forces do in fact represent a serious northern threat to regime forces. [This statement was designed to offset recurrent charges that the inability of the 4th Infantry Division to invade northern Iraq might have catastrophic consequences for the limited number of forces in the south.]

Eighth, a large and capable ground force has attacked to within 60 miles of Baghdad on multiple fronts, and they currently maintain readiness levels of their combat systems above 90 percent mission capable. As we speak, elements of that ground force are continuing the attack. The regime is in trouble, and they know it.

Ninth, in the past 24 hours, I have received reports that coalition forces are working with local Iraqis in the city of An Nasiriyah, and the death squads that operate—the squads of gangs, regime gangs that operate in that city—have come under fire. [Curiously, this somewhat diminishes the previous point, but it honestly reflects the situation.]

In the southeastern section of Basra, 600 Royal Marines of the 40 Commando made a classic infantry assault against *Fedayeen* Saddam and Ba'ath Party stalwarts.

The media's general perception of a flagging campaign was not diminished on March 31, the twelfth day of the campaign, despite the fact that ground forces were engaged with Iraqi troops around Al Hindiyah, about forty-eight miles south of Baghdad. There the 3rd Infantry Division seized a bridge over the Euphrates River prior to its demolition by the Iraqis. Explosive charges were in place, but the swift movement of the 3rd Infantry Division caught the Iraqis off-guard.

The conviction that the plan was behind schedule stemmed in part from fighting that continued in the rear, well behind the spearhead of the advance. A mixture of Republican Guard and militia units continued to offer sporadic resistance of varying degrees of intensity around Al Hilla and the city of An Nasiriyah. As an example, 100 miles to the south at As

Samawah, the 82nd Airborne Division used precision artillery counterfire to destroy an enemy D-30 artillery system. This is a Soviet-designed 122mm towed artillery piece, some of which came from Russia, some from Yugoslavia, while some were manufactured in Iraq. Designated the "Saddam" (what else?), the D-30 has a range of nine miles and a sustained rate of fire of four rounds per minute. A crew of seven is required for the D-30, which is generally regarded as having good performance. In precision counterfire, UAVs, Joint STARS, and other targeting systems, including counterbattery radar that calculates the position of the shooter from the trajectory of enemy incoming artillery shells, combine to provide near real-time intelligence. Counterbattery radar has improved and the United States can react almost immediately with accurate counterbattery fire.[8] In essence, U.S. precision artillery turns every enemy artillery crew into a target a few seconds after they fire their weapon.

While much was made of Iraqi attacks on coalition supply lines, the elements of the 7th Cavalry were raiding the supply routes and trains of the enemy, capturing 150 prisoners of war and destroying many vehicles and the omnipresent caches of weapons. (One streetwise soldier speculated that the weapons were more the product of graft than of military need and that Iraqi contracting officers bought far more weapons than were necessary to secure the "grease" on each contract.)

In air action, the coalition flew 2,000 sorties. Of these, 800 were strike sorties, some against fixed regime targets but most against "emerging targets" of the Republican Guard.[9] The relative shortage of tankers was overcome again by using them more intensively, despite the problems of crew fatigue and the never-ending maintenance needs of forty-year-old aircraft. Four hundred of the sorties were by tankers, which have transferred more than 20 million gallons of jet fuel since the beginning of Operation Iraqi Freedom.

A Marine Boeing AV-8B Harrier crashed while attempting to land on the amphibious assault ship USS *Nassau*. The pilot ejected and was recovered by one of the invaluable search and rescue helicopters, this one from the *Nassau*. Another Navy aircraft, a Lockheed Martin S-3B Viking, went off the deck of the USS *Constellation* after an arrested landing. The two pilots ejected and were rescued by a Sikorsky HH-60 helicopter. A search and rescue swimmer dropped into the water to help the pilots in the recovery process. Neither pilot was seriously injured.

In the CENTCOM briefing, rumors of 4,000 foreign suicide bombers crossing the border into Iraq inspired a series of questions among reporters who immediately wished to know what actions were being taken by special operation forces to deter them.

Brigadier General Vincent "Unflappable" Brooks responded that the well-equipped, highly mobile special operation forces would "deny the infiltrators freedom of movement in the western desert of Iraq"—Brook-speak for "we'll kill them."

The questions persisted. As an example, one questioner asked, "Back to the suicide [a suicide car bombing had just taken place] and the threat of another four thousand. Were coalition soldiers told ahead of time to prepare for that type of fighting? And what had been the effect of it becoming a reality on the morale of the soldiers? And secondarily, how many times would you say Iraqi civilians have been killed after being targeted by coalition soldiers because there was a threat they might be suicide attackers or they were driving where they should be and didn't stop?"

Translated, the questions meant: "Did you fail in the training of your soldiers? Are your soldiers terrified of the threat of suicide bombers? And how many innocent Iraqis have you murdered so far because of this threat?"

To this General Brooks responded that there was a heightened awareness of a threat by the soldiers and that morale was a complex issue, determined by many factors. He commented that casualties had occurred among Iraqi civilians when they were pushed in front as shields by irregular Iraqi forces. But, he emphasized, "we're not targeting them. No one's killing more Iraqis right now than the regime."[10]

The question of land mines was raised, and Brooks revealed that while Iraqi forces typically used them extensively, leaving them behind to wreak havoc on the Iraqi populace, the U.S. forces used land mines only as a temporary protective measure and recovered them after their use.

The most incisive question of the day was from Charles Henry of WTOP Radio, who asked if there was ever a competition between humanitarian and military tactical supplies in the flow of material into Iraq. The answer was that military tactical supplies would necessarily have priority until the conflict was over.

THE VIEW FROM THE OTHER SIDE

The halt brought about by the sandstorm and the need to let supplies catch up greatly heartened the information gatherers who constituted the anti-American Internet. Significant coalition losses were reported, including "more than 200 combat vehicles" and "70 helicopters disabled."

It was proudly announced that a number of "myths" had been disproved and among these was the efficacy of PGMs. It was noted that "the massed use of strategic and tactical precision guided munitions did not provide U.S. forces with a strategic advantage." And while it was admitted that PGMs did avoid civilian casualties, it was argued that the PGMs did not have sufficient power to destroy an intended target.

A second disproved myth was that modern high-tech weapons were superior to "older generation weapons." The GRU report argued that despite a twenty-five-to-thirty-year generation gap between American and Iraqi weapons, the latter were sufficient to enable the Iraqis to resist, confident that they could inflict heavy losses on the enemy.

The GRU view was that the coalition forces were at least 40 percent short of those required for victory in Iraq and that, as a result, the U.S. advance was characterized by disorganized and impulsive actions. (What the coalition forces regarded as getting inside the Iraq OODA loop was thus considered "impulsive.") The same commentary insisted that the coalition had failed every goal it had set during the nine days of war and now had no means of attaining victory.

The following day, after announcing a strike on a supply convoy to the 3rd Infantry Division that destroyed ten fuel trucks and an APC, the GRU reports indicated a conflict between General Franks and Secretary Rumsfeld that was going to result in a change in coalition command.

On March 30, a sort of "All Quiet on the Iraqi Front" message was distributed by IRAQWAR.ru. It noted that the coalition command had been surprised to find that Iraqi forces were better technically equipped than had been believed, emphasizing that there were adequate numbers of night-vision equipment distributed among Iraqi forces and that they were the "latest models manufactured in the U.S. and Japan." But a faint note of reality crept into the reporting on March 31. After noting that announced coalition casualties were far smaller than the actual amounts and that the American campaign was bogged down, it warned that "the Iraqi command is now in danger of underestimating the enemy."[11]

WHAT WENT RIGHT AND WHY

The U.S. Marine Corps continued to operate in an almost flawless manner, even though precedents were being broken and new records for long-distance movement (not in the traditional Marine Corps doctrine) and fighting were being established every day. The Marines are not a heavy fighting force. They are trained and equipped to move onshore, seize objectives, then turn to the Army for heavy sustaining forces.

The activities of the 1st Marine Division, as with all other units, were obscured in the early days of the war for security reasons. The 1st, which was "lighter" in armor than the 3rd Infantry Division, was given several missions on the southern end of the trek north to Baghdad, somewhat diluting its strength. Nonetheless, for the most part it maintained its position all the way to Baghdad, paralleling the 3rd Infantry Division on the eastern flank.

One of the keys to the 1st Marine Division success, as always, was the union of Marine air and ground in action, bringing about the modern dream of operational maneuver from the sea. Marine Corps Assistant Commandant General William Nyland commented on the ability of the Marine Corps to move 11,000 Marines, and all of the aviation, logistics, and sustainment assets only thirty days after being notified about going to war. Two Maritime Prepositioning Forces took only eighteen days to off-load needed cargo, with improvements coming every day.[12]

Within the first few days of combat, the Marines seized an airfield with a 9,000-foot-long runway that had been abandoned after being attacked during the 1991 Gulf War. Without attempting to repair the main runway, they began using it as a major refueling and rearming point for the highly effective Bell AH-1W attack helicopters. Colonel R. (Boomer) Milstead, Commander of the Marine Air Group 29, noted that the base soon became a "major logistical hub," pivotal for resupply operations as well.[13] Lockheed Martin KC-130 transports (flying from a taxiway, the runway still being unserviceable), Boeing CH-46 Sea Knights, and Sikorsky CH-53E Sea Stallion helicopters used it to transship materials to the most advanced forces. The Marines expanded on the concept with additional airports tied to the advancing ground forces.

The MEF had trained for just this sort of operation at 29 Palms, California, and upgraded their vehicles to meet the demands of desert warfare. To keep things moving, they ran a hose reel fuel system seventy miles from the Kuwait border, to replenish the FARP throughout the area. For forward resupply, they depended upon Lockheed Martin KC-130s. As a result the Marines were able to keep pace with the 3rd Infantry Division even though they were moving over rougher terrain against more intense resistance.

The Marines also made good use of their Pioneer and backpack Dragon Eye UAVs. The Hunter has a fourteen-foot wingspan and weighs up to 450 pounds, while the Dragon Eye is a product of Paul MacCready's genius. The forty-five-inch wingspan Dragon Eye is a five-pound backpackable modular UAV that gives Marine small-unit commanders the capability to see over the next hill and beyond the next building. After being hand-launched (or catapulted by a bungee cord), the Dragon Eye flies to a predetermined GPS waypoint, where its two full-motion, low-light, and infrared cameras can pick up information to send it back as much as six miles.

More mundane, the tried and true helicopters had operated well from shipboard, but as time passed the round-trip grew longer and the ability to adequately service the ground forces declined. The acquisition of the first airfield cut 2.5 hours from the average mission, and the reduction in flight time was reflected in a corresponding reduction in average maintenance requirements.

The conversion of an abandoned runway to a major logistics hub was not easy, for the Marines had to contend with Iraqi artillery fire. The austere working conditions were far different from those aboard ship. The constant problem of dust was intensified by a shortage of water, essential to clean sand out of helicopter engines. Cannibalization, the bane of all maintenance officers, became a way of life. Operationally, Iraqi antiaircraft fire remained a constant concern, for the low-flying Marine aircraft were perfect targets for the enemy gunners.

On the plus side, the air bases on land can operate twenty-four hours a day, while deck operations were more constrained and limited to a twelve-hour shift. The Marines looked forward to a cessation of hostilities and the conversion of all their operations into humanitarian relief missions.

One of the great Marine accomplishments was bringing the Boeing AV-8B Harrier to the level of capability that had been dreamed of ever since the Marines began using the aircraft in 1972.

Of the seventy-six Harriers in the theater, sixty were operated off two "Harrier Carriers," the USS *Bonhomme Richard* and the USS *Bataan*. The presence of the two amphibious warfare ships provided an immediate operating base near Kuwait, where the aircraft could refuel and rearm, hot or cold, and receive maintenance at all levels. It also permitted take-offs and landings under instrument conditions.

The Harrier is a demanding aircraft. Only one other V/STOL fighter ever came into operation, and that was the relatively primitive and now-retired (due to its dangerous operating characteristics) Yakovlev Yak-38 Forger. The Harrier has its roots in the British Hawker P. 1127 of 1960. After years of development it reached its current state of refinement as the Boeing (formerly McDonnell Douglas) AV-8B, a joint project with British Aerospace. Using the 20,280 pounds of vectored thrust of its Rolls-Royce Pegasus turbofan engine, the Harrier has a maximum speed of 547 knots and a maximum range of 900 miles. Its combat radius is 142 miles, and its forte is operation close behind the front lines.

During Desert Storm, sixty-six Harrier aircraft operated from shore, while another twenty operated from shipboard. During operations,

Harriers were based as close as thirty-five miles from the front lines. They flew 3,380 sorties and sustained a mission-capable rate of 90 percent.[14]

This was, until Operation Iraqi Freedom, the high tide of Harrier operations. In the intervening years the aircraft has come under close scrutiny because of its high accident rate and its maintenance difficulties. In the thirty-one years since it entered service, it has had 143 major noncombat accidents, killing forty-five Marines and destroying about one-third of the Harriers in service. In the period leading up to Operation Iraqi Freedom, maintenance difficulties have kept Harrier availability very low, with the result that Harrier pilots were able to log only about eight hours a month of flying time, about half the amount considered necessary to remain proficient in the aircraft. The aircraft has been grounded thirty-one times since 1990, an ominous record.

Yet all the problems seemed resolved in Operation Iraqi Freedom. The Harriers were able to take off from the carrier, fly a mission, go to a forward operating base (FOB) to rearm and refuel, fly a mission, and then return to the carrier. This doubled the availability of the aircraft.

The addition of the Litening II ER targeting pod greatly extended the Harrier's capability. The video downlink of the ISR version of the Litening pod was particularly valuable, for it enabled forward air controllers to see what the Harrier pilots saw and talk them to the targets.

The Litening and other Israeli products have caused some angry comment among the Arab nations, who insist that their use confirms the war in Iraq is part of a Zionist conspiracy. The technology of Israel and the United States is melded in a whole spectrum of weapons, including the Tactical Air-Launched Decoy (TALD), the USAF AGM-142 Have Nap missile, the U.S. Army's Hunter UAV, the Marine Corps Pioneer UAV, and many smaller components, including computers and armor for Bradley fighting vehicles.[15]

The versatility of the Harrier is matched by that of their carriers, the *Baatan* and the *Bonhomme Richard*. These 844-foot-long *Wasp*-Class Amphibious Assault Ships can launch Landing Craft Air Cushion vehicles, conventional landing craft, helicopters, and the Harrier. A crew of 1,108, including 104 officers, mans the twenty-knot vessel, which also has a 1,894-man Marine detachment. They are the largest amphibious ships in the world and give the U.S. Navy a powerful long-range striking force.

The success of these operations lends credence to the ongoing Navy arguments that sea-based operations can avoid the embarrassment of an ally (such as Turkey) suddenly denying bases. A host of diplomatic issues are bypassed, and an adequate sea-based capability would permit projecting U.S. power anywhere in the world, without concern for land bases. The aim of the Navy is to engage in operational maneuvers, "Forward from the Sea." According to the Navy vision, operate directly from the sea or from strategic distances. An example of this occurred when the 26th MEU flew its helicopters from the Mediterranean Sea into northern Iraq, while KC-130s brought in fuel, equipment, and personnel. This sort of stiletto attack, where the blade is inserted in the back of an enemy fighting force before it is aware that is under attack, is particularly important in wars such as that in Iraq, where the battlefield is noncontiguous and success depends upon networking and the ubiquitous C⁴ISR.

Although such arguments are compelling to the Navy, Air Force advocates point out that in every war far more tonnage is dropped and targets attacked by land-based airpower. Another perspective is that Operation Iraqi Freedom demonstrates once again that the U.S. military needs a wide spectrum of capability in all services. No one service or capability is the answer for every conflict. It is the combined arms effects of all services and coalition allies that produce victories.

The more ardent airpower enthusiast would embrace General Loh's view that bombers are far more independent than carrier task forces, which require constant replenishment of fuel, munitions, spare parts, and other supplies. General Loh also believes that bombers are far more independent of bases than carriers in the sense that they operate from bases beyond the theater of operations. He points out that a carrier task force has several ports and air bases ashore supporting it.[16]

In Operation Iraqi Freedom, the Marines blended personnel, training, aircraft, ships, and information dominance into a powerful force that fit perfectly into EBO. The Marines have long been famous for frontal attack, where their skill, bravery, and attrition would bludgeon any opposing enemy into submission. The bludgeon has been replaced by a rapier, allowing the Marines to fence adroitly within the enemy OODA cycle.

The Navy aviation assets were also in top form for Operation Iraqi Freedom, so much so that Rear Admiral David Nichols of the Naval Strike and Air Warfare Center (one of the "centers of excellence" that contributed so much to U.S. leadership) was quoted as saying that instead of thinking in terms of "lessons learned," the thinking should be of "what we validated."[17] This comment is congruent with USAF views on operations and has the effect of causing some to pause and review many planned technological advances that are on the drawing board to make sure that the current systems have been fully exploited before money is spent on new systems.

Admiral Nichols went on to amend his statement to the extent that the lack of big wing tankers was a major hurdle and that "the tanking piece was not an insignificant impact early in the war." Nichols believes that the tanker shortage was due more to the timing of operations than to the absolute number of tankers available, but that more tankers would have been welcome.

Operation Iraqi Freedom marked the debut of the Boeing F/A-18E/F Super Hornet, and Vice Admiral Michael Malone, Commander of the Naval Air Force at U.S. Pacific Fleet, stated, "The Super Hornet did very well. Its readiness numbers are what we expected and better. It's demonstrating that it's a marvelous strike platform. It's got great range. And its flexibility in being an airborne tanker is remarkable."[18]

The Super Hornets averaged thirty-five missions a day for sixteen days, half of which were strike missions. The balance of the missions were in-flight refueling, flown by F/A-18E "Strike Tanker" aircraft that transferred 2.3 million pounds of fuel to other aircraft.[19]

Vice Admiral Timothy Keating specifically cited the performance of the F/A-18E/F Super Hornet as one of the six most important things that "went right" in the conduct of Operation Iraqi Freedom.[20]

Nonetheless, the F/A-18 has been the subject of much criticism throughout its career, and an in-depth investigation is made of the aircraft in appendix 6.

Another maritime element that went right was the Navy special warfare efforts. Like all of the SOF activities, the exact record of Navy SEAL operations in the south has not been disclosed, but they were tasked in part with preventing the Iraqis from flooding the Gulf with oil. They succeeded in a remarkable operation with few casualties,[21] as is detailed in appendix 8. Many attribute the striking improvement in U.S. SOF capabilities to the progress made since the Nunn-Cohen Amendment to the 1987 Department of Defense Authorization Act. Sponsored by then Senators Sam Nunn and William Cohen, the act established the U.S. Special Operations Command. Subsequently the services and the commanders in chief of the various theaters began to enlarge the responsibilities of special forces and provide them with additional resources.

Other operational areas that are conducted with great skill and little fanfare are those of electronic countermeasures and Psyops.

In concert with Lockheed Martin P-3Cs used for ISR, one of VAQ-136's Northrop Grumman EA-6B Prowlers took off from the USS *Kitty Hawk* and fired an AGM-88 HARM against a SAM site in a preplanned attack. With the site destroyed, two Boeing F/A-18s struck a target near the site. In addition to its suppression of enemy air-defense missions, the aging Prowler fleet replaced the USAF EF-111 and serves as the only joint-service stand-off radar jammer. Prowler availability often determines whether or not a strike mission takes place, including those by stealth aircraft. (Some attribute the loss of the F-117A Nighthawk in Bosnia in

1999 to inadequate stand-off radar jamming because sufficient EA-6Bs were not available.)

The Prowlers, flown by joint USAF and Navy crews, operate off all five of the carriers in the Persian Gulf and the Mediterranean, and some operate from land bases as well. The Prowlers often work in conjunction with HARM-equipped Lockheed Martin F-16CJs to kill enemy defenses.

Mass leaflet drops (more than 40 million leaflets) seemed to have good results in persuading Iraqi military leaders to lay down their arms without fighting. The leaflets, instructing the Iraqi military how to surrender and avoid combat, how to position their equipment, and what to do with their arms, also cautioned the Iraqis not to obey orders to use weapons of mass destruction. In addition to leaflets, EC-130E Commando Solo aircraft broadcast messages to the Iraqi community.

A special salute must be given to the work of the Royal Australian Air Force Boeing F/A-18A, which was done superbly and aroused the admiration of U.S. counterparts.

WHAT WENT WRONG AND WHY

Despite all the statements to the contrary, the V Corps and the MEF outran their supply lines, and this not only hampered their forward movement but also exposed them to the possibility of dangerous counterattacks.

This situation was denied at all levels and in a variety of ways. The common rebuttal was that "while an individual soldier at a particular point might not get all three MREs (Meals, Ready to Eat) in a day, there is no general shortage." One could not expect anything less, for it is inconceivable that the top leadership would lend aid and comfort to the enemy (and the press) by admitting that there was a supply problem.

Yet there are myriad stories of units pleading for more ammunition—always ammunition first—and for other supplies, and while the delay outside of Baghdad may have been "part of the plan," it is far more likely that it was a fact of life brought about by the speed of the advance, the adverse weather, and the lack of sufficient intratheater airlift and ground logistic support.

Ground logistic support is still confined to relatively obsolete methods, and in the general transformation of the Army and Marines, where speed is now beginning to be held as a key factor in victory, attention must be given to developing new vehicles for ground supply that can keep up with the demand of modern battle.

Airlift, just as with helicopters and tankers, is not a glamorous part of the service, and in budgetary considerations it is usually put on the back burner when evaluated against the needs for new fighters or bombers.

If the Boeing C-17 had been procured in greater numbers and if the logistics effort had been fine-tuned to make use of theater tactical airlift capability (C-130s), the shortfall in ammunition, food, water, and supplies could have been ameliorated and perhaps not occurred at all.

Like the AWACSs, the C-17 program was in trouble most of its life. In December 1979, a "C-X" Task Force was formed to create the specifications for an aircraft that could meet U.S. force projection requirements by operating routinely into small, austere airfields of the type previously restricted to the much smaller Lockheed C-130. The C-X was to meld the ability of the Lockheed C-5 with that of the C-130, so that outsize cargo (including main battle tanks) could be carried into the tactical environment.

After a long and bitter competition, McDonnell Douglas was announced as the winner in August 1981. This distressed Lockheed, which till that time had a virtual monopoly on Air Force dedicated cargo turboprop and jet aircraft with its C-130, C-141, and C-5A. Low-rate production of the C-17 Globemaster III was not approved until December 1988, and the Initial Operating Capability (IOC) was not reached until January 1995.

All during this period, the C-17 became the subject of bitter attacks by Les Aspin, the Wisconsin Congressman who was Chairman of the House Armed Services Committee. He was abetted in this by Senator Sam Nunn, whose constituency included the Lockheed plant in Marietta, Georgia.

When General Loh was Commander of Aeronautical Systems Command in 1989, the C-17 was in such hot water that the potential buy was cut down to only forty aircraft and was referred to as "that turkey." The program went on and was resuscitated by the efforts of Don Koslowski, of McDonnell Douglas, among others. Loh points out that every weapon system goes through a period where micromanagement by Congress overwhelms common business sense. He says that the trick is to get through this period with tenacity and a few strategically located supporters, and you eventually wind up with a first-rate weapon system that becomes "the darling of the force, like the C-17, F-16, and, I predict, the F/A-22."[22]

Former Chief of Staff Merrill A. McPeak concurs, saying that there is a systemic problem with all major programs: "You take it back to Congress every year and get it reauthorized and reappropriated, and they usually muck with it in such a way you are always sweeping up broken glass. This is the sense in which, for any sufficiently large program, you do not have one 30-year program, but 30 one-year programs."[23]

When President Clinton took office, Aspin became Secretary of Defense, and he instructed McPeak that he was to fire five people responsible for the C-17. One was a female member (who shall be nameless here) of the Air Force Acquisition Staff; three were general officers and one was a very senior civilian. McPeak found a way to retain the female member of the acquisition staff and very reluctantly informed the other four that he would appreciate their tendering their resignations. They did so graciously.

Following this, the C-17 program gathered steam and proceeded rather smoothly, despite the fact that the quantity to be procured was constantly reduced, which drove up unit cost. At present there are 180 planned for procurement (up from 134 in 2002) and 92 in the inventory. Many say that it would have been better if there were 360 projected and 180 in the inventory today and, if there had been, the supply problem in Iraq might never have materialized. Decisions to procure more aircraft must be made soon to avoid gaps in the production line, which would greatly increase the cost of follow-on aircraft.

Air Force Chief of Staff General John P. Jumper states unequivocally that the C-17 was a star performer in Operation Iraqi Freedom, noting that it is revolutionary in the way in which it can deliver mobility "wholesale and retail." In its wholesale mode, it can pick up material anywhere in the world and fly it to the appropriate staging areas; in its equally capable retail mode, it can take off from anywhere in the world and fly directly to a desert strip in the heart of the war zone. He notes that strategic and tactical airlift are losing their meaning, becoming blurred as the capability of one aircraft encompasses both.[24] (A similar process occurred with bombing, where it became impossible to determine precisely what was "tactical" and what was "strategic" in bombing missions.)

Yet there was in fact a shortage of intratheater transport (including helicopters) and a consequent shortage of materials delivered to the troops. This puts the onus of blame directly back on the commanders, from Franks down through the ranks, who permitted a situation to develop in which troops short on ammunition might have been badly shot up by an aggressive and capable enemy.

Fortunately, that blame evaporates if those commanders, because of their ISR assets and common operating picture, were so confident in their knowledge of the battlefield, their assessment of the enemy, and their access to supportive airpower that the risk was regarded as negligible.

And that was the case. It was far more important to keep the enemy off-balance, and reversing the usual role of land and air forces was one way of doing this. Under Franks' plan, the ground forces became bait, luring the Iraqi forces out of their entrenched hiding positions to move to the attack. When they did so, they became immediate targets and were destroyed.

Joint STARS had a big role in this effort, but General McPeak, former USAF Chief of Staff, points out a lesser known aspect of Joint STARS, the paralyzing effect it has on the enemy who sits in the foxhole or inside the concealed tank and thinks, *I can sit here and die slowly if they get to me, or I can move and die immediately.*

In the end it did not matter much, for sitting or moving, there was nothing the Iraqis could do to prevent Baghdad's gates from being slowly pried open.

6

Air and Ground Actions, Working Together

OPERATION IRAQI FREEDOM:
April 1, 2, 3, and 4

The 1st Marine Division made a series of widespread attacks in six different towns in Central Iraq, hunting down paramilitary forces. In battles at Ad Diwaniyah and Ash Shatra (which is just north of An Nasiriyah), the Marines were joined by about one hundred indigenous tribal personnel to capture many prisoners of war, destroy bunkers, and remove explosives from a bridge, all with no coalition casualties.[1]

The first Iraqi ballistic missile fired against coalition forces in Iraq was intercepted by a PATRIOT PAC-3 missile about 1:00 A.M. EST.

Joint warfare took place in a totally unprecedented way when Northrop Grumman F-14Ds and Boeing F/A-18s from Carrier Air Wing 8 in the Mediterranean Sea supported the operations of the U.S. Army's 173d Airborne Brigade in northern Iraq. More than fifty missions were flown against SAM sites, artillery positions, and barracks. The concept of flying such long-range carrier-based missions to support inland ground operations was unthinkable prior to the advent of sophisticated command and control systems coupled to PGMs and midair refueling.

The Navy lost an F-14B from the *Kitty Hawk's* VF-154 when an engine failure was compounded by a fuel management problem. The crew members ejected safely and were recovered by a combat search and rescue helicopter and airlifted back to the *Kitty Hawk* thirteen hours after the accident.[2]

Moving from one combat area to another is customary for Marines, and the 24th MEU moved from Operation Enduring Freedom in Afghanistan to Operation Iraqi Freedom with its usual speed and style. More than 2,300 Marines were involved, along with four different types of helicopter, the Bell AH-1 and UH-1, the Boeing Vertol CH-46, and the Sikor-sky CH-53.[3]

The V Corps undertook "limited objective attacks" near Al Hillah, Karbala, and As Samawah. The attacks intended to create vulnerabilities in the Republican Guard defenses and to isolate remaining pockets of resistance for destruction. The familiarity of the names of the cities and of the nature of the mission led many observers to speculate again as to why coalition forces were still delaying their advance and wonder if this signified some problem in logistics or flank defense. Peter Graff from Reuters quoted two retired four-star generals, Barry McCaffrey and Ronald Griffith, divisional commanders in the 1991 Gulf War and military television commentators in Gulf War II, as saying that two or three more armored divisions and more artillery were essential and that the initial planning had been wrong. This created much controversy among their contemporaries, many of whom deemed their remarks ill-advised.

Actually, the progress of the V Corps had opened the gates to Baghdad. Three Brigade Combat Teams of the 3rd Infantry Division had destroyed six T-72 tanks, thirteen APCs, and fifteen antiaircraft weapons. Like an agile heavyweight fighter, the V Corps slammed body punches against the enemy, sapping its strength. The 1st Brigade Combat Team seized bridges. The 101st Airborne (Air Assault) Division continued to isolate enemy forces at the city of An Najaf. Units from the 82nd Airborne Division smashed enemy paramilitary forces at As Samawah. V Corps artillery, working with Air Force CAS aircraft, destroyed sixty enemy vehicles. All of this effort, combined with the daily decimation of enemy troops by coalition aircraft, was setting Baghdad up for the knock-out blow.

The ratio of Iraqi civilian casualties to coalition casualties was raised by reporters at the CENTCOM briefing. By April 1, the coalition had suffered about 100 casualties, compared to an estimated 500 to 700 Iraqi casualties. National Public Radio asked if, as CENTCOM had said, allied troops were prepared to pay a heavy price to take Baghdad, did this mean that five times as many Iraqi casualties would occur as the "heavy" coalition casualties? The CENTCOM response was that all casualties were to be held to a minimum as a matter of policy.

April 2 was Day 14 of Operation Iraqi Freedom, and CENTCOM began its briefings with a series of images depicting how exact the targeting and execution of bombing attacks was on Saddam International Airport. In one instance twenty-six designated targets were shown, followed by a slide showing those twenty-six destroyed with the buildings adjacent to the targeted point left unharmed. The audience of reporters was monumentally unimpressed. Instead the line of questioning centered around the reports of the recovery of PFC Jessica Lynch and the meaning of the term *red line*, which General Brooks explained as being "a term that characterizes that there may be a trigger line where the regime deems sufficient threat to use weapons of mass destruction."

Several key points that Brooks presented were overlooked in the questioning. These include the vast scope of special operation forces operating in the western desert. The special operation forces identified targets in the Iraqi 15th Mechanized Division for coalition aircraft, which included B-52Hs of the 457th Air Expeditionary Group from Fairford, England, and U.S. Navy aircraft from the carriers *Harry S. Truman* and *Theodore Roosevelt*, both positioned in the southern Mediterranean.[4] The implications of this long-distance, joint service cooperation by aircraft of vastly different performance of the U.S. Air Force and U.S. Navy, in combination with U.S. Army troops on the ground, were tremendous and symbolized the success of the coalition forces in general.

Heavily supported by the F-16s of the Air National Guard's 120th Expeditionary Fighter Squadron, SOF forces had seized the Haditha Dam on March 31. If planned Iraqi demolitions had been carried out, the waters would have flooded Karbala and beyond. CAS enabled the special operation forces to hold their position against a wide variety of attacks.

Brooks also gave a brief description of land force operations that should have served as a clue to coming events. He noted that the Republican Guard Baghdad Division had been destroyed by the 1st MEF, which also seized a bridge over the Tigris River, and that 5th Corps had attacked and effectively decimated both the Medina and the Nebuchadnezzar divisions. Paramilitary troops firing from the Ali Mosque in An Najaf were spared return fire from coalition troops out of respect for the mosque, which is reputedly the burial place of Ali, Muhammad's son-in-law.

The advances noted by Brooks brought the coalition forces to within thirty miles of Baghdad at two points, one to the southeast and one to the southwest. The most important result of these advances was the movement of Republican Guard forces from the north to defend Baghdad after the Medina and Baghdad divisions had been reduced to a shambles. When the Republican Guard forces moved, they were immediately attacked.

The effect of the air attacks was telling upon the morale of the Iraqi officers and men. Many fled to their homes, took off their uniforms, and waited for the end. In an interview in the *Christian Science Monitor* on April 18, one of the shocked Iraqi warriors blamed Saddam Hussein and his two sons, Qusay and Uday, for their poor military decisions, saying, "Every plan of Saddam was a disaster." Iraqi Army Major Saleh Abdullah Mahdi Al Jaburi said that in the first week of April his 4,000-man unit lost 800 men to air attacks.[5]

Saddam's officers understood that the general strategy was to inflict enough casualties on American forces that the people of the United States would rebel against the war, but this proved impossible to accomplish. The Iraqis found themselves being killed at a distance, all the while unable to respond.

Allied forces continued to work with Kurdish fighters in the north, even though the regime continued to warn the Kurds of repercussions if they assisted the Americans. The power of the regime's threats was much more evident to the south, where Ba'ath Party officials retained influence over the Iraqi populace even after the territory they previously commanded had been captured.

The media raised questions about the use of cluster bombs by coalition forces. Concern was expressed about the possibility of Iraqi civilians, particularly children, being harmed by unexploded bomblets. Particular emphasis was focused on the bomblets being the same color as food packages. (This had been true early in the campaign in Afghanistan but was no longer the case.) Boeing B-52Hs dropped six sensor-fused CBU-105 WCMD cluster bombs on Iraqi armor, the first time these have been used in combat. The ROE prohibit their use in populated areas. The dual-mode CBU-105s have inertial guidance and are heat seekers with the capability to compensate for wind as they direct themselves to the targets. CENTCOM's response was to emphasize the careful process of target and weapon selection that underlies every sortie to assure that minimum collateral damage is inflicted.

Coalition air activity escalated to more than 1,900 sorties, of which 900 were strike sorties. Some 540 sorties were flown against Republican Guard targets, continuing the accelerating dissolution of those units.

Two aircraft losses were reported, with a Sikorsky UH-60 Black Hawk crashing in central Iraq and a Boeing F/A-18C fighter going down at about 3:45 AM EST.[6]

The general sense of the ubiquity, pervasiveness, and success of the special operation forces was emphasized on April 3, Day 15 of Operation Iraqi Freedom. The ability of special operation forces to provide laser guidance to "on-call" aircraft was remarkable, and impossible for the Iraqi regime to counter. The availability of Lockheed Martin AC-130 Spectre gunships added immensely to SOF firepower. The AC-130s have a long loiter time and can provide coverage of hundreds of square miles on a standard mission. Across hundreds of miles of desert, other special operation forces raided key regime locations, including the Tharthar Palace, a luxurious residence of Saddam Hussein, on Baghdad's outskirts.

Two significant preemptive events took place in early April. On April 1, the British troops captured five SSN-2 Styx maritime missiles near the

Ash Shuaybah airport. The swift Iraqi Navy Osa I/II patrol boats were capable of firing the twenty-five-mile-range missiles, but most of these had been destroyed. They nonetheless presented a significant threat to coalition vessels. Then on April 3, other British forces seized fifty-six surface-to-surface short-range missiles near Al-Zubair. These were perhaps the most obvious evidence of the efficiency of getting inside the enemies' decision loop, for the missiles were captured before they could be used, even though their setup and firing time was very short.

A PATRIOT missile shot down a Navy F/A-18, killing its pilot. The blue-on-blue shroud of fratricide continued to hang over PATRIOT performance.

On April 3, the fifteenth day of the campaign, the gloves came off and American forces reached the southern outskirts of Baghdad. It was an incredible performance for coalition forces, advancing 350 miles in fifteen days, overcoming Iraqi resistance and huge sandstorms with equal ease.

The secret was in the air, of course. Coalition air force aircraft had performed two key functions. The first was the suppression of enemy mobile forces and the destruction of massed troops to decimate Republican Guard units before they could enter combat. The second was providing cover to the flanks and rear so that coalition ground forces could advance knowing they would not be cut off or ambushed from behind or the side. About 1,900 sorties were flown on April 3, with 850 of these being strike sorties, all using PGMs. Where in 1991 only a small percentage of bombs dropped had been precision-guided, in 2003 the majority were PGMs.

The world was amazed on April 4, Day 16, when the 3rd Infantry Division launched an attack on Saddam International Airport, only twelve miles from Baghdad. Despite Iraqi disclaimers that the Americans were nowhere in the vicinity, a hot firefight raged for four hours, with coalition armor outfighting that of the Iraqis and coalition airpower proving decisive. Within twenty-four hours, troops of the 101st Airborne Division arrived at what had been renamed the Baghdad International Airport. Sporadic resistance continued for some time.

Seizing the airport had both psychological and military importance. Despite statements from "Baghdad Bob" (Iraqi Minister of Information Mohammed Saeed al-Sahaf) that "we butchered the force present at the airport. We have retaken the airport! There are no Americans there," it was evident to the people of Baghdad that the Americans were on their doorstep in force. In military terms, aircraft began landing on the airfield as soon as areas were cleared for them to do so, alleviating some of the continuing supply problems.

Marine Bell AH-1W Super Cobra attack helicopters had proved to be effective all during the war, but one accidentally crashed in Central Iraq, killing both crew members.[7]

The RAF Tornados prepared to drop 1,000-pound bombs filled with concrete rather than explosives against targets that were in high-density civilian areas or were parked near a religious or cultural site of importance. The bombs retained the precision guidance systems and were intended to destroy enemy armor by kinetic energy alone, without causing collateral damage.

THE VIEW FROM THE OTHER SIDE

The reports from Russian intelligence, as represented on a variety of Internet sources, stressed the continuing stout resistance of Iraqi forces and seemed to say that the coalition forces were essentially stalled along the front. Kurdish efforts in the north were downplayed and their motives impugned. It was estimated that the current activity at various points on the long battlefield would continue for another four or five days, to be followed by a longer pause for rest, repairs, and reinforcement.

The April 2 collection of reports revealed the continued ignorance of the intelligence gatherers as to the mode of coalition operations; the fact that towns and other centers of resistance were bypassed was interpreted as meaning the coalition did not have the capability to engage Iraqi forces in combat. Areas occupied by coalition forces were described as territory "captured" and still containing as many as 30,000 active Iraqi troops. In one of their imaginative quotes, Major General Buford Blount is said to have reported "fierce Iraqi resistance" and that the Republican Guard had repelled all attempts to break through their lines. A hopeful prediction, reminiscent of Spring 1945 communiqués from Berlin, concluded the day's reporting, saying that "military analysts believe that today and tomorrow will decide the outcome of the attack on Baghdad that began two weeks ago. If the coalition forces fail to break the Iraqi defenses, then by the weekend, the U.S. will be forced to curtail all attacks and resort to positional warfare while regrouping forces and integrating them with the fresh divisions arriving from the U.S. and Europe." Further, a tactical pause of seven to fourteen days was supposed to lead to a reevaluation of all coalition battle plans.

April 3 reports were less sanguine, as the reports confirmed a twenty-five-kilometer advance by the 3rd Infantry Division in the last twenty-four days. Iraqi command and control degeneration was admitted, as was the loss of many tanks and artillery pieces. Hopes were now pinned on the

90–100,000 regular troops and militia "fighting" behind coalition lines. On April 4, the Russian reports indicated that the capture of Saddam International Airport did not surprise the Iraqi command and suggested that another sandstorm would "leave the coalition without its major advantage—the aviation, without which the coalition will be left one-on-one with a numerically superior enemy."[8]

There was an almost poignant envy in the tone of the Russian information-gathering system; the speed and efficiency of the coalition forces seemed to daze them.

WHAT WENT RIGHT AND WHY

General Franks' plan continued to go well, although the questions raised from the start about the desirability of having more "boots on the ground" remained pertinent. The "flow" of troops was obviously adequate, thanks to the overwhelming effects of coalition airpower, but it was generally accepted that more troops would have been helpful to suppress the Iraqi paramilitary forces' attacks on supply lines and to begin the transition to maintaining order and stability within captured territory.

The fluidity and the integration of U.S. and coalition forces in what was increasingly described as "interactive" rather than "joint" operations caused some outside observers to discuss the desirability of a future single armed service to replace the five U.S. military services that operate today. In the past such a concept was based primarily on the economies of scale to be obtained in uniforms, equipment, training, facilities, and so on. It was pointed out that if the several services can work together so smoothly, would it not make sense for them to truly combine, so that future operations would be even more closely integrated.

The idea, while attractive on the surface, is deeply foolish and flawed, for it overlooks the many ways in which the individual services specialize in operations that are not necessarily joint in nature but are nonetheless essential.

The work of the U.S. Navy in Operation Iraqi Freedom vividly illustrates this point, and each of the other services—Air Force, Army, Marines, and Coast Guard—has a similar portfolio of specialized activities that only they could provide.

Vice Admiral Timothy J. Keating gave a general background of what he believed "went right" for the Navy and coalition forces, then detailed the reasons that events occurred as they did.[9] He also pointed out how specialized activities, unique to the U.S. Navy, Marines, and Coast Guard, were able to conduct vital operations that no other service could do.

The first of Vice Admiral Keating's observations was in concert with General Franks' desire to move swiftly and preserve Iraqi assets for the people. The two GOPLATS (gas and oil platforms) seized by Navy SEALs initiated the general process of containing oil fires by coalition Explosive Ordnance Disposal (EOD) teams. While other elements of the special forces (Delta Force, SEALs, Air Force Special Operations, special forces–capable Marines and Rangers) are familiar and exercise with water-based operations, none have the natural inclination and resources to exploit them as does the Navy.

This flexibility and capability was demonstrated again in the de-mining of the Khor Abd Allah (KAA) waterway and the Umm Qasr port. The de-mining action was necessary for both military and compassionate reasons.

Ironically, mining countermeasures had been caught in the general decline of military budgets, and the USS *Inchon*, the last remaining dedicated mine warfare and support ship, had been decommissioned in July 2002. As an interim measure, the USS *Kearsarge* took over as the mine warfare command ship.

Mine Countermeasures Squadron 3 served as the combined task group commander and initiated mine countermeasures only twelve hours after the war began. Helicopter Mine Countermeasures Squadron HM-14, flying specially equipped Sikorsky MH-53E Sea Dragons, flew sidescan sonar surveys of the KAA and also conducted magnetic and acoustic sweep operations. (HM-14 also has Sikorsky SH-60B/F Seahawks, H-3 Sea Kings, and Boeing CH-46D Sea Knights on its roster.) Surface mine countermeasures ships moved in even as Royal Navy ships conducted gunfire support for U.K. troops onshore.

Coalition resources were limited but capable. The U.S. Navy had four mine sweepers available (the USS *Ardent, Cardinal, Dextrous,* and *Raven*), while the Royal Navy provided six (HMS *Blyth, Bangor, Brocklesby, Grimsby, Ledbury,* and *Sandown*), along with the mother ship, the RFA *Sir Belvidere*.

These ten ships used information from the MH-53s surveys to look for mines and investigate each of the many contacts. Water conditions were poor and made investigation difficult for the divers when minelike objects were discerned. A great deal of time was saved when prompt action intercepted camouflaged Iraqi vessels and removed more than 100 mines they were about to deploy.[10]

The mining operation was distinguished by two elements that support Vice Admiral Keating's point that individual services develop unique talents and core competencies. One of these was the first operational use of unmanned underwater vehicles (UUVs). These were operated by the

Navy's Very Shallow Water (VSW) detachment, which was based on the USS *Gunston Hall* before having a shore headquarters in Umm Qasr. The VSW detachment consists of Navy SEALs, Marine Corps Force Reconnaissance divers, Explosive Ordnance Disposal (EOD) divers, and the fascinating (and to some controversial) marine mammals, as well as the UUVs.

The second innovation was the first operational use of these marine mammals, dolphins, in the Navy's Marine Mammals System (MMS). The Navy has more than twenty dolphins in its program at San Diego. Two Atlantic bottlenose dolphins, one named Makai, a thirty-three-year-old male, and Tacoma, a twenty-two-year-old male, were flown to Iraq.[11] Through careful teamwork and ingenuity, the mammals were airlifted to pools on the beach and then were dispatched to clear mines in shallow and silted waterways. The dolphins proved to be invaluable to the mine-clearance operation. The mammals were subsequently placed in plastic swimming pools installed aboard a Navy LSD (Landing Ship Dock).

The dolphins have been trained to use their "onboard" sonar to detect mines and then mark them with floats. They are also taught to avoid touching the mines, so that there is no significant risk to the animals doing the work. The biggest hazard to the dolphins in Operation Iraqi Freedom was from local dolphins, known to be territorial, who might have tried to drive Makai and Tacoma away.

The REMUS (Remote Environment Monitoring Unit S) is a lightweight, low-cost, autonomous underwater vehicle, originally designed by the Woods Hole Oceanographic Institution but now available commercially only through Hydroid, Incorporated, of East Falmouth, Massachusetts. These were used in mine-hunting operations where humans and marine mammals could not operate effectively, i.e., in strong currents and extremely low visibility. Navy experts estimated that the use of UUVs expedited the clearance of the waterways by almost a week.

The marine mammals program has a long history, and the U.S. Navy likes to make an analogy between the trusted relationship of dogs and their handlers in the military and between dolphins and their handlers. The same elements of care, trust, and love apply in each case. There are those who protest to placing dolphins in jeopardy in hunting mines, but the counterargument is that just as in the case with guard dogs, the dolphins are used to save human lives and to carry out an important mission.

A second argument follows in that the marine mammals in the Navy's program get the finest possible diets and veterinary care and in many respects have a longer and higher-quality life than do their non-HMOed counterparts in the oceans.

In the mine-clearing process, the dolphins and the UUVs saved time by discriminating between mines and ordinary debris such as tires and fifty-five-gallon drums that littered the seabed. This made the divers' work far easier. The combination of divers, marine mammals, and UUVs enabled mine clearing to go on under conditions of heavy silt, strong currents, and minimal visibility that would have precluded diver-only operations.

Vice Admiral Keating stressed the Navy's flexibility in several matters, including the quick reaction of EOD teams in Operation Dogwood, the search for and retrieval of the remains of Lieutenant Nathan "O. J." White, whose Hornet had been shot down by a PATRIOT missile during a night CAS mission near Karbala. A UUV was flown in to the site to map the wreckage area and identify dive spots. The pilot's remains were found and returned to the USS *Kitty Hawk* for a memorial service.

Keating also emphasized the element of speed and the broad base of firepower in the fleet, pointing out that some eight hundred Tomahawks had been fired from thirty-five coalition ships and that one-third of these had been launched from submarines. Keating had directed the operations of more than fifteen submarines in his AOR where, prior to Operation Iraqi Freedom, only six had been allocated. Of the fifteen, twelve were U.S., two were British, and one was Danish. The Danish sub did not fire Tomahawks but furnished information and warning for the others.

The U.S. Coast Guard also distinguished itself. The Coast Guard cutter *Boutwell* had set many records in the past, including the largest at-sea rescue ever when she recovered more than 500 people from a burning cruise ship in 1980. In 2002, *Boutwell* seized over $100 million in cocaine during drug interdiction operations. In Operation Iraqi Freedom, *Boutwell* identified and seized cargoes prohibited by U.N. sanctions and helped intercept Iraqi mine-laying vehicles.

Evenhanded in his praise, Vice Admiral Keating pointed out the flexibility and the effectiveness of the Boeing F/A-18 Hornets and Super Hornets, particularly the latter's refueling capability.

The U.S. Army had similar arguments as to why a single integrated service might not be the best solution, and most of these centered around the amazing speed and flexibility with which "heavy" units, i.e., those equipped with Abrams tanks, Bradley Fighting Vehicles, and Paladin self-propelled artillery, were able to scoot up the length of Iraq much like Jeb Stuart's cavalry scooted through Virginia during the Civil War.

The very concept of "transformation" threatens proponents of the Abrams and the Bradley, both of which have had vehement critics over the years. The most significant advance in Army artillery, the massive Crusader system, was canceled because of its projected $9 billion cost and its ninety-seven-ton weight. This led to a difficult relationship between Army Chief of Staff General Eric K. Shinseki and Secretary of Defense Donald Rumsfeld.

The Army has picked an Interim Armored Vehicle, the Stryker, to provide transportability, speed, and maneuverability required by transformation. Equipped with eight wheels instead of tracks, the Stryker is intended to fill the capabilities gap between the "legacy" (read: "old") Abrams and Bradley systems and future combat systems. Manufactured by the General Dynamics' Land Division, the Stryker carries a 105mm gun in some of its many versions. (The Stryker is already being compared disadvantageously to the tried-and-true M113s, which are said to be faster and more powerful than the Stryker by its critics.)

However, the ability of both the Abrams and the Bradley to advance so far into Iraq so swiftly and suffer so little damage almost certainly has given them a new lease on life. The 1st Brigade Combat Team of the 3rd Infantry Division entered Iraq on March 20 and pushed straight forward toward Baghdad, including an initial thirty-hour first-increment run.

The Abrams already had an impressive combat pedigree. Some eighteen hundred were deployed in the 1991 Gulf War, and only nine were destroyed, with no tank crew member killed in the process. In Operation Iraqi Freedom, about half that number of tanks were employed. The Iraqi and Arab media claimed seventy M1 and two British Challenger tanks destroyed, but a postbattle analysis indicates that seven Abrams were destroyed, one by friendly fire from a Marine AH-1W Hellfire missile and one by rolling off a bridge when the driver was apparently killed by rifle fire. The widespread availability of RPGs seemed to have the greatest effect. Most but not all observers believe that none of the very effective Russian AT-14 Kornet antitank guided missiles was encountered, even though it was reported that twelve launchers and 200 missiles had been delivered to Iraq by Syria. Up to five M2 and M3 Bradleys were also claimed, but no confirmation of these losses has been issued.

An official report from the Tank and Automotive Command (TACOM) stated that there were "no catastrophic losses due to Iraqi direct or indirect fire weapons" but that several tanks were destroyed due to secondary effects attributed to Iraqi weapon systems. Most M1A1 losses were due to mechanical breakdown, with the vehicles subsequently being vandalized by Iraqis or stripped for parts by U.S. forces. At least one M1A1 was lost to friendly fire from a Bradley Fighting Vehicle. Another was deliberately destroyed after it was immobilized in Baghdad by an engine fire.[12]

The Abrams was so effective that in many instances, Iraqi troops abandoned their armored vehicles when the M1A1 arrived. It was very capable at a distance, in one instance destroying an enemy vehicle more than 4,100 meters away.

The swift, effective performance and relatively low losses place both the Abrams and the Bradley in a new light. The intensity of RPG fire was so great that it was widely speculated that the lighter, less heavily armored Stryker would have had far more losses. Advocates countered that the speed of the Stryker would have prevented this, but the general sense is that the survivability of both the Abrams and the Bradley is an endorsement of previous Army planning.

Official Army sources stated that twenty-three Bradley and Abrams vehicles had been damaged, but unofficial reports place the numbers much higher. According to retired Colonel David Hackworth, three Abrams were destroyed and twelve damaged beyond economical repair. He also stated that sixteen Bradleys had been destroyed and thirty-five more seriously damaged.[13] Hackworth also believes that three of the losses were from the Kornet guided missile. There is already talk of introducing improved anti-RPG armor to the sides of the Abrams to give it further safety, but concerns about weight may hinder this.

WHAT WENT WRONG AND WHY

As the coalition forces became more experienced in their successful tactics, the Iraqi forces were less and less able to fight on anything approaching an equal basis. The result was that fewer and fewer things seemed to go wrong for the coalition.

Nonetheless, the early arguments about the total number of troops being committed seemed to gain weight in spite of the accelerating successes of the coalition forces. The sentiment was echoed in the foreign press and in comments made by pro-Iraqi observers. Yet in the United States the criticism of Secretary Rumsfeld for deploying too few troops became muted in the face of the undeniable progress of V Corps.

Rumsfeld's reputation was very much on the line, for if General Franks' forces had suffered a reversal and been forced to either dig in or retreat, there is no question where the finger of blame would have pointed. As the situation developed, it appeared that Rumsfeld's initial judgment was sound—but only for the active combat stage of the campaign. Every day that passed, with its increase in prisoners of war, conquered territory to supervise, Iraqi civilians to care for, and guerrilla-style attacks and terrorism made it evident that Rumsfeld had indeed been wrong. The crisis would not be ended even "after" the military battles were won.

The coalition forces were then tasked to administer a gigantic state that had known only a dictatorship, where there was little commercial initiative except in the retail markets, and where the government had previously handled all the ordinary problems of city life—power, water, food supplies—inefficiently but with an iron hand. There was a tendency upon the part of an average Iraqi civilian to expect miracles from the coalition occupation troops and to object strongly and sometimes violently when those miracles were not immediately forthcoming.

Precision-Guided Munitions (PGMs)

The widespread use of PGMs was one of the fundamental differences between the 1991 and 2003 Gulf Wars, and the different types of PGM yielded some surprising results.

By design, specification, and testing, LGBs were supposed to be the most accurate type of PGM. The bombs are usually standard general purpose (GP) bombs that become LGBs by the addition of a guidance kit. Included in the kit are a computer-control group (CCG), guidance canards (small control surfaces) placed on the front of the warhead to steer the bomb, and a wing assembly attached to the aft end of the bomb to turn it into a glider of sorts. Unlike missiles, the bombs are free-fall devices and are not connected electronically to the aircraft. Each bomb has an internal semiactive guidance system that detects reflected laser energy and guides the weapon to a target that is illuminated by an external laser source. The illumination can be provided by another aircraft, by a UAV, by the drop aircraft itself, or by a ground source.[14]

The delivery aircraft drops the LGB, which acquires the laser-designated target, and onboard guidance provides commands to the control surface to "fly the bomb" directly into the target.

LGBs vary in size from 500 to 5,000 pounds. Some, such as the GBU-28, are designed to "bust bunkers," i.e., drill their way through reinforced concrete structures and then explode.

Other PGMs use the GPS. A GPS receiver takes information from four satellites (of the twenty-four-satellite constellation) and uses it to calculate its position—longitude, latitude, and altitude—on Earth. There are also a variety of GPS-guided bombs, ranging from the MOAB, which stands officially for Massive Ordnance Air Blast and unofficially for "Mother Of All Bombs," down to much smaller weapons. The 21,000-pound thermobaric MOAB was not used in Operation Iraqi Freedom. The GPS weapon of choice was the JDAM, which was dropped from a wide variety of platforms. It has an inertial guidance system, into which information is inserted from the aircraft, and a GPS system for increased accuracy.

On balance, the LGB should be more accurate than the GPS-type bomb, but this was not always the experience in Operation Iraqi Freedom (or, for that matter, during Operation Enduring Freedom in Afghanistan). This was for a variety of reasons, some technical, some operator-induced.

There were a disturbing number of LGB duds and misses. The LGBs did not work as well under actual operating conditions as in testing. Some misses were attributed to weapons being released at low grazing angles and extended ranges from intended targets. In addition, pilots were accustomed to ignoring the wind during LGB drops. It became evident that winds do affect LGB accuracy at long ranges.

Analysis of the bombing reveals that while it may be economical, simply strapping kits on existing bombs in the inventory may not be the best way to conduct operations. Research and development is already under way to develop smaller bombs that are designed from the start to be precision-guided and which would have better flight characteristics. The Boeing Company is developing the so-called Small Diameter Bomb (SDB), which will allow aircraft to carry more munitions to more targets and strike them more accurately with less collateral damage.

The increased number of bombs compounds the difficulty of an enemy confronting American power. If some rogue nation were to create a crisis that required a military solution, ten B-2s could arrive unannounced, carrying eighty SDBs each, and with the expected excellent C⁴ISR effectively snuff the military capability of the enemy with 800 lethal strikes in a matter of minutes.

Thus has the RMA created the basis for the RDA. It may be that one further example, beyond Iraq, will be necessary to make sure that these two important revolutions are perceived properly by all our potential enemies.

This point is driven home by the example of the April 7 B-1B raid in the following chapter.

7

A Thunder Run into Baghdad

April 5, 6, 7, and 8

In an armored thrust far more dramatic than even Rommel's June 1940 drive to the sea in France, the 3rd Infantry Division sent 26 M1A1 Abrams tanks and ten Bradley Fighting Vehicles on a twenty-five-mile run through the streets of south and central Baghdad, stunning not only the Iraqis but the world. Early reports indicated that the aptly named "Thunder Run" killed two to three thousand Iraqis who had attempted to interfere with the raid. Never did the morale, information, and propaganda value of embedded reporters prove to be of greater value than in this almost arrogant plunge into the heart of the regime.

The armored spearhead, which paraded within two miles of Saddam's famous bunker and onto his favorite military parade ground, burst the bubble of media and public discontent over the "slow progress" of the war, demonstrating that under the umbrella of absolute air dominance, coalition forces could move when and where they wished to move, even in the heart of Saddam's citadel, Baghdad.

In the previous days, fighting sandstorms and units of the Republican Guard, Marines to the east and Army units to the west had punched to the edge of the ancient city. The V Corps controlled the corridor from Karbala to Baghdad, while the 1st MEF controlled the corridor from Salman Pak to Baghdad. In the process, both forces accepted the nibbling attacks of Iraqi paramilitary forces on their flanks. Saddam's Fedayeen militiamen's attacks were not without effect; the advance would have gone more swiftly and with greater confidence if there had not been one. But the actual difference in results was negligible: despite the attacks and the overblown concerns about them, the coalition forces had used speed to brush by defenses that certainly would have caused greater casualties (on both sides) *if* the coalition had fought as Saddam had wished them to fight.

The coalition advance was not unlike the United States' island-hopping strategy during World War II, when thousands of Japanese soldiers were bypassed on Pacific "fortresses," unable to leave or be supplied and no longer a threat. (The Japanese were marooned by water, the Iraqis by the threat of airpower pounding any movement.) Instead of slugging it out, the coalition relied on its airpower to provide CAS, on a rapid-reacton basis. Ground and airborne forward air controllers (FACs) in a wide variety of aircraft, including A-10s, F-15Es, F-16s, F-14Bs, and F/A-18s, provided round-the-clock cover in and over Baghdad, all armed with the silver bullets of PGMs.[1]

The Iraqi paramilitary forces had one great advantage, the profligate way in which ammunition, guns, and other equipment had been spread around Iraq, stored in hospitals, schools, churches, and elsewhere, and all easily accessed. Any paramilitary force of any size could find all the light weapons, RPGs, and ammunition it required in almost any neighborhood.

Even as the sudden spate of good news reduced their numbers, the die-hard media prophets of doom cited the Fedayeen attacks as precursors of a bitter, Stalingrad-like battle in Baghdad itself, where the morale of the Republican Guard was supposed to be lifted by the efforts of the paramilitary, which were often feeble and cowardly, such as the militiaman who snapped off a few shots at American troops, then jumped into a civilian car laden with women and children to be driven away.

There were some technological antidotes to the Fedayeen activities. When a captured Iraqi mentioned that a gathering of Iraqi forces was expected at the racetrack at Ad Diwaniyah, an Army Hunter drone was sent to verify the information. Not long after, both Army artillery and USAF A-10s were firing on the 500 Iraqi fighters gathered there.[2]

While the storm gathered around Baghdad, northern Iraq was effectively monitored and controlled by a relatively small number of special forces, who were focused primarily on denying the Iraqis any movement of ballistic missiles, and the 173rd Airborne Brigade. To this point in the war, the Iraqi missiles were the equivalent of a "fleet-in-being" tying down more forces than their destructive potential warranted because their political potential was so great. John Chalmers of Reuters asked if reports were true that the special operation forces had destroyed both an oil pipeline and a rail line between Iraq and Syria. General Brooks, the briefing officer, declined to comment specifically but emphasized the desire to preserve the oil infrastructure of Iraq.

Special forces also denied free movement of Iraqi forces along the road systems, using their own weaponry where required but calling on airpower to destroy enemy armor if necessary.

Officers conducting the CENTCOM briefing continued to be pressed on noncombat issues, the most volatile of which were the unaccounted-for explosions inside Baghdad that had caused civilian casualties. The sources of the explosions had not yet been found, with CENTCOM leaning to the explanation that they were caused by Iraqi SAMs falling back to earth and blowing up. Attention was directed to a variety of stories of suicide bombers. A report that received great attention was of an air attack on a convoy of Russian diplomats leaving Baghdad by road to the north.

On Day 18, April 6, it was reported that British forces had found the remains of Ali Hasan al-Majid, known familiarly as "Chemical Ali," the architect of the genocidal "Anfal" campaign against the Kurds in 1988. Postwar reports indicated that Hasan might in fact still be alive.

Fratricide reared its ugly head again at Kalak, in northern Iraq, when aircraft, reportedly USAF F-15Es, attacked a convoy of Kurdish fighters and U.S. special forces personnel. Eighteen Kurds were killed and forty-four were wounded; there were no U.S. casualties. The strike was supposedly made in response to a request by special forces to attack a tank that loomed ahead of the coalition column.

U.S. and British Psyops continued at its intense pace, with more than 40 million leaflets delivered and with continued radio and television broadcasting of the coalition message. This was often described as an attempt to win the hearts and minds of the Iraqi people but was in many ways dedicated more to deterring lower-level Iraqi leaders from implementing orders to use weapons of mass destruction. A supplement to Psyops was the accelerating attempts to restore water and power. General Brooks took it as a good sign of progress on the water front that in some areas the Iraqis were washing their cars.

Elements of the 82nd Airborne Division pulled out all the stops in an attack on Fedayeen positions in Karbala, using AH-64 Apaches along with A-10s, F-16s, and F/A-18s to hammer the Hammurabi Armored Division. The Apaches also gave the coordinates for a strike by the U.S. Army's Tactical Missile System.[3]

April 7, Day 19, saw the incredible potential displayed in an attack in which C⁴SIR, PGMs, highly trained and confident airmen, and the B-1B bomber combined to attempt to decapitate the regime. Reliable reports indicated that Saddam Hussein and his two sons were going to attend a meeting in a restaurant in the al Mansur section of western Baghdad. Four

2,000-pound JDAMs were dropped, and a sixty-foot crater replaced the target. The success of the effort is still unknown at this writing, but it was a first-class demonstration of the flexibility and power of modern warfare.

An F-15E of the 333rd Fighter Squadron crashed, possibly due to the ingestion of a MANPAD missile. Major William R. Watkins and Captain Eric B. Das were killed.

Analysis of the previous days' shocking armored foray into Baghdad indicated that a similar force could now go into the city and hold any desired terrain. More than 100 armored vehicles of the 3rd Infantry Division's 2nd Brigade Combat Team secured the Republican Palace, which was the official seat of government for Saddam.[4] One side effect was that newly liberated Iraqi citizens seem to wish to avenge themselves on Saddam's regime by looting government buildings of virtually any commodity, including many that were previously nailed down.

Iraqi casualties were high, with an estimated 600 killed and seventy armed (not armored) vehicles destroyed. The small but heavily armed trucks, nicknamed "technicals" by the coalition, were driven into an unequal contest against Abrams and Bradleys and were destroyed before their guns could have any effect. It was obvious that the Iraqi troops employing the unarmored vehicles had been grossly misinformed about their chances for survival in such an encounter.

The Marines continued their advance in the ancient Babylonian Diyala River Valley, crossing the Diyala River and taking the al-Rashid airport in southeast Baghdad after destroying a concentrated force of Iraqi tanks, armored vehicles, technicals, and artillery.

In Basra, the U.K. forces concluded their efforts to wipe out remaining pockets of Ba'ath Party officials and regime forces. The immediate effect was to unleash a collective sigh of relief from the Iraqi people in Basra, who had been kept under the regime's thumb until the moment of the British victory. Later the sighs would be replaced by complaints about the speed and scope of relief efforts.

Objections were raised by reporters at CENTCOM to a series of coalition actions that included aircraft attacks on the Al-Jazeera offices, where one person died, the Abu Dhabi television office, and the Palestine Hotel, where most of the reporters were staying. The Palestine Hotel was struck by cannon fire from a tank, killing two journalists and wounding several others. General Brooks' response was that all such incidents were regrettable, but that combat operations were under way and that the objective of removing the regime had priority. He further stated that when Americans were fired upon, they would return fire.

THE VIEW FROM THE OTHER SIDE

The initial Russian analysis of the presence of coalition forces so close to Baghdad was that they were going to halt their offensive and conduct siege warfare. The "extraordinary dispersion" of coalition forces was assessed as an advantage for the coming Iraqi counterattacks. The Internet assessment also charged the Americans with rape and looting.

However it was noted on April 6 that a "quickly changing" situation was developing as coalition forces advanced on Baghdad. Saddam International Airport was under severe attack, and the American forces were barely holding on. Lieutenant General T. Michael Moseley's comments on the effect coalition airpower had on Iraqi forces were dismissed as being "probably connected with severe pressure put on the American military command by American financial groups that desperately needed good news from the U.S.–Iraqi front by the end of the financial week."[5]

The now-famous "Thunder Run" was given a masterful spin, being portrayed as a desperate attempt by coalition forces to capture top officials of Saddam Hussein's regime. The attempt, according to the Russian viewpoint, ended in the ejection of coalition forces from the city. IRAQWAR.RU quoted General Franks as saying the results of the attack were "paltry" and the casualties "unacceptable."

The following day, however, the Internet quotes were far more subdued, admitting that U.S. units were in place in Baghdad and that Iraqi opposition was confined to that of autonomous groups, with no apparent organized central control. The IRAQWAR.RU analytical center suspended efforts to comment on the war after April 8.[6]

WHAT WENT RIGHT AND WHY

The first and most obvious answer as to what went right was the success of General Franks' plan to use swift ground forces in conjunction with air supremacy and information dominance to completely out-think and out-fight the Iraqi military. Speed had almost replaced firepower as the *sine qua non* of a mechanized infantry division for the long move north to Baghdad, but once the heavily armed and armored Abrams and Bradleys were in the city the awesome firepower of both dominated the battleground. None of the senior U.S. leaders would accept that a gamble had been made in spreading the numerically few forces to Baghdad so swiftly. The official view was that the risks were more than acceptable because of the unparalleled information and aerospace dominance, a view confirmed by the April 7 attack by a Boeing B-1B on Saddam Hussein. The execution of the attack spoke volumes for the successful way in which the war was being run.

There is probably no weapon system in the world that had a more prolonged conception or attenuated gestation, nor after finally coming into existence as a production aircraft suffered more sustained criticism (much of it from within the U.S. Air Force itself) over the years, than the Boeing (formerly Rockwell) B-1B.*

The first studies for the aircraft began in the early 1960s. The new bomber was intended to replace what was then regarded as an aging B-52, and the studies engendered a number of projects with great acronyms, including *SLAB* (Subsonic Low Altitude Bomber), *ERSA* (Extended Range Strike Aircraft), *AMPSS* (Advanced Manned Precision Strike System), and *AMSA* (Advanced Manned Strategic Aircraft).

It was not until November 1969 that a formal RFP (Request for Proposal) was issued to contractors and Boeing, Convair (later General Dynamics), and Rockwell International (formerly North American) responded.

Rockwell won the competition for the B-1 bomber, which first flew on December 23, 1974. Four prototypes of the supersonic low-level swing-wing bomber were built and speeds of Mach 2 were reached. Production contracts for a limited number of aircraft were placed, but President Jimmy Carter elected to cancel the program on June 30, 1977, on the basis that its role could be accomplished by ALCMs but also with the secret knowledge that stealth aircraft were on the horizon.

President Ronald Reagan, for a variety of political and military reasons, reinstated the program with an order for 100 B-1Bs, a modified version with less supersonic capability. The first flight of the B-1B took place on October 18, 1984, and the production aircraft were rapidly delivered.[7]

The B-1B has a top speed of Mach 1.2, a maximum operating weight of 477,000 pounds, and an intercontinental range. Although initially planned as a nuclear strike bomber, it now functions as a precision strike system and routinely carried twenty-four JDAM bombs in Iraq. It became the "JDAM truck," but it also had a very accurate bomb/nav system for dropping "dumb" bombs.

The career of the B-1B was dogged by accidents and by a consistent failure of the defensive electronic suite to perform as specified. Yet it came into its own over Afghanistan and especially in Operation Iraqi Free-

---

* The author confesses to a bias for the aircraft, having received two demonstration flights in the airplane that (1) convinced me of its capability and (2) proved to me that the incredible skills of its professional crew members compensated for many of the deficiencies in its defensive electronic suite.

dom, where fewer than a dozen B-1Bs delivered half the total weight of bombs dropped during the Iraqi campaign. In the process, they came to be viewed in a new light by some, as the backbone of the U.S. bomber force. In 2001, Secretary Donald Rumsfeld ordered the U.S. Air Force to retire some thirty-three B-1Bs, in order to provide funds to upgrade the remaining aircraft in the fleet. Now this order may be rescinded and new upgrades approved, as the B-1B has moved from being a back-bench player to first string. One of the factors in this change in attitude was the sensational attack of April 7, 2003.

Only eleven B-1Bs (officially named the Lancer but inevitably called the Bone by its crew) were deployed to take part in Operation Iraqi Freedom, but they did a disproportionate share of the bomb dropping. In the course of the campaign, they flew 432 sorties and dropped 2,250 tons of bombs, almost all precision-guided.

Each "Bone" has a name bestowed upon it by its crew, and *Seek and Destroy*, part of the 405th AEW, was engaged in in-flight refueling when it was notified of an emerging target by an E-3 AWACS aircraft. The B-1B and its crew of four are part of the 34th Bomb Squadron, 28th Bomb Wing, from Ellsworth Air Force Base, South Dakota. The wing is commanded by Colonel James Kowalski, who was serving in Operation Iraqi Freedom as Commander of the 405th AEW.

The AWACS action was based on orders from the U.S. CAOC at Prince Sultan Air Base, and these in turn were received from CENTCOM, where thirty-three minutes before a tip on Saddam's presence at the restaurant had been carefully vetted with all sources of ISR and deemed credible. Although this has not been officially confirmed, the tip probably came from special forces personnel on the ground in Baghdad.

Told that "this is a big one" by an AWACS controller, the four-man B-1B crew began the highly coordinated tasks required of each crew member— Aircraft Commander Chris Wachter; pilot Captain Sloan Hollis; Lieutenant Colonel Fred Swan, Weapon Systems Officer (Offensive); and Lieutenant Joe Runci, Weapon Systems Operator (Defensive). Each man knew that they had twelve minutes to complete all of their tasks and drop the four bombs they were directed to use.

Among their tasks was locating the exact target (the al-Saa restaurant), probing enemy air defenses, confirming all decisions with the AWACS controllers, arming and setting the fuse on the specified weapons (two were to be instant; two were to be delayed JDAMs), and, finally, placing the exact coordinates of the target in the bombs' guidance mechanisms. (While still in the bomb bay, the JDAM receives constant updating from the aircraft's avionic system. Once released, the inertial guidance system takes over and, with periodic GPS updates, guides the bomb to its target.)

In the air, the B-1B was backed up by the AWACS and by Lockheed Martin F-16CJs, which would have been used to suppress any enemy missile sites that were detected. There was also a Northrop Grumman EA-6B Prowler, which does double duty for the Air Force and the Navy in electronic countermeasures.

The B-1Bs fly with images of virtually the whole of Iraq captured electronically, so the coordinates were compared with the map and the high-definition images to make sure that they were correct. The coordinates themselves were received over the radio and written down, then transmitted back to an AWACS controller for verification. They were then entered into the weapon system and rechecked to be sure they corresponded exactly to those received. The crew was given two targets, with specific coordinates for each one—technically there were two DMPIs, two desired mean points of impact. The distance between the two DMPIs has been estimated as between 50 and 100 yards.

The stakes were high, but so was the risk of collateral damage, and precision was the byword. In the twelve minutes after their receipt, all of the bomb-run checklist items were completed, and then the first two GBU-31 Version 3 hard target penetrator JDAMs were released by the automatic mode of the bombing system. The aircraft was flying close to 30,000 feet (an altitude made possible by the previous suppression of SAMs) and at about five hundred knots at the time of release.

These 2,000-pound bombs were the standard BLU-109 penetrator equipped with the JDAM kit. They were intended to blast through the restaurant and reach the bunkers beneath where the meeting was to take place. Three seconds later, two of the standard GBU-31 Version 1 JDAMs were released. Because of the difference in their case design, the standard JDAMs have more explosive power than the penetrators. All four bombs followed direct paths to the targets, destroying them.

Unofficial reports indicate that more than a dozen bodies were removed from the wreckage by Iraqi personnel. At this writing, the debris is being carefully analyzed to determine if Saddam Hussein was killed in the attack.

Whether or not Hussein was killed, the almost unbelievably good (by any previous standard) forty-five minutes required for the "kill chain" to be exercised is still considered much too long by USAF leaders, who want to reduce the time so that in the future emerging targets will be attacked in one minute or less. (The Chief of Staff, General Jumper, stressing the need for compatible data links, says that there is still too much "fat finger and conversation time," "fat finger" referring to manually typing in information.)

The B-1B dropped the bombs on the al-Saa restaurant, then went on to hit seventeen other targets in two target groups, separated by about two hundred miles. The first group received nine bombs and the second eight. The other targets included an airfield, a SAM site, fielded forces, and artillery.

Individual crew members were asked how they felt about the mission. The Weapon System Officer responsible for the bombing, Colonel Crawford, said that there was no time for much personal reflection and that the crew reverted to training. Crawford has flown for twenty years and spent the last fifteen in the B-1, which he regards as a great system that "works as advertised."

All of the crew members praised the lethality and survivability of the airplane and went on to stress that "any crew in the B-1 force could have done this mission, because we've been trained to it over the last few years." They also made a point of praising the maintenance personnel and the munitions people who make up the weapons back at the base.

In both Operation Enduring Freedom (Afghanistan) and Operation Iraqi Freedom, the B-1Bs have maintaining about 90 percent mission-capable (i.e., available to perform the assigned role), rates, a fact credited to the high morale and hard work of the maintenance crews who often had to cannibalize parts between aircraft. In Enduring Freedom, the B-1B became a star, dropping some 40 percent of the total bomb tonnage while flying only 5 percent of the missions.

Perhaps more remarkable even than the accuracy and the number of weapons dropped was the emergence of the B-1Bs MTI radar as first-rate equipment. In General Jumper's words, "The B-1B has remarkable MTI radar capability: once up out of weeds and flying at a decent altitude, the MTI radar proved to be extremely able, and its signal was integrated with the Joint STARS signal during sand storms."[8]

The B-1B maintained its high mission-ready numbers during Operation Iraqi Freedom, and this was the more remarkable because at least one of the "Bones" was over Iraq twenty-four hours a day, seven days a week. Normally, one is over the target, one departing en route home, and one en route to the target. If required, all three could attack at a given time, making seventy-two JDAMs available on a moment's notice. On a typical mission, the B-1B may put three weapons on a target, to ensure a kill.

The work is tiring; the crews fly every third day, on sorties that range from nine to almost sixteen hours. Sleep is at a premium, but once a mission starts, the adrenaline is pumping, for even though Iraqi air defenses were erratic, there was still danger from the multiple SAM launches.

The crews and their leaders are conscious of the importance of accurate targeting and the precise delivery of weapons, both in the effect they have on enemy capabilities and in the difference that precision bombing makes in avoiding civilian casualties. During World War II, the combined bombing campaigns of all the combatant nations killed more than 1 million civilians, sometimes as many as 70,000 in a single raid. After seventy-eight days of NATO bombing in Serbia in 1999, there were about 500 civilians killed, while an estimated 800 died in Afghanistan, a number that Major General David Deptula, Director of Plans and Programs at Air Combat Command Headquarters at Langley Air Force Base, Virginia, questions. Deptula believes that the figure is high and bases his estimate on his service as Director of the Air Operations Center during the first three months of Operation Enduring Freedom.[9]

His skepticism is based on the care with which attacks are planned to avoid collateral damage. Target folders and databases are created for targets all over the world, often many years in advance. A new software tool, the Fast Assessment Strike Tool–Collateral Damage (FAST–CD) examines the target, its surrounding terrain, the direction and angle of attack, and the characteristics of the munitions proposed for the strike.

Each weapon creates a damage pattern; that of the Hellfire missile, with its 40-pound warhead would be small; the damage from a 2,000-pound bomb could carry out to more than 600 feet from the point of impact.

The FAST–CD program then generates a "probable damage field" (described as something that looks like insects hitting a car windshield at high speed) for the attack.

If it looks like collateral damage will result, the analysts using FAST–CD recommend against hitting the target or else provide suggestions for alternate routes, times, points of impact, weapons, or fusing that will result in less (and, if possible, no,) collateral damage.[10]

As a result of the Bones' sterling performance, a number of upgrades may be forthcoming in the future budgets. The most important would be a fully automated data link, so that targeting data could be placed directly in the weapons, bypassing the crew interface and cutting minutes off the "kill-chain" time. The existing ground surveillance radar could be upgraded to pick out targets as small as one foot in diameter. The effective ALE-55 fiber-optic towed decoy could be incorporated. A Litening II pod could be added, even though the B-1B is very susceptible to the drag induced by external stores and even though the installation would require an exception to START I treaty provisions. A new electronic countermeasures suite, possibly similar to that used in the F/A-18E/F, might be added. And, as with all the bombers, modifications to permit carriage of the new SDBs would enhance its versatility.

It thus evolves that a major part of what went right with Operation

Iraqi Freedom resides in a weapon system that has borne the brunt of criticism for many years but has always been, in fact, a powerful and effective aircraft.

WHAT ELSE WENT RIGHT?

The Joint Forces CAOC in Prince Sultan and the similar arrangements at the $40 million Operations Center at the Al-Udeid Air Base near Doha, Qatar, worked remarkably well. They were efficiently laid out and well integrated, but for the future General Jumper sees that sensor data from many different platforms will be collated, overlaid, and furnished in a single comprehensive digital picture where every threat is clearly visible.

The success of the CAOC was no accident. The facilities had received some barbed comments about excessive cost and their lavish technologies, but they worked like a charm. For the first time in the history of warfare, the combatants of all services shared the same picture, the common operating picture, of what was happening, and this led to a transformation of the concept of "jointness" among services transcending into what really became interactive operations, a goal so remote that although it was talked about, it was never really considered achievable before.

In previous wars, the AOC did not always get the very best officers, and for a good reason. There was a natural tendency for the very best officers to be given the command of combat units. Both General Ryan and General Jumper wanted to be sure that in the event of a war in Iraq, the CAOC in Prince Sultan would have the very best people on hand to interpret events and transmit their conclusions about them. Both men insisted that the CAOC be treated as a weapon system, one with a lethal capability. (The CAOC's weapon system designation is AN-USQ-163 "Falconer.")

To this end they preselected the general officers and the colonels who would be assigned (sometimes against their real wishes, for many would have preferred to lead a combat unit) to the CAOC. Their selections went so far as to consider the personalities of each of those selected and make sure that compatible people were assigned to work together.[11] The AOC concept is so important that schools have been established to train specialists to run the standardized facilities.

General Moseley found it necessary to develop two equal staffs. One, the "C' staff, handled functions for the coalition or combined forces and included officers from all the services and countries involved in the operation, including the U.S. Army, Navy, Marines, Royal Air Force, and

Royal Australian Air Force. The other, designated "AFFOR" (Air Force Forces), was dedicated to supporting the Air Force in the region. He also built up the alternate CAOC at Al-Udeid, which ultimately became the prime CAOC for the theater. The CAOC at Al-Udeid received the most modern equipment and can operate with fewer personnel than the one at Prince Sultan, which over time was emptied of equipment.

Just as the Navy was able to increase its power and mobility despite a drastic reduction in the number of ships it possessed, so did the Air Force accommodate reality by creating the hotly disputed AEF concept. The AEF jettisoned years of standard operating procedures. Air Force Chief of Staff General Mike Ryan was the original father of the AEF idea, but it has been continually refined by the current Chief, General Jumper. It has become the Air Force's standard method of "presenting Air Force forces" and conducting deployed operations.

The purpose of the reorganization was to create an organizational structure and rotational deployment schedule to allow the U.S. Air Force to meet worldwide demands without placing undue stress upon its people and equipment.

Ten AEFs of about 175 aircraft and 20,000 people were established. Each one is composed of fighter aircraft along with all the associated support aircraft and units needed to enable it to project power in the field. The mix of aircraft can vary and be tailored for the prospective mission, but the fighting force was to be capable of deployment to anywhere in the world in forty-eight hours. The AEFs rotate on a fifteen-month training and deployment cycle, and most personnel deploy for ninety-day increments in the cycle.

Besides their economic use of assets, the AEFs were needed to bring some predictability into the lives of Air Force personnel, who were caught up in a 300 to 400 percent increase in temporary overseas duty assignments at a time when the overall force was cut. One result was a large increase in the number of people deciding to leave the service because it was too disruptive to family life. The AEF was intended to have predictable schedules of overseas deployments that would be followed rigorously, enabling personnel to deploy for ninety days at a time and know when they would be at home and when they would be away.

Operation Iraqi Freedom required the deployment of the resources from eight of the AEFs to field four AEFs of force structure in the field for the war, where the system worked beautifully in terms of striking power. The concept of rotation was temporarily given up, however, to meet the demands of Operation Iraqi Freedom, and this was accepted by the personnel. Steps are already being taken to reinstate the normal rotation process with the establishment of two transitional AEFs (Blue and

Silver) to put the deployment schedule back on track by March 2004. Personnel in those AEFs, 1, 2, 9, and 10, who were identified to support Operation Iraqi Freedom but did not deploy will make up the bulk of those going to the Blue and Silver deployments.

The great success of the AEF in Operation Iraqi Freedom was its economy. Under ordinary circumstances, about 120,000 personnel would have been required to support the level of air operations achieved in Operation Iraqi Freedom. Using the AEF concept reduced this number by more than one-half.[12]

Much went right with the Combat Search and Rescue (CSAR) efforts, one of the most demanding jobs of the coalition, which, as with other elements of the services, operated jointly and effectively in Operation Iraqi Freedom. A complete account of CSAR ops known at the time of this writing may be found in appendix 6.

During the war, the use of the Israeli Military Industries TALD was so successful that the U.S. Navy initiated an order for an improved version that could fly farther than sixty miles. The original TALD is a glider, but the improved version will be jet-powered and can have a GPS flight plan preprogrammed and do such tasks as dropping chaff and broadcasting deceptive radio signals.

As a final note on what went right, one has to point to the equipment issued to the individual combat soldiers, which was superb for the most part. This includes the Kevlar armor, the night-vision equipment, and the weaponry. A nation so focused on advanced air and space technology might have somehow overlooked how important it is to keep the tip of the spear as well equipped as possible. Such was not the case, and despite the discomfort of wearing the protective gear, the weight of the equipment, and other essential gear, the average soldier went into battle superbly confident that he (or she) was well outfitted for the task.

Two incidents show what can go right even when things were going very wrong. On April 8, an A-10 from the 110th Fighter Wing and piloted by Major James Ewald was shot down and Ewald was forced to eject near the Baghdad Airport. He was rescued when a Bradley fighting vehicle from the 54th Engineer Battalion pulled up and the Bradley commander shouted, "Hey, pilot dude, come out, we're Americans," took Major Ewald aboard, and brought him back to friendly territory. The story sounds apocryphal but is not. The second incident came the same day when another A-10 was badly shot up by enemy flak. Although the aircraft was severely damaged, with controls shot away and an inoperative hydraulic system, Captain Kim Campbell, of the 23rd Fighter Group, call sign "K.C." for Killer Chick, brought her aircraft back using "manual reversion" procedures to land safely at a base in southern Iraq, a physically difficult feat.

Captain Campbell, a graduate of the U.S. Air Force Academy, is one of 114 active duty female fighter or bomber pilots on duty in the U.S. military.

WHAT WENT WRONG AND WHY

The most devastating, least explainable, and highest priority "what went wrong" candidate is without question fratricide, the sad killing of friendly forces by friendly fire. Reduced to a cliché by the phrase *blue on blue*, fratricide remains a seemingly impossible problem to solve.

Friendly troops have killed each other since ancient times; it has been mentioned in Greek and Roman accounts. Napoléon's army suffered greatly from the effects of amicicide, as it is sometimes known. Fratricide looms larger in recent wars because with the decline in casualties it has become a significant percentage of the total. During World Wars I and II, Korea, and Vietnam, fratricide occurred on a far larger absolute scale but because of the heavy casualties in those conflicts was a much smaller percentage of the losses. In World Wars I and II and in Korea, fratricide accounted for about 2 percent of those killed in action (KIA). In Vietnam, the percentage rose to almost 3 percent. In the 1991 Gulf War, of the total of 146 coalition casualties, 35—or 24 percent—were from "friendly fire." This shocked and horrified the coalition military leaders, and an intensive but obviously not 100 percent successful effort was made to reduce the possibility of fratricide occurring. Early assessments of fratricide deaths in Operation Iraqi Freedom indicate that it is running at about 10 percent (15 dead out of 150 casualties), with an additional 20 deaths still being investigated.[13]

There are many reasons for fratricide, and not least is the pressure, fear, and confusion implicit in combat. Modern combat has become "modern combat" with the speed of battle intensified by the electronic revolution. Accuracy in battle has always been a problem, but where in the past accuracy was compromised by relatively large problems (the identification of an enemy force moving up on the front—Blücher at Waterloo, for example), it can now be reduced to the absurdity of deaths occurring because a single number was entered incorrectly on a computer keyboard.

The increase in the speed of battle means an increase in the speed of decision making, and this adds to the probability of error. And in addition to being swifter, battle is now so fluid that it is "frontless," with the emphasis on deep penetration, rapid maneuver, and heavy firepower on demand.[14] No longer will the enemy be found only ahead, across a half-mile of barbed wire and shell holes; now he is going to be anywhere at any time as the maneuver units move through his territory.

After the 1991 war, significant changes were made in the training and the education of the soldier as a result of the efforts of the Army's multiservice Combat Identification Task Force. The task force improved training manuals and created videos that helped identify both problems and possible solutions to fratricide.

A similar effort was made in the areas of command and control to improve situational awareness and fire control discipline—two areas that were blamed for friendly fire incidents in Operation Iraqi Freedom.

But it was hoped that the answer would lie in technology, and more than $175 million was spent over ten years by the Department of Defense to create the Battle Field Combat Identification System (BCIS). It was to be a sophisticated version of IFF that has been around since World War II. Unfortunately, BCIS proved to be both too expensive and insufficiently reliable and was dropped in 2001.

Other technological advances were less sophisticated. These range from the almost simplistic thermal tape, applied like duct tape to vehicles, the Budd light (visible only through night-vision optics and named for the inventor, not for the beer), the DARPA light, and increased use of GPS. The two lights are battery-powered infrared beacons that can be identified from the air and the ground but are somewhat limited in range.

Unfortunately, the progress in antifratricide devices did not match the speed of warfare and the totally foreseeable but inevitable and unpreventable increase in the number of electronic systems operating in the battlefield. This, as noted previously, was offered by some as a primary cause for the PATRIOT shooting down the Tornado and the F/A-18 aircraft. The fear of chemical or biological armed tactical weapons prevents a "Weapons Tight" rule of engagement.

Others believe that those accidents and other similar incidents were not because of any technological deficiencies but stemmed instead from the traditional problem areas of training and fire-control discipline.

The range of fratricide incidents is a measure of its complexity. At the extreme left on a predictability scale was the appalling incident in which Sergeant Asan Akbar, a thirty-one-year-old convert to the Muslim religion, allegedly "fragged" 101st Airborne (Air Assault) Division command tents by rolling grenades into them. Major Gregory Stone and Captain Christopher Scott were killed. Akbar was taken into custody and is awaiting trial. In the center of the scale are the misidentification of one British tank by another and the attack by F-14Bs on a Kurdish convoy rather than an Iraqi tank. At the far right are the two inexplicable PATRIOT missile shoot-downs of friendly aircraft. Ranged along the scale are a wide variety of incidents, from individual soldiers shooting at the wrong person in a night fight to the F-16 locking on and attacking the PATRIOT missile site.

Somewhat ironically, the unit most well equipped to avoid friendly fire, the 4th Infantry Division, was forced by political circumstances to miss most of the major battles. The 4th Infantry Division had received Combat Identification Panels (CIPs) along with instructions on their use, and some three thousand were installed on front-line vehicles. The CIP is visible from the front, rear, and sides of the vehicles, day and night, to the thermal sighting systems used by coalition forces. The technology is almost laughably simple: the panels indicate a square cool spot on an otherwise "hot" vehicle. The panels were used in addition to a visible beacon called the Phoenix Light, and Glo Tape, which is detectable by infrared illuminators.

At a higher level of complexity, the 4th Infantry Division was equipped with Force XXI Battle Command Brigade-and-Below (FBCB2), which improves situational awareness by using a radio-based network to depict the location of all friendly forces on a computer map. A more sophisticated variant of this, Blue Force Tracking (BLUFOR), does the same thing via GPS.[15] The systems are joined via a Tactical Internet—another example of modern warfare. The Tactical Internet uses a Single-Channel Ground and Airborne Radio System and Enhanced Position Location Reporting System radios, which are line-of-sight.

The U.S. Army had about 8,000 of the FBCB2 systems on hand and provided 1,000 systems to other Army, Marine, and U.K. units, so that they could hook into the network. These sets were the GPS variant.[16]

The problem of fratricide will be intensively addressed in the coming years, but past experience indicates that along with the transformation of the armed services there has to be a transformation in research activities directed to fratricide. Previous efforts have had numerous constraints placed on the study process, each one reflecting a point of view of one or another of the military services. All the services placed budget restraints on the search, despite the expenditure of a huge amount of money. Future research perhaps should be conducted outside the military service sphere, with each of the services providing consulting and, of course, having the final say on the system or systems it adopts.

Sadly, it may be that the prevention of fratricide has reached a point of diminishing returns, where any new technology for preventing friendly fire accidents accidentally presents the enemy with a chance to inflict casualties in greater numbers than those caused by fratricide. A system that prevents one tank firing against another for even a second might be superb, if the other tank was a friendly, but fatal if it was not. A similar hazard exists in any split-second delay by a PATRIOT battery in determining whether the target is a friendly aircraft or an incoming tactical ballistic missile. To avoid this, the requirement for any new antifratricidal device must specify that existing capabilities must not be downgraded but improved.

General Jumper has pointed out that while any incident of fratricide is deplorable, the general problem of fratricide in Operation Iraqi Freedom may prove, upon close analysis, to be not as great as appears on the surface. He notes that there was more close contact with the enemy in Operation Iraqi Freedom than at any time since Vietnam. The ground forces were always moving forward, always in contact, perhaps not always with the Republican Guard but engaged at some level with the Fedayeen or the paramilitary. As a result it was a constant close air support situation, and fratricide, in proportion to the number of CAS missions, may be a much lower percentage than currently thought.[17]

Others would contend that the most significant "what went wrong" element was already emerging and that was the failure to provide a sufficient number of MPs to handle the emerging problems of resistance. General Bernard Trainor says that there was an "unforgivable lack of preparation to provide postcombat security, stability, and services, i.e., there was no preparation to bring order out of chaos . . . The problem was poor planning, lack of troops, and the need for a more robust Military Police/Civil Affairs capability."[18] Some of the difficulties may have led to the early replacement of Lieutenant General (Ret.) Jay Garner with an experienced professional civilian diplomat, L. Paul Bremer.

Brigadier General (Ret.) David Grange takes a somewhat different viewpoint, noting the value and volume of the humanitarian aid that followed on the very heels of the forces. He points out that immediate needs were met on a "retail basis," with the supply, for example, of individual bottles of water to the thirsty Iraqis, but that larger needs needed on a "wholesale basis" with the supply of entire water purification plants, were not met as soon as required.[19]

Still others would say that the greatest failure was the diplomatic efforts prior to the war, which resulted in a series of humiliating rebuffs that would have caused the removal of any secretary of state with less stature than Colin Power. The serial failures with European powers, with the United Nations, and even with Turkey may have long-term effects in terms of the United States public image and, in particular, the image of President Bush. Some military analysts attribute the disaster to the inability of the National Security Council to merge viewpoints and give effective oversight of the fused applications of all the instruments of national power. The interagency squabbles over General Jay Garner's efforts as head of Iraq's Office for Reconstruction and Humanitarian Assistance and Garner's hurried and unseemly replacement by L. Paul Bremer are cited as examples of a major failure by the NSC staff.

In this regard, General Grange notes that the public, as a whole, deserves a much better explanation of why we went to war, expanding the rationale beyond the need to contain the probability of Iraqi weapons of mass destruction and moving on to real underlying issues such as the desire to change the status quo in the Middle East.[20] The need to revitalize the economy of the Muslim world requires that an entire new value system be put in place, one in which hatred of the non-Muslim world is replaced by a reasoned self-interest in improving the lot of Muslim people. (Scholars such as Professor Bernard Lewis would disagree with this, arguing that the problem lies deeper, at the very core of Islamic belief. If this is the case, the future is indeed bleak for Muslims and for everyone else.)

These shortcomings must be balanced against the indisputable diplomatic success that kept Operation Iraqi Freedom confined to a regional conflict. General Grange points out that the holding actions against North Korea, Afghanistan, and the cartels in Colombia and guerrillas in the Philippines were very well done.[21] There was only a token intervention by Syria, but it was quickly contained, as evidenced by the reported return of Saddam Hussein from that country. Grange also noted that the border with Syria should have been shut down sooner and more effectively.

MISSING FACTORS

Maritime air operations would have been unquestionably enhanced if the U.S. Navy had possessed aircraft with true stealth capabilities. Then Secretary of Defense Richard Cheney terminated a multibillion-dollar contract program for the A-12 Avenger aircraft on January 7, 1991. The cancellation was subsequently challenged by the contractors (the McDonnell Douglas/General Dynamics team), but the dollar amounts and the legality of the cancellation are not the point here. The point is the absence of stealth capability in current U.S. Navy aircraft, a deficiency that has left the field of stealth to the U.S. Air Force's Northrop Grumman B-2A Spirit and Lockheed Martin F-117A Nighthawk.

It has been twelve years since the A-12 cancellation, and in that interval the Navy might have at least procured navalized versions of the Lockheed Martin F-117A. Today, instead of having a stealth aircraft capability, the

Navy has two reminders of the A-12: the largest program cancellation in history and the largest lawsuit ever filed against the Department of Defense.

The Navy could also have profited from a fully developed team of UAVs and unmanned combat aerial vehicle (UCAVs). Each of the other services used either or both of the new-type vehicles, and the Navy's failure to employ them extensively may reflect a problem within the Navy culture regarding unmanned aircraft, or it may simply be a blind spot that is being repaired by the work of the Office of Naval Research. The Marine Dragon Eye UAV is one example of that work.

PHASING DOWN

The actual combat phase of Operation Iraqi Freedom was essentially over as Saddam Hussein's regime fled, going underground or fleeing the country. As the war moved into a new phase, fratricide remained a problem, but a more obvious danger emerged: the assassination of coalition force members by those who remained under Saddam's shadowy control, however ill-defined that it was.

8

Lessons Learned and the Fight to Win the Peace

OPERATION IRAQI FREEDOM
April 9 and on

In an image echoing the morbid photograph of Benito Mussolini hanging by his heels in the Piazza Loreto in Milan, an enormous statue of Saddam Hussein was toppled in Firdos Square in Baghdad on April 9. To many Iraqis and Arabs, this was a more definitive statement that the war had been lost than all the Psyops broadcasts and leaflets put together.

When Mussolini was deposed in 1943, Fascism collapsed throughout Italy like a pricked balloon. In 1945 Hitler committed suicide, and Nazi Germany surrendered a little more than a week later. In both instances, despite the instantaneous evaporation the hated ruling party, all government agencies continued operations because the traditional, professional, essentially nonpolitical bureaucracy continued to function well. The reins of government passed, but the mechanisms government remained in place. In neither country did any resistance movement (not even the so-called "Werewolf" movement of the Nazis) appear.

Iraq was far different, for Saddam Hussein had seen to it that almost every public office was held by a member of the Ba'ath Party and many important offices held by either a relative or a fellow tribesman from the Tikrit area. The Ba'ath Party collapsed with Saddam's fall and, with it, much of Iraq's public service. Unlike the case in Germany and Italy, there was no "faceless bureaucracy" to keep services going. Instead, those members of the Ba'ath Party who could expect only punishment from the coalition went underground to continue fighting, no matter how futile it might be, establishing a resistance movement that promises to grow in power, feeding on reports that Saddam still lives.

And this would prove to be a critical difference, so great was Saddam's

161

reputation for personal revenge, for murdering on the slightest provocation, that both loyalists and ordinary people still lived in fear. The possibility of Saddam's return, however slight it might be in real life, was sufficient to inspire the hard core of his followers to still resist.

(Another critical difference might have been the hammering administered to the German public by the Royal Air Force and the U.S. Army Air Forces: by May 1945, most Germans were convinced of the power—and the deadly serious intent—of their opponents.)

The Ba'ath Party's ideology was a pan-Arab, secular nationalism. Only about 10 percent of the Iraqi population belonged, but like the Nazi Party, the Ba'ath Party was well organized, beginning with small cells in every village. From these were recruited leaders for regional and national command positions. The Ba'ath Party came to power on February 8, 1963, and five years later General Hasan al-Bakr, a Tikriti and friend of Saddam, came to power. Two years later Saddam engineered a successful coup to become Iraq's dictator for thirty-three long and terror-filled years.

Iraq was impoverished by twenty-two years of wars, U.N. sanctions, and the systematic pillaging of every source of revenue by Saddam Hussein and his most intimate colleagues. One by-product of this was the "revenge" looting by Iraqi citizens after they were convinced that Saddam's reign was in fact over and they could invade government and party buildings with impunity and even the many palaces and estates of the ruling establishment. So desperate was their poverty that they would steal barrels filled with uranium-poisoned residue, emptying them for use as water barrels.

As a result, even though there was still more fighting to do throughout Iraq, the coalition forces had to turn almost immediately to what was termed *stability operations*, which included ordinary police work and the reconstruction of needed water, power, and fuel facilities. The 3rd Infantry Division's combat troops almost overnight had to switch their mindset from combat operations to becoming the custodians of public order, and it speaks well of the education, training, and intelligence of coalition troops that they were able to do as well as they did. When errors were made, they were usually on the side of being too permissive or too trusting and too often resulted in U.S. casualties.

In the north, where up to this point a relatively few airborne troops, special operation forces, and Kurdish elements had secured large areas of the country, three important cities remained under Iraqi control for a few more days: Kirkuk, Mosul, and Tikrit. The latter, envisaged as perhaps the equivalent of the mythic Nazi "Alpine Redoubt," was where die-hard members of the Ba'ath Party were supposed to rally for a bloody last stand. Elsewhere in Iraq, the opposition continued at greater and lesser levels of intensity.

The 101st Airborne Division was employed to squelch Iraqi resistance in areas that the 3rd Infantry Division had bypassed on its whirlwind march to Baghdad. In the south, the United Kingdom's 1st Armored Division moved north to link up with the 1st MEF.[1]

The entire 5th Corps of the Iraqi Army surrendered on April 11, allowing Mosul and Kirkuk to pass uneventfully into coalition hands. The Iraqi 5th Corps, which had numbered some one hundred thousand during the 1991 Gulf War, had only about fifteen thousand troops. Even so, the surrender brought the total prisoners of war in coalition hands up to only about 20,000, far short of the original estimates of 50,000 for which preparations were made. As occurred elsewhere, the Iraqi soldiers apparently just wandered home, glad to avoid having been killed by the overwhelming power of the coalition attack but potentially candidates for an Iraqi resistance movement. Air and ground attacks forced about twenty-five hundred Iraqi soldiers to abandon their positions defending Tikrit, turning the last major Iraqi city over to the 26th MEI just two days later.[2]

In the ensuing weeks, there would continue to be violent civil unrest, even as the level of fighting subsided—but never quite died out. Coalition special operation forces were especially effective in obtaining surrenders in several areas where pockets of military resistance remained. The Iraqis, their communications cut off and their supplies running low, were relieved to find a peaceful way out of their predicament without the fear of incurring Saddam's wrath. Others, stiffened by radical foreign volunteers, continued to mount sneak attacks.

Although there were continued reminders from CENTCOM that operations were continuing, each of the services and many military thinkers began examining the brilliant Operation Iraqi Freedom Campaign and formulating "lessons learned" that could be applied to the future. The first task in this process is gathering data, and Lieutenant General Moseley (who was selected to become a four-star general and Vice Chief of Staff of the U.S. Air Force) issued the first data compilation, dated April 30, 2003. In it he laid out the initial statistics of the air war that had been such an important component of the victory. These figures were subsequently updated as information flowed in, so that by April 25, 2003, the coalition was shown to have flown almost 50,000 fixed-wing missions, of which the U.S. Air Force flew roughly thirty thousand, the Navy ninety-five hundred, the Marines fifty-five hundred, and the Royal Air Force and Royal Australian Air Forces about five thousand. Of the missions some 36 percent were strike sorties, 20 percent tanker missions, and 25 percent airlift missions, with 4 percent miscellaneous.[3]

This was the era of what Major General David Deptula calls "Mass Precision"; never in history has so much accurate firepower been placed on an adversary in such a compressed period of time. Persistent (i.e., platforms with long loiter times) ISR and persistent precision strike capability were the keys to success. He notes, however, that BDA in Operation Iraqi Freedom lagged events by several days.[4]

Moseley's report shows that some 28,820 munitions were dropped, of which 19,060 were precision-guided, an amazing 66 percent. All told, the munitions amounted to about fourteen thousand tons. The aerial refueling figures were equally impressive, with 417,137,233 gallons of fuel being off-loaded by tankers of all the services. Another 195,753,818 gallons of jet fuel were provided by land- and ship-based sources.

Moseley's report was studded with commentary to make the raw statistics a little bit more understandable. The 417-plus million gallons of fuel were noted as being able to keep a Boeing 737-300 flying for 11.9 years. He also noted some firsts, including the use of the CBU-105 and CBU-107 weapons, the use of an AGM-86D CALCM with a hard target penetrator, the first drop of a JDAM by an F-14D, and one of the first combat deliveries of "dumb" bombs by the B-2. The F-14D was modified on-ship to use the JDAM, while the B-2 flew from Whiteman Air Force Base, Missouri, with eighty standard 500-pound Mk 82s that were dropped with good effect on an Iraqi garrison.[5]

Eventually all of the services and the Department of Defense will release more comprehensive statistical reports and all will have compiled substantial "lessons learned" papers. In the following pages, initial thoughts on the lessons learned on various aspects of Operation Iraqi Freedom have been compiled from some of the most authoritative sources in the country. Naturally enough, they reflect in many ways both "what went right" and "what went wrong" covered previously herein.

One measure of how well things went is that many of the first conclusions drawn indicate that it will take time and careful consideration to exploit to the full the current capability of the coalition armed forces and that some of the planned investment in radical new technologies might well be deferred until this is done.

Not everyone agrees on every point as to what lessons were learned, but there was a surprising degree of consensus on most elements. One unusual aspect that reflects the general tenor of the war is that while the viewpoints are for the most part "joint" rather than reflecting the interests of a particular service, there are still lessons pointed out that underline the value (and the interests) of a particular service.

WEAPONS OF MASS DESTRUCTION

From the point of view of military operations, the Iraqi failure to use weapons of mass destruction as the various red lines (where weapons of mass destruction were expected to be deployed) were approached was a blessing. While chemical or biological weapons could have been overcome, they would have impeded progress, perhaps for weeks. Most believed that Saddam did not possess nuclear weapons, but if he did possess and use them, the war would still ultimately have been won, but at far greater cost to both the coalition and the Iraqis, and with global repercussions impossible to foresee. It is possible that Iraqi leaders still possessed weapons of mass destruction but were deterred from their use by repeated coalition warnings that to do so would be a war crime.

The primary military objective for discovering Iraqi weapons of mass destruction was to prevent their use. Politically, the inability to find weapons of mass destruction began to be a curse from the very first days of the war, when there was report after report that weapons of mass destruction might have been discovered—only to find out in each case that they were not. A genuine discovery would have meant vindication of the claims of President Bush. Unfortunately, Saddam Hussein had the time to transport any weapons of mass destruction that he retained to Syria or other states during the long buildup to Operation Iraqi Freedom. Nonetheless, the failure to this time to find any definite evidence presents the coalition, and particularly the Bush administration, with a sticky problem that may never be resolved in the eyes of opponents to the war on Iraq, which makes general diplomatic approval of further preemptive military action against other countries, such as as Syria, Iran, and even North Korea, almost impossible to obtain. The failure to find weapons of mass destruction was in fact the only offset to the RDA brought about by the crushing real-time immediate superiority of coalition arms, and this may have been considerably offset by the discovery of the mobile labs and the critical equipment for enriching uranium found under a rosebush in an Iraqi scientist's garden.

Despite the contretemps of missing weapons of mass destruction, there were ample lessons to be learned from Operation Iraqi Freedom as it unfolded.

LESSONS LEARNED

The first lesson that each of the services sought to impress upon themselves was that the triumph in Iraq should not go to their heads and that future wars would almost undoubtedly be far more difficult and costly. With this lesson came concerns that the American public might not have the same cautionary point of view and that the easy success in Iraq might raise levels of expectation to a point that could not be met in a war with a more competent opponent.

There were many other lessons as well. The first of these was that Operation Iraqi Freedom demonstrated the preferred way to fight a war, regardless of the skill of the opponent. The formula included complete information dominance through C⁴ISR, and complete air dominance, including loitering platforms equipped with PGMs, with both of these used in combination with swift-moving powerful land forces. This was a one-two-three punch that the Iraqis could not withstand and, in fact, no other armed force in the world could withstand.

This has been called a "new air-land dynamic" by retired Vice Admiral Arthur Cebrowski, who characterized it as discovering a new "sweet spot" in the relationship between air and land warfare. The term quickly caught on.[6]

Yet the sweet spot was a combination that even many senior Army personnel did not understand when complaints were made about insufficient troops. In the words of General "Chuck" Horner, "It is necessary for ground commanders to know that the primary maneuver force on the battlefield is the aircraft overhead, be it a B-2A or Joint STARS. The ground commander's task is now to maneuver in such a way that it either fixes the enemy troops into position or makes him move so that he is now vulnerable to air strikes."[7]

All of this was made possible by the deployment of highly trained, well-equipped, well-motivated armed services composed entirely of volunteers, men and women of the highest character, brave in battle and compassionate in victory.

Arriving at this war-winning formula was difficult, time-consuming, and expensive. However, it was extremely worthwhile, for it established the highest benchmark of military prowess in history. More important than anything else, it is only this style of warfare—short of resorting to nuclear weapons—that can win the global war on terrorism in which the United States, and the rest of the non-Muslim world, finds itself.

Just like Operation Iraqi Freedom itself, the lessons to be learned from the war are complex, interrelated, and sometimes contradictory. The lessons that we learn will have to be calibrated in the light of the fact that current and potential enemies to the United States will also learn from Operation Iraqi Freedom. As previously noted, such enemies may not be as inept as Iraq or have such totally counterproductive leadership. They may instead be skillful and well led, and it is not inconceivable that an emerging enemy might have a huge population and sizable industrial base. It is against such very real possibilities that the lessons learned must be applied not only to future operations but also to future defense budgets. A balance must be sought between the need to fully exploit all that has been achieved to date and the need to improve our weapon systems in the future, and this will take careful research on the part of the military, careful consideration on the part of Congress, and full support of the American people.

For the coalition forces, some lessons learned apply to all services of all nations, some to one or more services, and some to other agencies. And as previously suggested, some also apply to the Congress of the United States and therefore to the American public.

As for the lessons learned by the services, in the words of former Air Force Chief of Staff General Michael E. Ryan, many of the lessons were not really "learned" but were in fact "demonstrated"[8] as the product of doctrine, years of training, and practical expertise. The coalition professionals have been involved in refining the operational art of warfare for as long as twenty years, and many of the flag officers of Operation Iraqi Freedom were the colonels and lieutenant colonels who ran combat units in Desert Storm. The victory in Operation Iraqi Freedom was one for military systems that stress rationalism, transparency, accountability, and professionalism,[9] traits that must be maintained at whatever cost in the future and traits that are difficult to keep after easy victories.

LESSONS FOR THE COALITION

The most obvious lesson was one that had been the most difficult to learn over centuries of warfare, and that is that joint and true combined operations can work well only if the concept is adhered to through all levels from the Commander in Chief down to the newest enlisted person. The promise of true joint operations was signaled early on when the Coalition Forces Land Component (CFLC) Commander was given jurisdiction over both the Army and the Marines. A similar signal was the assignment of USAF Major General Daniel Leaf as a liaison officer to the CFLC. General Moseley would be promoted to four-star general and Vice Chief of Staff of the Air Force.

Joint or combined operations usually work well in exercises but tend to fray in actual combat. This proved not to be the case in Operation Iraqi Freedom, with the small but highly efficient British aerial refueling fleet being a shining example. When the increase in sortie rate precipitated an in-flight refueling problem because of the general tanker shortage, the RAF tankers provided the U.S. Navy with superb service, one that had the pilots in U.S. carrier wardrooms (already discontent with the shortage of Air Force tankers) buzzing with excited approval.

One of the peak points in combined operations occurred early in the war with the seizure of the oil fields and offshore oil platforms in southern Iraq. Perhaps at once the most delicate and most dangerous of operations went off flawlessly, with both regular and special forces of the United States and the United Kingdom meshing to prevent all but the most minor damage.

Another lesson learned was that the heavy investment in the weapon systems of the armed services has paid off handsomely, with all but a very few systems turning in stellar performances. The most expensive and the riskiest of this long series of investments were in the persistent and enduring C4 ISR systems, yet it was here that the payoff was greatest, for the coalition forces had insight into the Iraqi defenses at every level, while denying all information to the enemy.

It takes courage as well as foresight to back the spending of billions of dollars on space systems, for it is almost impossible to be certain of the wartime effectiveness of a huge galaxy of dedicated satellite systems, no matter how many studies are made. These systems are expensive to operate, requiring dedicated organizations to function twenty-four hours a day, every day, most of the time under routine, even boring, conditions.

The first decisions to create these expensive satellite systems were made many decades ago. The research and development costs are extremely high, and the extensive investment in ground facilities to monitor and govern the satellites has to be made relatively early in the program, long before any results are possible. There is no assurance of success until long after the expensive process of inserting the satellites into their orbits begins. Each insertion is costly and fraught with risk, for despite the years of experience, things can and do go wrong with launch systems. Depending upon the system involved, it may take months before the satellite, or system of satellites, is adjusted so that it begins transmitting the data it is designed to provide.

Once the system is established in position, it takes additional time to familiarize the users with the system's potential. But as noted previously, General Moseley had some fifty satellites at his disposal, many of them "tweaked" to customize their utility and all providing millions of bits of data to everyone from General Franks to an individual SOF soldier in the field.

The development of UAVs and UCAVs was both less costly and less risky than that of satellite systems, and the unmanned vehicles returned results far out of proportion to the expenditures. While everyone agrees that UAVs are the wave of the future and that investment in research, development, and production should be increased, there is a difference of opinion on the UCAVs. Many experts are predicting that in the future manned aircraft "mother ships" will govern the combat of UCAVs in many forms—stealth fighters, stealth bombers, stealth reconnaissance. Others feel that UCAVs both are too expensive and lack the essential human element for combat. The first commander of the U.S. Air Force's Air Combat Command, General John Michael Loh, takes vehement exception to UCAVs, believing that Operation Iraqi Freedom showed that unmanned combat vehicles are a liability on the modern battlefield. While Loh strongly supports UAVs such as the Predator and the Global Hawk, he feels that the track record of the unmanned cruise missile was deplorable, citing that several fell in Saudi Arabia, Turkey, and Iran. Others crashed in Iraq and caused unnecessary civilian casualties. Loh believes that "we need a person in the loop in the terminal phase of a weapon attack to make damn sure it hits where we want it to hit and does not cause civilian casualties or an international incident that will adversely affect the campaign as these unmanned combat systems did in Iraq."[10]

Of all the decisions made as long as a decade ago, one of the least commented on yet most effective was the decision to equip almost all U.S. forces with the very best night-fighting equipment available so that they can in truth "Own the Night," as the U.S. Army proudly claims. As a result, U.S. and other coalition forces can maneuver at night with almost the same degree of visibility as they possess during the day, putting them at a great advantage over enemy forces not equipped with similar devices. The equipment includes both low-light-level devices and thermal sensing devices. At one end of the size scale they range from the ubiquitous night-vision goggles to the boxy-looking thermal sight on an M4 rifle that portrays an enemy soldier as a black outline against a milky-white background. Slightly larger is the Lightweight Laser Designator Range finder, which resembles a video camera but can illuminate a target many miles away by day or by night, using laser or infrared technology. The laser can designate targets for aircraft ranging above.

Armored vehicles carry their own array of equipment, including variations on the tried-and-true Forward-Looking Infra-Red (FLIR) that has been used on the B-52 and other aircraft for decades but is now miniaturized for use on smaller vehicles. The image of the FLIR has been refined to provide a well-defined outline by which the operator can identify specific types of equipment, rather than just the familiar blur on the radar screen. Night-fighting equipment, such as the old Low Altitude Navigation and Targeting Infra-Red for Night (LANTIRN) system or the new Litening

II targeting pod, is fitted to a variety of aircraft and UAVs. Other aircraft, including the Lockheed Martin AC-130 Spectre and Sikorsky MH-53 Pave Low helicopters, have their own suites of night-fighting equipment.

There is a valid concern that relatively low-cost second-generation night-vision equipment will be available for future enemies to use and that this will somewhat redress the balance of night-fighting capability. The answer to this is not easy, for even improving U.S. and coalition equipment would not maintain the current degree of advantage.

Stealth is another extremely expensive technology to incorporate in weapon systems, and it is an expensive way to fight a war, given the maintenance facilities and man-hours required to keep the aircraft stealthy. Yet both the Lockheed Martin F-117A Nighthawk and Northrop Grumman B-2A Spirit did splendidly, with four of the B-2As flying from Diego Garcia, while others operated from halfway around the world at their home station, Whiteman Air Force Base, Missouri. The Boeing B-1B, which is regarded as "slightly stealthy," also did remarkably well.

Just as with night-vision equipment, stealth remains at once a great advantage and a significant hazard, for if an inexpensive technological counter to stealth is found, the heart of the United States' bomber fleet will be destroyed. The great capability (and the great expense) of stealth aircraft led to their being procured in very small numbers. Some fifty-two Nighthawks and twenty-one Spirits remain in service, but if they should be deprived of their stealth capability, they would become vulnerable and only marginally useful, and the brunt of the bombing load would fall on the reduced B-1B fleet, currently projected to be about three dozen combat-ready aircraft and about forty-four combat-ready B-52s. Even when equipped with cruise missiles and PGMs, such a fleet would be too small to conduct major operations over an extended period or to handle two simultaneous conflicts.

Perhaps not the ultimate in robotics but the ultimate in sensible self-preservation is the "Packbot," a robot used in Iraq to search buildings for enemy soldiers or equipment. Equipped with remote infrared and optical cameras, Packbots are radio-controlled by operators who see the robot's camera view through a helmet-mounted eyepiece. Sergeant First Class Tim South, Special Projects Noncommissioned Officer for the Rapid Equipping Force South, said that the tread-driven Packbot can climb stairs and right itself if flipped over.[11]

Of the many U.S. and coalition weapon systems listed in appendix 1, all proved themselves without a shadow of a doubt, with the exception of the Apache and the PATRIOT, and even these two systems were quite capable in most circumstances. The Apache's difficulties are largely chalked up to their being used without adequate battlefield preparation, while the PATRIOT's tragic incidents of fratricide are still being intensively investigated. Both the Apache and the PATRIOT did well in many instances, and both still have strong adherents.

ARMY LESSONS LEARNED–OR DEMONSTRATED

The American army entered the arena with some dissension in the ranks at the very highest levels. Secretary Rumsfeld did not attempt to hide his distaste for the Army Chief of Staff, General Erik K. Shinseki, and although the reports were denied on all sides, initially had difficulty working with General Franks. (Rumsfeld did not attend Shinseki's retirement ceremony, an unsubtle rebuff.)

The difficulty stemmed in part from Shinseki's apparent inability to share—or to share to the extent desired—Secretary Rumsfeld's enthusiasm for transforming the services. Shinseki was an advocate of more boots on the ground when that idea was not popular.

The Army has a long history of fielding large units equipped with heavy equipment, intended for large-scale military encounters with similarly equipped opponents. The Air Force transformed from its historic pattern of wings of aircraft of a homogenous type—bombers, fighters, etc.—into the AEF concept, a much more flexible organization. The Army has found it more difficult to follow this pattern of downsizing into smaller units capable of dealing with the types of regional wars generally predicted for the future.

Yet one of the first lessons learned from Operation Iraqi Freedom was that the very equipment destined to be phased out in the future, the "legacy" Abrams tanks and Bradley fighting vehicles, proved to be essential in the quick dash from the sea to Baghdad and, more important, in maintaining an authoritative presence after arriving in the Iraqi capital. (*Legacy* is a current value-laden buzzword used to avoid designating older equipment as obsolete.)

A visible armored behemoth is intimidating in a way that an unseen Predator is not, and the power to intimidate is often as important as the power to destroy. Although the numbers of M1A1s and M1A2s and Bradleys will probably be reduced in the future in favor of newer, lighter vehicles, they will now no doubt remain in much greater numbers than previously planned. Further, they will continue to receive major upgrades, particularly in trying to defend against the ubiquitous RPGs.

The Army, which had encountered difficulties in using CAS in Afghanistan, did much better in Operation Iraqi Freedom, especially after the first thirty-six hours of fighting, when a better understanding was obtained on the establishment of more realistic fire support coordination lines. It was obvious that embedded FAC were essential and that Army UAVs were more effective when combined with Air Force assets.

The integration of UAVs of the various services into the overall C⁴SIR picture is a perfect example of the long-sought elimination of "stovepipes" of information rising from the source (Predator, Hunter, U-2, etc.) directly to the top of its own command chain, without being integrated at a lower level to maximize its use. One great lesson of Operation Iraqi Freedom was that for maximum utility all of the intelligence information has to be integrated into a "common operational picture" and analyzed at an operational level, eliminating the "stovepipes."

The use of "kill boxes" helped the CAS efforts. Kill boxes were areas designated in which aircraft could strike targets without the requirement of close control. The CAS, in conjunction with the excellent use of artillery (especially the Paladin system) and the Lockheed Martin Vought Multiple Launch Rocket System, proved to be overwhelming to Iraqi defenders, who were almost always already depleted by air strikes.

It is probable that the Apache Long Bow will no longer be seen as capable of CAS on its own but will instead be used in concert with other CAS aircraft and artillery. The lesson learned was that helicopters have limited utility until defenses are suppressed on the battlefield, and this has vast implications for not only future budgets but also the makeup of future Army organizations.

In general, while the Army benefited, as did all the services, from the new spaced-based technology, much of the success stemmed from basic doctrine and training. The logistic effort by the Army was expensive but paid off superbly. Prepositioned equipment can sit idle for months in foreign warehouses, but when it is needed, it is on hand and there is no six months' delay for sea lift.

The success of the Army training efforts was evident in many areas, but two highlights were the cooperation of regular Army units and the special forces and the conduct of urban combat. The value of an all-volunteer force was never more evident than in the intelligent manner in which ordinary soldiers handled the menace of suicide bombers after the main combat operations had concluded. They managed, for the most part, to implement procedures that distanced themselves from the hazard of the suicide bomber without unduly inconveniencing or antagonizing a population rather easily antagonized.

The same level of intelligence and training kept soldier-on-soldier fratricide casualties very low.

NAVY LESSONS LEARNED–OR DEMONSTRATED

To the vast satisfaction of the Naval High Command, aircraft carriers once again proved themselves to be both essential and effective. The deployment of five carrier battle groups (three in the Persian Gulf and two in the Mediterranean) was in itself a statement of such unrivaled power that no nation, or combination of nations, in the history of the world could match. These carrier task forces require the permission of no nation to take up station in international waters, a factor worth its weight in gold in times of crisis.

The Navy faced the problem of a tanker shortage in a straightforward manner. The USS *Abraham Lincoln* and USS *Constellation* (the *Connie* on the last cruise of its illustrious career) had been on station in the Persian Gulf for the longest times and were designated to receive the available USAF strategic tanker support. The USS *Kitty Hawk*, as previously noted, undertook to provide its own tanker support with the use of Lockheed Martin S-3s and (later) Boeing F/A-18E Super Hornet tankers.

Tanking operations had been tested during Operation Southern Watch, and typically the Hornets would tank on both outbound and inbound routes, increasing the amount of on-station time for CAS operations. The tankers themselves would launch and recover after each tanking evolution, meaning that there was constant traffic on the carrier decks.

Just as with the Army, "legacy" equipment proved itself equal to the task. The veteran Northrop Grumman E-2C Hawkeye (the prototype of which was first flown on October 21, 1960) command and control aircraft were essential in filling the critical communication gaps caused when AWACS aircraft could not operate from some of the foreign bases that had been counted on.[12] The Hawkeyes maintained communication among Army, Air Force, Marine, and British units, and the Navy's tactical air arm in CAS operations.

In a similar way, the workhorse Northrop Grumman EA-6B Prowler was the only aircraft in Operation Iraqi Freedom that combined electronic counterwarfare jamming equipment and the capability to fire the HARM to suppress enemy air defenses. The Prowlers, supported with firepower from F/A-18s and F-16s, provided coverage for both stealth and conventional bombers and fighters over Baghdad.

There are an insufficient number of Prowlers, and the armed services need a replacement as soon as possible, in greater numbers, with greater capability, or a completely new approach to electronic warfare.

Two other "legacy" systems, the Northrop Grumman F-14 and the Lockheed Martin P-3, also did stellar work.

In general, the Navy leaves Operation Iraqi Freedom with a strong hand for maintaining a large carrier force in the present and developing newer, longer-range, more autonomous carriers in the future. Two hard-learned lessons from Operation Iraqi Freedom were that that future carrier forces will require both stealth aircraft and UAVs of types yet to be defined. This, like the Army's retention of heavy armor, causes immense budget problems that will not be easily resolved.

One lesson that the Navy taught the other services was that of public relations. There is no better public image possible than that provided by the sight of hardworking crews on the decks of aircraft carriers launching or recovering one powerful jet aircraft after another, moving among the deadly dangerous array of jet engines, propellers, rockets, and bombs with greater grace and precision than any ballet corps could muster. Then the Navy perhaps topped all PR efforts of all time with the dramatic sight of President George W. Bush flying into the *Abraham Lincoln* in the co-pilot's seat aboard a Lockheed Martin S-3B Viking. It was a political coup for the President and a PR coup for the Navy. The aircraft, the very first "Navy One," was piloted by Commander John P. "Loose" Lussier, a veteran instructor pilot.

MARINE LESSONS LEARNED–OR DEMONSTRATED

The U.S. Marines' debarking from ships and racing forward across the desert to Baghdad (a distance roughly comparable to that from Camp Pendleton to San Francisco), sometimes fighting more and tougher battles than the 3rd Infantry Division faced, was such a remarkable epic that it should be added to the Halls of Montezuma and the Shores of Tripoli in Marine lore.

In the process, the Marines went in three short weeks from an invasion force breaching Iraqi territory, to a blitzkrieg juggernaut chewing up the Republican Guard, to a peacekeeping force patrolling hostile streets. In the process, an Army CFLC Commander was accepted, but the Marines continued to depend heavily on its organic CAS and tanker equipment.

The integration of Marine and naval air forces is scheduled for the future in a cost-cutting move. This will be opposed by loyalists in both services and may be an instance where esprit and tradition will be valued more highly than dollar savings.

Making full use of C4SIR and USAF interdiction capabilities, the Marines focused on Baghdad (in General Trainor's words) as "the jewel in the crown," accepting risks to their lines of communication (LOC). Troop training and fire discipline were superb, as was their performance in mobile operations in urban terrain.

One area in which the Marines rose to the occasion, and which reflects the dedication and training of the enlisted personnel, was in the highly effective use of the Boeing AV-8B Harrier, which was brought forward as the Marines advanced and was kept flying despite all the problems incident to forward deployment to unprepared areas. Time after time, it involved the application of the sheer mechanical genius of the crew chiefs whose long hours of work had the Harriers ready in time for the next sortie. Still, the very success of the AV-8B argues strongly for the follow-on STOVL versions of the F-35.

AIR FORCE LESSONS LEARNED–OR DEMONSTRATED

Success can present dilemmas, and this was certainly the case with the U.S. Air Force in Iraq. The success of the Northrop Grumman B-2A Spirit stealth bomber and the surprisingly (to all but insiders in the B-1B community) stellar work of the Boeing B-1B (which dropped more precision-guided bombs than any other aircraft) have to make Air Force planners reconsider future options for fighters and bombers.

All three bombers—the B-52, B-1B, and B-2A—demonstrated the value of long-range aircraft power projection, and the first two also showed the value of high–loiter time aircraft in the new age of C⁴ISR and PGMs. Such aircraft lessen the demand for the already-critical in-flight refueling assets and offer commanders a capability reminiscent of that found during the time when the Strategic Air Command maintained a fleet of nuclear bombers airborne twenty-four hours a day.

Existing plans call for the introduction of a new bomber into the fleet in 2030, relying in the interval upon B-52s that will be approaching seventy years of service, B-1Bs that will be about forty-five years old, and youngster B-2As only thirty-eight years of age. Some are saying that the performance of the bombers in Operation Iraqi Freedom really calls for the much earlier introduction of a supersonic or hypersonic stealth bomber with a nonrefueled intercontinental range, able to appear over foreign trouble spots within a few hours of an emergency occurring. An alternative to this is already on the drawing boards, an enlarged version of the Boeing X-45 UCAV.

Others have a diametrically opposed view, stating that the already-demonstrated efficiency and capability of the bombers mean that the United States can get by with an even smaller force and still have ample means for any emergency. (This is perhaps true if we continue to fight small wars against less well equipped enemies and fight them sequentially. An all-out war with a major power would be completely different.)

At the heart of the problem is the immense funding required to procure 267 Lockheed Martin F-22As and a larger number of Lockheed Martin F-35s over the next decade. It is here that Air Force opinion is sharply divided. The Air Force has been behind the procurement of the F-22A/B for more than a decade, and it still sees the aircraft as absolutely indispensable for achieving air supremacy in any future conflict. Declines in defense spending—and increases in F-22 program costs—have caused a gradual reduction in the number of aircraft to be procured from over 600 down to the current 267–381 range.

Opponents to the F-22A/B claim that there is no fighter in the world that can match the current Boeing F-15C and that a fleet of 100 "silver bullet" F-22s would be more than adequate for any enemy apt to emerge in the next twenty or thirty years.

General John Michael Loh has definite views on the situation, stating that "the Air Force leadership continues to undervalue and downplay the significant, almost overwhelming contribution of the bomber fleet and bomber crews, particularly the B-1, in both Afghanistan and now Iraq. In Iraq, clearly the B-1, B-52, and, to a less extent, the B-2 were the real workhorses and centerpiece of our victory. The B-1 dropped more bombs than any other aircraft and, because of its extremely long endurance, was able to rapidly retarget and attack the safe house where Saddam and his sons were said to be present. The B-52s also played a significant role. Combined, all three bombers totally overshadowed the contributions of the Navy, Army, and other Air Force attack aircraft in terms of percentage of weapons delivered and targets destroyed, particularly time-sensitive targets.

"Bombers fit perfectly in the new way of waging war in a network-centric real-time targeting System of Systems, because bombers provide longtime dwell over the target area with their long endurance to provide the 'Engage' link in the Find, Fix, Target, Track, Engage, Assess kill chain. The Air Force has not fully appreciated the long endurance characteristic of bombers. It does recognize the long-range capability. Now based in the region as the B-1 was based in Oman, we can exchange range for loiter time with huge bomb loads to be able to respond rapidly to reduce the time lines for Find-to-Engage significantly.

"Don't get me wrong. I fully support our fighter fleet and the need for 381 F/A-22s and F-35 Joint Strike Fighters. They are far more efficient to operate and maintain and have much more operational flexibility for multiple roles and scenarios. . . . The Air Force can also underscore its long-

A conventional air-launched cruise missile being loaded into a B-52 *(Courtesy: Air Force Magazine)*

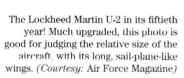

A Lockheed Martin F-117A Nighthawk stealth fighter touches down, its brake-chute blossoming with a reassuring tug. *(Courtesy:* Air Force Magazine)

Photos like these, showing the exact impact of precision-guided weapons, did not have the effect upon blasé reporters the way they did during the 1991 Gulf War. *(Courtesy:* Air Force Magazine)

The Lockheed Martin U-2 in its fiftieth year! Much upgraded, this photo is good for judging the relative size of the aircraft, with its long, sail-plane-like wings. *(Courtesy:* Air Force Magazine)

A group of special forces troops relax before a mission. Their equipment is superb, as is their training. *(Courtesy:* Air Force Magazine)

Two Lockheed Martin F-16 "Vipers" taxiing out. Officially the "Fighting Falcon," pilots prefer the name "Viper" for the tough little aircraft. *(Courtesy:* Air Force Magazine*)*

The United States Air Force flies many compassionate missions; here a Boeing C-17A Globemaster III taxis in, loaded with humanitarian supplies. *(Courtesy:* Air Force Magazine*)*

A night-vision photo of the first troops ready to enter Baghdad *(Courtesy:* Air Force Magazine*)*

Blowing bubbles works with kids, no matter from what nation. *(Courtesy:* Air Force Magazine*)*

Burned-out Iraqi tanks, like this T-55, litter the countryside, mute evidence of the overwhelming coalition air superiority. *(Courtesy:* Air Force Magazine*)*

A Sikorsky HH-60 helicopter in a steep bank *(Courtesy:* Air Force Magazine*)*

Men of the 173rd Airborne Brigade boarding the Boeing C-17A Globemaster III from which they would make their historic jump into northern Iraq *(Courtesy: U.S. Air Force)*

They say that the hardest part of a paratrooper's mission is the waiting; for most people, it would be the long leap into the dark over enemy territory. *(Courtesy: U.S. Air Force)*

Staff Sgt. Jason M. Smith of the 392nd Air Expeditionary Wing refuels an A-10 Thunderbolt on April 3, 2003. *(Courtesy: U.S. Air Force)*

U.S. Army Sikorsky HH-60 Blackhawk helicopters ferry in equipment on April 2, 2003, at a forward base in southern Iraq. *(Courtesy: U.S. Army)*

At Ramstein Air Base, Germany, a sixty-six-ton Abrams tank is loaded into the cavernous interior of the tried-and-true Lockheed Martin C-5B Galaxy. The aircraft is from the 17th Airlift Squadron, Charleston Air Force Base, South Carolina. The tank was flown directly to a captured base in northern Iraq. *(Courtesy: U.S. Air Force)*

Soldiers assigned to the 1st Infantry Division, 63rd Armored Regiment provide security from a M1A1 Abrams Battle Tank and a M2A3 Bradley fighting vehicle in Kirkuk, Iraq, on April 18, 2003. *(Courtesy: U.S. Army)*

The Iraqi dust made for colorful sunsets; here U.S. Army Blackhawks take off for a mission. *(Courtesy: U.S. Army)*

A U.S. Army security-forces member provides security at a power plant in Baghdad on April 15, 2003. *(Courtesy: U.S. Army)*

The stealthy lines of the Northrop Grumman B-2A Spirit are evident in this shot of the cockpit area. *(Courtesy: U.S. Air Force)*

A Bradley Infantry Fighting Vehicle crew with the 24th Infantry Division from Ft. Riley, Kansas, takes a break in central Iraq. The crew is part of the land force that had moved in thirty-two hours what had taken ninety-six hours during the 1991 Gulf War. *(Courtesy: U.S. Army)*

Against the backdrop of a burning oil well, a well-trained Army soldier stands with his machine gun. *(Courtesy: U.S. Army)*

The Lockheed Martin EC-130H Compass Call aircraft engaged in very successful electronic-warfare operations. *(Courtesy: U.S. Air Force)*

If you look closely, you can see the intent face of the boom operator reflected in the windshield as he carefully refuels a Boeing F-15E Strike Eagle. *(Courtesy: U.S. Air Force)*

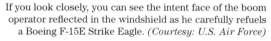

Ground crewmen make the last essential checks as an armed Lockheed Martin F-16 prepares to taxi out for takeoff. *(Courtesy: U.S. Air Force)*

General Tommy Franks traveled throughout the Middle East in a Boeing C-40B. He is shown here with Brigadier General Rick Rosboro. *(Courtesy: U.S. Air Force)*

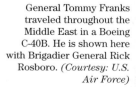

The Navy and the Air Force use different methods to refuel; when KC-135Rs are scheduled to refuel Navy aircraft, they equip the boom with a special basket device to accommodate the Navy technique. *(Courtesy: U.S. Navy)*

A beautiful Marine Sikorsky CH-53 taxis, following instructions for parking. *(Courtesy: U.S. Marine Corps)*

President George W. Bush made history with his morale-raising trips to the troops. *(Courtesy: U.S. Air Force)*

A 398th Air Expeditionary Group "Rivet Joint" aircraft takes off. The RC-135 conducts electronic surveillance of the battlefield. *(Courtesy: U.S. Air Force)*

Soldiers standing by at a Patriot missile battery *(Courtesy: U.S. Air Force)*

The Iraqi soldiers in prisoner-of-war camps had a great advantage over their colleagues who were not yet captured, for they were not being continuously bombed. *(Courtesy: U.S. Air Force)*

An experienced hand in loading aircraft, Tech Sgt. Dennis Washington of the 86th Expeditionary Contingency Response Group signals a forklift operator to approach and unload a C-17. The 86th was one of the first units to enter northern Iraq. *(Courtesy: U.S. Air Force)*

Captain Jennifer Wilson, a B-2A Spirit pilot, is the first female B-2 pilot to fly a combat mission. *(Courtesy: U.S. Air Force)*

In a too-often repeated scene, a wounded soldier is assisted aboard a Lockheed Martin C-130. *(Courtesy: U.S. Air Force)*

standing role in long-range power projection with the B-1, B-52, and B-2 in the fight for a bigger role in transformation and efficiency, particularly when contrasted with the Navy carrier battle groups and their dependence upon very short-legged fighters that do not match up with the FFTTEA real-time system, and are enormously expensive to operate and support compared to bombers.

"I'm a fighter general that supports airpower in all its forms, both fighter and bomber capabilities. It is because the Air Force fears that if it pushes bomber growth, it will come at the expense of the F/A-22."

Loh's opinion is supported by General Horner, who asks if the need for the F-22 is diminished, given that the F-35 can carry bombs about as well but for less cost.[13] The F-35 is needed because of its international sales promise, but its very existence may reduce the number of F-22A/Bs procured to about one hundred aircraft.

Loh is also critical of past procurements of Low Density/High Demand (LD/HD) systems, Pentagonese for assets that are few in number but for which there are many requirements. These include most of the information-gathering aircraft and range from the Predator to the U-2.* The difficulty, besides the inadequate number of aircraft, is the strain the current high operational tempo puts on crew members. The true heroes of network-centric warfare are, of course, the crews who operate the scarce LD/HD systems,[14] some of whom have averaged more than 210 days a year away from home since the mid-1990s.

The Lockheed Martin fighters (F-22A/B and F-35 Joint Strike Fighter) are not the only bulges in the Air Force budget. Additional funds are required for the Boeing C-17, which did absolutely remarkable work but is still not available in sufficient quantities, and for a new tanker, the Boeing 767, to replace the older KC-135. Despite the C-17's able performance, it became obvious in Iraq that it would be highly desirable to have a transport with similar qualities to the C-17 but with stealth characteristics.

Yet even the costs of these programs fade against the realization that the space satellite systems are also aging and will need to be replaced with new, more technologically advanced systems over the next three decades.

Therefore, one of the major lessons learned by the Air Force was that the thinking and planning that went into the creation of the current mix of highly effective weapon systems will have to be intensified in the future, so as to make the budget not only accommodate the maintenance

---

* The complete list includes the Predator, Joint STARS, RC-135 Rivet Joint, HH-60, EC-130H Compass Call, EC-130E ABCCC, HC-130, E-3 AWACS, and U-2.

of what are now by definition "legacy" systems but also provide the wherewithal for their replacement.

LESSONS TO BE LEARNED BY THE PUBLIC AND BY CONGRESS

The American public and the American Congress can well learn some lessons from Operation Iraqi Freedom. The first is that previous investments in the defense of the United States have paid off handsomely and that cuts, particularly in such critical areas as the gathering of "humint"—human intelligence—were costly in the extreme, placing the United States at risk for such events as the terrorist attacks of September 11, 2001.

The second is that we are engaged in a global War against Terrorism. This war will be of indeterminate length, and it can be won only by maintaining over all our future enemies the same degree of advantage that we enjoyed in Iraq. To do so will require us to invest in our future defenses at a rate higher than has been the case for almost all of the two previous decades. The increase does not have to be of the dramatic nature of World War II, when defense spending consumed a substantial portion of the GDP. But defense spending does have to be a significantly higher percentage than is currently spent (about 3.4 percent), rising to perhaps 6 or 7 percent by 2008. After being sustained at that rate for a few years, the costs could easily drop back down to the 3–4 percent range—given that China or a revived Russia does not emerge as a potential foe.

The increase is necessary not only for new equipment. The United States must face the fact that transformation or not, an increase in the total number of regular service personnel is required, particularly for such elite branches as the special forces, SEALS, Rangers, Air Force Special Operations, and so on. It must be recognized that only so many special operation forces can be derived from the current force structure.

The military is currently far too small for the number of current operations plus the need for homeland defense. Any increase in operations will stretch our forces beyond the breaking point. Many of the existing forces are tired.

The special operation forces have been deployed extensively in Afghanistan and Iraq and elsewhere around the world. In addition, too many Guardsmen and Reservists have been called to duty too often for too long. The entire concept of a National Guard or Reserve force is impractical if the components of those forces are required to be constantly or even repeatedly on duty. In mid-July, Secretary of Defense Rumsfeld announced a call for a sweeping reorganization of the National Guard and

Reserve forces to address these needs. If they do find a·way to address the needs without an expansion of regular military forces, it will be a major administrative miracle.

The hard fact is that there must be at least a temporary increase in the total number of active-duty regular military service members to accommodate current and future requirements. Over time, the transformation of the military may permit a general reduction in the forces, perhaps to a point lower than the current level, but this will take years, and it is unfair to demand constant overseas combat duty from a relatively few people. In addition, there is every possibility that combat may be expanded, from obvious points of interest such as Syria, Iran, and North Korea to less probable areas in the Philippines, Indonesia, or South America. (General of the Army Omar Bradley stated that Korea was the wrong war in the wrong place at the wrong time. In fact, every war is just that— and we have to be prepared to accept it.)

The American public and the American Congress must react to the fact that the nation is at war with a vicious enemy and will be for many years to come. Congress must make the necessary legislative provisions to create the forces that will protect it, even though those provisions carry a cost with them. The alternative cost, failure to win the War against Terrorism, is so ghastly that it does not bear consideration.

And what might our future enemies have learned from Operation Iraqi Freedom? General Bernard Trainor makes an interesting speculation that the events leading up to Operation Iraqi Freedom may induce future opponents to wage "Lawfare" against us, using legal and international stratagems to prevent the United States from exercising its might.[15]

Future enemies almost certainly learned that there are only a few ways to deal with U.S. military might. The first has been adopted by North Korea, and that is the possession of and threat to use nuclear weapons. A second choice is to form an alliance with a strong country, perhaps Russia or China, and to operate under its protection. The third is to ally itself to and support asymmetric warfare such as terrorism, as Iran and Syria have done.

Overall, a new approach to American security is required. John Warden suggests that we must have an explicitly stated U.S. Grand Strategy that is equivalent in its simplicity and endurance as mutually assured destruction was during the Cold War. That strategy should have or address the following elements:

1. It is in the vital interest of the United States for the world to be sufficiently peaceful to allow unhindered commerce with the majority of states and peoples.

2. The United States has no desire for territorial expansion or exercising control over entities outside its borders.
3. The United States will only intervene in areas outside its borders when there is a clear and present danger to itself or to global peace and security.
4. The United States believes that the best route to peace for itself and the world is to maintain a military capability that far exceeds in effect that possessed by any other powers, individually or in combination.
    - It believes that this capability should be such as to make any rational would-be aggressor unlikely to do anything that would lead to a U.S. military response.
    - It believes that this capability makes it difficult or impossible for any aggressor to attack the United States directly.
    - It believes that this capability is difficult or impossible to defend against and that it provides very high probability of military success at very low cost.

The heart of this set of beliefs is the creation of a force that will be based on the current potential of the United States, which is widely believed to be at a beginning level and has an almost asymptotic growth curve ahead of it. The United States' security force should have the following characteristics:

1. It will capitalize on the unique American strengths in technology, organizational flexibility, and individual agility.
2. It will not only keep up with but also spur technological progress.
3. It will be a multipurpose force, able to defeat the most potent aggressors, separate third party combatants, and provide relief to disaster victims.
4. It will combine so many different types of offense and defense that it presents an overwhelming challenge to potential aggressors.
5. It will be able to accomplish its objectives with a minimum loss of life and a low risk of failure and at a fraction of the time and expense required today.
6. It will cost less than the current mix of forces and provide more security.
7. In essence, this will be a force that creates the future of warfare, rather than a force that reacts to it.[16]

Elaborate, extensive, long-running, and effective plans to stimulate the economies of the Muslim world will be equally important in fighting terrorism. While not a mission of the military, such a program is vital to the accomplishment of the military mission.

The sad truth is that the failure to create such a technologically advanced force will leave the United States with two alternatives, neither of which is acceptable. The first is accepting defeat by the terrorists. The second is the indiscriminate use of nuclear weapons to defeat terrorism on a grand scale but with incalculable collateral losses.

The creation of such a force is within the capability of the American economy, the answer to the question of whether it is within the capability of the American government depends upon the concept of transformation spreading to other agencies.

A GOVERNMENT TRANSFORMED

The ability of the United States to lead and to win the war on terrorism depends upon much greater integration and planning on the part of the national security apparatus. All of the elements of national power—diplomatic, economic, and military—must view the conflict not from the time the first bomb is dropped but from the time the President makes the first speech on the crisis until the time the last American leaves the country in question. We are at present using a World War II organizational structure in the environment of the twenty-first century. The State Department, the Department of Defense, the CIA, and the NSC simply do not plan together well until a crisis is ongoing. The Department of Defense is at the beginning of its massive transformation, and all of its allied organizations must undergo a similar change to cope with the realities of the twenty-first century. The focus must be shifted, so that all of these agencies work together equally well prior to a crisis and also after the crisis is passed. There must be no Turkey before the next war, nor any postwar instability after it.

Had this needed transformation taken place five years ago, the precrisis planning in regard to Iraq would have resulted in much greater postconflict success than we see today. Plans for restoring civil security, basic services, and political structure are just as important as plans for kill boxes for force application or logistics to keep forces flowing.

There has been a distinct shift in the nature of operations in the last ten years. Analysis of Desert Storm, Deliberate Force, Allied Force, Enduring Freedom, and now Iraqi Freedom shows that the air forces are increasingly the principal means of securing the defeat of the enemy during hostilities, while the preponderant task of the surface forces is administering the posthostility security mission.[17]

In practical terms, it falls to the lot of the Army to take on the additional planning, organizing, training, and equipping for the posthostility security mission, and this must be considered when examining the Army's force structure and budget requests. This is entirely unfair. The Army and the Marines should not be tasked with the permanent nation-building responsibility. Instead, an international group should be created to do this essential task.

CONCLUSION

Operation Iraqi Freedom was a brilliant military success, accomplished in spite of a series of what were either diplomatic disasters or simple foreign intransigence, based on resentment of U.S. primacy in economic and military matters.

Far more went right than went wrong, but it is important to recognize that this was the first time any nation in history had fought a war in so compelling a manner and that some errors were inevitable.

Far more important than anything else is the recognition that the methods used in Operation Iraqi Freedom can be immensely improved in the future, so that there may be a genuine Pax Americana established, one unmarred by terrorist threats or aggressive warfare by one state upon another.

APPENDIX ONE

WEAPON SYSTEMS

AIRCRAFT

Fairchild Republic A-10A/OA-10A Thunderbolt II
Service: U.S. Air Force
Mission: Battlefield support
Crew: 1
Engines: Two 9,065-lb static thrust General Electric TF34-GE-100 turbofans
Span: 57 ft. 6 in.
Length: 53 ft. 4 in.
Height: 14 ft. 8 in.
Weight, empty: 28,000 lbs.
Max. Armament: 16,000 lbs.
Max. Takeoff Weight: 51,000 lbs.
Max. Speed: 368 kts.
Cruise Speed: 300 kts.
Radius, with 9,500 lbs. of weapons: 250 nautical miles (nm), loitering for 1 hr 45 min.
Armament:
GAU-8 seven-barrel Gatling cannon firing up to 3,900 rounds/min.
Up to 16,000 lbs. of up to 6 AGM-65 Maverick unguided rocket pods, precision-guided bombs such as the GBU-10, GBU-12, and GBU-16
Entered service: 1976

Sixty rugged, reliable ground-support "Warthogs" accompanied American troops closely throughout the campaign. The aircraft's design, originally tooled with Warsaw Pact opponents in mind, features a high degree of redundancy and several hundred pounds of titanium armor. It attacked targets with a variety of AGM missiles like the AGM-65 Maverick and fired hundreds of thousands of 1-pound rounds of 30mm ammunition. (The depleted-uranium core of the 30mm round is controversial for its possible contribution to postwar illnesses.) Although many aircraft were struck by ground fire and several severely damaged by short-range SAMs, only one was lost and that pilot was rescued.

Lockheed Martin AC-130 Spectre
Service: U.S. Air Force
Mission: Close-support gunship

Crew: 13
Engines: Four 4,910-shp Rolls-Royce (formerly Allison) T56-A-15 turboprops
Span: 132 ft. 7 in.
Length: 99 ft.
Height: 38 ft. 6 in.
Weight, empty: 76,469 lbs.
Max. Takeoff Weight: 175,000 lbs.
Max. Speed: 325 kts.
Cruise Speed: 300 kts.
Range with max. payload: 1,780 nm
Armament:
2 20mm (3,000 rounds) or 1 25mm Gatling cannon
1 40mm Bofors cannon (256 rounds)
1 105mm howitzer (100 rounds)
Principal sensor: (U) AN/APQ-180 radar

This modified Hercules transport orbits its ground target while firing its array of small, medium, and large cannons. First used in the 1960s during the Vietnam War, this design has been upgraded several times. Radar and electrooptical sensors allow all-weather targeting, and the aircraft has several defensive subsystems to defeat ground-launched missiles. One of the most reliable combatant aircraft in Iraqi Freedom, the eight AC-130s achieved a 91 percent mission-capable rate while operating over armored formations and attacking targets in Baghdad itself. One AC-130 sank an Iraqi patrol craft after being vectored in by a P-3C Orion.

Bell Helicopter Textron AH-1W
Service: U.S. Marine Corps
Mission: Antitank helicopter
Crew: 2
Engines: Two 1,890-shp General Electric T700-GE-401 turboshafts
Rotor diameter: 48 ft.
Length, rotors turning: 58 ft.
Height: 14 ft. 3 in.
Weight, empty: 10,300 lbs.
Max. Takeoff Weight: 24,750 lbs.
Cruise Speed: 152 kts.
Range: 320 nm
Endurance: 3 hours
Armament:
1 M197 20mm three-barrel Gatling (750 rounds)
4 AGM-114 Hellfire or 4 BGM-71 TOW II antitank missiles
2.75-in. and 5-in. rocket pods
Entered service: 1986

Boeing MH-6/AH-6 "Little Bird"
Service: U.S. Army
Mission: Special operations support
Crew: 2
Engine: One 425-shp Allison 250-C30 turboshaft

Rotor diameter: 27 ft. 4 in.
Length, rotors turning: 32 ft. 1 in.
Height: 11 ft. 2½ in.
Weight, empty: 1,591 lbs.
Max. Takeoff Weight: 3,550 lbs.
Cruise Speed: 152 kts.
Range: 330 nm
Armament:
Precision-guided: 4 BGM-71 TOW II antitank missiles
2 AGM-114 Hellfire antitank missile pods
Nonprecision: 2 M260 2.75-in Hydra 70 rocket pods
2 M134 7.62mm six-barrel Gatling gun pods
2 12.7mm machine-gun pods
2 40mm Mk 19 grenade launchers
Self-defense: 2 FIM-92 Stinger AAM

Boeing (formerly McDonnell Douglas) AH-64A/D Apache and Apache Longbow

Service: U.S. Army
Mission: Antitank helicopter
Crew: 2
Engines: Two 1,890-shp General Electric T700-GE-701C turboshafts
Rotor diameter: 48 ft.
Length, rotors turning: 58 ft. 3 in.
Height: 16 ft. 3 in. to top of radome
Weight, empty: 11,800 lbs.
Max. Takeoff Weight: 22,280 lbs.
Cruise Speed: 139 kts.
Range: 220 kts.
Endurance: 3.3 hours
Armament:
1 M230 30mm Chain Gun (1,200 rounds)
Up to 16 AGM-114 Hellfire antitank missiles
2.75-in. and 5-in. rocket pods
Entered service: 1985 (A), 1998 (D)

Two hundred and fifty Apaches were deployed to the region: the TADS (AN/ASQ-170) and the PNVS (AN/AAQ-11) Northrop Grumman mmw Longbow radar.

Boeing (formerly McDonnell Douglas)/BAe Systems AV-8B Harrier II

Service: U.S. Marine Corps
Mission: VSTOL attack
Crew: 1
Engine: One 23,400-lb. static thrust Rolls-Royce F402-RR-408 Pegasus turbofan
Span: 30 ft. 4 in.
Length: 47 ft. 9 in. (II Plus variant)
Height: 11 ft. 7¾ in.
Weight, empty: 12,500 lbs.
Max. Armament: 13,235 lbs.

Max. Takeoff Weight: 29,750 lbs.
Max. Speed: 547 kts.
Radius, with 4 1,000-lb. bombs, 2 missiles, and 2 drop tanks: 401 nm
Armament:
GAU-12/U five-barrel 25mm Gatling cannon (300 rounds) inpod
4 precision-guided AGM-65 Maverick AGM
5 nonprecision 1,000-lb. Mk 83 or 15 Mk 82 500-lb. bombs
Principal sensor: (−8B+)AN/APG-65 I-band
Entered service: 1985 (−8B), 1993 (−8B+)

Boeing (formerly Rockwell) B-1B Lancer (or, more commonly, Bone)
Service: U.S. Air Force
Mission: Long-range conventional bomber
Crew: 4 (pilot, copilot, offensive and defensive systems officers)
Engines: Four 30,780-lb. static thrust General Electric F101-GE-102 turbofans
Span, swept: 73 ft.
Span, unswept: 137 ft.
Length: 146 ft.
Height: 34 ft.
Weight, empty: 192,000 lbs.
Max. Takeoff Weight: 477,000 lbs.
Max. Speed: Mach 1.2 at sea level
Cruise Speed: Mach 0.83 at low level
Range: "Intercontinental"
Armament:
Precision-guided: Up to 24 GBU-31 2,000-lb. JDAMs
AGM-154 Joint Stand-Off Weapon
Nonprecision: Up to 84 Mk 82 500-lb. bombs or 30 CBU-87/89 cluster and CBU-97 sensor-Fused weapons
Principal sensor: AN/APQ-164 I/J-band radar
Entered service: 1986

Northrop Grumman B-2A Spirit
Service: U.S. Air Force
Mission: Long-range stealth bomber for high-value targets
Crew: 2 (pilot, copilot)
Engines: Four 17,300-lb. static thrust General Electric F118-GE-100 turbofans
Span: 172 ft.
Length: 69 ft.
Height: 17 ft.
Weight, empty: 153,700 lbs.
Max. Takeoff Weight: 336,500 lbs.
Max. Speed: Mach 0.8
Cruise Speed: Mach 0.78 at 37,000 ft.
Range with 32,000-lb. Payload: 6,000 nm
Armament:
Precision-guided: Up to 16 GBU-31 2,000-lb. JDAM
8 GBU-37 4,700-lb deep-penetration near-precision
8 AGM-154 Joint Stand-Off Weapons

Nonprecision: Up to 80 Mk 82 500-lb. or 16 Mk 84 2,000-lb. bombs or 36 CBU-87/89 cluster and CBU-97 sensor-fused weapons
Principal sensor: AN/APQ-181 J-band radar
Entered service: 1997

Boeing B-52H Stratofortress
Service: U.S. Air Force
Mission: Long-range conventional and nuclear-weapon bomber
Crew: 5 (pilot, copilot, navigator, radar navigator, defensive systems officer)
Engines: Eight 17,000-lb. static thrust Pratt & Whitney TF33-P-3 turbofans
Span: 185 ft.
Length: 157 ft. 7 in.
Height: 40 ft. 8 in.
Weight, empty: 195,000 lbs.
Max. Takeoff Weight: 488,000 lbs.
Cruise Speed: Mach 0.77
Range: 8,811 nm
Armament:
Precision-guided: Up to 12 AGM-86B/C ALCM conventional cruise missiles GBU-31; 2,000-lb. JDAM
AGM-154 Joint Stand-Off Weapon
AGM-142 Have Nap AGM
Nonprecision: Up to 51 Mk 82 500-lb. or 18 Mk 84 2,000-lb. bombs
CBU-87/89 cluster and CBU-97 sensor-fused weapons
Entered service: 1962 (H)

Lockheed Martin C-130H Hercules
Service: U.S. Air Force
Mission: Theater tactical transport
Crew: 5
Engines: Four 4,591-eshp Rolls-Royce (formerly Allison) T56-A-15 turboprops
Span: 132 ft. 7 in.
Length: 97 ft. 9 in.
Height: 38 ft. 1 in.
Weight, empty: 81,000 lbs.
Max. Payload: 42,673 lbs.
Max. Takeoff Weight: 155,000 lbs.
Max. Speed: 325 kts.
Cruise Speed: 300 kts.
Range with max. Payload: 1,780 nm
Loadings: 5 463L standard freight pallets
92 ground troops
74 litter patients + 5 attendants
64 paratroopers
Entered service: 1958 (A), 1974 (H)

Lockheed Martin C-130J-30 Hercules
Service: Royal Australian Air Force
Mission: Theater tactical transport

Crew: 5
Engines: Four 6,000-eshp (running at 4,591 shp) Rolls-Royce-Allison AE2100D turboprops
Span: 132 ft. 7 in.
Length: 112 ft. 9 in.
Height: 38 ft. 10 in
Weight, empty: 79,291 lbs.
Max. Payload: 38,060 lbs.
Max. Takeoff Weight: 175,000 lbs.
Max. Speed: 347 kts.
Cruise Speed: 339 kts.
Max. Range: 2,968 nm
Loadings: 7 463L standard freight pallets
128 ground troops
97 litter patients + 2 attendants
92 paratroopers
Entered service: 2001

Boeing C-17 Globemaster III
Service: U.S. Air Force
Mission: Heavy-lifting, intercontinental, and intratheater transport
Crew: 3 (2 pilots, 1 loadmaster)
Engines: Four 40,440-lb. static thrust Pratt & Whitney F117-PW-100 turbofans
Span: 169 ft. 9 in.
Length: 173 ft. 11 in.
Height: 55 ft. 1 in.
Weight, empty: 277,000 lbs.
Max. Payload: 170,000 lbs.
Max. Takeoff Weight: 585,000 lbs.
Max. Speed: Mach 0.875
Cruise Speed: Mach 0.77
Range with 160,000-lb. Payload: 2,403 nm
Loadings: 18 463L standard freight pallets
1 M1A1 or -A2 Abrams heavy tank
154 ground troops
48 litter patients + 102 ambulatory patients
102 paratroopers
Entered service: 1995

Northrop Grumman C-2A(R) Greyhound
Service: U.S. Navy
Mission: Carrier Onboard Delivery (COD) transport
Crew: 4
Engines: Two 4,910-shp Allison T-56-A-425 turboprops
Span: 80 ft. 7 in.
Length: 56 ft. 10 in.
Height: 15 ft. 10½ in.
Weight, empty: 36,346 lbs.
Max. Payload: 10,000 lbs. (land-based), 8,600 lbs. carrier ops

Max. Takeoff Weight: 57,500 lbs.
Max. Speed: 310 kts.
Cruise Speed: 260 kts.
Range with 8,600-lb. Payload: 1,043 nm
Loadings: 12 litter patients
26 passengers
Entered service: 1987

Lockheed Martin C-5B Galaxy
Service: U.S. Air Force
Mission: Heavy-lifting intercontinental transport
Crew 3 (2 pilots, 1 loadmaster)
Engines: Four 41,000-lb. static thrust General Electric TF39-GE-1C turbofans
Span: 222 ft. 9 in.
Length: 247 ft. 10 in.
Height: 65 ft. 1 in.
Weight, empty: 374,000 lbs.
Max. Payload: 291,000 lbs.
Max. Takeoff Weight: 840,000 lbs.
Max. Speed: 497 kts.
Cruise Speed: 450 kts.
Range with max. Payload: 2,986 nm
Loadings: 36 463L standard freight pallets
2 M1A1 or -A2 Abrams heavy tanks
6 AH-64 Apache helicopters
3 CH-47 Chinook helicopters
75 passengers in upper deck + 275 in lower deck
270 troops
Entered service: 1971

Lockheed Martin C-141B Starlifter
Service: U.S. Air Force
Mission: Intercontinental transport and medevac
Crew 5–6 (2 pilots, 2 flight engineers, 1 loadmaster, 1 navigator added for air-drops). Medevac adds 2 flight nurses, 3 medical technicians
Engines: Four 20,250-lb. static thrust Pratt & Whitney TF33-P-7 turbofans
Span: 160 ft.
Length: 168 ft. 10 in.
Height: 39 ft. 3 in.
Weight, empty: 148,120 lbs.
Max. Payload: 90,880 lbs.
Max. Takeoff Weight: 343,000 lbs.
Max. Cruise Speed: 491 kts.
Normal Cruise Speed: 430 kts.
Range: 2,575 nm
Loadings: 13 463L standard freight pallets
200 troops
155 paratroopers

103 litters and 14 seats
Entered service: 1979

McDonnell Douglas C-9

Service: U.S. Air Force, U.S. Navy
Mission: Short-haul and medevac transport
Crew: 10 (2 pilots, crew chief, 2 attendants, 5 medical attendants)
Engines: Two 14,500-lb. static thrust Pratt & Whitney JT8D-9 turbofans
Span: 93 ft. 5 in.
Length: 119 ft. 4 in.
Height: 27 ft. 6 in.
Weight, empty: 59,706 lbs.
Max. Payload: 32,444 lbs.
Max. Takeoff Weight: 110,000 lbs.
Max. Speed: 501 kts.
Cruise Speed: 438 kts.
Range with max. Payload: 1,452 nm
Loadings: 40 patients
Entered service: 1973

Boeing CH-46E Sea Knight

Service: U.S. Navy, U.S. Marine Corps
Mission: Fleet replenishment and troop movement
Crew: 4
Engines: Two 1,770-shp General Electric T58-GE-16 turboshafts
Rotor diameter (each): 51 ft.
Length, rotors turning: 84 ft. 4 in.
Height: 16 ft. 8 in.
Weight, empty: 15,537 lbs.
Max. Payload: 5,166 lbs.
Max. Takeoff Weight: 24,300 lbs.
Cruise Speed: 145 kts.
Range: 132 nm
Loadings: 22 troops + 2 aerial gunners
15 litter patients + 2 attendants
Entered service: 1962 (original), 1978 (D/E)

Boeing CH-47 Chinook

Service: U.S. Army
Mission: Heavy-lifting support
Crew: 4
Engines: Two 3,750-shp Textron Lycoming T55-L-712 turboshafts
Rotor diameter (each): 60 ft.
Length, rotors turning: 84 ft. 4 in.
Height: 18 ft. 8 in.
Weight, empty: 22,452 lbs.
Max. Payload (internal): 14,356 lbs.
Max. Takeoff Weight: 50,000 lbs.
Cruise Speed: 138 kts.

Mission radius (internal load only): 100 nm
Loadings: 44 troops
24 litter patients + 2 attendants
Entered service: 1962 (original), 1984 (D)
   Chinooks were used to deploy the 101st Air Assault Division to northern Iraq.

Sikorsky CH-53D Sea Stallion

Service: U.S. Marine Corps
Mission: Medium-lifting deployment and resupply
Crew: 4
Engines: Two 3,925-shp General Electric T64-GE-413 turboshafts
Rotor diameter: 72 ft. 3 in.
Length, rotors turning: 88 ft. 3 in.
Height: 24 ft. 11 in.
Weight, empty: 23,600 lbs.
Max. Payload (internal): 8,000 lbs.
Max. Takeoff Weight: 42,000 lbs.
Cruise Speed: 160 kts.
Mission radius (internal load only): 578 nm
Loadings: 37 troops
24 litter patients + 4 attendants
Entered in service: 1966

Sikorsky CH-53E Super Stallion

Service: U.S. Marine Corps
Mission: Heavy-lifting deployment and resupply
Crew: 4
Engines: Three 4,360-shp General Electric T64-GE-416 turboshafts
Rotor diameter: 79 ft.
Length, rotors turning: 99 ft. 3 in.
Height: 28 ft. 4 in.
Weight, empty: 32,226 lbs.
Max. Payload (internal): 30,000 lbs.
Max. Takeoff Weight: 69,750 lbs.
Cruise Speed: 138 kts.
Mission radius (internal load only): 540 nm
Loadings: 55 troops
24 litter patients + 2 attendants
Entered in service: 1981

Northrop Grumman E-2C Hawkeye

Service: U.S. Navy
Mission: Carrier-based Airborne Early Warning
Crew: 5
Engines: Two 5,100-eshp Allison T56-A-427 turboprops
Span: 80 ft. 7 in.
Length: 57 ft. 8¾ in.
Height: 18 ft. 3¾ in.
Weight, empty: 40,484 lbs.

Max. Takeoff Weight: 54,426 lbs.
Max. Cruise Speed: 374 kts.
Cruise Speed: 259 kts.
Ferry Range: 1,541 nm
Principal sensor: AN/APS-145 radar
Entered service: 1971

    AEW missions were carried out by the E-2C squadrons embarked on the six Navy carriers deployed in support of Operation Iraqi Freedom. VAW-117, deployed in the Persian Gulf onboard USS Nimitz toward the end of the war, is equipped with the USG-3 system. E-2s are the only airborne nodes in the Cooperative Engagement Capability (CEC) system. CEC allows all sensor information to be seen by all "shooters" as a single picture.

Boeing E-3A Sentry
Service: U.S. Air Force
Mission: Airborne Warning and Control System (AWACS)
Crew: 21 (4 flight, 17 mission specialists)
Engines: Two 21,000-lb. static thrust Pratt & Whitney TF33-PW-100 turbofans
Span: 145 ft. 9 in.
Length: 152 ft. 11 in.
Height: 41 ft. 9 in.
Weight, empty: 171,000 lbs.
Max. Takeoff Weight: 347,000 lbs.
"Optimized" Cruise Speed: Mach 0.78
Cruise Speed: 259 kts.
Range: 5,000 + nm
Endurance, unrefueled: 8 hours
Principal sensor: AN/APY-2 radar
Entered service: 1991

Northrop Grumman E-8C Joint STARS
Service: U.S. Air Force
Mission: Airborne ground surveillance and battle management
Crew: 21
Engines: Two 18,000-lb. static thrust Pratt & Whitney JT3D-3B turbofans
Span: 145 ft. 9 in.
Length: 152 ft. 11 in.
Height: 42 ft. 6 in.
Weight, empty: 171,000 lbs.
Max. Takeoff Weight: 336,000 lbs.
Max. Speed: Mach 0.84
Cruise Speed: 259 kts.
Endurance with one refueling: 20 hours
Principal sensor: AN/APY-3 radar
Entered service: 1991

Northrop Grumman EA-6B Prowler
Service: U.S. Navy
Mission: Carrier-based Electronic Warfare

Crew: 4
Engines: Two 10,400-lb. static thrust Pratt & Whitney J52-P408 turbofans
Span: 53 ft.
Length: 59 ft. 10 in.
Height: 16 ft. 8 in.
Weight, empty: 32,162 lbs.
Max. Takeoff Weight: 61,500 lbs.
Max. Speed: 532 kts.
Cruise Speed: 419 kts.
Range, max. external load: 955 nm
Principal sensor: AN/ALQ-99F
Entered service: 1972

Lockheed Martin EP-3 Aries II
Service: U.S. Navy
Mission: Signals intelligence (SIGINT) reconnaissance
Crew: 22
Engines: Four 4,900-shp Rolls-Royce (formerly Allison) T56-A-14 turboprops
Span: 99 ft. 6 in
Length: 116 ft. 7 in.
Height: 33 ft. 7 in.
Weight, empty: 76,469 lbs.
Max. Takeoff Weight: 139,760 lbs.
Max. Speed: 411 kts.
Cruise Speed: 328 kts.
Range with 3 hours on station: 1,346 nm
Entered service: 1990

Lockheed Martin EC-130 Commando Solo
Service: U.S. Air Force
Mission: Psychological warfare broadcasting
Crew: 11
Engines: Four 4,910-shp Rolls-Royce (formerly Allison) T56-A-15 turboprops
Span: 132 ft. 7 in.
Length: 99 ft.
Height: 38 ft. 6 in.
Weight, empty: 76,469 lbs.
Max. Takeoff Weight: 175,000 lbs.
Max. Speed: 325 kts.
Cruise Speed: 300 kts.
Range with max. Payload: 1,780 nm

Boeing (formerly McDonnell Douglas) F/A-18C/D Hornet
Service: U.S. Navy, U.S. Marine Corps
Mission: Multirole attack and fighter
Crew: 1 (C), 2 (D)
Engines: Two 17,700-lb. static thrust General Electric F404-GE-402 turbofans
Span: 40 ft. 5 in.
Length: 56 ft.

193

Height: 15 ft. 4 in.
Weight, empty: 23,832 lbs.
Normal Payload: 13,700 lbs.
Max. Takeoff Weight: 51,900 lbs.
Max. Speed: Mach 1.8
Radius, attack: 470 nm
Armament:
Precision-guided: AIM-9 Sidewinder AAM
AIM-120 AMRAAM AAM
AGM-65 Maverick AGM
AGM-84D Harpoon ASM
AGM-84E SLAM AGM
AGM-88 HARM antiradar missile
AGM-154 JSOW AGM
GBU-32 JDAM 1,000-lb. bomb
GBU-10 Paveway II 1,985-lb. bomb
Unguided: Mk 82 500-lb., Mk 83 1,000-lb., or Mk 84 2,000-lb. bombs
M61 six-barrel 20mm Gatling cannon
Principal sensor: AN/APG-65/-73
Entered service: 1989

Boeing F/A-18E/F Super Hornet
Service: U.S. Navy, U.S. Marine Corps
Mission: Multirole attack and fighter
Crew: 1 (E), 2 (F)
Engines: Two 22,000-lb. static thrust General Electric F414-GE-400 turbofans
Span: 44 ft. 11 in.
Length: 60 ft. 4 in.
Height: 16 ft.
Weight, empty: 30,591 lbs.
Max. Payload: 17,750 lbs.
Max. Takeoff Weight: 66,000 lbs.
Max. Speed: Mach 1.8
Radius, attack: 660 nm
Armament:
Precision-guided: AIM-9 Sidewinder AAM
AIM-7 Sparrow AAM
AIM-120 AMRAAM AAM
AGM-65 Maverick AGM
AGM-84D Harpoon ASM
AGM-84E SLAM AGM
AGM-88 HARM antiradar missile
AGM-154 JSOW AGM
GBU-32 JDAM 1,000-lb. bomb
GBU-10 Paveway II 1,985-lb. bomb
Unguided: Mk 82 500-lb., Mk 83 1,000-lb., or Mk 84 2,000-lb. bombs
M61 six-barrel 20mm Gatling cannon
Principal sensor: AN/APG-73
Entered service: 2001

Northrop Grumman F-14D Tomcat ("Bombcat")
Service: U.S. Navy
Mission: Multirole attack and fighter
Crew: 2
Engines: Two 27,000-lb. static thrust General Electric F110-GE-400 turbofans
Span, swept: 38 ft. 2½ in.
Span, unswept: 64 ft. 1½ in.
Length: 62 ft. 8 in.
Height: 16 ft.
Weight, empty: 43,735 lbs.
Normal Payload: 14,500 lbs.
Max. Takeoff Weight: 74,349 lbs.
Max. Speed: Mach 2.38
Cruise Speed: Mach 0.78
Range: 1,600 nm
Armament:
Precision-guided: AIM-9 Sidewinder AAM
AIM-54 Phoenix AAM
AIM-7 Sparrow AAM
AIM-120 AMRAAM AAM
GBU-32 JDAM 1,000-lb. bomb
GBU-10 Paveway II 1,985-lb. bomb
Unguided: Mk 82 500-lb., Mk 83 1,000-lb., or Mk 84 2,000-lb. bombs
M61 six-barrel 20mm Gatling cannon
Principal sensor: AN/APG-65/-73
Entered service: 1972

Boeing F-15C Eagle
Service: U.S. Air Force
Mission: Air-superiority fighter
Crew: 1
Engines: Two 25,000-lb. static thrust Pratt & Whitney F100-PW-220 turbofans
Span: 42 ft. 9¾ in.
Length: 63 ft. 9½ in.
Height: 18 ft. 5½ in.
Weight, empty: 28,600 lbs.
Max. Takeoff Weight: 68,000 lbs.
Max. Speed: Mach 2.5
Cruise Speed: Mach 0.75
Range: 686 nm
Armament:
Precision-guided: AIM-9 Sidewinder AAM
AIM-7 Sparrow AAM
AIM-120 AMRAAM AAM
Unguided: M61 six-barrel 20mm Gatling cannon
Principal sensor AN/APG-63/-70
Entered service: 1979

Boeing F-15E Strike Eagle
Service: U.S. Air Force
Mission: Dual-role fighter
Crew: 2
Engines: Two 29,000-lb. static thrust Pratt & Whitney F100-PW-229 turbofans
Span: 42 ft. 9¾ in.
Length: 63 ft. 9½ in.
Height: 18 ft. 5½ in.
Weight, empty: 45,000 lbs.
Normal Payload: 23,000 lbs.
Max. Takeoff Weight: 81,000 lbs.
Max. Speed: Mach 2.5
Cruise Speed: Mach 0.75
Range: 686 nm
Armament:
Precision-guided: AIM-9 Sidewinder AAM
AIM-120 AMRAAM AAM
AGM-65 Maverick AGM
AGM-84D Harpoon ASM
AGM-84E SLAM AGM
AGM-88 HARM antiradar missile
AGM-130 AGM
AGM-154 JSOW AGM
GBU-32 JDAM 1,000-lb. bomb
EGBU-15 glide bomb
GBU-10 Paveway II 1,985-lb. bomb
Unguided: Mk 82 500-lb. or Mk 84 2,000-lb. bombs
M61 six-barrel 20mm Gatling cannon
Principal sensor: AN/APG-70
Entered service: 1989

Lockheed Martin F-16C Fighting Falcon
Service: U.S. Air Force
Mission: Dual-role fighter
Crew: 1
Engine: One 29,000-lb. static thrust Pratt & Whitney F100-PW-229 or General Electric F110-GE-129 turbofan
Span: 32 ft. 9 in.
Length: 49 ft. 5 in.
Height: 16 ft. 9 in.
Weight, empty: 18,917 lbs.
Normal Payload: 15,900 lbs.
Max. Takeoff Weight: 42,300 lbs.
Max. Speed: Mach 2
Range: 677 nm
Armament:
Precision-guided: AIM-9 Sidewinder AAM
AIM-120 AMRAAM AAM
AGM-65 Maverick AGM

AGM-88 HARM antiradar missile
AGM-154 JSOW AGM
GBU-31 JDAM 2,000-lb. bomb
Unguided: Mk 82 500-lb. or Mk 84 2,000-lb. bombs
M61 six-barrel 20mm Gatling cannon
Principal sensor: AN/APG-68(V)
Entered service: 1989

Lockheed Martin F-117A Nighthawk
Service: U.S. Air Force
Mission: Stealth attack
Crew: 1
Engines: Two 9,040-lb. static thrust General Electric F404-GE-F1D2 turbofans
Span: 43 ft. 4 in.
Length: 65 ft. 11 in.
Height: 12 ft. 5 in.
Weight, empty: 29,500 lbs.
Normal Payload: 5,000 lbs.
Max. Takeoff Weight: 52,500 lbs.
Max. Speed: Mach 0.9
Range: 500 nm
Armament:
Precision-guided: GBU-31 JDAM 2,000-lb. bomb
GBU-27A penetrating bomb
EGBU-15 glide bomb
Entered service: 1989

Boeing KC-10 Extender
Service: U.S. Air Force
Mission: Tanker/transport
Crew: 3–6 (pilot, copilot, engineer + 3 refueling crew)
Engines: Three 52,500-lb. static thrust General Electric CF6-50C2 turbofans
Span: 165 ft. 4 in.
Length: 181 ft. 7 in.
Height: 58 ft. 1 in.
Weight, empty: 241,027 lbs.
Max. Payload:
    As tanker: 356,065 lbs.
    As transport: 169,409 lbs.
Max. Takeoff Weight: 590,000 lbs.
Max. Speed: 530 kts.
Cruise Speed: 490 kts.
Range with max. Payload/Cargo: 3,797 nm
Range for refueling, 200,000 lbs. off-load: 1,910 nm
Loadings: 17 463L pallets + 75 passengers
27 463L pallets
Entered service: 1982

Lockheed Martin KC-130 Hercules
Service: U.S. Marine Corps
Mission: Tactical tanker/transport
Crew: 6 (2 pilots, operator, flight engineer, first mechanic, loadmaster)
Engines: Four 4,591-eshp Rolls-Royce (formerly Allison) T56-A-15 turboprops
Span: 132 ft. 7 in.
Length: 97 ft. 9 in.
Height: 38 ft. 4 in.
Weight, empty: 83,300 lbs.
Max. Payload: 42,673 lbs.
Max. Takeoff Weight: 175,000 lbs.
Max. Speed: 315 kts.
Range:
    As tanker carrying 45,000 lbs. of fuel: 1,000 nm
    As transport carrying 38,258 lbs.: 2,875 nm
Loadings: 5 463L standard freight pallets
3,600 U.S. gallon fuel bladder
92 ground troops
74 litter patients + 5 attendants
64 paratroopers
Entered service: 1956

Boeing KC-135R Stratotanker
Service: U.S. Air Force
Mission: Tanker/transport
Crew: 4 (pilot, copilot, navigator, boom operator)
Engines: Four 22,000-lb. static thrust CFM International F108-CF-100 turbofans
Span: 130 ft. 10 in.
Length: 134 ft. 6 in.
Height: 38 ft. 4 in.
Weight, empty: 98,466 lbs.
Max. Payload:
    As tanker: 203,288 lbs.
    As transport: 89,000 lbs.
Max. Takeoff Weight: 322,500 lbs.
Max. Speed: 508 kts.
Cruise Speed: 461 kts.
Range for refueling, 120,000 lbs. off-load: 1,000 nm
Loadings: 17 463L pallets & 75 passengers
27 463L pallets
Entered service: 1982

Lockheed Martin MC-130H Combat Talon
Service: U.S. Air Force
Mission: Special operations
Crew: 7
Engines: Four 4,910-shp Rolls-Royce (formerly Allison) T56-A-15 turboprops
Span: 132 ft. 7 in.
Length: 99 ft.

Height: 38 ft. 6 in.
Weight, empty: 72,892 lbs.
Max. Takeoff Weight: 155,000 lbs.
Max. Speed: 325 kts.
Cruise Speed: 300 kts.
Range with max. Payload: 1,780 nm
Principal sensor: AN/APQ-170 radar
Loadings: 77 troops
57 litter patients
52 paratroopers
Entered service: 1966 (E), 1991 (H)

Boeing MH-47E Chinook SOF
Service: U.S. Army
Mission: Special operations
Crew: 3
Engines: Two 4,110-shp Textron Lycoming T55-L-714 turboshafts
Rotor diameter (each): 60 ft.
Length, rotors turning: 98 ft. 11 in.
Height: 18 ft. 9 in.
Weight, empty: 26,094 lbs.
Max. Payload (internal): 14,356 lbs.
Max. Takeoff Weight: 54,000 lbs.
Cruise Speed: 138 kts.
Mission radius with 12,000-lb. payload: 300 nm
Loadings: 44 troops
24 litter patients + 2 attendants
Principal sensor: AN/APQ-174 J-band radar
Entered service: 1990

Sikorsky MH-53J Pave Low
Service: U.S. Air Force
Mission: SOF and combat SAR
Crew: 6
Engines: Two 4,330-shp General Electric T64-GE-100 turboshafts
Rotor diameter: 72 ft. 3 in.
Length, rotors turning: 88 ft. 3 in.
Height: 24 ft. 11 in.
Weight, empty: 33,226 lbs.
Max. Takeoff Weight: 54,000 lbs.
Cruise Speed: 143 kts.
Range: 548 nm
Loadings: 38 troops
Entered service: 1988 (J)

Sikorsky HH-60G/MH-60 Pave Hawk
Service: U.S. Air Force
Mission: Combat SAR and SOF
Crew: 3–4

199

Engines: Two 1,620-shp General Electric T700-GE-701C turboshafts
Rotor diameter: 53 ft. 8 in.
Length, rotors turning: 64 ft. 10 in.
Height: 16 ft. 10 in.
Weight, empty: 12,330 lbs.
Max. Takeoff Weight: 22,000 lbs.
Max. Speed: 150 kts.
Range: 324 nm
Endurance: 2.33 hours
Armament: 2 M134 7.62mm three-barrel Miniguns
Entered service: 1987

Bell Helicopter Textron OH-58D
Service: U.S. Army
Mission: Scout and light attack
Crew: 2
Engine: One 750-shp Allison T703-AD-700 turboshaft
Rotor diameter: 35 ft.
Length, rotors turning: 42 ft. 2 in.
Height: 12 ft. 9½ in.
Weight, empty: 2,825 lbs.
Max. Takeoff Weight: 4,500 lbs.
Max. Speed: 128 kts.
Cruise Speed: 110 kts.
Range: 300 nm
Endurance: 3 hours
Armament:
1 M197 20mm three-barrel Gatling (750 rounds)
4 AGM-114 Hellfire antitank missiles or 4 FIM-92 Stinger AAM
2 Hydra 70 2.75-in. rocket pods
Entered service: 1986

Lockheed Martin P-3C Orion
Service: U.S. Navy
Mission: Antisubmarine and maritime surveillance
Crew: 11
Engines: Four 4,900-shp Rolls-Royce (formerly Allison) T56-A-14 turboprops
Span: 99 ft. 6 in.
Length: 116 ft. 7 in.
Height: 33 ft. 7 in.
Weight empty: 61,491 lbs.
Max. Weapons Load: 20,000 lbs.
Max. Takeoff Weight: 139,760 lbs.
Max. Speed: 411 kts.
Cruise Speed: 328 kts.
Range with 3 hours on station: 1,346 nm
Armament:
AGM-84D Harpoon antiship cruise missile
AGM-84E SLAM AGM

AGM-65 Maverick AGM
Mk-46 antisubmarine torpedo
Mk-50 ASW torpedo
2 × 2,000-lb. or 4 × 1,000-lb. mines
Mk 82 500-lb. bombs
Principal sensor: AN/APS-137 I-band radar
Entered service: 1969

General Atomics RQ-1A/MQ-1 Predator A
Service: U.S. Air Force
Mission: Unmanned reconnaissance
Engine: One 100-hp Rotax 914 four-cylinder piston engine
Span: 48 ft. 9 in.
Length: 28 ft. 9 in.
Weight, empty: not available
Payload: 450 lbs.
Max. Takeoff Weight: 2,250 lbs.
Ceiling: 25,000 ft.
Range: 400 nm
Endurance: 24 hours
Armament: 2 AGM-114 Hellfire antitank missiles

AAI RQ-2B Pioneer
Service: U.S. Marine Corps
Mission: Unmanned reconnaissance
Engine: One 26-hp Sachs SF2-350 two-cylinder piston engine
Span: 17 ft.
Length: 14 ft.
Weight, empty: not available
Payload: 75 lbs.
Max. Takeoff Weight: 452 lbs.
Ceiling: 15,000 ft.
Endurance: 5 hours

Northrop Grumman RQ-4 Global Hawk
Service: U.S. Air Force
Mission: Unmanned High-Altitude, Long-Endurance (HALE) reconnaissance
Engine: One 7,600-lb. static thrust Rolls-Royce-Allison AE 3007H turbofan
Span: 116 ft.
Length: 44 ft.
Height: 15 ft. 3 in.
Weight, empty: 9,200 lbs.
Payload: 2,000 lbs.
Max. Takeoff Weight: 25,600 lbs.
Ceiling: 65,000 ft.
Endurance: 24–36 hours

AAI RQ-5 Hunter
Service: U.S. Marine Corps
Mission: Unmanned reconnaissance
Engine: Two 68-hp four-cylinder piston engines
Span: 29 ft.
Length: 23 ft.
Weight, empty: not available
Payload: 250 lbs.
Max. Takeoff Weight: 1,600 lbs.
Ceiling: 15,000–20,000 ft.
Endurance: 11.6 hours

AAI RQ-7A Shadow 200
Service: U.S. Army
Mission: Unmanned reconnaissance
Engine: One Rotax 914 four-cylinder piston engine
Span: 12 ft. 9 in.
Length: 11 ft.
Weight, empty: not available
Payload: 56 lbs.
Max. Takeoff Weight: 327 lbs.
Ceiling: 15,000 ft.
Endurance: 5–6 hours

Lockheed Martin S-3B Viking
Service: U.S. Navy
Mission: Multipurpose surveillance/targeting/ECM/SAR/tanker
Crew 2–4
Engines: Two 9,275-lb. static thrust General Electric TF34-GE-400B turbofans
Span: 68 ft. 8 in.
Length: 53 ft. 4 in.
Height: 22 ft. 9 in.
Weight, empty: 29,000 lbs.
Weapons Load: 3,958 lbs.
Max. Weight 52,539 lbs.
Max. Speed: 450 kts.
Cruise Speed: 370 kts.
Range: 2,300 nm
Armament:
AGM-65 Maverick AGM
AGM-84D Harpoon ASM
AGM-84E SLAM
Entered service: 1982

Sikorsky SH-60 Seahawk
Service: U.S. Navy
Mission: Medium lifting/utility/assault
Crew: 3 (pilot, copilot, sensor operator)
Engines: Two 1,870-shp General Electric T700-GE-701C turboshafts

Rotor diameter: 53 ft. 8 in.
Length, rotors turning: 64 ft. 10 in.
Height: 16 ft. 10 in.
Weight, empty: 13,648 lbs.
Max. Takeoff Weight: 21,110 lbs. (ASW)
Max. Speed: 145 kts.
Range: 380 nm
Endurance: 3.5–6 hours
Armament: 3 Mk-46 or Mk-50 torpedoes
Entered service: 1983

Sikorsky UH-1N/Model 212 Huey
Service: U.S. Air Force, Navy, Marine Corps
Mission: Utility
Crew 2 (pilot, copilot)
Engines: Two 1,250-shp Pratt & Whitney Canada T400-CP-400 turboshafts
Rotor diameter: 48 ft.
Length, rotors turning: 41 ft. 10¾ in.
Height: 13 ft. 5 in.
Weight, empty: 5,997 lbs.
Max. Takeoff Weight: 10,500 lbs.
Cruise Speed: 100 kts.
Range: 231 nm
Armament:
GAU-17 7.62mm three-barrel Minigun
2.75-in. rocket pods
GAU-16 0.50-cal. machine gun
M240 7.62mm lightweight machine gun
Entered service: 1971

Sikorsky UH-60L Blackhawk
Service: U.S. Army
Mission: Assault transport
Crew: 3 (pilot, copilot, crew chief)
Engines: Two 1,870-shp General Electric T700-GE-701C turboshafts
Rotor diameter: 53 ft. 8 in.
Length, rotors turning: 64 ft. 10 in
Height: 16 ft. 10 in.
Weight, empty: 11,605 lbs.
Max. Takeoff Weight: 17,527 lbs. (22,000 lbs. alternate max.)
Max. Speed: 159 kts.
Cruise Speed: 112 kts.
Range: 1,150 nm
Endurance: 2.33 hours
Armament: 2 M134 7.62-mm three-barrel Miniguns
Entered service: 1989 (L)

Lockheed Martin U-2 Dragon Lady
Service: U.S. Air Force
Mission: High-altitude reconnaissance
Crew: 1
Engine: One 19,000-lb. static thrust General Electric F118-GE-101 turbofan
Span: 103 ft.
Length: 63 ft.
Height: 16 ft.
Weight, empty: 14,300 lbs.
Max. Takeoff Weight: 41,000 lbs.
Max. Speed: 413 kts.
Cruise Speed: 373 kts.
Range: 3,913 nm
Endurance: 10 + hours
Principal sensor: ASARS-2
Entered service: 1956

MISSILES AND BOMBS

AGM-114 Hellfire
Variants: AGM-114B/C, AGM-114F, AGM-114K, AGM-114L
Span (all variants): 1 ft. 1 in.
Diameter (all variants): 7 in.
Weight:
    AGM-114B/C/K: 100 lbs.
    AGM-114F: 107 lbs.
    AGM-114L: 110 lbs.
Speed: Mach 1.3
Range:
    AGM-114B/C: 8,000 meters
    AGM-114K: 7,000 meters
    AGM-114L: 9,000 meters
Warhead:
    18 lbs. shaped-charge
    20 lbs. tandem antiarmor
    Thermobaric
Number used in OIF: 562

    From NAVAIR China Lake Public Affairs

    Marine assault units in Operation Iraqi Freedom are packing Hellfire missiles equipped with a new metal-augmented-charge (MAC) warhead designed, developed, and built at Naval Air Systems Command (NAVAIR) China Lake [in less than a year].

    Hellfire is used by the Army, Navy, and Marines. The current Hellfire version—AGM-114 Hellfire II—has expanded its original antiarmor target set to include close-air support, urban assault, and antiship missions.

    Unlike conventional warheads, which have a sharp pressure spike that decays rapidly, the MAC has a sustained pressure wave. That pressure propagates throughout a structure to extend the lethal effects of the warhead detonation.

AGM-65A-K Maverick
Span: 2 ft. 4 in.
Diameter: 1 ft.
Length: 8 ft.
Weight: 462 lbs. (AGM-65A/B/D/H)
Warhead:
    WDU-20/B 125-lb. shaped-charge
    AGM-65E/F/G/K: 637–70 lbs.
    WDU-24/B 300-lb. blast fragmentation
Speed: Mach 1.3
Range: 8 nm
Number used in OIF: 918

AGM-84H SLAM (ER)
Span: 3 ft.
Diameter 1 ft. 1.5 in
Length: 14 ft. 4 in.
Weight: 1,600 lbs.
Warhead: 800-lb. penetrating blast-fragmentation
Speed: Mach 0.85
Range: 150 nm
Number used in OIF: 3

AGM-86C/D CALCM
Span: 12 ft.
Diameter: 2 ft. 0.5 in.
Length: 20 ft. 9 in.
Weight: 3,150 lbs. (AGM-86C)
Warhead:
    2,000-lbs. (Block 0)
    3,000-lb. (Block 1) blast-fragmentation
    -D hard-target penetrator
Speed: 478 kts.
Range: 600 nm
Number used in OIF: 153

AGM-88
Span: 3 ft. 8 in.
Diameter: 10 in.
Length: 13 ft. 8 in.
Weight: 800 lbs.
Warhead: 146-lbs blast-fragmentation WDU-21/B or WDU-37/B
Speed: Mach 2 +
Range: >8 nm
Number used in OIF: 408

AGM-130
Fin Span: 4 ft. 11 in.
Diameter: 1 ft. 6 in.
Length: 12 ft. 10.5 in.
Weight: 2,910 lbs.
Warhead: 2,000-lb. (B) Mk 84 bomb or (C) BLU-109/B penetrator
Range: 21.6 nm
Number used in OIF: 4

AGM-154 SOW
Span: 8 ft. 10 in
Diameter: 1 ft. 1.1 in.
Length: 14 ft.
Weight: 1,065 lbs.
Warhead: 2,000 lbs. (A/D) 145 BLU-97 submunitions, (C/E) BROACH penetrator
Range:
    Low-altitude: 14.6 nm
    High-altitude: 34.8 nm
Number used in OIF: 253

BGM-71D/E/F TOW
Span (all variants): 1 ft. 5.7 in.
Diameter (all variants): 6 in.
Length: 5 ft. 0.2 in.
Weight: 47.5 lbs. BGM-71D
Warhead: 13 lb. shaped-charge
    50-lb. BGM-71E/F
    13.5-lb. explosively formed projectile
Speed: 300 mps
Range: 3,750 m

BGM-109C/D Tomahawk
Variant: Block III TLAM
Span: 8 ft. 9 in.
Diameter: 1 ft. 8.4 in.
Length: 18 ft. 3 in., with booster 20 ft. 6 in.
Weight: 2,900 lbs. (missile only); 3,500 lbs. (with booster)
Warhead: 1,000-lb. WDU-25/B unitary or bomblet
    Block III: 700 lbs.
Speed: 478 kts.
Range: 675 nm
    Block III: 870 nm
Number used in OIF: 802

FGM-148 Javelin
Fin Span: 1 ft. 3 in.
Diameter: 5 in.
Length: 3 ft. 6.6 in.
Weight: 26.1 lbs.

Warhead: 18.6-lb. shaped-charge
Range: 2,500 m

MGM-140/164A ATACMS/ATACMS Block II
Fin Span: 4 ft. 7 in.
Diameter: 2 ft.
Length: 13 ft.
Weight: 3,687 lbs. (MGM-140A); 2,910 lbs. (MGM-140B)
Warhead: 275 lbs. 275 M74 APAM submunition
Range: More than 92 nm (Block I), 162 nm (MGM-140B)

MIM-104C/D PATRIOT PAC-2
Fin Span: 3 ft.
Diameter: 1 ft. 4 in.
Length: 17 ft.
Weight: 1,984 lbs.
Warhead: 200-lb. blast-fragmentation with proximity fuse
Range: 86 nm

MIM-104C/D PATRIOT PAC-3
Fin Span: 1 ft. 7.7 in.
Diameter: 1 ft. 4 in.
Length: 17 ft. 0.7 in.
Weight: 688 lbs.
Warhead 161-lb. hit-to-kill blast-fragmentation with proximity fuse
Range: 8.1 nm

MLRS M26/M26A1 Rocket
Diameter: 9 in.
Length: 13 ft.
Weight: 677 lbs.
Warhead: 340 lbs., 644 M77 dual purpose grenades (M26)
    518 M77 (M26A1)
Range: 17.3 nm (M26), 24.3 nm (M26A1 ERR)

GBU-10/B Paveway I/II
Weight: 1,985 lbs.
Warhead: Mk 84 bomb; -10H/B has BLU-109/B (I-2000) earth-penetrator with KMU-351/B guidance kit
Range: 8 nm
Circular error probable (CEP): 9m
Number used in OIF: 236

GBU-12/B Paveway I/II
Weight: 603 lbs.
Warhead: Mk 82 bomb with KMU-388/B guidance kit
Range: 5.2 nm
Circular error probable (CEP): 9m
Number used in OIF: 7,114 (by far the most of any individual PGM)

GBU-16/B Paveway II
Weight: 1,000 lbs.
Warhead: Mk 83 bomb with KMU-455/B guidance kit
Range: 8 nm
Circular error probable (CEP): 9m
Number used in OIF: 1,223

GBU-24/B Paveway III LLLGB (Low-Level Laser Guided Bomb)
Weight: 2,350 lbs.
Warhead: MK 84 bomb
   GBU-24A/B/E: BLU-109/B penetrator
   GBU-24C/D: BLU-116/B Advanced Unitary Penetrator (AUP)
Range: More than 10 nm
Number used in OIF: 24

GBU-27/B Paveway III for F-117
EGBU-27 GPS/LGB similar with GPS
Weight: 2,170 lbs.
Range: More than 10 nm
Number used in OIF (GBU-27/B): 11
Number used in OIF (EGBU-27 GPS/LGB): 98

GBU-28/B Paveway III Bunker Buster
Weight: 4,676 lbs.
Warhead: BLU-113/B penetrator/bomb
Range: More than 7.6 nm
Number used in OIF: 1

GBU-15 Electro-Optical Guided Bomb (EOGB) with cruciform wing
Weight: 2,450 lbs.
Warhead: 2,000-lb. Mk 84 bomb or BLU-109/B penetrator
Range: 13 nm
Circular error probable (CEP): 3m

GBU-31/B JDAM (Joint Direct Attack Munition)
Weight: 2,036 lbs.
Warheads:
   GBU-31(V)1/B, GBU-31(V)2/B: Mk 84 bomb with KMU-556/B guidance kit
   GBU-31(V)3/B: BLU-109/B with KMU-557/B guidance kit
   GBU-31(V)4/B: BLU-109/B with KMU-558/B guidance kit
Number used in OIF: 5,086

GBU-32/B JDAM (Joint Direct Attack Munition)
Weight: 1,000 lbs.
Warhead: Mk 83 bomb with KMU-559/B guidance kit
Number used in OIF: 768

GBU-35/B JDAM *(Joint Direct Attack Munition)*
Weight: 1,000 lbs.
Warhead: BLU-110/B with KMU-559/B guidance kit
Number used in OIF: 675

GBU-37/B GAM *(GPS-Aided Munition)*
Weight: 5,000 lbs.
Warhead: BLU-113/B penetrator/bomb
Number used in OIF: 13

GBU-38/B JDAM *(Joint Direct Attack Munition)*
Weight: 500 lbs.
Warhead: Mk 82 bomb

CBU-87/B CEM *(Combined Effects Munition)*
CBU-103/B when fitted with Wind-Corrected Munitions Dispenser (WCMD) k
Tail kit for greater accuracy
Weight: 950 lbs. including 202 3.4-lb. BLU-97/B
Number used in OIF (CBU-87/B): 118
Number used in OIF (CBU-103/B): 818

CBU-89/B *"Gator" AntiPersonnel/Antitank Mine*
CBU-104/B when fitted with Wind-Corrected Munitions Dispenser (WCMD) k
Tail kit for greater accuracy
Weight: 700 lbs. including 72 4.3-lb. BLU-91/B antitank munitions or 22 3.7-lb. BLU-92/B antipersonnel munitions

CBU-97/B SFW *(Sensor-Fused Weapon) Antitank*
CBU-105/B when fitted with Wind-Corrected Munitions Dispenser (WCMD) k
Tail kit for greater accuracy
Weight: 914 lbs. including 10 BLU-108/B, each consisting of four "Skeet" sensor-fused submunitions
Number used in OIF (CBU-105/B): 88

CBU-99/B *Rockeye II Antitank*
Weight: Includes 247 Mk 118 submunitions
Number used in OIF: 182

CBU-107/B PAW *(Passive Attack Weapon) WCMD (Wind-Corrected Munitions Dispenser)*
Weight: 1,000 lbs. with 3,750 nonexplosive penetrator rods to disable without explosion
Number used in OIF: 2

Mk 82 *Unguided Bomb*
Length: 5 ft. 6 in.
Diameter: 10.75 in.
Weight: 500 lbs.
Number used in OIF: 5,504

Mk 83 Unguided Bomb
Length: 9 ft. 11.5 in.
Diameter: 1 ft. 2 in.
Weight 1,014 lbs.
Number used in OIF: 1,692

Mk 84 Unguided Bomb
Length: 10 ft. 9 in.
Diameter: 1 ft. 6 in.
Weight: 2,039 lbs.
Number used in OIF: 6

M117 Unguided Bomb
Weight: 750 lbs.
Number used in OIF: 1,625

LAND VEHICLES AND ARMOR

The number of Army mechanized equipment actually on the ground is thought to be roughly 814 M1 Abrams and 549 M2 Bradleys.

U.S. Tracked Combatants

M1 Abrams
Combat weight: 126,000 lbs.
 139,080 lbs. (M1A2 with depleted uranium armor)
Length, gun forward: 32 ft. 3 in. (A2)
Width: 12 ft. (3.65 m) with skirts
Height: 9 ft. 6 in. (2.89 m) to top of cupola
Ground clearance: 19 in. (center), 17 in. (sides)
Crew: 4 (commander, gunner, loader, driver)
Armament:
120mm/46-caliber M256 smoothbore gun with 40 rounds MPAT (Multi-Purpose Anti-Tank), M830 HEAT (High-Explosive Anti-Tank), and M829 APFSDS-T
7.62mm M240 coaxial machine gun
7.62mm M240 machine gun for loader (10,800 rounds total)
12.7mm M2 machine gun for commander (1,000 rounds)
Range: 230 nm
Number used in OIF: Approximately 850

M2 Bradley IFV
Crew: 9 (3 vehicle, 6 dismounts)
Weight: 67,000 lbs. combat-loaded
Length: 21 ft. 2 in.
Width: 10 ft. 6 in.
Height: 9 ft. 9 in.
Ground clearance: 18 in.

Armament:
Turret-mounted BGM-71 TOW antitank missile—2 in launchers, 5 in reserve
M242 25mm Bushmaster cannon, 300 ready rounds, 600 reserve
Coaxial M240C 7.62mm machine gun, 800 ready rounds, 1,400 reserve
Range: 261 nm

M3 Bradley CFV
Crew: 5 (3 vehicle, 2 dismounts)
Weight: 67,000 lbs. combat-loaded
Length: 21 ft. 2 in.
Width: 10 ft. 6 in.
Height: 9 ft. 9 in.
Ground clearance: 18 in.
Armament:
Turret-mounted BGM-71 TOW antitank missile, 2 in launchers, 10 in reserve
M242 25mm Bushmaster cannon, 300 ready rounds, 1,200 reserve
Coaxial M240C 7.62mm machine gun, 800 ready rounds, 3,400 reserve
Range: 261 nm

M113A3 Armored Personnel Carrier
Net weight: 23,880 lbs.
Combat weight: 27,180 lbs.
Full-armor weight: 31,000 lbs.
Length: 17 ft. 5 in.
Width: 8 ft. 10 in.
Height with air-defense machine gun: 8 ft. 3 in.
Ground clearance: 17 in.
Crew: 2 (commander, driver) + 11 troops
Armament: 12.7mm M2 HB machine gun with 2,000 rounds
Range: 269 nm

AAV7 USMC Amphibious Personnel Carrier
Variants:
    AAVC7A1: Command vehicle
    AAVR7A1: Recovery vehicle
Weight:
    Combat-equipped, 50,758 lbs.
    Loaded, 21 troops: 56,743 lbs.
    Loaded, 10,000 lbs.: 60,758 lbs.
Length: 26 ft.
Width: 10 ft. 9 in.
Height: 10 ft. 8 in.
Ground clearance: 16 in.
Crew: 3
Cruising Range:
    Land at 25 MPH: 261 nm
    Water at 2600 RPM: 7 hours
Armament:

HBM2: .50-caliber machine gun
MK 19 MOD3 40 MM machine gun

M4 C2V (Command and Control Vehicle)
Length: 24 ft. 2 in.
Width: 9 ft. 9 in.
Height: 9 ft.
25 procured and program ended in 1990s
15 taken out of storage and issued to units in Iraq

M6 Linebacker Forward-area Air Defense
Weight: 59,800 lbs.
Length: 21 ft. 4 in.
Height: 8 ft. 6 in.
Ground clearance: 18 in.
Armament:
Turret-mounted four-tube FIM-92A Stinger launcher with 10–11 missiles
M242 Bushmaster 25mm cannon with 600–900 rounds
Coaxial M240C 7.62mm machine gun with 1340–3600 rounds

M7 Fire Support Team Vehicle (FIST)
Weight: 60,000 lbs. combat-loaded
Length: 21 ft. 2 in.
Width: 10 ft. 6 in.
Height: 9 ft. 9 in.
Ground clearance 18 in.
Armament:
Turret-mounted M242 Bushmaster 25mm cannon
Coaxial M240C 7.62mm machine gun

M1068 Standard Integrated Command Post System (SICPS)
Base Weight: 23,398 lbs.
   Combat-loaded: 27,130 lbs.
   Maximum: 31,000 lbs.
Length: 19 ft. 1½ in.
Width: 8 ft. 9¾ in.
Height: 8 ft. 6 in.
Crew: 4 (commander, driver, 2 command post operators)
Range: 269 nm

U.S. Wheeled Combatants

AGMS 6 × 6
Operator: Special Operation Forces
Avenger
Mission: Air-defense system
Crew: 2 (driver and gunner)
Weight: 8,600 lbs.
Length: 16 ft. 3 in.

Width: 7 ft. 2 in.
Height: 8 ft. 8 in.
Ground clearance: 16 in.
Armament:
8 Stinger missiles in 2 launch pods, reload 8 missiles in less than 3 minutes
1.50-caliber M3P machine gun with 200 rounds ammunition

LAV-25 8 × 8 Light Armored Vehicle
Variants: LAV-A, LAV-AC, LAV-AD, LAV-AT, LAV-L, LAV-M, LAV-PC, LAV-R, LAV-105
Crew 3 (commander, gunner, driver) + 6 troops
Combat weight: 28,200 lbs.
Length: 21 ft.
Width: 8 ft. 2 in.
Height: 8 ft. 10 in.
Ground clearance: 16 in.
Armament:
Turret-mounted 25mm M242 Chain Gun with 210 ready rounds, 420 stowed
7.62mm M240 coaxial mg with 440 ready rounds
7.62mm mg on pintle mount with 220 ready rounds
Range: 357 nm

M1117 4 × 4 Armored Security Vehicle (ASV)
Crew: 3
Weight: 12,428 lbs.
Length: 20 ft. 5 in.
Width: 8 ft. 5 in.
Height: 8 ft. 6 in.
Range: Over 348 nm
Armament: 1 40mm MK 19 Grenade Launcher
1 12.7mm M2 machine gun

M973 Small Unit Support Vehicle (SUSV), aka "Tonka Toy"
Curb weights:
    Front vehicle: 6,041 lbs.
    Rear vehicle: 3,880 lbs.
Payload:
    Front vehicle: 1,389 lbs.
    Rear vehicle: 3,549 lbs.
Trailer: 5,512 lbs.
Length: 22 ft. 8 in.
Width: 6 ft. 1½ in.
Height: 8 ft. ½ in.
Crew and passengers:
    Front vehicle: 6 (with driver)
    Rear vehicle: 11
Maximum trailer weight: 2500 kg
Range: 179 nm

U.S. Artillery

M109A6 Paladin
Mission: Self-propelled artillery
Crew: 4 (accompanying M992 FAASV-5)
Weight: 63,615 lbs.
Length: 32 ft. 3 in.
Width: 10 ft. 4 in.
Height with air-defense machine gun: 10 ft. 7 in.
Ground clearance: 18 in.
Armament: 155mm/39-cal. M284 rifled howitzer, 37 conventional rounds, 2 Copperhead rounds
Extended Range: 30 km with HE RAP and M203 propellant
Max. Unassisted Range: 22 km
Max. Rate of Fire: 4 rounds/min for three minutes
Sustained Rate of Fire: 1 rd/min (dependent on thermal warning device)

M270 MLRS
Crew: 3
Weight:
    Empty: 44,509 lbs.
    Combat: 55,536 lbs.
Length: 22 ft. 5 in.
Width: 9 ft. 9 in.
Height: 19 ft. 5 in. (elevated)
Ground clearance: 17 in.
Armament: 12 227mm rocket cells, salvo in < 1 minute
Range: 261 nm

M119 105mm towed howitzer
Weight: 4,100 lbs. (1869.7 kg)
Length with tube in firing position: 20 ft. 9 in. (6.32 m)
Maximum Range:
    With Charge 71: 1,500 meters
    With Charge 81: 4,000 meters
    With M913 rocket-assisted projectile: 19,000 m

M198 155mm towed howitzer
Weight: 15,758 lbs.
Length:
    Firing: 36 ft. 2 in.
    In tow: 40 ft. 6 in.
Weight: 15,758 lbs.
Bore: 155mm/39 calibers
Maximum Effective Range:
    Conventional ammunition: 22,400 meters
    Rocket-assisted projectile 30,000 meters
Rate of Fire:

Maximum: 4 rounds per minute
Sustained: 2 rounds per minute

U.S. Support and Supply vehicles, Tracked

M992 Field Artillery Ammunition Support Vehicle (FAASV)
Weight: 57,500 lbs.
Length: 22 ft. 3 in.
Width: 10 ft. 4 in.
Height: 10 ft. 6 in.
Ground clearance: 14½ in.
Crew: 4 with M109A3/A5, 5 with Paladin
Munitions resupply load:
90 155mm projectiles with 96 propelling charges and 104 fuses
3 Copperhead projectiles

M9 ACE Armored Combat Earthmover
Weight, gross: 55,000 lbs.
Length: 20 ft. 5 in.
Height: 8 ft. 9 in.
Ground clearance: 13½ in.
Trench width: 5 ft. 2 in.
Vertical wall: 1 ft. 6 in.
Tilt dozing: 5 degrees
Bowl capacity: 8.7 cu. yds.
Range: 174 nm

M88 Hercules Recovery Vehicle
Crew: 4
Weight: 140,000 lbs.
Ground clearance: 17 in.
Boom capacity: 70,000 lbs.
Vehicle hoisting capability:
    Spade up: 12,000 lbs.
    Spade down: 70,000 lbs.
Range: 243 nm

M104 Wolverine Heavy Assault Bridge
Weight without bridge: 103,000 lbs.
Weight with bridge: 124,000 lbs.
Crew: 2
Gap Crossing Length: 78 ft. 9 in.
Mission Load Class (MLC): 70.0 tons
Deployment Time: Less than 5 minutes
Recovery Time: 10 minutes (5 minutes to engage, 5 minutes to store in Travel Mode)

215

U.S. Support and Supply Vehicles, Wheeled

M-Gator 6 × 6
Weight (including fuel): 1,450 lbs.
Maximum Cargo Load: 1,250 lbs.
Length: 9 ft.
Width: 5 ft.

After-action comments: "Soldiers are very appreciative of this asset. They believe the vehicle could benefit from greater power and the ability to tow a trailer. They would like to be able to mount a crew-served weapon for personal protection ... It would be very difficult to get the units to return to the days before the M-Gator ... and I wouldn't want to be the one who tries to take it away."

Prowler ATV (4 × 4)
Weight: 795 lbs.

MK48 LVS
Curb Weight: 24,500 lbs.
    With MK14: 40,300 lbs.
    MK15: 50,550 lbs.
    MK16: 40,550 lbs.
    MK17: 47,200 lbs.
Payload Capacity:
On Road:
    With MK14: 45,000 lbs.
    MK15: 20,000 lbs.
    MK16: 46,000 lbs.
    MK17: 39,000 lbs.
Off Road:
    With MK14: 25,000 lbs.
    MK15 and 17: 20,000 lbs.
Length:
    MK48: 19 ft. 10.5 in.
    With MK14 or Mk: 17: 38 ft.
    MK15: 37 ft.
    MK16: 33 ft. 2 in.
Height: 8 ft. 6 in.

M809 Family of 6 × 6 5-ton trucks
Variants:
M246 Tractor Wrecker 5 Ton 6X6 W/W W/E
M246A2 Tractor Wrecker 5 Ton 6X6 W/W W/E
M812A1 Transporter Bridge Floating
M813/813A1 Cargo 5 Ton 6X6 LWB W/E (A1 with drop sides)
M814 Cargo 5 Ton 6X6 XLWB W/E (with and without winch)
M816 Wrecker 5 Ton 6X6 W/Winch W/E
M817 Dump 5 Ton 6X6 W/E
M818 Tractor 5 Ton 6X6 W/E (with and without winch)

M819 Tractor Wrecker 5 Ton 6X6 W/W W/E
M820/M820A2 Van Expansible 5 Ton 6X6 (A2 with hydraulic lift gate)
M821 Stake 5 Ton 6X6 W/Winch W/E

M915 Family of semi-tractors
Variants:
M915/M915A1/A2 6 X 4 Tractor Line Haul 50,000 GVW
M916M916A1/A2 6 X 6 Tractor LET 66,000 GVW W/Winch
M920 8 X 6 Tractor MET 75,000 GVW W/W

M839 Family of 6 × 6 5-ton trucks
Variants:
M924/M924A1 Cargo 5 Ton 6X6 LWB W/E
M925/M925A1/A2 Cargo Drop Sides 5 Ton 6X6 W/W W/E
M926/M926A1 Cargo 5 Ton 6X6 LWB W/W W/E
M927/M927A1/A2 Cargo 5 Ton 6X6 XLWB W/E
M928/M928A1/A2 Cargo 5 Ton 6X6 XLWB W/W W/E
M929/M929A1/A2 Dump 5 Ton 6X6 W/E
M930/M920A1/A2 Dump 5 Ton 6X6 W/Winch W/E
M931/M931A1/A2 Tractor 5 Ton 6X6 W/E
M932/M932A1/A2 Tractor 5 Ton 6X6 W/Winch W/E
M934/,934A1/A2 Van Expansible 5 TON 6X6
M935M935A1/A2 Van Expansible 5T 6X6 W/Hyd. Lift. Gate
M936/M936A1/M936A2 Wrecker 5 Ton 6X6 W/Winch W/E

Heavy Expanded-Mobility Tactical Truck (HEMTT) Family
M977 basic vehicle:
Weight: 38,300 lbs.
Payload: 22,000 lbs.
Length: 33 ft. 5 in.
Width: 8 ft.
Wheelbase: 17 ft. 6 in.
Range: 261 nm
Variants:
M977 Cargo TAC 8X8 Heavy Expanded MOB W/W W/Lt. Crane
M978 Tank Fuel Service 2500 Gal. 8X8 Heavy Expanded MOB
M983 Tractor TAC 8X8 Heavy Expanded MOB W/WN W/Crane
M984/M984A1 Wrecker TAC 8X8 Heavy Expanded MOB W/Winch
M985 Cargo TAC 8X8 Heavy Expanded MOB W/Med. Crane
M985E1 Cargo 8X8 57000 GVW High Mobility
M1120 8X8 HVY EXP MOB W/Load Handling System

M998 High-Mobility Multipurpose Wheeled Vehicle
Basic vehicle:
Weight, empty: 5,200 lbs.
Payload: 2,500 lbs.
Weight, gross: 7,700 lbs.
Length: 15 ft.
Width: 7 ft. 1 in.

Height: 6 ft.
Ground clearance: 16 in.
Range: 261 nm
Variants:
M998 Cargo/Troop carrier
M1038 Cargo/Troop carrier with winch
M1025 Armament: carrier
M1026 Armament: carrier with winch
M1037 Shelter carrier
M1042 Shelter carrier with winch
M1043 Armament: carrier, USMC, with supplemental armor
M1044 Armament: carrier, USMC, with supplemental armor and winch
M966 TOW ATGM carrier with 6 missiles
M1036 TOW ATGM carrier, armored, with winch
M1045 TOW ATGM carrier with supplemental armor
M1046 TOW ATGM carrier with supplemental armor and winch
M996 Ambulance, 2-litter, basic armor
M997 Ambulance, 4-litter, basic armor
M1035 Ambulance, 2-litter, soft top
M1037 Shelter Carrier
M1042 Shelter Carrier, with winch
M1069 Prime mover for M119-towed 105mm howitzer

M1097 Heavy HMMWV
Basic M1097 Shelter Carrier
Basic vehicle:
Weight, empty: 5,200 lbs.
Payload: 4,400 lbs.
Weight, gross: 10,300 lbs.
Length: 15 ft. 10½ in.
Width: 7 ft. 1 in.
Height: 6 ft.
Variants:
M1113 Heavy HMMWV with 5,150-lb. Payload
M1114 Up-armored HMMWV with GVW of 12,100 lbs.
M1116 USAF security version of M1114

M1000/M1070 Heavy Equipment Transport System (HETS)
Weight:
    Tractor: 40,000 lbs.
    Trailer: 51,000 lbs.
Payload: 140,000 lbs.
Length:
    Tractor: 29 ft. 10 in.
    Trailer: 51 ft. 10 in.
Max. width: 12 ft.
M1074 Palletized Loading System (PLS)
Weight:
    Tractor: 40,000 lbs.

Trailer: 51,000 lbs.
Payload:
    Truck: 33,000 lbs.
    Trailer: 33,000 lbs.
Length:
    Truck: 31 ft. 11 in.
    Trailer: 27 ft. 3½ in.
Max. width: 8 ft.
Ground clearance: 15½ in.
Range: 292 nm
Variants:
M1074 Cargo HVY PLS Transport 15–16.5 Ton 10X10 W/MHE W/E
M1075 Cargo Heavy PLS Transport 15–16.5 Ton 10X10
M1076 Trailer Palletized Loading System (PLS) 8X20
M1077A1 Bed Cargo: Demountable PLS 8X20 (Flatrack)

FMTV 4 × 4 Light Tactical Vehicle
Basic M1078, drop-side tray, 2 doors
Weight, empty: 20,300 lbs.
    Payload: 5,000 lbs.
    Trailer: 21,000 lbs.
Weight, loaded: 25,300 lbs.
Length: 21 ft. 3 in.
Width: 8 ft. 0 in.
Height: 8 ft. 10 in.
Ground clearance: 22 in.
Variants:
M1078 Cargo 4X4 LMTV W/E
M1079 Van LMTV W/E
M1081 Cargo 2.5 Ton 4X4 LMTV W/E LAPES/AD
M1082 Trailer Cargo LMTV with drop sides

FMTV 6 × 6 Medium Tactical Vehicle
Basic M1083 drop-side tray, rear-mounted crane, 2 doors
Length: 23 ft. 2 in.
Width: 8 ft. 0 in.
Height: 8 ft. 10 in.
Ground clearance: 22 in.
Wheelbase: 14 ft. 9 in.
Weight, empty: 23,600 lbs.
Payload: 10,000 lbs.
Trailer: 21,000 lbs.
Weight, loaded: 33,500 lbs.
Variants:
M1083 Cargo MTV W/E
M1084 Cargo MTV W/MHE W/E
M1085 Cargo MTV LWB W/E
M1086 Cargo LWB W/MHE W/E
M1087 Van Expansible MTV W/E

M1088 Tractor MTV W/E
M1089 Wrecker MTV W/W W/E
M1090 Dump MTV W/E
M1093 Cargo 5 TON 6X6 MTV W/E LAPES/AD
M1094 Dump 5 TON 6X6 MTV W/E LAPES/AD
M1095 Trailer Cargo MTV with drop sides

U.K. Combatants

Challenger II Main Battle Tank
Combat weight: 137,789 lbs.
Length, gun forward: 37 ft. 9 in.
Width: 11 ft. 6 in.
Height: 8 ft. 3 in.
Ground clearance: 19 in. (center), 17 in. (sides)
Crew: 4 (commander, gunner, loader, driver)
Armament:
120mm/-caliber L30 rifled gun with 52 rounds HESH (High-Explosive Squash Head) and APFSDS-T
7.62mm Chain Gun coaxial machine gun
7.62mm M240 machine gun for loader (10,800 rounds total)
12.7mm M2 machine gun for commander (1,000 rounds)
Range: 243 nm
Number used in OIF: 120

Scimitar Armored Reconnaissance Vehicle
Combat weight: 17,791 lbs.
Length: 16 ft. 1 in.
Width: 7 ft. 4 in.
Height: 6 ft. 10½ in.
Ground clearance: 13¾ in.
Crew: 3
Vehicle Armament:
Turret-mounted 30mm L21 Rarden cannon with 160 rounds
Coaxial 7.62mm GPMG with 3,000 rounds
Variants:
Sabre (nearly identical with lower-profile turret)
Spartan
Sultan C2

Warrior Combat Fighting Vehicle
Weight: 52,900 lbs.
Length: 20 ft. 9½ in.
Width: 9 ft. 11½ in.
Height: 9 ft. 2 in.
Ground Clearance: 19.3 in.
Crew: 3 (driver, commander, gunner) + 7 fully equipped soldiers
Armament: Turret-mounted BGM-71 TOW antitank missile, 2 in launchers, 4 in reserve

30mm L21 Rarden cannon with 160 rounds
Coaxial M240C 7.62mm machine gun, 800 ready rounds, 1,400 reserve
Variants:
Milan carrier
Recovery vehicle
Engineer combat vehicle
Artillery command post
Number deployed: 150

AS90 Braveheart 155mm self-propelled howitzer
Weight: 92,595 lbs.
Length: 31 ft. 10 in.
Width: 10 ft. 10 in.
Height: 9 ft. 10 in.
Crew: 5 or 4 (driver, commander, layer, loader)
Armament:
155mm/39-caliber (52-caliber barrel in a few), 48 rounds carried
Burst rate of fire: 3 rounds in 10 seconds
Intense rate of fire: 6 rounds per minute for 3 minutes
Sustained rate of fire: 2 rounds per minute
Maximum Range, 39-caliber: 24,700 meters
30,000 meters extended range
52-caliber: 30,000 meters
40,000 meters extended range
Road Range: 350 km
Number deployed: 32

Combat Engineering Tractor (CET)
Weight: 37,500 lbs.
Length: 24 ft. 9 in.
Height: 8 ft. 9 in.
Crew: 2
Armament: 1 × 7.62 machine gun
Road Range: 259 nm

All Terrain Mobility Platform (ATMP) 6 × 6
Weight: 2,821 lbs.
Length: 13 ft. 8 in.
Width: 5 ft. 8 in.
Height: 5 ft. 3 in.
Ground clearance: 13.4 in.
Range: 287 nm

The Truck Utility Medium (Heavy Duty) TUM(HD)
Truck Utility Heavy (TUH)
TUH: GVW Loaded 11,685 lbs.
Payload: 3,086 lbs.
TUM (HD): GVW Loaded 8,499 lbs.
Payload: 3,086 lbs.

DROPS 8 × 6 Demountable Rack Offload and Pickup System (DROPS)
with flatrack Payload (similar to PLS and LVS). The IMMLC is used
primarily as an ammunition carrier in support of AS90.
Curb weight: 30,953 lbs.
Loaded weight: 70,548 lbs. (MMLC); 72,664 lbs. (IMMLC)
Max. Load: 36,376 lbs.
Length: 29 ft. 11 in.
Width: 8 ft. 2½ in. (MMLC); 9 ft. 6 in. (IMMLC)
Height: 10 ft. 5 in.
Number deployed: 6 per Royal Support Regiment

U.K. AIRCRAFT

Sentry AEW1 command and control aircraft
(See U.S. Boeing E-3 Sentry, which is very similar)

Tornado GR4 bomber/reconnaissance aircraft
Crew: 2
Engines: Two 15,900-lb. static thrust afterburning Turbo Union RB199-103 turbo-
fans
Span:
  Fully spread: 45 ft. 7 in.
  68-deg. sweep: 28 ft. 2 in.
Length: 54 ft. 10 in.
Max. Speed: 1,263 kts. (Mach 2.2) at 36,000 ft.; 617 kts. (Mach 0.93) at sea level
Armament:
1 × 27mm Mauser cannon and up to 18,000 lbs. of ordnance
Paveway 2 or 3 laser-guided bombs, ballistic or retarded "dumb" 1000-lb. bombs
Cluster Bomb Units (CBU)
Storm Shadow stand-off attack missile
Brimstone antitank
Air Launched Anti-Radiation Missile (ALARM)
Sidewinder AAM
Entered service: 1981 (GR 1), 1999 (GR4)
Number used in OIF: 30

Jaguar GR3 attack/reconnaissance aircraft
Crew: 1
Engines: Two 8,040-lb. static thrust Turbomeca/Rolls-Royce Adour 106
Span: 28 ft. 6 in.
Length: 55 ft. 2 in.
Max. Speed: 918 kts. (Mach 1.4) at 36,000 ft.
Armament:
2 30mm Aden guns and up to 10,000 lbs. of stores
Paveway 2 and 3 laser-guided bombs
1,000-lb. retard and free-fall bombs
CBU-87 cluster bombs

CRV-7 rocket pods
2 AIM-9L Sidewinder AAM
Entered Service: 1973
Number used in OIF: 4

Harrier GR7 attack aircraft

Crew: 1
Engine: One 21,750-lb. static thrust Rolls-Royce Pegasus Mk 105 vectored thrust turbofan or (GR7A, GR9A) one 24,750-lb. static thrust Pegasus Mk 107 vectored thrust turbofan
Span: 30 ft. 4 in.
Length: 46 ft. 4 in.
Max. Speed: 575 kts.
Armament: Two 25mm cannon on under-fuselage stations
Up to 2 Storm Shadow stand-off attack missiles
Paveway 2 and 3 laser-guided bombs
Brimstone antiarmor missiles
16 Mk 82 (500-lb.) or 6 Mk 83 (1,000-lb.) bombs or 4 Maverick air-ground missiles
2 AIM-9L Sidewinder or Advanced Short-Range AAM (ASRAAM) missiles
Entered service: 1990 (GR7)
Number used in OIF: 18

Tornado F3 air-defense aircraft

Crew: 2
Engine: Two 16,410-lb. static thrust afterburning Turbo Union RB199-34R Mk 104 turbofans
Span:
    Fully spread: 45 ft. 7 in.
    68-deg. sweep: 28 ft. 2 in.
Length: 61 ft. 3 in.
Max. Speed: 1,265 kts. (Mach 2.2) at 40,000 ft.
Armament: 1 × 27mm Mauser cannon and 4 Skyflash or AIM-120 AMRAAM Medium-Range AAM and 4 AIM-9L Sidewinder or ASRAAM Short-Range AAM
Entered service: 1986
Number used in OIF: 14

VC-10 tanker aircraft

Crew: 6
Engine: Four 22,500-lb. Rolls-Royce Conway 301 turbofans
Span: 146 ft. 2 in.
Length:
    C1K: 158 ft. 8 in.
    K3/K4: 171 ft. 8 in. (excluding nose probe)
Cruise Speed:
    C1K: 450 kts.
    K3/K4: 504 kts.
Loadings:
    K317: 1,960 lbs. of fuel for transfer
    K41: 49,914 lbs. of fuel for transfer

Entered service: 1966
Number used in OIF: 8

Tristar K1/KC1 tanker aircraft
Crew: 6
Engines: Three 50,000-lb. static thrust Rolls-Royce RB211-524B4 turbofans
Span: 164 ft. 6 in.
Length: 164 ft. 2.5 in.
Max. Speed: 474 kts. at 30,000 ft.
Loadings: 160 passengers (KC1), 260 passengers (K1)
97,000 lbs. (KC1); 300,000 lbs. total fuel
Entered service: 1985

Hercules transport aircraft
(similar to U.S. Lockheed Martin C-130 H except for longer fuselage)

Nimrod maritime patrol aircraft
Crew: 13 (2 pilots, flight engineer, 2 navigators, 1 Air Electronics Officer
[AEO], 3 "wet-men" Air Electronic Operators monitoring sonobuoys, 4 "dry-men"
Air Electronic Operators)
Engines: Four 12,140-lb. static thrust Rolls-Royce RB168-20 Spey 250 turbofans
Span: 114 ft. 10 in.
Length: 126 ft. 9 in.
Max. Speed: 500 kts.
Armament: Internal bay for up to 9 torpedoes, bombs, and depth-charges
AIM-9L Sidewinder AAMs can also be carried
Entered service: 1969 (as the MR1)
Number used in OIF: 6

Chinook helicopters
(similar to U.S. Boeing CH-47 Chinook)

Puma helicopter
Engines: Two 1,435-shp Turbomeca Turmo 111C4 turboshafts
Rotor diameter: 49 ft. 2½ in.
Length, rotors turning: 59 ft. 6½ in.
Max. Speed: 142 kts.
Accommodation: Up to 20 passengers/troops or 7,055 lbs. underslung load
Entered service: 1971

Gazelle helicopter
Engine: One 592-shp Turbomeca/Rolls-Royce Astazou 111N turboshafts
Rotor diameter: 34 ft. 5 in.
Length, fuselage: 31 ft. 3 in.
Max. Speed: 143 kts.
Cruise Speed: 126 kts.
Range: 362 nm
Entered service: 1971

Sea King helicopter
Crew: 4
Engines: Two 1,660-shp Rolls-Royce H1400-1 Gnome turboshafts
Rotor diameter: 62 ft.
Length: 55 ft. 9¾ in.
Max. Speed: 124 kts. at sea level
Range: 243 nm
Accommodation: Up to 19 passengers
Entered service: 1977

Lynx Helicopter AH7 and AH9
Crew 2 (3 with door gunner)
Engines: Two 850-shp Rolls-Royce Gem 41 turboshafts
Weight (max. takeoff): 10,500 lbs.
Length (fuselage): 39 ft. 7 in.
Height: 11 ft. 2 in.
Max. Speed: 178 kts.
Cruise Speed: 125 kts.
Range: 478 nm
Combat radius: Approximately 54 nm with 2-hour loiter
Accomodation: 10 troops
Armament: (when fitted) 8 × TOW antiarmor missiles
2–4 7.62mm GPMG machine guns
Number used in OIF: 6

COMBATANT SHIPS

Kitty Hawk–*class conventionally propelled Aircraft Carriers (CV)*
Builders:
CV 63—New York Shipbuilding Corp., Camden, NJ
CV 64—New York Naval Shipyard, Brooklyn, NY
Displacement, full load: 81,985 tons
Length, overall: 1,062.5 ft.
Flight Deck Width: 252 ft.
Beam: 130 ft.
Draft: 37 ft.
Engines: Eight boilers, 4 geared steam turbines, 280,000 shp on four shafts
Speed: 30 + kts.
Crew:
   Ship's Company: 3,150
   Air Wing: 2,480
Armament:
   RIM-7 Sea Sparrow launchers
   3 20mm Phalanx CIWS mounts
Aircraft:
   F-14 Tomcat (12) (A model in CV 63, D model in CV 64)
   F/A-18C Hornet (36)

EA-6B Prowler (4)
E-2C Hawkeye (4)
S-3B Viking (8)
SH-60F CV-Helo (4)
HH-60H Seahawk(2)
C-2A Greyhound (2) on Constellation

NAME	Hull #	Laid Down	Launched	Comm.	Age (yrs.) at OIF Start	Deployed to
KITTY HAWK	CV 63	12/27/1956	5/21/1960	4/29/1961	41.9	Arabian Gulf
CONSTELLATION	CV 64	9/14/1957	10/8/1960	10/27/1961	41.4	Arabian Gulf

Nimitz–class nuclear-propelled Aircraft Carriers (CVN)
Builder: Newport News Shipbuilding Co., Newport News, VA.
Displacement, full load:
   Nimitz: 101,097 tons
   Theodore Roosevelt: 103,300 tons
   Abraham Lincoln: 104,017 tons
   Harry S. Truman: 101,378 tons
Length, overall: 1,092 ft. (*Nimitz*, 1,089 ft. 6 in.)
Flight Deck Width: 252 feet
Beam: 134 feet
Draft: 38 ft. 5 in. (*Nimitz* 37 ft. before refit)
Engines: Two nuclear reactors, 280,000 shp on four shafts
Speed: 30 + kts.
Crew:
   Ship's Company: 3,200
   Air Wing: 2,480
Armament:
   2–3 RIM-7 Sea Sparrow launchers
   3–4 20mm Phalanx CIWS mounts
Aircraft:
Nimitz:
   F-18E Super Hornet (24)
   F/A-18A and C Hornet (24)
   EA-6B Prowler (4)
   E-2C Hawkeye (4)
   S-3B Viking (8)
   SH-60F CV-Helo (6)
   HH-60H Seahawk (2)
Theodore Roosevelt:
   F-14D Tomcat (10)
   F/A-18C Hornet (24)
   F/A-18B Hornet (12)—USMC
   EA-6B Prowler (4)
   E-2C Hawkeye (4)
   S-3B Viking (8)

SH-60F CV-Helo (6)
HH-60H Seahawk (2)
C-2A Greyhound (2)
Abraham Lincoln:
F-14D Tomcat (12)
F/A-18E Super Hornet (12)
F/A-18C Hornet (24)
EA-6B Prowler (4)
E-2C Hawkeye (4)
S-3B Viking (8)
SH-60F CV-Helo (6)
HH-60H Seahawk (2)
C-2A Greyhound (2)
Harry S. Truman:
F-14A Tomcat (10)
F/A-18C Hornet (24)
F/A-18A Hornet (12)—USMC
EA-6B Prowler (4)
E-2C Hawkeye (4)
S-3B Viking (8)
SH-60F CV-Helo (6)
HH-60H Seahawk (2)
C-2A Greyhound (2)

NAME	Hull #	Laid Down	Launched	Comm.	Age (yrs.) at OIF Start	Deployed to	Desert Shield/Storm
NIMITZ	CVN 68	6/22/1968	5/13/1972	5/3/1975	27.9	Arabian Gulf	
THEODORE ROOSEVELT	CVN 71	10/31/1981	10/27/1984	10/25/1986	16.4	Mediterranean	Y
ABRAHAM LINCOLN	CVN 72	11/3/1984	2/13/1988	11/11/1989	13.4	Arabian Gulf	
HARRY S. TRUMAN	CVN 75	11/29/1993	9/7/1996	7/25/1998	4.7	Mediterranean	

Ticonderoga–*class Guided-Missile Cruisers (CG)*
Builders: Ingalls Shipbuilding, Pascagoula, MS, and Bath Iron Works, Bath, ME
SPY-1 Radar and Combat System Integrator: Lockheed Martin
Displacement, full load: 9,600 tons
Length: 567 feet
Beam: 55 feet
Draft: 31 ft. 6 in.
Engines: Four General Electric LM 2500 gas turbines, 80,000 shp on two shafts
Speed: 30 + kts.
Crew: 24 officers, 340 enlisted
Aircraft: 2 SH-60 Sea Hawk (LAMPS III)
Armament:
122 Vertical Launch System cells for RIM-66/67/156/161 Standard SAM
AGM-84D Harpoon antiship missiles
RUM-139 Vertical Launch ASROC (VLA) ASW

BGM-109 Tomahawk land-attack missiles
6 Mk-46 torpedoes (2 × 3-tube mounts)
2 5-in./54-cal. Mk-45 (lightweight gun)
2 20mm Phalanx CIWS

NAME	Hull #	Laid Down	Launched	Comm.	Age (yrs.) at OIF Start	Remarks	Deployed to	Desert Shield/Storm
VALLEY FORGE	CG 50	4/14/1983	6/23/1984	1/18/1986	17.2		Arabian Gulf	Y
BUNKER HILL	CG 52	1/11/1984	3/11/1985	9/20/1986	16.5	Tomahawk	Arabian Gulf	Y
MOBILE BAY	CG 53	6/6/1984	8/22/1985	2/21/1987	16.1	Tomahawk	Arabian Gulf	Y
SAN JACINTO	CG 56	7/24/1985	11/14/1986	1/23/1988	15.2	Tomahawk	Mediterranean	Y
PRINCETON	CG 59	10/15/1986	10/2/1987	2/11/1989	14.1		Arabian Gulf	Y
NORMANDY	CG 60	4/7/1987	3/19/1988	12/9/1989	13.3		Arabian Gulf	Y
COWPENS	CG 63	12/23/1987	3/11/1989	3/9/1991	12.0	Tomahawk	Arabian Gulf	
CHOSIN	CG 65	7/22/1988	9/1/1989	1/12/1991	12.2		Arabian Gulf	
SHILOH	CG 67	8/1/1989	9/8/1990	7/18/1992	10.7	Tomahawk	Arabian Gulf	
ANZIO	CG 68	8/21/1989	11/2/1990	5/2/1992	10.9		Mediterranean	
CAPE ST. GEORGE	CG 71	11/19/1990	1/10/1992	6/30/1993	9.7	Tomahawk	Mediterranean	

Arleigh Burke–*class* Guided Missile Destroyers (DDG)
Builders: Bath Iron Works, Bath, ME, and Ingalls Shipbuilding, Pascagoula, MS
SPY-1 Radar and Combat System Integrator: Lockheed Martin
Displacement, full load:
    DDG 51 through 71: 8,315 tons
    DDG 72 through 78: 8,400 tons
    DDG 79 and later: 9,200 tons
Length:
    DDG 51–78: 505 feet
    Flight IIA (DDG 79–98): 509 ft. 6 in.
Beam: 59 ft.
Draft: 30 ft. 7 in.
Engines: Four General Electric LM 2500-30 gas turbines, 100,000 shp on two shafts
Speed: 30 + kts
Crew: 23 officers, 300 enlisted
Aircraft:
    DDG 51–78: None; LAMPS III electronics installed on landing deck for coordinated DDG 51/helo-ASW operations
    DDG 79 and later: 2 SH-60 Seahawk LAMPS III helicopters
Armament: 90 Vertical Launch System cells for:
    RIM-66/67/156 Standard SAM
    AGM-84D Harpoon antiship missiles
    RUM-139 Vertical Launch ASROC (VLA) ASW
    BGM-109 Tomahawk land-attack missiles
6 Mk-46 torpedoes (2 × 3-tube mounts)
1 5-in./54-cal. Mk-45 (lightweight gun)
2 20mm Phalanx CIWS

NAME	Hull #	Laid Down	Launched	Comm.	Age (yrs.) at OIF Start	Remarks	Deployed to
ARLEIGH BURKE	DDG 51	12/6/1988	9/16/1989	7/4/1991	11.7	Tomahawk	Mediterranean
JOHN S. McCAIN	DDG 56	9/3/1991	9/26/1992	7/2/1994	8.7	Tomahawk	Arabian Gulf
MITSCHER	DDG 57	2/12/1992	5/7/1993	12/10/1994	8.3		Mediterranean
PAUL HAMILTON	DDG 60	8/24/1992	7/24/1993	5/27/1995	7.8	Tomahawk	Arabian Gulf
FITZGERALD	DDG 62	2/9/1993	1/29/1994	10/14/1995	7.4		Arabian Gulf
BENFOLD	DDG 65	9/27/1993	11/9/1994	3/30/1996	7.0		Arabian Gulf
MILIUS	DDG 69	8/8/1994	8/1/1995	11/23/1996	6.3	Tomahawk	Arabian Gulf
DONALD COOK	DDG 75	7/9/1996	5/3/1997	12/4/1998	4.3	Tomahawk	Mediterranean
HIGGINS	DDG 76	11/14/1996	10/4/1997	4/24/1999	3.9	Tomahawk	Arabian Gulf
O'KANE	DDG 77	5/8/1997	3/28/1998	10/23/1999	3.4	Tomahawk	
PORTER	DDG 78	12/2/1996	11/12/1997	3/20/1999	4.0	Tomahawk	Mediterranean
OSCAR AUSTIN	DDG 79	10/9/1997	11/7/1998	8/19/2000	2.6	Tomahawk	Mediterranean
WINSTON CHURCHILL	DDG 81	5/17/1998	4/17/1999	3/10/2001	2.0	Tomahawk	Mediterranean

Spruance–*class Destroyers (DD)*

Builder: Ingalls Shipbuilding, Pascagoula, MS
Displacement, full load: 8,040 tons
Length: 563 ft.
Beam: 55 ft.
Draft: 29 ft.
Engines: Four General Electric LM 2500 gas turbines, 80,000 shp on two shafts
Speed: 30 + kts
Crew: 30 officers, 352 enlisted
Aircraft: 2 SH-60 Seahawk LAMPS III helicopters
Armament:
8 AGM-84D Harpoon (from 2 quad launchers)
BGM-109 Tomahawk from VLS or Armored Box Launcher
RUM-139 Vertical Launch ASROC (VLA) missiles from VLS
6 Mk-46 torpedoes (from 2 triple tube mounts)
2 5-in. 54-cal. Mk-45 (lightweight gun)
2 20mm Phalanx CIWS

NAME	Hull #	Laid Down	Launched	Comm.	Age (yrs.) at OIF Start	Remarks	Deployed to	Desert Shield/Storm
OLDENDORF	DD 972	12/27/1974	10/21/1975	3/4/1978	25.0		Arabian Gulf	Y
BRISCOE	DD 977	7/21/1975	12/15/1976	6/3/1978	24.8	Tomahawk	Mediterranean	
STUMP	DD 978	8/22/1975	4/30/1977	8/19/1978	24.6			
DEYO	DD 989	10/14/1977	1/20/1979	3/22/1980	23.0	Tomahawk	Mediterranean	
FLETCHER	DD 992	4/24/1978	6/16/1979	7/12/1980	22.7	Tomahawk	Arabian Gulf	

Los Angeles–*class Nuclear-propelled Attack Submarines (SSN)*
Builders: Newport News Shipbuilding Co., Newport News, VA, and General Dynamics Electric Boat Division
Displacement, submerged:
    Through 718: 6,084 tons
    719 to 756: 6,145–6,190 tons
    757 and later: 6,927 tons
Length: 362 ft.
Beam: 33 ft.
Draft: 32 ft.
Engines: One nuclear reactor, 35,000 shp total (est) on one shaft
Speed: 20 + kts.
Crew: 13 officers, 121 enlisted
Armament:
Up through 618: 4 torpedo tubes for:
    UGM-109 Tomahawk land-attack
    Mk-48 torpedoes
719 and later: 12 VLS tubes for UGM-109 Tomahawk
4 torpedo tubes for MK-48 torpedoes

NAME	Hull #	Laid Down	Launched	Comm.	Age (yrs.) at OIF Start	Remarks
BREMERTON	SSN 698	5/6/1976	7/22/1978	3/28/1981	22.0	
AUGUSTA	SSN 710	4/1/1982	1/21/1984	1/19/1985	18.2	Tomahawk
HONOLULU	SSN 718	11/10/1981	9/24/1983	7/6/1985	17.7	
PROVIDENCE	SSN 719	10/14/1982	8/4/1984	7/27/1985	17.6	Tomahawk
PITTSBURGH	SSN 720	4/15/1983	12/8/1984	11/23/1985	17.3	Tomahawk
KEY WEST	SSN 722	7/6/1983	7/20/1985	9/12/1987	15.5	Tomahawk
LOUISVILLE	SSN 724	9/16/1984	12/14/1985	11/8/1986	16.4	Tomahawk
NEWPORT NEWS	SSN 750	3/3/1984	3/15/1986	6/3/1989	13.8	
SAN JUAN	SSN 751	8/16/1985	12/6/1986	8/6/1988	14.6	Tomahawk
PASADENA	SSN 752	12/20/1985	9/12/1987	2/11/1989	14.1	
BOISE	SSN 764	8/25/1988	3/23/1991	11/7/1992	10.4	
MONTPELIER	SSN 765	5/19/1989	4/6/1991	3/13/1993	10.0	Tomahawk
TOLEDO	SSN 769	5/6/1991	8/28/1993	2/24/1995	8.1	Tomahawk
COLUMBIA	SSN 771	4/21/1993	9/24/1994	10/9/1995	7.4	Tomahawk
CHEYENNE	SSN 773	7/6/1992	4/3/1995	9/13/1996	6.5	Tomahawk

Oliver Hazard Perry–*class Guided-Missile Frigates (FFG)*
Builders: Bath Iron Works, Bath, ME; Todd Shipyards, Seattle, WA; and Todd Shipyards, San Pedro, CA
Displacement, full load: 4,100 tons
Length: 445 feet (453 feet with LAMPS III modification)
Beam: 45 ft.
Draft: 24 ft. 6 in.

Engines: Two General Electric LM 2500 gas turbines, 41,000 shp total on one shaft
Speed: 29 kts.
Crew: 17 officers, 198 enlisted
Aircraft: 2 SH-60 (LAMPS III)
Armament:
Mk-13 Mod 4 launcher for:
36 RIM-66 SM-1 MR SAM
4 AGM-84 Harpoon antiship missiles
6 MK-46 torpedoes(2 × 3-tube mounts)
1 76mm/62-cal. MK-75 rapid-fire gun
1 20mm Phalanx CIWS

NAME	Hull #	Laid Down	Launched	Comm.	Age (yrs.) at OIF Start	Deployed to	Desert Shield/Storm
THACH	FFG 43	3/6/1982	12/18/1982	3/17/1984	19.0	Arabian Gulf	
VANDEGRIFT	FFG 48	10/13/1981	10/15/1982	11/24/1984	18.3	Arabian Gulf	Y
GARY	FFG 51	12/18/1982	11/19/1983	11/17/1984	18.3	Arabian Gulf	
CARR	FFG 52	3/26/1982	2/26/1983	7/27/1985	17.6	Mediterranean	
HAWES	FFG 53	8/26/1983	2/18/1984	2/9/1985	18.1	Mediterranean	Y
REUBEN JAMES	FFG 57	11/19/1983	2/8/1985	3/22/1986	17.0	Arabian Gulf	
RODNEY M. DAVIS	FFG 60	2/8/1985	1/11/1986	5/9/1987	15.9	Arabian Gulf	

Avenger–class Mine Countermeasures Ships (MCM)
Builders: Peterson Shipbuilders, Sturgeon Bay, WI, and Marinette Marine, Marinette, WI
Displacement, full load: 1,312 tons
Length, overall: 224 ft. 4 in.
Beam: 39 ft.
Draft: 11 ft. 6 in.
Engines: Four Isotta-Fraschini ID36 SS-6V AM diesels, 2,720 bhp on two shafts with controllable-pitch propellers
Speed:
Maximum: 13.5 kts.
Mine-hunting speed: 5 kts.
Crew: 72
Sensors: SQQ-32 mine detection sonar
SLQ-48(V) Mine Neutralization System

NAME	Hull #	Laid Down	Launched	Comm.	Age (yrs.) at OIF Start	Deployed to
SENTRY	MCM 3	10/8/1984	9/20/1986	9/2/1989	13.5	Suez
DEVASTATOR	MCM 6	2/9/1987	6/11/1988	10/6/1990	12.5	Suez
SCOUT	MCM 8	6/8/1987	5/20/1989	12/15/1990	12.3	Suez

ARDENT	MCM 12	10/22/1990	11/16/1991	2/18/1994	9.1	Arabian Gulf
DEXTEROUS	MCM 13	3/11/1991	6/20/1992	7/9/1994	8.7	Arabian Gulf
CHIEF	MCM 14	8/19/1991	6/12/1993	11/5/1994	8.4	Suez

Osprey–*class Coastal Minehunters (MHC)*
Builders: Intermarine USA, Savannah, GA, and Avondale Industries, Inc., Gulfport, MS
Displacement, full load: 895 tons
Length, overall: 187 ft. 10 in.
Beam: 35 ft. 11 in.
Draft: 9 ft. 6 in.
Engines: Two Isotta-Fraschini ID36 SS-6V AM diesels, 1,160 bhp driving two Voith-Schneider vertical cycloidal propellers, two 180-bhp hydraulic motors for mine hunting, one 180-hp bow thruster
Speed: 12 kts.
Crew: 51
Weapons: 1 30mm or 40mm gun
Sensors:
SQQ-32 mine detection sonar
SLQ-48(V) Mine Neutralization System

NAME	Hull #	Laid Down	Launched	Comm.	Age (yrs.) at OIF Start	Deployed to
CARDINAL	MHC 60	2/1/1994	3/9/1996	10/18/1997	5.4	Arabian Gulf
RAVEN	MHC 61	11/15/1994	9/28/1996	9/5/1998	4.5	Arabian Gulf

Cyclone–*Class Patrol Coastal Ships (PC)*
Builder: Bollinger Shipyards, Inc., Lockport, LA
Displacement, full load: 341 tons
Length: 170 ft. 7 in.
Beam: 25 ft.
Draft: 7 ft.
Engines: Four Paxman Valenta diesels, 13,400 bhp on four shafts
Speed: 35 kts.
Crew: 28 + 9 SEALs
Armament:
2 Stinger SAMs in twin mounting
2 25mm Mk-88 Sea Snake cannon in single mounts
2 40mm Mk-19 grenade machine guns in single mounts
2 12.7mm machine guns in single mounts
2 7.62mm machine guns in single mounts

NAME	Hull #	Laid Down	Launched	Comm.	Age (yrs.) at OIF Start	Deployed to
CHINOOK	PC9	6/16/1993	2/26/1994	1/28/1995	8.1	Arabian Gulf
FIREBOLT	PC10	9/17/1993	6/10/1994	6/10/1995	7.8	Arabian Gulf

Hamilton–*class High-Endurance Cutters* (WHEC)
Builder: Avondale, New Orleans, LA
Displacement, full load: 3,250 tons
Length, overall: 378 ft.
Beam: 42 ft. 8 in.
Draft: 20 ft.
Engines: CODOG (2 Pratt & Whitney FT.4-A6 gas turbines, 28,000 shp, and two Fairbanks Morse 38TD8 1/8 diesels, 7,200 bhp) on two shafts with controllable-pitch propellers
Speed: 29 kts.
Crew: 148–165
Armament:
1 76mm/62-cal. OTO Melara dual-purpose gun
2 40mm Mk-19 grenade launchers in single mounts
2 25mm Mk-38 Sea Snake Cannon in single mounts
2 .50-cal. machine guns in single mount
6 12.75-in. (324mm) Mk-46 torpedos in 2 × 3-tube mounts
Helicopters extendable helicopter hangar for HH 65

NAME	Hull #	Laid Down	Launched	Comm.	Age (yrs.) at OIF Start	Deployed to
DALLAS	WHEC 716	2/7/1966	10/1/1966	10/26/1967	35.4	Arabian Gulf
BOUTWELL	WHEC 719	12/12/1966	6/17/1967	6/14/1968	34.8	Arabian Gulf

Island–*class Patrol Boats*
Builder: Bollinger Shipyards, Inc., Lockport, LA
Displacement, full load: 155–165 tons
Length, overall: 110 ft.
Beam: 21 ft.
Draft: 7 ft. 4 in.
Engines: Two Alco-Paxman Valenta 16 RP200 diesels, 6,200 bhp on two shafts
Speed: 26 kts.
Crew: 16
Weapons: 1 25mm Bushmaster low-angle cannon
2 7.62mm M60 machine guns in single mounts

NAME	Hull #	Laid Down	Launched	Comm.	Age (yrs.) at OIF Start	Deployed to
AQUIDNECK	WPB 1309		6/14/1986	9/26/1986	16.5	Arabian Gulf
BARANOF	WPB 1318	6/8/1987	1/15/1988	5/20/1988	14.8	Arabian Gulf
WRANGE: LL	WPB 1332	10/17/1988	5/26/1989	6/24/1989	13.7	Arabian Gulf
ADAK	WPB 1333	11/25/1988	6/30/1989	11/17/1989	13.3	Arabian Gulf
GRAND ISLE	WPB 1338	6/18/1990		12/14/1990	12.3	Arabian Gulf
BAINBRIDGE ISLAND	WPB 1343	12/3/1990	4/19/1991	6/14/1991	11.8	Arabian Gulf
PEA ISLAND	WPB 1347	4/29/1991		11/1/1991	11.4	Arabian Gulf
KNIGHT ISLAND	WPB 1348	10/3/1991		12/6/1991	11.3	Arabian Gulf

Amphibious Warfare Ships

Blue Ridge–*Class Amphibious Command Ship (LCC)*
Builder: Newport News Shipbuilding Co., Newport News, VA
Displacement, full load: 18,874 tons
Length, overall: 634 ft.
Extreme Beam: 108 ft.
Draft: 27 ft.
Engines: Two Foster Wheeler boilers, 1 General Electric steam turbine, 22,000 shp on one shaft
Speed: 21.5 kts.
Crew: 201 officers, 1,083 enlisted
Aircraft: All helicopters except the CH-53 Sea Stallion can be carried

NAME	Hull #	Laid Down	Launched	Comm.	Age (yrs.) at OIF Start
MOUNT WHITNEY	LCC20	1/8/1969	1/8/1970	1/16/1971	32.2

Tarawa–*Class Amphibious Assault Ships (LHA)*
Builder: Ingalls Shipbuilding, Pascagoula, MS
Displacement, full load: 39,400 tons
Length: 820 feet
Beam:
    Waterline: 106 feet
    Extreme width: 131 ft. 10 in.
Draft: 25 ft. 11 in.
Flight deck:
Length: 820 ft.
Width: 118 ft. 1 in.
Engines: Two boilers, two geared steam turbines, 70,000 shp total on two shafts
Speed: 24 kts.

Crew:
  Ship's Company: 82 officers, 882 enlisted
  Marine Detachment: 1,900 +
Armament:
2 RIM-116 21-cell RAM launchers
2 Phalanx 20mm CIWS mounts
4 25mm Mk 38 Sea Snake cannon
3 .50-cal. machine guns
Aircraft, depending on mission:
  6 AV-8B Harrier attack
  12 CH-46 Sea Knight helicopters
  4 CH-53E Sea Stallion helicopters
  3 UH-1N Huey helicopters
  4 AH-1W Super Cobra helicopters
Landing Craft:
4 LCU-1600 class LCU
Up to 2 LCAC may be carried

NAME	Hull #	Laid Down	Launched	Comm.	Age (yrs.) at OIF Start	Deployed to	Desert Shield/Storm
NASSAU	LHA 4	8/13/1973	1/28/1978	7/28/1979	23.6	Arabian Gulf	Y
SAIPAN	LHA 2	7/21/1972	7/18/1974	10/15/1977	25.4	Mediterranean	
TARAWA	LHA 1	11/15/1971	12/1/1973	5/29/1976	26.8	Arabian Gulf	Y

Wasp–class Amphibious Assault Ships (LHD)
Builder: Ingalls Shipbuilding, Pascagoula, MS
Displacement, full load: 40,530 tons
Length: 844 feet
Beam:
  Waterline: 106 feet
  Extreme width: 140 ft.
Draft: 25 ft. 11 in.
Engines: Two boilers, two geared steam turbines, 70,000 shp total on two shafts
Speed: 24 kts.
Crew:
  Ship's Company: 104 officers, 1,004 enlisted
  Marine Detachment: 1,894
Armament:
2 RIM-116 21-cell RAM launchers
2 Phalanx 20mm CIWS mounts
3 25mm Mk-38 Sea Snake cannon
3 .50-cal. machine guns
Aircraft, depending on mission
6 AV-8B Harrier attack
12 CH-46 Sea Knight helicopters

4 CH-53E Sea Stallion helicopters
3 UH-1N Huey helicopters
4 AH-1W Super Cobra helicopters
Landing craft: Up to 3 LCAC may be carried

NAME	Hull #	Laid Down	Launched	Comm.	Age (yrs.) at OIF Start	Deployed to
KEARSARGE	LHD 3	2/6/1990	3/26/1992	10/16/1993	9.4	Arabian Gulf
BOXER	LHD 4	4/18/1991	8/7/1993	2/11/1995	8.1	Arabian Gulf
BATAAN	LHD 5	6/22/1994	3/15/1996	9/20/1997	5.5	Arabian Gulf
BONHOMME RICHARD	LHD 6	4/18/1995	5/17/1997	8/15/1998	4.6	Arabian Gulf
IWO JIMA	LHD 7	12/12/1997	3/25/2001	6/30/2001	1.7	Arabian Gulf

Austin–*Class Amphibious Transport Dock (LPD)*
Builders: Ingalls Shipbuilding, Pascagoula, MS; Lockheed Shipbuilding, Seattle, WA; and New York Naval Shipyard, Brooklyn, NY
Displacement, full load: 16,900 tons
Length, overall: 568 ft. 9 in.
Beam: 84 ft.
Draft: 23 ft.
Well deck:
    Length: 393 ft. 8 in.
    Width: 52 ft. 3 in.
Flight deck area: 15,000 ft^2 (1,394 m^2)
Engines: Two boilers, two De Laval steam turbines, 24,000 shp on two shafts
Speed: 20 kts.
Crew: 425
    930 troops in some ships
    840 troops and 90 flag in others
Armament: 2 20mm Mk-15 Mod 2 Phalanx Gatling-type CIWS
3 25mm Mk-39 Sea Snake chain guns
Helicopters: flight deck with 2 landing spots and hangar
Landing craft: 3 LCAC or 9 LCM-6

NAME	Hull #	Laid Down	Launched	Comm.	Age (yrs.) at OIF Start	Deployed to	Desert Shield/Storm
NASHVILLE	LPD 13	3/14/1966	10/7/1967	2/14/1970	33.1	Arabian Gulf	
PONCE	LPD 15	10/31/1966	5/30/1970	7/10/1971	31.7	Arabian Gulf	
AUSTIN	LPD 4	2/4/1963	6/27/1964	2/6/1965	38.1	Arabian Gulf	
DULUTH	LPD 6	12/18/1963	8/14/1965	12/18/1965	37.3	Arabian Gulf	
CLEVELAND	LPD 7	11/30/1964	5/7/1966	4/21/1967	35.9	Suez	
DUBUQUE	LPD 8	1/25/1965	8/6/1966	9/1/1967	35.6	Mediterranean	Y

Anchorage–*class Dock Landing Ships* (LSD)
Builder: Ing Alls, San Diego, CA
Displacement, full load: 14,000 tons
Length, overall: 553 ft. 6 in.
Beam: 85 ft.
Draft: 18 ft. 5 in.
Docking well:
 Length: 430 ft.
 Width: 50 ft.
Engines: Two boilers, two steam turbines, 24,000 shp on two shafts
Speed: 22 kts.
Crew: 358 + 330 troops
Armament: 2 20mm Mk-15 Phalanx Gatling-type CIWS
Helicopters: removable flight deck

NAME	Hull #	Laid Down	Launched	Comm.	Age (yrs.) at OIF Start	Deployed to	Desert Shield/Storm
ANCHORAGE	LSD 36	3/13/1967	5/5/1968	3/15/1969	34.0	Arabian Gulf	Y
PORTLAND	LSD 37	9/21/1967	12/20/1969	10/3/1970	32.5	Arabian Gulf	Y

Whidbey Island–*class Dock Landing Ships* (LSD)
Builders: Lockheed Shipbuilding, Seattle, WA, and Avondale Shipyards, New Orleans, LA
Displacement, full load: 15,704 tons
Length, overall: 609 ft. 5 in.
Beam: 84 ft.
Draft: 20 ft.
Docking well:
 Length: 440 ft.
 Width: 50 ft.
Engines: Four Colt-Pielstick 16PC 2.5 V400 diesels, 33,600 bhp on two shafts
Speed: 20 kts.
Crew: 342
 500 troops
Armament: 2 20mm Mk-15 Phalanx Gatling-type CIWS
Helicopters: landing area
Landing craft: 4 LCAC or 21 LCM-6

NAME	Hull #	Laid Down	Launched	Comm.	Age (yrs.) at OIF Start	Deployed to	Desert Shield/Storm
GUNSTON HALL	LSD 44	5/26/1986	6/27/1987	4/22/1989	13.9	Arabian Gulf	Y
COMSTOCK	LSD 45	10/27/1986	1/16/1988	2/3/1990	13.1	Mediterranean	
TORTUGA	LSD 46	3/23/1987	9/15/1988	11/17/1990	12.3	Arabian Gulf	
RUSHMORE	LSD 47	11/9/1987	5/6/1989	6/1/1991	11.8	Mediterranean	
ASHLAND	LSD 48	4/4/1988	11/11/1989	5/9/1992	10.9	Arabian Gulf	

Harpers Ferry–*class Dock Landing Ships (LSD)—Cargo Variant*
Builder: Avondale Industries, Inc., New Orleans, LA
Displacement, full load: 16,695 tons
Length, overall: 609 ft. 5 in.
Beam: 84 ft.
Draft: 20 ft.
Engines: Four Colt-Pielstick 16PC 2.5 V400 diesels, 33,600 bhp on two shafts
Speed: 21.6 kts.
Crew: 400
    400 troops
Armaments: 2 20mm Mk-15 Phalanx Gatling-type CIWS
Helicopters landing area

NAME	Hull #	Laid Down	Launched	Comm.	Age (yrs.) at OIF Start	Deployed to
CARTER HALL	LSD 50	33,553.0	34,244.0	34,972.0	7.5	Arabian Gulf
PEARL HARBOR	LSD 52	34,726.0	35,119.0	35,945.0	4.8	Arabian Gulf

Class: LCAC 1
Builder: Textron Marine and Land Systems/Avondale Industries, Inc., Gulfport, MS
Displacement:
    Light: 87.2 tons
    Full load: 170–182 tons
Length: 87 ft. 11 in.
Beam: 47 ft.
Engines: Four Avco-Lycoming TF-40B gas turbines (two for propulsion/two for lift.); 16,000 hp sustained; two shrouded reversible pitch airscrews; four double-entry fans, centrifugal or mixed flow (lift.)
Speed: 40 + knots (46 + mph; 73.6 kph) with full load
Range: 200 miles at 40 kts. with Payload
300 miles at 35 kts. with Payload
Crew: 5
Load Capacity: 60 tons / 75 ton overload
Military lift: 24 troops or 1 MBT
Armament: 2 12.7mm machine guns
Gun mounts will support:
    M-2HB .50-cal machine gun
    Mk-19 Mod3 40mm grenade launcher
    M-60 machine gun

JOHN ERICSSON	T-AO 194	3/15/1989	4/21/1990	3/18/1991	12.0
KANAWHA	T-AO 196	7/13/1989	9/22/1990	12/6/1991	11.3
PECOS	T-AO 197	2/17/1988	9/23/1989	7/6/1990	12.7
GUADALUPE	T-AO 200	7/9/1990	10/5/1991	9/25/1992	10.5
YUKON	T-AO 202	5/13/1991	2/6/1993	3/25/1994	9.0
PATUXENT	T-AO(D) 201	10/16/1991	7/23/1994	6/21/1995	7.7
RAPPAHANNOCK	T-AO(D) 204	3/29/1992	1/14/1995	11/7/1995	7.4

Sacramento–*class* Combat Support Ships (T-AOE)

Builders: Puget Sound Naval Shipyard and New York Shipbuilding Corp., Camden, NJ
Displacement, full load. 53,138 tons
Length: 796 ft. overall
Beam: 107 ft.
Draft: 39 ft. 4 in.
Engines: Four boilers, two steam turbines, 100,000 shp on two shafts
Speed: 27.5 kts.
Crew: 52 officers, 627 enlisted
Armament:
1 8-tube NATO Sea Sparrow launcher Mk-29
2 Mk-15 Phalanx Gatling-type CIWS
Helicopters: 2 UH-46 Sea Knight

NAME	Hull #	Laid Down	Launched	Comm.	Age (yr.) at OIF Start	Deployed to
CAMDEN	AOE 2	2/17/1964	5/29/1965	4/1/1967	36.0	Arabian Gulf

Supply–*class* Combat Support Ships (AOE)

Builder: National Steel and Shipbuilding Co., San Diego, CA
Displacement, full load: 48,800 tons
Length: 754 feet
Beam: 107 feet
Draft: 40 ft.
Engines: Four GE LM2500 gas-turbines, 105,000 shp on two shafts
Speed: 25 kts.
Crew: 40 officers, 627 enlisted
Armament:
1 8-tube NATO Sea Sparrow launcher Mk-29
2 Mk-15 Phalanx Gatling-type CIWS
Helicopters: 3 CH-46E Sea Knights

NAME	Hull #	Laid Down	Launched	Comm.	Age (yr.) at OIF Start	Deployed to
RAINIER	AOE 7	5/31/1990	9/28/1991	1/21/1995	8.2	Arabian Gulf
ARCTIC	AOE 8	12/2/1991	10/30/1993	9/11/1995	7.5	Mediterranean
BRIDGE	AOE 10	8/2/1994	8/24/1996	8/5/1998	4.6	Arabian Gulf

Safeguard–*class Rescue and Salvage Ship (ARS)*
Builders: Peterson Builders, Sturgeon Bay, WI
Displacement, full load: 3,200 tons
Length: 255 ft.
Beam: 51 ft.
Draft: 15 ft. 5 in.
Engines: Four Caterpillar geared diesels, 4,200 bhp on two shafts
Speed: 13.5 kts.
Crew: 7 officers, 92 enlisted
Salvage capability: 7.5-ton capacity boom forward
40-ton capacity boom aft
Heavy lifting: Capable of a hauling force of 150 tons
Diving Depth: 190 feet (57.9 meters), using air
Armament:
2 Mk-38 25mm chain guns
2 .50-cal. machine guns in single mounts

NAME	Hull #	Laid Down	Launched	Comm.	Age (yr.) at OIF Start	Deployed to
GRASP	ARS 51	5/2/1983	4/21/1984	12/14/1985	17.3	Arabian Gulf
GRAPPLE	ARS 53	4/25/1984	12/8/1984	11/15/1986	16.3	Arabian Gulf

Gopher State–*class Crane Ship (T-ACS)*
Builder: Norship Co, Norfolk, VA
Displacement: 31,500 long tons
Length: 610 feet
Beam: 78 feet
Draft: 31 feet
Engines: Two boilers, steam turbines, 17,500 shp on one shaft
Speed: 17.0 kts.
Crew: 35 civilian + 6 military

NAME	Hull #	Conversion Started	Launched	Comm.	Age (yr.) at OIF Start
GOPHER STATE	T-ACS 4	10/20/1985		10/23/1986	16.4
CORNHUSKER STATE	T-ACS 6	3/2/1986		4/12/1987	15.9

Powhatan–*class Fleet Ocean Tug (ATF)*
Builder: Marinette Marine, Marinette, WI
Displacement: 2,000 long tons
Length: 226 feet
Beam: 42 feet
Draft: 15 feet
Engines: Two GM EMD 20-645F7B diesels, 7,680 bhp, sustained on two shafts, Kort hozzles, bow thruster; 300 hp (224 kW)
Speed: 15 kts.
Crew: 16 civilian + 4 Navy

NAME	Hull #	Laid Down	Launched	Comm.	Age (yr.) at OIF Start
CATAWBA	ATF 168	12/14/1977	9/22/1979	5/28/1980	22.8

Wright–*class Aviation Support Ships (T-AVB)*
Builder: Ingals Shipbuilding, Pascagoula, MS
Displacement, full load: 23,872 tons (15,694 tons deadweight)
Length: 602 ft. overall
Beam: 90 ft.
Draft: 34 ft. (to summer freeboard)
Engines: Two boilers, two steam turbines, 30,000 shp on one shaft
Speed: 23.6 kts.
Crew: 41 civilian
Helicopters landing area

NAME	Hull #	Laid Down (as merchant)	Launched (as merchant)	Comm.	Age at OIF Start	Deployed to	Desert Shield/Storm
CURTISS	T-AVB4	4/12/1968	12/28/1968	8/18/1987	15.6	Arabian Gulf	Y
WRIGHT	T-AVB3	6/24/1968	7/29/1969	5/13/1985	17.9	Arabian Gulf	Y

MERCHANT-MANNED EQUIPMENT SUPPLY SHIPS

ALGOL-Class Fast Sealift Ships
Builders: Rotterdamsche D.D. Mij N.V., Rotterdam, the Netherlands; Rheinstahl Nordseewerke, Emden, West Germany; and A.G. Weser, Bremen, West Germany
Displacement: full load: 61,297 tons (32,295 deadweight tons)
Length: 946 ft. 6 in. overall
Beam: 105 ft. 8 in.
Draft: 36 ft. 9 in.
Engines: Two boilers, two steam turbines, 120,000 shp on two shafts = 33 kts.
Crew: 45 civilian + 56 troops
Helicopters flight deck

NAME	Hull #	Conversion Started	Comm.	Age (yr.) at OIF Start
ALGOL	T-AKR 287	10/12/1981	6/19/1983	19.8
BELLATRIX	T-AKR 288	10/21/1981	9/10/1983	19.5
DENEBOLA	T-AKR 289	5/4/1983	9/9/1984	18.5
POLLUX	T-AKR 290	5/21/1983	3/30/1985	18.0
ALTAIR	T-AKR 291	1/31/1983	11/12/1984	18.4
REGULUS	T-AKR 292	6/29/1983	8/27/1984	18.6
CAPELLA	T-AKR 293	10/21/1981	7/1/1983	19.7
ANTARES	T-AKR 294	10/5/1981	7/12/1983	19.7

Shugart–class Large, Medium-Speed Roll-on/Roll-off Ship
Builders: National Steel and Ship Building Co., San Diego, CA and Newport News Shipbuilding, Norfolk, VA
Displacement: 56,177 long tons
Length: 907 feet
Beam: 105 ft. 6 in.
Draft: 34 ft. 10 in.
Engines: One Burmeister & Wain 12L90 GFCA diesel, 46,653 hp(m) on one shaft, bow and stern thrusters
Speed: 24 kts.
Crew: 50 civilians

NAME	Hull #	Conversion Started	Launched	Comm.	Age (yr.) at OIF Start
SHUGHART	T-AKR 295	11/22/1993	4/13/1996	5/7/1996	6.9
YANO	T-AKR 297	5/1/1994	9/26/1995	2/8/1997	6.1
STOCKHAM	T-AKR 299	7/10/1994	2/19/1996	10/25/1997	5.4

Gordon–class Large, Medium-Speed Roll-on/Roll-off Ship
Builder/Converter: Newport News Shipbuilding, Norfolk, VA
Displacement: 54,298 long tons (21,709 deadweight)
Length: 956 feet
Beam: 105 ft. 8 in.
Draft: 34 ft. 10 in.
Engines: One Burmeister & Wain 12K84EF diesel, 26,000 hp(m) and Two Burmeister & Wain 9K84EF diesels, 39,000 hp(m), on three shafts (center cp prop), bow thruster
Speed: 24 kts.
Crew: 50 civilians

NAME	Hull #	Laid Down	Launched	Comm.	Age (yr.) at OIF Start
GORDON	T-AKR 296	10/8/1993	9/2/1994	1/31/1995	8.1
GILLILAND	T-AKR 298	10/15/1993	3/27/1995	5/24/1997	5.8

Bob Hope–*class Large, Medium-Speed Roll-on/Roll-off Ship*

Builder: Avondale Industries, Westwego, LA
Displacement: 63,055 long tons
Length: 950 feet
Beam: 106 feet
Draft: 34 feet
Engines: Four Colt Piclstick 10 PC4.2 V diesels, 65,160 hp, two shafts (cp props)
Speed: 24 kts.
Civilian complement: 30

NAME	Hull #	Laid Down	Launched	Comm.	Age (yr.) at OIF Start
BOB HOPE	T-AKR 300	6/5/1995	1/18/1997	9/30/1997	5.5
FISHER	T-AKR 301	4/15/1996	10/21/1997	8/4/1999	3.6
SEAY	T-AKR 302	3/24/1997	6/25/1998	3/28/2000	3.0
MENDONCA	T-AKR 303	11/3/1997	5/25/1999	1/30/2001	2.1
PILILAAU	I-AKR 304	6/29/1998	1/29/2000	7/24/2001	1.7
BRITTIN	T-AKR 305	5/3/1999	11/11/2000	7/11/2002	0.7

Watson–*class Large, Medium-Speed Roll-on/Roll-off Ship*

(6 ships assigned to APSRON 4, but only 3 confirmed to have been loaded in U.S.)
Builder: NASSCO, San Diego, CA
Displacement: 63,969 long tons
Length: 950 feet
Beam: 106 feet
Draft: 34 feet
Engines: Two GE Marine LM gas turbines, 64,000 hp, two shafts (cp props)
Speed: 24 kts.
Civilian complement: 30

NAME	Hull #	Laid Down	Launched	Comm.	Age (yr.) at OIF Start
WATSON	T-AKR 310	5/23/1996	7/26/1997	6/23/1998	4.7
RED CLOUD	T-AKR 313	6/29/1998	8/7/1999	1/18/2000	3.2
WATKINS	T-AKR 315	8/24/1999	7/28/2000	3/2/2001	2.1

HSV-1X JOINT VENTURE High-Speed Vessel

Builder: Incat Australia, Tasmania
Vessel Name: Joint Venture—Hull Number 050
Date Completed: November 21, 1998
Vessel Type: 96-meter Evolution 10 wave-piercing catamaran
Operator: U.S. Army Tank-Automotive and Armaments Command (TACOM)

Some more on the HSV (wording is U.S. Army's):
The Army in October 2001 leased the 313-foot aluminum catamaran to test the capabilities of commercial high-speed watercraft technology and will accept delivery in November of a second leased vessel, the TSV-1X Spearhead. The Australian-built *Joint Venture* travels at speeds up to 40 knots, approximately four times faster than current Army watercraft. It can carry 850 short tons and accommodate 363 personnel, including crew. Theater Support Vessels (TSVs) promise to change the way the Army gets to the fight.

To Date III MEF use of a contracted WestPAC HSV for theater support has shown: One Battalion, one Lift. Keeping combat power intact with Marines and equipment together. Load and unload times under one hour.
The capacity to transport over 400 tonnes of equipment, along with passengers; 750 tonnes Maximum Deadweight: 970 soldiers/Marines in comfortable airline-style reclining seats and 152 HMMWVs or 12 AAVPs and 20 LAVs. Multiple load combinations of tractor trailers, water tankers, etc., in vehicle deck with RO/RO vehicles/trailers.
Note: Current Air Mobility Command strategic airlift support (AMC) to move same number of Marines and equipment would require 14 to 17 military aircraft spread out over a 14-to-17-day period. Combined > 40,000 square feet of storage space. HSV configured for "field conditions," berthing/hotel service trailers were added for soldiers/Marines to meet mission specific needs.

TSV-1X Spearhead

Vessel Name: USAV TSV-1X SPEARHEAD ACTD—Hull Number 060
Builder: Incat, Tasmania, Australia
Date Completed: November 19, 2002
Vessel Type: 98-meter (321 ft. 6 in.) Evolution 10B wave-piercing catamaran
Speed: Reached 48.7 kts. in Arabian Gulf
Operator: U.S. Army Tank-Automotive and Armaments Command (TACOM)

CW3 Patrick S. May, Commander, USAV Spearhead, comments: "The reception of the TSV is amazing, and all eyes are on the Spearhead in every port. We've given hundreds of tours to everyone from the casual observer to generals.
"We have sailed a total of 29,305 nautical miles and our operations to date have covered most of the western part of the CENTCOM Theater from Jordan to Kuwait. We have carried 751 troops and hauled over 1320 pieces of military cargo, just about everything in the inventory except for tracks, all of which were already on the battlefield when we arrived."

Additional Support Ships for Movement of cargo, including Maritime Prepositioning Ships	
T-AK 2062	MV American Cormorant (Combat Prepositioning Force)
T-AK 3000	MV Cpl. Louis J. Hauge Jr. (MPS 2)
T-AK 3001	MV Pfc. William B. Baugh (MPS 2)
T-AK 3002	MV Pfc. James Anderson Jr. (MPS 2)
T-AK 3003	MV 1st Lt. Alex Bonnyman (MPS 2)
T-AK 3004	MV Pvt. Franklin J. Phillips (MPS 2)
T-AK 3005	SS Sgt. Matej Kocak (MPS 1)
T-AK 3006	SS Pfc. Eugene A. Obregon (MPS 1)
T-AK 3007	SS Maj. Stephen W. Pless (MPS 1)
T-AK 3008	MV 2nd Lt. John P. Bobo (MPS 1)
T-AK 3015	USNS 1st Lt. Harry L. Martin (MPS 1)
T-AK 3017	USNS Gysgt Fred W. Stockham (MPS 2)
T-AK 4396	MV Bernard F. Fisher (Logistics Prepositioning Force)
T-AK 4496	MV LTC John U.D. Page (Combat Prepositioning Force)
T-AK 4544	Sgt. Edward A. Carter, Jr. (Combat Prepositioning Force)
T-AK 4638	Pitsenbarger (Logistics Prepositioning Force)
T-AK 9655	MV Green Ridge (Logistics Prepositioning Force)
T-AKR 10	Cape Island (RRF)
T-AKR 1001	Adm. William M. Callaghan (RRF)
T-AKR 11	Cape Intrepid (RRF)
T-AKR 112	Cape Texas (RRF)
T-AKR 113	Cape Taylor (RRF)
T-AKR 2044	Cape Orlando (RRF)
T-AKR 5022	Cape John (RRF)
T-AKR 5051	Cape Ducato (RRF)
T-AKR 5051	Cape Gibson (RRF)
T-AKR 5052	Cape Douglas (RRF)
T-AKR 5053	Cape Domingo (RRF)
T-AKR 5054	Cape Decision (RRF)
T-AKR 5055	Cape Diamond (RRF)
T-AKR 5062	Cape Isabel (RRF)
T-AKR 5066	Cape Hudson (RRF)
T-AKR 5067	Cape Henry (RRF)
T-AKR 5068	Cape Horn (RRF)
T-AKR 5069	Cape Edmont (RRF)
T-AKR 5075	Capo Johnson (RRF)
T-AKR 5076	Cape Inscription (RRF)
T-AKR 5082	Cape Knox (RRF)
T-AKR 5083	Cape Kennedy (RRF)
T-AKR 7	Comet (RRF)
T-AKR 9666	Cape Vincent (RRF)
T-AKR 9678	Cape Rise (RRF)
T-AKR 9679	Cape Ray Cape R

T-AKR 9701	Cape Victory (RRF)
T-AKR 9711	Cape Trinity (RRF)
T-AKR 9960	Cape Race Cape R
T-AKR 9961	Cape Washington (RRF)
T-AKR 9962	Cape Wrath (RRF)
T-AO 187	USNS Henry J. Kaiser (Logistics Prepositioning Force)
T-AOT 5084	Chesapeake (Logistics Prepositioning Force)
	MV Tellus Faust

BRITISH WEAPONS USED IN OPERATION IRAQI FREEDOM

45 ALARM antiradar
27 Storm Shadow stand-off attack missiles
780 precision bombs
140 nonprecision bombs
(about the same ratio as U.S. attacks)

Thanks to Steve Llanso.

UNITED NATIONS SECURITY COUNCIL PROVISIONAL
7 NOVEMBER 2002
ORIGINAL: ENGLISH

United Kingdom of Great Britain and Northern Ireland and United States of America: draft resolution

[Adopted as Resolution 1441 at Security Council meeting 4644, November 8, 2002]

The Security Council,
Recalling all its previous relevant resolutions, in particular its resolutions 661 (1990) of 6 August 1990, 678 (1990) of 29 November 1990, 686 (1991) of 2 March 1991, 687 (1991) of 3 April 1991, 688 (1991) of 5 April 1991, 707 (1991) of 15 August 1991, 715 (1991) of 11 October 1991, 986 (1995) of 14 April 1995, and 1284 (1999) of 17 December 1999, and all the relevant statements of its President,
Recalling also its resolution 1382 (2001) of 29 November 2001 and its intention to implement it fully,
Recognizing the threat Iraq's non-compliance with Council resolutions and proliferation of weapons of mass destruction and long-range missiles poses to international peace and security,
Recalling that its resolution 678 (1990) authorized Member States to use all necessary means to uphold and implement its resolution 660 (1990) of 2 August 1990 and all relevant resolutions subsequent to resolution 660 (1990) and to restore international peace and security in the area,
Further recalling that its resolution 687 (1991) imposed obligations on Iraq as a necessary step for achievement of its stated objective of restoring international peace and security in the area,
Deploring the fact that Iraq has not provided an accurate, full, final, and complete disclosure, as required by resolution 687 (1991), of all aspects of its programmes to develop weapons of mass destruction and ballistic missiles with a range greater than one hundred and fifty kilometres, and of all holdings of such weapons, their components and production facilities and locations, as well as all other nuclear programmes, including any which it claims are for purposes not related to nuclear-weapons-usable material,
Deploring further that Iraq repeatedly obstructed immediate, unconditional,

and unrestricted access to sites designated by the United Nations Special Commission (UNSCOM) and the International Atomic Energy Agency (IAEA), failed to cooperate fully and unconditionally with UNSCOM and IAEA weapons inspectors, as required by resolution 687 (1991), and ultimately ceased all cooperation with UNSCOM and the IAEA in 1998,

Deploring the absence, since December 1998, in Iraq of international monitoring, inspection, and verification, as required by relevant resolutions, of weapons of mass destruction and ballistic missiles, in spite of the Council's repeated demands that Iraq provide immediate, unconditional, and unrestricted access to the United Nations Monitoring, Verification and Inspection Commission (UNMOVIC), established in resolution 1284 (1999) as the successor organization to UNSCOM, and the IAEA, and regretting the consequent prolonging of the crisis in the region and the suffering of the Iraqi people,

Deploring also that the Government of Iraq has failed to comply with its commitments pursuant to resolution 687 (1991) with regard to terrorism, pursuant to resolution 688 (1991) to end repression of its civilian population and to provide access by international humanitarian organizations to all those in need of assistance in Iraq, and pursuant to resolutions 686 (1991), 687 (1991), and 1284 (1999) to return or cooperate in accounting for Kuwaiti and third country nationals wrongfully detained by Iraq, or to return Kuwaiti property wrongfully seized by Iraq,

Recalling that in its resolution 687 (1991) the Council declared that a ceasefire would be based on acceptance by Iraq of the provisions of that resolution, including the obligations on Iraq contained therein,

Determined to ensure full and immediate compliance by Iraq without conditions or restrictions with its obligations under resolution 687 (1991) and other relevant resolutions and recalling that the resolutions of the Council constitute the governing standard of Iraqi compliance,

Recalling that the effective operation of UNMOVIC, as the successor organization to the Special Commission, and the IAEA is essential for the implementation of resolution 687 (1991) and other relevant resolutions,

Noting the letter dated 16 September 2002 from the Minister for Foreign Affairs of Iraq addressed to the Secretary-General is a necessary first step toward rectifying Iraq's continued failure to comply with relevant Council resolutions,

Noting further the letter dated 8 October 2002 from the Executive Chairman of UNMOVIC and the Director-General of the IAEA to General Al-Saadi of the Government of Iraq laying out the practical arrangements, as a follow-up to their meeting in Vienna, that are prerequisites for the resumption of inspections in Iraq by UNMOVIC and the IAEA, and expressing the gravest concern at the continued failure by the Government of Iraq to provide confirmation of the arrangements as laid out in that letter,

Reaffirming the commitment of all Member States to the sovereignty and territorial integrity of Iraq, Kuwait, and the neighbouring States,

Commending the Secretary-General and members of the League of Arab States and its Secretary-General for their efforts in this regard,

Determined to secure full compliance with its decisions,

Acting under Chapter VII of the Charter of the United Nations,

1. *Decides* that Iraq has been and remains in material breach of its obligations under relevant resolutions, including resolution 687 (1991), in particular through Iraq's failure to cooperate with United Nations inspectors and the IAEA, and to complete the actions required under paragraphs 8 to 13 of resolution 687 (1991);

2. *Decides*, while acknowledging paragraph 1 above, to afford Iraq, by this resolution, a final opportunity to comply with its disarmament obligations under relevant resolutions of the Council; and accordingly decides to set up an enhanced inspection regime with the aim of bringing to full and verified completion the disarmament process established by resolution 687 (1991) and subsequent resolutions of the Council;

3. *Decides that*, in order to begin to comply with its disarmament obligations, in addition to submitting the required biannual declarations, the Government of Iraq shall provide to UNMOVIC, the IAEA, and the Council, not later than 30 days from the date of this resolution, a currently accurate, full, and complete declaration of all aspects of its programmes to develop chemical, biological, and nuclear weapons, ballistic missiles, and other delivery systems such as unmanned aerial vehicles and dispersal systems designed for use on aircraft, including any holdings and precise locations of such weapons, components, sub-components, stocks of agents, and related material and equipment, the locations and work of its research, development and production facilities, as well as all other chemical, biological, and nuclear programmes, including any which it claims are for purposes not related to weapon production or material;

4. *Decides* that false statements or omissions in the declarations submitted by Iraq pursuant to this resolution and failure by Iraq at any time to comply with, and cooperate fully in the implementation of, this resolution shall constitute a further material breach of Iraq's obligations and will be reported to the Council for assessment in accordance with paragraphs 11 and 12 below;

5. *Decides* that Iraq shall provide UNMOVIC and the IAEA immediate, unimpeded, unconditional, and unrestricted access to any and all, including underground, areas, facilities, buildings, equipment, records, and means of transport which they wish to inspect, as well as immediate, unimpeded, unrestricted, and private access to all officials and other persons whom UNMOVIC or the IAEA wish to interview in the mode or location of UNMOVIC's or the IAEA's choice pursuant to any aspect of their mandates; further decides that UNMOVIC and the IAEA may at their discretion conduct interviews inside or outside of Iraq, may facilitate the travel of those interviewed and family members outside of Iraq, and that, at the sole discretion of UNMOVIC and the IAEA, such interviews may occur without the presence of observers from the Iraqi Government; and instructs UNMOVIC and requests the IAEA to resume inspections no later than 45 days following adoption of this resolution and to update the Council 60 days thereafter;

6. *Endorses* the 8 October 2002 letter from the Executive Chairman of UNMOVIC and the Director-General of the IAEA to General Al-Saadi of the Government of Iraq, which is annexed hereto, and decides that the contents of the letter shall be binding upon Iraq;

7. *Decides* further that, in view of the prolonged interruption by Iraq of the presence of UNMOVIC and the IAEA and in order for them to accomplish the tasks set forth in this resolution and all previous relevant resolutions and notwithstanding prior understandings, the Council hereby establishes the following

revised or additional authorities, which shall be binding upon Iraq, to facilitate their work in Iraq:

—UNMOVIC and the IAEA shall determine the composition of their inspection teams and ensure that these teams are composed of the most qualified and experienced experts available;
—All UNMOVIC and IAEA personnel shall enjoy the privileges and immunities, corresponding to those of experts on mission, provided in the Convention on Privileges and Immunities of the United Nations and the Agreement on the Privileges and Immunities of the IAEA;
—UNMOVIC and the IAEA shall have unrestricted rights of entry into and out of Iraq, the right to free, unrestricted, and immediate movement to and from inspection sites, and the right to inspect any sites and buildings, including immediate, unimpeded, unconditional, and unrestricted access to Presidential Sites equal to that at other sites, notwithstanding the provisions of resolution 1154 (1998);
—UNMOVIC and the IAEA shall have the right to be provided by Iraq the names of all personnel currently and formerly associated with Iraq's chemical, biological, nuclear, and ballistic missile programmes and the associated research, development, and production facilities;
—Security of UNMOVIC and IAEA facilities shall be ensured by sufficient United Nations security guards;
—UNMOVIC and the IAEA shall have the right to declare, for the purposes of freezing a site to be inspected, exclusion zones, including surrounding areas and transit corridors, in which Iraq will suspend ground and aerial movement so that nothing is changed in or taken out of a site being inspected;
—UNMOVIC and the IAEA shall have the free and unrestricted use and landing of fixed- and rotary-winged aircraft, including manned and unmanned reconnaissance vehicles;
—UNMOVIC and the IAEA shall have the right at their sole discretion verifiably to remove, destroy, or render harmless all prohibited weapons, subsystems, components, records, materials, and other related items, and the right to impound or close any facilities or equipment for the production thereof; and
—UNMOVIC and the IAEA shall have the right to free import and use of equipment or materials for inspections and to seize and export any equipment, materials, or documents taken during inspections, without search of UNMOVIC or IAEA personnel or official or personal baggage;

8. *Decides* further that Iraq shall not take or threaten hostile acts directed against any representative or personnel of the United Nations or the IAEA or of any Member State taking action to uphold any Council resolution;

9. *Requests* the Secretary-General immediately to notify Iraq of this resolution, which is binding on Iraq; demands that Iraq confirm within seven days of that notification its intention to comply fully with this resolution; and demands further that Iraq cooperate immediately, unconditionally, and actively with UNMOVIC and the IAEA;

10. *Requests* all Member States to give full support to UNMOVIC and the IAEA in the discharge of their mandates, including by providing any information related

to prohibited programmes or other aspects of their mandates, including on Iraqi attempts since 1998 to acquire prohibited items, and by recommending sites to be inspected, persons to be interviewed, conditions of such interviews, and data to be collected, the results of which shall be reported to the Council by UNMOVIC and the IAEA;

11. *Directs* the Executive Chairman of UNMOVIC and the Director-General of the IAEA to report immediately to the Council any interference by Iraq with inspection activities, as well as any failure by Iraq to comply with its disarmament obligations, including its obligations regarding inspections under this resolution;

12. *Decides* to convene immediately upon receipt of a report in accordance with paragraphs 4 or 11 above, in order to consider the situation and the need for full compliance with all of the relevant Council resolutions in order to secure international peace and security;

13. *Recalls*, in that context, that the Council has repeatedly warned Iraq that it will face serious consequences as a result of its continued violations of its obligations;

14. *Decides* to remain seized of the matter.

Annex

Text of Blix/El-Baradei letter

International Atomic Energy Agency

**United Nations Monitoring, Verification
and Inspection Commission**

The Director General

The Executive Chairman
_____

8 October 2002

Dear General Al-Saadi,

During our recent meeting in Vienna, we discussed practical arrangements that are prerequisites for the resumption of inspections in Iraq by UNMOVIC and the IAEA. As you recall, at the end of our meeting in Vienna we agreed on a statement which listed some of the principal results achieved, particularly Iraq's acceptance of all the rights of inspection provided for in all of the relevant Security Council resolutions. This acceptance was stated to be without any conditions attached.

During our 3 October 2002 briefing to the Security Council, members of the Council suggested that we prepare a written document on all of the conclusions we reached in Vienna. This letter lists those conclusions and seeks your confirmation thereof. We shall report accordingly to the Security Council.

In the statement at the end of the meeting, it was clarified that UNMOVIC and the IAEA will be granted immediate, unconditional and

253

unrestricted access to sites including what was termed "sensitive sites" in the past. As we noted, however, eight presidential sites have been the subject of special procedures under a Memorandum of Understanding of 1998. Should these sites be subject, as all other sites, to immediate unconditional and unrestricted access, UNMOVIC and the IAEA would conduct inspections there with the same professionalism.

H.E. General Amir H. Al-Saadi
Advisor
Presidential Office
Baghdad
Iraq

We confirm our understanding that UNMOVIC and the IAEA have the right to determine the number of inspectors required for access to any particular site. This determination will be made on the basis of the size and complexity of the site being inspected. We also confirm that Iraq will be informed of the designation of additional sites, i.e. sites not declared by Iraq or previously inspected by either UNSCOM or the IAEA, through a Notification of Inspection (NIS) provided upon arrival of the inspectors at such sites.

Iraq will ensure that no proscribed material, equipment, records or other relevant items will be destroyed except in the presence of UNMOVIC and/or IAEA inspectors, as appropriate, and at their request.

UNMOVIC and the IAEA may conduct interviews with any person in Iraq whom they believe may have information relevant to their mandate. Iraq will facilitate such interviews. It is for UNMOVIC and the IAEA to choose the mode and location for interviews.

The National Monitoring Directorate (NMD) will, as in the past, serve as the Iraqi counterpart for the inspectors. The Baghdad Ongoing Monitoring and Verification Centre (BOMVIC) will be maintained on the same premises and under the same conditions as was the former Baghdad Monitoring and Verification Centre. The NMD will make available services as before, cost free, for the refurbishment of the premises.

The NMD will provide free of cost: (a) escorts to facilitate access to sites to be inspected and communication with personnel to be interviewed; (b) a hotline for BOMVIC which will be staffed by an English speaking person on a 24 hour a day/seven days a week basis; (c) support in terms of personnel and ground transportation within the country, as requested; and (d) assistance in the movement of materials and equipment at inspectors' request (construction, excavation equipment, etc.). NMD will also ensure that escorts are available in the event of inspections outside normal working hours, including at night and on holidays.

Regional UNMOVIC/IAEA offices may be established, for example, in Basra and Mosul, for the use of their inspectors. For this purpose, Iraq will provide, without cost, adequate office buildings, staff accommodation, and appropriate escort personnel.

UNMOVIC and the IAEA may use any type of voice or data transmission including satellite and/or inland networks, with or without encryption capability. UNMOVIC and the IAEA may also install equipment in the field with the capability for transmission of data directly to the BOMVIC, New York and Vienna (e.g. sensors surveillance cameras). This will be facilitated by Iraq and there will be no interference by Iraq with UNMOVIC or IAEA communications.

Iraq will provide, without cost, physical protection of all surveillance equipment and construct antennae for remote transmission of data, at the request of UNMOVIC and the IAEA. Upon request by UNMOVIC through the NMD, Iraq will allocate frequencies for communications equipment.

Iraq will provide security for all UNMOVIC and IAEA personnel. Secure and suitable accommodations will be designated at normal rates by Iraq for these personnel. For their part, UNMOVIC and the IAEA will require that their staff not stay at any accommodation other than those identified in consultation with Iraq.

On the use of fixed-wing aircraft for transport of personnel and equipment and for inspection purposes, it was clarified that aircraft used by UNMOVIC and IAEA staff arriving in Baghdad may land at Saddam International Airport. The points of departure of incoming aircraft will be decided by UNMOVIC. The Rasheed airbase will continue to be used for UNMOVIC and IAEA helicopter operations. UNMOVIC and Iraq will establish air liaison offices at the airbase. At both Saddam International Airport and Rasheed airbase, Iraq will provide the necessary support premises and facilities. Aircraft fuel will be provided by Iraq, as before, free of charge.

On the wider issue of air operations in Iraq, both fixed-wing and rotary, Iraq will guarantee the safety of air operations in its air space outside the no fly zones. With regard to air operations in the no-fly zones, Iraq will take all steps within its control to ensure the safety of such operations.

Helicopter flights may be used, as needed, during inspections and for technical activities, such as gamma detection, without limitation in all parts of Iraq and without any area excluded. Helicopters may also be used for medical evacuation.

On the question of aerial imagery, UNMOVIC may wish to resume the use of U-2 or Mirage overflights. The relevant practical arrangements would be similar to those implemented in the past.

As before, visas for all arriving staff will be issued at the point of entry on the basis of the UN Laissez-Passer or UN Certificate; no other entry or exit formalities will be required. The aircraft passenger manifest will be provided one hour in advance of the arrival of the aircraft in Baghdad. There will be no searching of UNMOVIC or IAEA personnel or of official or personal baggage. UNMOVIC and the IAEA will ensure that their personnel respect the laws of Iraq restricting the export of certain items, for example those related to Iraq's national cultural heritage. UNMOVIC and the IAEA may bring into, and remove from, Iraq all of the items and materials they require, including satellite phones and other equipment. With respect to samples, UNMOVIC and IAEA will, where feasible, split samples so that Iraq may receive a portion while another portion is kept for reference purposes. Where appropriate, the organizations will send the samples to more than one laboratory for analysis.

We would appreciate your confirmation of the above as a correct reflection of our talks in Vienna.

Naturally, we may need other practical arrangements when proceeding with inspections. We would expect in such matters, as with the above, Iraq's co-operation in all respects.

Yours sincerely,
[Signed]
Hans Blix
Mohamed El-Baradei
Executive Chairman
Director General
United Nations Monitoring,
International Atomic Energy Agency
Verification and Inspection Commission

ELEMENTS OF THE INFORMATION-GATHERING SYSTEM

While all satellite systems are critical, only Milstar will be discussed briefly here to give some idea of the immense importance of information gathering and communication systems to the war. Milstar is not as well known (or understood) as the GPS, but its role in communications was crucial. These are all unclassified systems, less sophisticated than some of the highly classified "black" systems that are operating, and whose existence may not be revealed for decades, if ever.

The Milstar Satellite Communication System consists of a constellation of three satellites in low-inclined geosynchronous orbit that provides worldwide coverage between 65 degrees North and 65 degrees South latitude. It orbits at an altitude of 22,300 miles. Each of the satellites in the system is 51 feet long and 116 feet wide and weighs 10,000 pounds.

Milstar provides a secure, jam-resistant worldwide C² (Command and Control) for all forces at all levels of conflict; it links command authorities to ground forces, ships, aircraft, and submarines. Before its deployment it was roundly criticized as too expensive, unnecessary, and certain to fail.

In Operation Iraqi Freedom, *Milstar 5*, in geosynchronous orbit over the Indian Ocean, proved indispensable in providing clandestine communications with the shadowy special operations forces operating throughout Iraq, including those that helped free PFC Lynch. It also gave the Navy Tomahawk missiles target information, provided the MEFs with secure communications, and enabled the new Global Hawk UAV to operate effectively over Iraq. It also improved "jointness," for it enabled the ATOs to be sent to Navy vessels in six seconds—instead of being delivered via a floppy disk, as in 1991. *Milstar 5* also routed communications to *Milstar 4*, which sent the information to Milstar terminals on the surface.

Ironically, the unit most suited for operation with Milstar, the 4th Infantry Division, was delayed by Turkish recalcitrance and entered the war late.

As an indication as to the relative expense of satellite systems, a fifth and final Milstar satellite was added to the constellation on April 8, 2003. The satellite cost $800 million, while the launch vehicle (a Titan IV/Centaur) cost $468 million.

The very utility of the satellites has placed so many demands upon them that existing systems of communication are becoming stressed.

Other indispensable satellite systems include the following.

DEFENSE METEOROLOGICAL SATELLITE PROGRAM (DMSP)

DMSP satellites are used to collect air, land, sea, and space environmental data to support strategic and tactical military operations. Orbit altitude is 500 miles. The satellites are 20.2 feet long and 4 feet wide and weigh 1,750 pounds. They orbit the Earth in about 12 hours, covering an area 1,800 miles wide.

The DMSP is operated by the National Polar-Orbiting Operational Satellite System (NPOESS) program office. The first launch took place in the early 1960s and was classified until 1973. It was used during the Vietnam conflict.

DEFENSE SUPPORT PROGRAM (DSP)

The DSP is an early-warning spacecraft in geosynchronous orbit. It uses infrared sensors to sense heat from missile and booster plumes to provide an alert of a ballistic missile attack on the United States or its forces. Warning data is fed to North American Aerospace Defense Command (NORAD) and the U.S. Strategic Command (STRATCOM), which operates the system.

The satellite has a diameter of 22 feet, is 32.8 feet high with its solar panels deployed, weighs 5,000 pounds, and orbits at a height of 22,000 miles.

DSP was invaluable in Desert Storm, even though it was not designed to track tactical ballistic missiles.

DEFENSE SATELLITE COMMUNICATION SYSTEM (DSCS)

This communication satellite operates at 22,000 miles' altitude in a geosynchronous orbit to transmit superhigh frequency high-priority command and control communications.

The satellite has a solar span of thirty-eight feet and a central body approximately six by six by seven feet in size and weighs about twenty-six hundred pounds. A constellation consists of five primary and five residual DSCS satellites. It provides worldwide high-bandwith satellite communications for a host of government agencies, including the White House.

GLOBAL POSITIONING SYSTEM (GPS)

The GPS system has been described in the text. The worldwide navigation satellite system is operated by Air Force Space Command. Its orbit altitude is about 12,600 miles.

There are three different GPS satellites in orbit (II/IIA and IIR) and they vary in size. The II has a body eight by six by ten feet, with solar arrays with a span of thirty-seven feet.

The GPS satellites orbit the Earth every twelve hours and transmit signals so accurate that they can be figured to within one-millionth of a second.

POLAR MILSSATCOM

This system is designed to provide secure communications in the North Pole region, above 65 degrees North latitude. The orbit altitude is 23,500 feet, and it augments the Milstar system.

There are many other classified satellites that cannot be discussed here.

In addition to satellites, the information gathering and dispersing system uses a wide variety of manned and unmanned aircraft, most of which have been described at greater length elsewhere in the book and in appendix 1.

APPENDIX FOUR

APACHES AT ANACONDA

Operation Anaconda was a plan devised in February of 2002 to trap al Qaeda fighters who were attempting to gather their forces near the 10,000-foot Shah-I-Kot mountains of eastern Afghanistan. They had taken a severe drubbing at Kandahar and elsewhere and sought the security of remote areas to regain their strength. They were observed gathering in Shah-e-Kot Valley near Gardez.

In December of 2001, other al Qaeda fighters had managed to survive the bombing of Tora Bora and escape. This time the United States was determined to put about American-trained Afghan soldiers and as many as 200 highly trained special forces from Australia, Canada, Denmark, Germany, and Norway into the area. These troops were to rouse the al Qaeda and force them to retreat to a point where American forces of the 101st Airborne and 10th Mountain Divisions held key positions, along with special operation forces. The entire operation was planned and led by Major General Franklin L. Hagenback, who believed it would take about seventy-two hours to accomplish what he termed a "classic hammer and anvil" maneuver.

Unfortunately, the number of al Qaeda fighters was not known, and estimates varied from a few hundred to a few thousand. The operation was considered to be purely within the Army's purview and apparently was not coordinated adequately with the coalition's air component. According to at least one source, the Combined Air Operations Staff was not made aware of Operation Anaconda until twenty-four hours before it was to begin.[1]

Things began to unravel almost from the March 2, 2002, start, as three elements of the encircling coalition forces ran into unexpectedly tough resistance. Trucks carrying some 450 Afghan and coalition troops came under heavy mortar fire as they moved toward Sirkanel. When Army Apache helicopters joined in the battle, they were badly hit. The same scenario was repeated at two other points, with the coalition forces pinned down by mortar fire and RPGs, both specialties of the war in Afghanistan. A 2,000-pound "thermobaric" bomb was dropped to deprive the cave it hit of oxygen. One American soldier was killed and sixteen more were wounded.

The following day, U.S. aircraft dropped 270 bombs on the Taliban and al Qaeda force. Nonetheless, conditions deteriorated, as the al Qaeda were on familiar turf and had ample supplies of weapons and munitions. On March 4, the day the battle was supposed to have been concluded, an attempt was made to

261

insert troops by helicopters near a point in the mountains called Takur Gar. This appeared to be a perfect location for an observation post; unfortunately, the point was under the observation of al Qaeda fighters positioned in a well-concealed bunker system just over the ridge. Their armament included a heavy machine gun.

The insertion was rebuffed with heavy fire. A Navy SEAL team MH-47 Chinook helicopter was damaged in the attempt when a RPG struck the side of the aircraft and machine-gun bullets cut both hydraulic and fuel lines. As the Chinook departed, Petty Officer 1st Class Neil C. Roberts slipped on the oil-slicked ramp and fell from the helicopter. Another crew member fell but was tethered and so could be hauled back inside. Roberts was down, alone, in the midst of an enemy force. Although no one was there to witness the action, it is believed that Roberts defended himself with his automatic weapon until he was killed by enemy gunfire.

The SEAL team managed to crash-land over four miles from where Roberts had fallen. Air support was called in, and the SEAL team fought its way back to reach Roberts. Unaware of the fact that Roberts was dead, two additional helicopters were dispatched. One survived heavy fire to insert six members of a combat element, then returned to its base.

The six SEALs ran into heavy fire; one man was killed and two wounded in the first moments of the battle. The remainder disengaged, contacting an AC-130 overhead for fire support.

The next rescue effort came with two MH-47Es and a twenty-three-man Ranger quick reaction force moved into the same hot spot near Takur Ghar. The al Qaeda forces were waiting, and one MH-47 as it attempted to land near the site was shot down by a RPG. Four men were killed at once and others were wounded.

The Rangers deployed to attack the al Qaeda bunkers, calling in air support. Air Force aircraft arrived within minutes to bomb and strafe the bunker area. The second contingent of Rangers was inserted some twenty-four hundred feet to the east and two-thousand feet farther down the mountain. They had to make an arduous two-hour climb in three feet of snow to engage the enemy.

Air Force F-15E Strike Eagles called in to strafe the al Qaeda positions at the top of the ridgeline that were only a few yards from coalition lines provided CAS for fourteen hours. It was the first time F-15Es had used guns for CAS. When it appeared that gunfire was not going to stifle the al Qaeda gunfire, the F-15Es dropped JDAMs that destroyed the bunker. The Rangers then stormed the area, killing the remaining al Qaeda forces and capturing the position.

When darkness fell, four additional helicopters arrived and managed to get in to treat the wounded and extract the troops.[2] By the time the Battle of Takur Ghar ended, eight men had died.

The allied fighting force had now grown to about two-thousand, and air support expanded to include Boeing B-1B and Northrop Grumman B-2A bombers, Boeing F-15 fighters, Lockheed Martin AC-130 gunships, and Apache helicopters. The Afghan leader, General Zia Lodin, had pulled his troops out of battle on March 3 and did not get back into the fight until three days later, but then with an additional 1,000 troops.

The execution for Operation Anaconda was now the inverse of what had been planned. Instead of Afghan troops forcing the al Qaeda into a coalition trap, coalition forces were now going to move into the area where the enemy was located. The number of American troops continued to climb, ultimately reaching 1,200.

Airpower was now applied as it should have been before the battle began. A-

10s worked the battlefield over at low level, and more than 2,000 bombs were dropped on al Qaeda positions from B-52s and Boeing F/A-18 Hornets. Although five out of six Apaches had been damaged in the original attack, they were now to conduct operations in a properly prepared battlefield.[3] What had been planned as a seventy-two-hour operation lasted for another fourteen days before the remnants of the dug-in enemy either were killed or managed to escape.

The fight with the al Qaeda was over, but there were more difficulties to come. Major General Hagenback published an article in an issue of *Field Artillery* in which he criticized Air Force CAS techniques in the battle. While praising Navy and Marine pilots, he took a severe view of Air Force support.

This precipitated a series of responses and some closed-door meetings that resulted in Hagenback's later stating that his remarks were taken out of context.

Former Chief of Staff Merrill A. McPeak was an ardent advocate for the integration of the military services under one command in joint operations, and his motto for this was "COMMAND WORKS: Everything Else Sort of Works." By this he meant that when the various services, with their equipment, were under the control of a single individual, operations worked smoothly. When the various services we merely "attached" to a commander, things didn't work as well. He regards this as particularly true of CAS. McPeak's language is colorful, and he salted this comment with an old phrase: "One stupid general is better than two smart generals" when it comes to command.[4]

The arguments about Anaconda are important for two reasons. First, they reinforced the concept, proved again in Iraq, that operating Apache helicopters requires preliminary battlefield support and works best in concert with fixed-wing aircraft and artillery. The second is that subsequent Army/Air Force cooperation in Iraq was extremely smooth: the Anaconda lesson had been learned.

APPENDIX FIVE

"A PLATFORM OF LAST RESORT"—OVERVIEW OF THE NAVY'S F/A-18E/F PROCUREMENT PROGRAM

On May 6, 2003, the USS *Abraham Lincoln* returned to its home port of Everett, Washington, after nearly ten months at sea. The *Lincoln* spent much of this latest deployment in the Persian Gulf, supporting Operations Southern Watch and Iraqi Freedom. When the *Lincoln* departed the United States in July 2002, it carried on its deck the future of naval aviation—the Boeing F/A-18E Super Hornet, assigned to the "Eagles" of Fighter Attack Squadron 115 (VFA-115). The Super Hornet's first combat deployment was a landmark event in the history of an ambitious procurement program that began more than a decade ago. Though comprehensive analyses of the F/A-18E's combat performance are still pending, initial reports indicate that the aircraft performed superbly and met the performance criteria it had been designed to fulfill. If subsequent analysis reinforces these claims, the F/A-18E/F may very well prove its proponents correct and turn out to be one of the most successful procurement programs in DOD history.

The Super Hornet was conceived in 1988 as a joint Navy–McDonnell Douglas concept study of an upgraded F/A-18 called "Hornet 2000." Though the Navy showed interest in the upgraded Hornet, it was not a priority project. At the time, the Navy's primary aviation procurement priority was the General Dynamics/McDonnell Douglas A-12 Avenger. The A-12 was intended to be a stealthy, delta-winged replacement for the venerable Grumman A-6E Intruder heavy attack plane, the "long rifle" of naval aviation for nearly thirty years. However, the A-12 was canceled by then Defense Secretary Dick Cheney, for seemingly innumerable reasons, many related to funding.[1]

The cancellation of the A-12 left a large gap in the Navy's plans to modernize its aviation branch. With no A-12s and with the A-6E quickly reaching the end of its service life, the Navy needed to find a new way of maintaining its long-range strike capability. The Navy's initial response was to aim lower, starting a project called A-X, which was to provide an aircraft that could fill the strike gap left by the A-6 at a lower cost than the A-12. The A-X quickly became the A/F-X, as the Navy realized that they would have to replace the aging F-14 Tomcat as well and that shrinking budgets would mean that they had a better chance of getting the aircraft they needed if they asked for a dual-role strike fighter. The A/F-X (in whatever form it took) was to be the Navy's major new-build strike fighter that would take naval aviation well into the twenty-first century. In addition to the

265

A/F-X, the Navy intended to upgrade an existing airframe to supplement the A/F-X and sustain a potent strike capability until the A/F-X came on-line. However, the Navy's bad luck with regard to obtaining a new aircraft persisted, and the A/F-X program was terminated in the Clinton Administration's 1993 Bottom-Up Review. The F/A-18E/F, already in Engineering and Manufacturing Development at the time, remained unscathed by the Bottom-Up Review.[2]

In 1990–91, the Navy and the Office of the Secretary of Defense (OSD) participated in a series of Major Aircraft Reviews (MARs) to determine the best course of action with regard to the major upgrade program to supplement the A/F-X. Among the aircraft proposals examined in the MARs were three versions of the Grumman F-14 Tomcat—the Advanced Tomcat 21, Super Tomcat 21, and F-14D Quickstrike—and two versions of the McDonnell Douglas F/A-18 Hornet: the F/A-18E/F and the F/A-18F(AW), an all-weather strike variant of the Super Hornet. The Navy and OSD also examined proposals for an upgraded A-6 Intruder and a navalized version of the Air Force's new F-22 Advanced Tactical Fighter, known as the NATF.[3]

All alternatives but the Super Hornet and the Quickstrike Tomcat were ruled out on the grounds of cost (NATF and both Tomcat 21s), survivability issues (A-6), and potential for foreign sales. In this latter category, McDonnell Douglas's strong client base for the F/A-18A-D worked to the Super Hornet's advantage. Another requirement at the time was that the aircraft be compatible with Marine Corps aviation objectives, another factor that worked in favor of the Super Hornet, since the Marines have been operators of the original Hornet since its introduction in the early 1980s. (The Marines subsequently chose to forgo the Super Hornet in favor of the S/VTOL version of the Joint Strike Fighter.) In the end, the Navy deemed the F-14D Quickstrike costlier, less reliable, and less survivable than the Super Hornet and chose to proceed with the F/A-18E/F.

The design requirements for the F/A-18E/F focused on five specific criteria: range, payload, weapons "bringback," survivability, and, perhaps most important, growth. In every area, the E/F is superior to the older C/D model Hornet.

The Super Hornet's unrefueled combat radius is 520 nm, whereas the latest-model C/D Hornets have only a 369 nm radius. In addition, the Super Hornet has been cleared to carry a buddy refueling store that will allow it to refuel other aircraft, including other Super Hornets. Having a high-performance tanker aircraft means that a buddy store–outfitted E/F can get to a refueling point faster than the much slower S-3 Viking currently tasked with aerial refueling, and tanker rendezvous will take less time. The Super Hornet is also capable of taking on fuel from any hose-and-drogue-outfitted refueling platform.

In terms of payload, the Super Hornet has eleven weapons and sensor stations rather than the C/D's nine.

Weapons bringback is the ability of an aircraft to return to the carrier without having to jettison external stores, such as costly, unspent precision ordnance, in order to reach an acceptable landing weight. The C/D's bringback load is limited to 5,523 pounds, while the E/F can bring back up to 9,000 pounds of ordnance, fuel, or mission-specific sensor pods. The significance of bringback capability is that it allows aircrews to return costly precision weapons to a ship's arsenal for future use, rather than dumping these weapons into the ocean just so the aircraft can get back aboard the carrier. In this regard, the Super Hornet provides more bang for the Navy's buck, in the most literal sense.

In terms of survivability, the Super Hornet features a reduced radar cross-signature and carries an improved Electronic Countermeasures (ECM) system. Further upgrades to the Super Hornets' ECM suite will be made possible by the last design feature: space.

The most unique feature of the Super Hornet is that it was designed with empty space within the fuselage to accommodate several decades' worth of avionics and weapon system upgrades. While some new systems replace old ones, many are supplemental and require additional space to house all the associated "black boxes," not to mention power sources and cooling units. The Super Hornet was designed specifically with these future needs in mind, something the C/D Hornet can no longer offer. The old Hornet has grown as much as it can.[4]

The Super Hornet program has been repeatedly praised for consistently being on or ahead of schedule, as well as on-budget, which has been the case since the program began. One reason the program was able to move so quickly from the start was the decision of McDonnell Douglas and the Navy to market the F/A-18E/F as a modification of an existing system, the F/A-18C/D, rather than a "new start" program. This decision had an incredible impact on the course the Super Hornet would take on its way to operational deployment.

By classifying the Super Hornet as an Engineering Change Proposal (ECP), the Navy/McDonnell Douglas team bypassed the costly (in terms of money and time) prototyping, demonstration, and fly-off phase known as Milestone I. Systems in Milestone I generally have long gestation periods, as the F-22/YF-23 and Joint Strike Fighter competitions illustrate. There is a considerable amount of debate over the ethics of marketing the Super Hornet as an ECP when it is essentially a new aircraft. While having the outward appearance of a larger C/D model Hornet, the Super Hornet has a different wing, fuselage, tailplanes, engines, and intakes, as well as many different components of lesser significance. The presence of so many new major components makes it difficult to argue that the Super Hornet is simply a modification to the C/D airframe. However, the obvious design commonality between the C/D and the E/F lends some credibility to the claim of modifications.

Opponents of the Super Hornet have persisted in claiming that the Navy/McDonnell Douglas (Navy/Boeing, from mid-1997 on, as Boeing and McDonnell Douglas merged) team finessed established DOD procurement procedures by their characterization of the nature of the Super Hornet in order to obtain approval for the program without having to go through the risky, high-cost prototype phase. Some have gone so far as to state that the team's bypassing of the Milestone I phase of development amounts to "nothing less than a conscious assault on the checks and balances of the Constitution."[5]

Proponents of the Super Hornet argue that regardless of ethical questions surrounding the bypass of Milestone I, the Navy needs this airplane. Aside from the single-engine Joint Strike Fighter (naval aviators generally prefer the safety of two engines for "blue water" operations), the Super Hornet is the only aircraft program that will allow the Navy to face the challenges of the twenty-first century. This will be hard to do with systems that were designed to meet the challenges of the 1980s and 1990s such as the F/A-18C/D. The Super Hornet is prepared to meet these challenges head-on, as its participation in the recent war in Iraq shows.

On September 29, 1995, the first EMD Super Hornet was revealed to the public during a roll-out ceremony at McDonnell Douglas' St. Louis plant. The first aircraft, a single-seat F/A-18E known as "E1" (there were seven EMD aircraft, five E models and two F models, each numbered in accordance with their production), began flight testing on November 29, 1995, initiating a rigorous 4.5-year test program.

Though the test program concluded with no crashes or major mishaps, it was not entirely without problems. The first problem encountered during flight testing was known as "wing drop." First experienced on a March 4, 1996 test flight during high-speed, high angle of attack (AOA) maneuvering, wing drop resulted in a sudden and uncontrolled loss of lift under one wing, causing the wing to "drop" and roll the aircraft. This problem, the result of a design flaw, could have seriously degraded the Super Hornet's close-in dogfighting performance if uncorrected. Critics of the program later seized upon the wing drop problem and argued that had the F/A-18E/F gone through a prototype phase, wing drop could have been detected and corrected before flight testing began.

With the assistance of engineers at NASA's Langley Research Facility, the McDonnell Douglas/Navy team discovered the cause of the problem and went about finding a way to correct it. In November 1997, test flights were conducted with the wing-fold joint fairings (which cover the hinges that allow the Super Hornet's wings to fold for carrier storage) removed, a measure that seemed to eliminate the wing drop anomaly completely. Since the fairing would be needed on the operational Super Hornets, a porous fairing that would allow air to pass through mesh screens in the wing-fold joint was developed and fitted to the test aircraft. This development saved the E/F program from possible termination and allowed flight testing to continue on schedule.[6]

In November 1996, another potentially serious problem was encountered by an E/F on a test flight out of Naval Air Station Patuxent River. While the aircraft was flying a supersonic profile, one of its General Electric F414 engines experienced a compressor stall, which resulted in shutdown of the engine. The pilot safely recovered on a single engine, but the test fleet was grounded while the problem was determined and a fix put in place. The problem was solved in under two months. The compressor stall was the result of fatigue cracks in the compressor's stator vanes, a problem corrected by fitting more robust stator vanes to the engines of the test fleet. All seven EMD aircraft were quickly cleared for flight, and aircraft F1 went on to log the type's first carrier landing aboard the USS *John Stennis* on January 18, 1997.[7]

The last major development problem came a bit later in the program, when excessive noise and vibration in the underwing stores area was detected in 2000. This problem prompted the Government Accounting Office (an organization with a long history of opposition to the Super Hornet) to recommend a delay of full-rate production, but a suitable fix was found in repositioning of the store racks, again saving the program and keeping it on schedule. In fact, full-rate production commenced on February 15, 2000.[8]

The most common criticism of the F/A-18E/F is that it offers little improvement over the aircraft it is supposed to replace. This criticism is valid in many regards. The Super Hornet lacks the combat radius of both the A-6 and the F-14. However, when the Super Hornet was given the green light, the Department of Defense's projected threat assessments took the collapse of the Soviet Union to heart and assumed that the long-range aerial threat to carrier battle groups (the raison d'étre of the F-14) will continue to diminish and that the Navy's power-projection role will focus more on littoral-area warfare, requiring less of a deep inland strike capability, like that of the A-6. Also, the Super Hornet is criticized as being less maneuverable than the C/D Hornet in certain flight profiles. Among the most vocal critics (and a powerful congressional opponent) of the F/A-18E/F has been Senator Russell Feingold of Wisconsin.

The problem with the critics of the Super Hornet is that they fail to ask (let alone begin to answer) the question, "If not the Super Hornet, than what?" Most viable alternatives were ruled out in 1991 as too costly, too vulnerable to enemy defenses, or both. As with many defense programs in times of scarce budget resources, the Super Hornet represents an acceptable compromise. In an article on turn-of-the-century fighter procurement, Professor Williamson Murray of the Army War College rightly calls the F/A-18E/F a "platform of last resort."[9] Having had a succession of strike fighter proposals rejected, the Navy took what it could get to fill the capability gap left by the retirement of the A-6, cancellation of the A-12 and A-F/X, and the ongoing phaseout of the F-14.

Thanks to Joe Copalman.

PERSONNEL RECOVERY IN OPERATION IRAQI FREEDOM

As a matter of policy, the United States never deploys military forces anywhere in the world without providing a capability to rescue or recover personnel who may become isolated in enemy territory or, in fact, captured. This mission is called "Personnel Recovery" and is inclusive of all the efforts that our nation will make with all of its instruments of power to recover our young men and women. It is a national imperative backed up by a robust rescue capability and the willingness to use it and is inclusive of what we used to call combat search and rescue (CSAR).

Traditionally, the U.S. Air Force has maintained the largest and most robust rescue force. During the Iraq conflict, its rescue forces of HH-60s, MC-130s, and pararescuemen (PJs) deployed from Moody Air Force Base, Nellis Air Force Base, and Patrick Air Force Base. Arriving in the theater, they were dispersed at several locations. In addition, they moved forward with coalition ground forces as the units advanced into Iraq. When the Iraqi airfield at Talil was taken on April 4 one of the first flying units to arrive was a detachment of rescue helicopters.[1] Supporting communications capability was soon set up, and their crews went on immediate alert. As special operation forces from the United States, Great Britain, and Australia seized other airfields in the west and north, other detachments did the same.

Naval Reserve helicopter rescue units, veterans of combat in Desert Storm, were also activated and deployed to the region. Their locations in the Gulf and Mediterranean have also not yet been reported. The sailors from Helicopter Rescue Squadron 4 based at Norfolk, Virginia, and from Helicopter Rescue Squadron 5 from San Diego, California, deployed with 180 personnel and eight HH-60H Seahawk helicopters.[2]

The Army, Marines, and special operation forces do not have preformed rescue squadrons. However, embedded in their tactical units are designated teams of helicopters and personnel that are responsive for immediate rescue. The Marines have "tactical recovery of aircraft and personnel" (TRAP) teams. The Army calls its designated units "disaster assistance response teams" (DART). Some of the teams come from the 5th Battalion of the 158th Aviation Regiment and are called "Raptors." They are organized to move with attack helicopter units on deep attacks and provide an immediate rescue capability for any downed aircrews.[3]

"It's an American thing," said CWO 5 Warren Aylworth, tactical operations officer with the Raptors. "We always want to get our people out. We take that more seriously all the time."[4]

The special operation forces designate helicopters for rescue duties within each formed assault element or task force. This is a preplanned element of the operation so that when their capabilities are needed, it is almost a seamless operation.

Taken in the aggregate, the rescue capabilities among the coalition forces were significant.

The Air Force and Navy rescue units in the region were under the operational or tactical control of the theater Joint Search and Rescue Center (JSRC) that was co-located with the CAO Center at Prince Sultan Airbase in Saudi Arabia. This was the largest JSRC in history. This gave the JSRC direct access to units that could actively search for and locate missing personnel or provide critical support to any task force designated for a recovery mission. The JSRC had reporting to it numerous subordinate rescue coordination centers located with various component headquarters. These headquarters actually directed rescue or recovery missions as they occurred.

Based on information in open sources, it appears that the rescue forces were not overly busy performing combat recoveries, although fifty-five assorted missions were executed at the direction of the JSRC.[5] They saved seventy-three personnel and participated in twenty other rescues. The available data indicate that five fixed-wing coalition aircraft (a British Tornado, F-14, F-18, F-15E, and A-10) were downed in enemy territory.

Looking closely at these losses, CENTCOM officials reported that the Tornado was downed by a PATRIOT missile on March 23. Both crew members, Flight Lieutenant Kevin Main and Flight Lieutenant David Williams from 9 Squadron forward based at Ali Al Salem in Kuwait, were killed. It is unclear at this point how or why the missile battery targeted the Tornado. Proper communication, navigation, and traffic control procedures should have prevented such an unfortunate turn of events.[6]

A similar incident occurred less than twenty-four hours later when another allied aircraft, this time an F-16, was targeted by a PATRIOT missile unit. Unfortunately for the PATRIOT site, this particular F-16 was equipped to locate and destroy enemy SAM batteries. Assuming that the site was an enemy position trying to shoot him down, the pilot launched a missile at it. The missile did considerable damage to the radar equipment but did not kill the missile crew.[7]

As events were unfolding in Iraq, a terrible tragedy in Afghanistan reminded us that American forces—including rescue elements—were still engaged in that remote nation. On March 23 a USAF HH-60G from the 41st Rescue Squadron based at Moody Air Force Base, Georgia, crashed, killing all six troops on board. It went down on a night mission to evacuate two Afghani children with head injuries.[8]

The F-14 was lost on April 1. Navy sources reported that it was forced down by a mechanical failure involving the fuel system. Assigned to Fighter Squadron 154 aboard the *Kitty Hawk*, the aircraft was over southern Iraq when the crew safely ejected.[9]

Air Force rescue crews scrambled for the F-14 crew who landed southwest of An Nasiriyah. Escorted by A-10s, the HH-60s entered Iraq and recovered the men. "Once we heard the guys coming to get us it was a great feeling," said the pilot,

Lieutenant Chad Vincelette.[10] This was a classic CSAR mission.

Disaster struck the *Kitty Hawk* again the next day when an F-18 from Fighter Squadron 195 aboard that ship was downed southwest of Baghdad. Rescue forces responded and joined other aircraft that were intensively searching for the pilot. But Lieutenant Nathan White had been killed. Two weeks later, a spokesman for CENTCOM stated that White was downed by a PATRIOT missile, as was the Tornado crew on March 23.[11]

Concerned about the incidents of surface-to-air fratricide, the Chairman of the Joint Chiefs of Staff, General Richard Myers, said, "We'll have to investigate each one of them, see if it was a breakdown in our techniques or our procedures or if there was a technical breakdown that we have to shore up."[12]

On April 6, an Air Force F-15E from the 333rd Fighter Squadron based at Seymour Johnson Air Force Base, North Carolina, went down near Mosul. Specifically designed for low-level attack, the aircraft was apparently flown into the ground. A rescue task force of helicopters and A-10s launched and proceeded to the crash site even though enemy air defenses in the area were numerous and active. But contact was never made with the two crew members, and on April 23, the Department of Defense announced that the pilot, Captain Eric Das, and weapons systems operator, Major William Watkins III, had been killed. Their bodies were later recovered.[13]

On April 8, two A-10s were hit by enemy fire while supporting the advance of the 3rd Infantry Division just south of Baghdad. The first A-10 was struck by a SAM. The pilot was able to fly away from the area before he ejected. He was spotted floating to the ground and rescued by U.S. Army forces in the area.

The second A-10 was hit by AAA fire. One engine was destroyed and the flight controls were damaged. But the A-10 is designed to survive severe battle damage, and the pilot was able to land at the recently seized Talil Air Base. This saved the aircraft and removed the need for another rescue mission.[14]

Overall in the war, allied fixed-wing aircraft flew 15,825 strike sorties.[15] Only the one A-10 was lost to enemy action, for a loss rate of .0063 percent. This continues a trend of ever fewer aircraft lost per combat sortie that reaches back to World War II. Many reasons can be cited for this trend: better built aircraft, better tactics, better support equipment such as electronic jamming pods and decoy flares, better crew training, and a well-established ability to seize air superiority by quickly destroying an opponent's ability to offer any significant aerial resistance.

In contrast, the Iraqis did claim numerous coalition aircraft shot down. At one point early in the war, they even staged what appeared to be the capture of allied airmen who parachuted into the Tigris River in downtown Baghdad. The event was duly covered by the Al-Jazeera satellite television channel as Iraqi troops combed the reeds growing along both banks and fired their rifles into the water in a vain attempt to flush out hiding allied airmen. When queried, both U.S. and British spokesmen denied that any aircraft or personnel were missing.[16]

The Iraqi air defenses did achieve some level of success. Numerous UAVs were shot down, reflecting their ever-increasing use by the United States and its allies.[17] Orbiting at low altitudes and slow speeds, they made easy targets. From a Personnel Recovery perspective, their losses were unimportant, because UAVs do not need rescue operations.

Combined, the effects of these two historical developments mean less business for the rescue forces and reinforce the obvious—the best Personnel Recovery tactic is to prevent any manned aircraft from being shot down.

Under the larger tasking of Personnel Recovery, the dedicated rescue forces were used on several occasions for medical evacuation of ground personnel. In another action on March 23, a rescue task force of HH-60s, A-10s, and an HC-130 tanker scrambled to recover an Army special forces team that had critically wounded personnel and was trapped near Baghdad. Reminiscent of the recoveries of special forces teams along the Ho Chi Minh Trail during the war in Southeast Asia, the A-10s covered the helicopters as their crews extracted the endangered troops. Enemy reaction was fierce as the helicopters approached the location of the soldiers. But the A-10s were able to provide suppression support as the helicopters swooped in and made recovery. The HC-130 was then able to descend below the low clouds to refuel the helicopter so that it could return to its home base.[18]

This same scenario was repeated almost verbatim on April 7, as another trapped Army team was recovered by a similar rescue task force. Said one Air Force rescue pilot, "It really comes back to that cliché that we don't leave anybody behind."[19]

The most dramatic Personnel Recovery event of the conflict was the operation to rescue Army PFC Jessica Lynch on April 2. She had been taken prisoner several days prior when her unit, a maintenance company, was ambushed. Several fellow soldiers were killed, and five others were taken prisoner.

But this operation was not mounted by rescue forces per se, although a few Air Force PJs were in the task force. It was a direct action mission carried out by Navy SEALs who were directly supported by Army Rangers. A large Marine diversionary action was carried out nearby and included an air strike by AV-8 Harriers who attacked a Ba'ath Party headquarters.

The large joint force ground element was inserted by Marine CH-53 and CH-46 helicopters as a large armada of Air Force AC-130 gunships, Marine AH-1W attack helicopters, and Army MH-6 "Little Birds" circled above to provide immediate fire support. Moving quickly, the substantial force neutralized the area. They then entered an enemy held-hospital in the city of An Nasiriyah and recovered Lynch from her incarceration.[20] In terms of audacity, it rivaled the great Sontay raid into North Vietnam in 1970—although unlike that raid, it actually freed an American. And it showed to the world the lengths to which the United States would go to rescue its personnel.

At the same time, another task force of mostly intelligence personnel was combing through liberated Iraqi intelligence centers and prisons looking for an American naval pilot still missing from the first Gulf War in 1991. Captain Michael Speicher had gone down on the first night of the conflict. He never made contact with search aircraft or elements and his position was not precisely known until his wreckage was found after the war. Initially classified as KIA, he was reclassified as "missing in action, captured," by the Secretary of the Navy in October 2001.[21]

All efforts to date have failed to locate Speicher. However, what appear to be his initials were found scratched into a cell wall in the Hakimiyah prison in Baghdad. His case remains open even after all remaining missing from the current war have been found.[22]

Rotary-wing (helicopter) losses were higher than the fixed-wing losses. The data are still being collected, but initial open reports indicate that as many as fifteen helicopters were lost, although that number includes both combat and noncombat losses.

Most crews were recovered by intraservice rescue operations. A special forces MH-53 was the first allied aircraft loss of the war. Its crew was picked up by another special forces helicopter and recovered to their home base. The aircraft itself was destroyed.[23]

The same day, a U.S. Marine CH-46E from Helicopter Squadron 268 crashed in Kuwait as it was ferrying troops to Umm Qasr in southern Iraq. All fourteen aboard, American and British, were killed. There was no rescue operation.[24]

An AH-64 Apache was lost at the beginning of combat operations. Assigned to the 11th Aviation Brigade, it was shot down as Army forces began their move into Iraq. Its crew was recovered by other Army units.[25]

A second AH-64, this one assigned to the 1st Battalion of the 227th Aviation Regiment, went down in a multibattalion raid against enemy armor units near Karbala on March 24. This was designed as a classic "deep-strike" mission, something that Army aviation has been developing for several years. Retired U.S. Army General Wesley Clark described it on CNN:

This was the first Army doctrinal deep attack mission. We've trained this mission for about eighteen years. It was designed to go against the Soviets. We applied it against the 2nd Brigade of the Medina Division. We had good results on this mission. We took out a bunch of T-72s, artillery and infantry. On the other hand, it was a firefight, and we took return fire.[26]

The Apache was downed by concentrated and massive enemy small-arms fire. Other Army helicopters tried to recover the crew but were shot off by enemy forces in the area. The crew of two, CWO 2 Ronald Young and CWO 2 David Williams, was captured.[27]

In addition, in the raid the Apache battalions of the 11th Aviation Regiment had many aircraft heavily damaged. One enemy commander used a simple expedient to defend against the Apaches. Seeing them in flight, he used his cell phone to call nearby units and warn them of the advancing helicopters. Alerted, they were able to concentrate their fire against the interlopers. As they tried to hover and direct their precision missiles against Iraqi targets, numerous helicopters suffered heavy damage from the massed guns of the enemy units. Army planners had not dedicated forces to eliminate or suppress the guns so that the Apaches could safely operate. It was an expensive lesson.

The aviation unit commanders adjusted their tactics. Subsequent raids were preceded by Air Force and Navy attack aircraft's beating down the guns and achieving a level of air superiority sufficient for the helicopter to operate. Said the V Corps Commander, Lieutenant General William Wallace, "We learned from our mistakes, we adjusted and adapted based on what we learned, and we still used the Apache helicopter in a significant role during the course of the fight."[28]

On March 21, two Royal Navy Sea King helicopters collided over the northern Arabian Gulf. Six British and one U.S. personnel were killed. It was a noncombat loss but tragic nonetheless.[29]

Nine days later, a UH-1N assigned to Marine Helicopter Squadron 169 crashed on takeoff at night from a forward operating location in southern Iraq. Three troops on board were killed. A fourth Marine was critically wounded and evacuated by rescue forces.[30]

On April 1, a Marine AV-8 Harrier crashed while trying to land at night aboard the USS *Nassau*. The pilot successfully ejected and was recovered by a Navy search and rescue helicopter.[31]

On April 2, a UH-60 from the 2nd Battalion of the 3rd Aviation Regiment was shot down by small-arms fire near Karbala. Six on board were killed. There was no rescue effort and the bodies were recovered by a ground team.[32]

An AH-1W assigned to Marine Helicopter Squadron 267 crashed in Central Iraq on April 3, killing its two crew members. This was not a combat loss.[33]

In the Mediterranean, a U.S. Navy CH-46E crashed during deck-to-deck resupply operations. The crew was rescued by local rescue elements.[34]

As the war sped toward its inevitable conclusion, allied intelligence sources searched in vain for the soldiers captured with PFC Lynch and the two helicopter pilots shot down in the massive AH-64 raid on March 24. Had the soldiers been positively located, undoubtedly another special forces raid would have been mounted to rescue them. But as Marine Task Force Tripoli moved north toward Tikrit, an Iraqi civilian approached one of the lead elements and told them that seven Americans were being held in a small village just to the north. Moving cautiously, the Marines entered the village and freed the soldiers, the five from PFC Lynch's unit and the two Apache crew members. Said one of the pilots, CWO 2 Ronald Young, "We feel like we won the lottery of life." All seven were in good condition, although three had been wounded in the process of being captured.[35]

Undoubtedly, other aircraft will be lost as our forces continue to occupy Iraq. But rescue forces will remain in place as long as they are needed to perform both combat rescue and other personnel recovery missions.

The history is being collected and studied for "lessons learned." This will take time and careful analysis. But certain points do seem to be surfacing.

1. The best Personnel Recovery device is the prevention of loss. Air superiority means ever fewer aircraft shot down. The increasing use of UAVs puts fewer aircrews at risk. But the massed guns at low level still are a serious threat to helicopters.
2. Aerial fratricide is still a concern. Procedures have to be adjusted to ensure that "friendly" air defenses do not destroy aircraft and vice versa.
3. Ground forces are now primed and ready to recover downed aircrews.
4. Recent changes in operational concepts may mean that more "support" personnel may be at risk of being isolated in "enemy" territory.
5. Our rescue forces are well directed and ready to respond to *whoever* needs their services.
6. Personal Recovery is a national priority.

Thanks to Darrel Whitcomb.

APPENDIX SEVEN

U.S. NAVY ORDER OF BATTLE–OPERATION IRAQI FREEDOM

US NAVAL FORCES IN THE PERSIAN GULF, ARABIAN SEA, RED SEA, AND EASTERN MEDITERRANEAN AS OF MARCH 20, 2003

The list below covers all US Navy Ships operating in the Central Command Area of Operations and involved in Operation Iraqi Freedom **as of March 20, 2003.** Warships from other nations as well as ships from other US military branches are not included (except for HSV-X1 as this ship is a combined Army-Navy project). Also not included are ships underway to the region when the operation started (e.g. the USS *Nimitz* [CVN 68] Battle Group).

Aircraft Carrier Battle Groups (CVBG)		
USS *Kitty Hawk* (CV 63) CVBG	USS *Kitty Hawk* (CV 63) USS *Chancellorsville* (CG 62) USS *Cowpens* (CG 63) USS *John S. McCain* (DDG 56) USS *O'Brien* (DD 975) USS *Cushing* (DD 985) USS *Gary* (FFG 51) USS *Vandegrift* (FFG 48) USS *Bremerton* (SSN 698)	Carrier Air Wing (CVW) 5: VF-154 (F-14A) VFA-27 (F/A-18C) VFA-192 (F/A-18C) VFA-195 (F/A-18C) VAQ-136 (EA-6B) VAW-115 (E-2C) VS-21 (S-3B) HS-14 (HH/SH-60H/F)

USS *Constellation* (CV 64) CVBG	USS *Constellation* (CV 64) USS *Valley Forge* (CG 50) USS *Bunker Hill* (CG 52) USS *Higgins* (DDG 76) USS *Milius* (DDG 69) USS *Thach* (FFG 43) USS *Columbia* (SSN 771) USS *Rainier* (AOE 7)	Carrier Air Wing (CVW) 2: VF-2 (F-14D) VMFA-323 (F/A-18C) VFA-151 (F/A-18C) VFA-137 (F/A-18C) VAW-116 (E-2C) VAQ-131 (EA-6B) VS-38 (S-3B) HS-2 (SH-60F/HH-60H)
USS *Theodore Roosevelt* (CVN 71) CVBG	USS *Theodore Roosevelt* (CVN 71) USS *Anzio* (CG 68) USS *Cape St. George* (CG 71) USS *Arleigh Burke* (DDG 51) USS *Porter* (DDG 78) USS *Winston Churchill* (DDG 81) USS *Carr* (FFG 52) USNS *Arctic* (T-AOE 8)	Carrier Air Wing (CVW) 8: VF-213 (F-14D) VFA-201 (F/A-18A) VFA-15 (F/A-18C) VFA-87 (F/A-18C) VAQ-141 (EA-6B) VAW-124 (E-2C) VS-24 (S-3B) HS-3 (SH/HH-60F/H)
USS *Abraham Lincoln* (CVN 72) CVBG	USS *Abraham Lincoln* (CVN 72) USS *Mobile Bay* (CG 53) USS *Shiloh* (CG 67) USS *Paul Hamilton* (DDG 60) USS *Fletcher* (DD 992) USS *Crommelin* (FFG 37) USS *Honolulu* (SSN 718) USS *Camden* (AOE 2)	Carrier Air Wing (CVW) 14: VF-31 (F-14D) VFA-115 (F/A-18E) VFA-25 (F/A-18C) VFA-113 (F/A-18C) VAQ-139 (EA-6B) VS-35 (S-3B) VAW-113 (E-2C) HS-4 (SH/HH-60F/H)
USS *Harry S. Truman* (CVN 75) CVBG	USS *Harry S. Truman* (CVN 75) USS *San Jacinto* (CG 56) USS *Oscar Austin* (DDG 79) USS *Mitscher* (DDG 57) USS *Donald Cook* (DDG 75) USS *Briscoe* (DD 977) USS *Deyo* (DD 989) USS *Hawes* (FFG 53) USS *Pittsburgh* (SSN 720) USS *Montpelier* (SSN 765) USNS *Mount Baker* (T-AE 34) USNS *Kanawha* (T-AO 196)	Carrier Air Wing (CVW) 3: VF-32 (F-14B) VMFA-312 (F/A-18C) VFA-37 (F/A-18C) VFA-105 (F/A-18C) VAW-126 (E-2C) VAQ-130 (EA-6B) VS-22 (S-3B) HS-7 (HH/SH-60H/F)
	**Amphibious Ready Groups (ARG)**	
USS *Tarawa* (LHA 1) ARG	USS *Tarawa* (LHA 1) USS *Duluth* (LPD 6) USS *Rushmore* (LSD 47)	HMM-161
USS *Nassau* (LHA 4) ARG	USS *Nassau* (LHA 4) USS *Austin* (LPD 4) USS *Tortuga* (LSD 46)	HMM-263

Amphibious Task Force East	USS *Saipan* (LHA 2) USS *Kearsarge* (LHD 3) USS *Bataan* (LHD 5) USS *Ponce* (LPD 15) USS *Portland* (LSD 37) USS *Gunston Hall* (LSD 44) USS *Ashland* (LSD 48)	HMH-464 (CH-53E) HMM-162 (CH-46E) HMM-365 (CH-46E) HML/A-269 (UH/AH-1N/W) VMA-223 (AV-8B) VMA-542 (AV-8B)
Amphibious Task Force West	USS *Boxer* (LHD 4) USS *Bonhomme Richard* (LHD 6) USS *Cleveland* (LPD 7) USS *Dubuque* (LPD 8) USS *Anchorage* (LSD 36) USS *Comstock* (LSD 45) USS *Pearl Harbor* (LSD 52)	VMA-211 (AV-8B) VMA-311 (AV-8B)

Other US Navy Warships in the Area of Operations

HSV-X1 Joint Venture	USS *Chinook* (PC 9)	USS *Firebolt* (PC 10)
USS *Augusta* (SSN 710)	USS *Providence* (SSN 719)	USS *Newport News* (SSN 750)
USS *San Juan* (SSN 751)	USS *Boise* (SSN 764)	USS *Toledo* (SSN 769)
USS *Cheyenne* (SSN 773)	USS *Mount Whitney* (LCC 20)	USS *Ardent* (MCM 12)
USS *Dextrous* (MCM 13)	USS *Cardinal* (MHC 60)	USS *Raven* (MHC 61)

Other Military Sealift Command Ships in the Area of Operations

USNS *Comfort* (T-AH 20)	USNS Algol (T-AKR 287)	USNS Altair (T-AKR 291)
USNS Capella (T-AKR 293)	USNS Pililaau (T-AKR 305)	USNS Brittin (T-AKR 305)
USNS *Sirius* (T-AFS 8)	USNS Shughart (T-AKR 295)	USNS Bob Hope (T-AKR 300)
USNS Dahl (T-AKR 312)	USNS *Spica* (T-AFS 9)	USNS Gordon (T-AKR 296)
USNS Yano (T-AKR 297)	USNS Gilliland (T-AKR 298)	USNS Watson (T-AKR 310)
USNS Watkins (T-AKR 315)	USNS *Walter S. Diehl* (T-AO 193)	USNS Catawba (T-ATF 168)
USNS *Henry J. Kaiser* (T-AO 187)	USNS Chesapeake (T-AOT 5084)	MV Green Ridge (T-AK 9655)
MV Bernard F. Fisher (T-AK 4396)	USNS Pitsenbarger (T-AK 4638)	USNS Sgt. E. A. Carter, Jr. (T-AK 4544)
MV LTC John U. D. Page (T-AK 4496)	MV American Cormorant (T-AK 2062)	USNS Gysgt F. W. Stockham (T-AK 3017)
MV Pvt. F. J. Phillips (T-AK 3004)	MV 1st LT Alex Bonnyman (T-AK 3003)	MV Pfc. James Anderson, Jr. (T-AK 3002)
MV Pfc. William B. Baugh (T-AK 3001)	MV Cpl. L. J. Hauge, Jr. (T-AK 3000)	USNS 1st LT Harry L. Martin (T-AK 3015)
MV 2nd LT John P. Bobo (T-AK 3008)	SS Maj. Stephen W. Pless (T-AK 3007)	SS Pfc. E. A. Obregon (T-AK 3006)
SS Sgt. Matej Kocak (T-AK 3005)		

Source: http://navysite.de/navy/iraqi-freedom.htm

SPECIAL OPERATIONS FORCES AT THE AL FAW PENINSULA

The conduct of special operations is always cloaked in secrecy. The view the general population has of special operations is conditioned by the media, particularly films, in which hardy single warriors conduct Rambo-like operations on their own against largely incompetent enemies.

In truth, special operations are conducted with the utmost professionalism against able and well-prepared enemies who must be overcome with shock, surprise, and overwhelming firepower.

The first and to date the best documented account of special operations is that of the combined forces used to secure the oil fields and pipelines on the Al Faw peninsula.

Seizure of these facilities was critical to the conduct of the war, to the future of Iraq, and to the environment. General Franks had put a great deal of emphasis on the southern and northern oil fields. He wanted to prevent the destruction of the desalinization plant and avoid the ecological disaster that would result from the discharge of millions of gallons of oil into the waters adjacent to the peninsula. The polluted water would have its counterpart in the polluted air from burning oil fields, and there was concern about the effect this would have on the air intakes of combat ships in the Gulf.

Saddam Hussein had planned for the destruction of the facilities and the discharge of oil into Gulf waters but was caught by the surprise opening of the war, in which ground action preceded air action.

The coalition special forces tasked to protect the oil fields and the GOPLATs in the Gulf had planned for weeks on how to forestall Saddam. The original intent was to put forces in first to seize the oil fields, because it was well known that the Iraqis had put charges on the wellheads. Yet over time, the planning flip-flopped on numerous occasions, with the date and the time of the attack changing as well as the sequence in which the targets would be attacked.

The difficulty was that the small, highly qualified force of special operations personnel could only be in one spot at a time. A decision had to be made as to the relative value of putting in an Army special forces team on the ground in western Iraq as a part of the anti–tactical ballistic missile efforts rather than concentrating on preserving the southern oil fields. At the same time, the advance of the ground forces had to be supported.

On March 19, the decision was made to put forces into the oil field facilities on the Al Faw peninsula and onto the GOPLATs on the next day. The success of the March 20 action would depend upon air and information dominance. The responsibility for the success of the operations rested on the shoulders of three officers. Colonel Frank Kisner, Combined Joint Special Operations Air Component Commander, was the single Air Commander for all special air operations in the theater. The overall Commander of the mission was Captain Bob Harward, a Navy SEAL in command of the Naval Special Warfare Task Group. Colonel Randy O'Boyle was the Air Mission Commander. It was his job to manage the assets so that the Al Faw peninsula could be seized. All three reported to Brigadier General Gary Harrel, Combined Force Special Operations Command Component Commander.

Fortunately, according to Colonel Kisner, air detachments in the southwest of Iraq had been made available, despite the high demand for their services, for two rehearsals of the operation. The rehearsals were absolutely essential to permit the sequencing of such a large force in such a short time into what was considered a high-threat area.

O'Boyle says that the most important sequencing task was placing the Navy SEALs in the right spot at the right time so that they could carry out the critical initial assault of the operations—seizing and securing the oil-field infrastructure. In completing the task, the most difficult work was synchronizing the infiltration of U.S. forces and the British Royal Marine Commandos, which had not worked together before.

This synchronization was essential, because while only the Navy SEALs could go in with the speed and precision to seize the pumping stations at night, their numbers were too small to hold the area the next day. It was vital to have follow-on forces of significant size and capability to finish up and hold the target the next day.

As Air Mission Commander, O'Boyle flew in a Lockheed Martin AC-130 Spooky gunship, because the UHF line of sight radio communications were essential because of the close proximity of friendly forces to the target area. The AC-130s are brilliant in their support of special forces action with precise fire, and O'Boyle was awed by the professionalism and ability of the thirteen-man crew. The Al Faw peninsula mission was so important that it received all of the critical assets it asked for in terms of strike aircraft. The AC-130 gunships were in particularly high demand all over the theater but were always available to O'Boyle for the execution of the mission.

Part of O'Boyle's job was to compensate for the slips in timing that occurred because of incredibly bad weather and the enemy reaction to the attack.

The gunships participated three times, twice in rehearsals. Realistic rehearsals are a signature note of special operations. They were extremely valuable in refining the plan and particularly in accustoming the ground team, the SEALs, and the United Kingdom's Royal Marines to working together. The rehearsals lessened the effect of the communication differences between U.S. and U.K. forces.

As the time for action grew near, the rehearsals became more difficult because the participants, particularly the Royal Marines, were wanted for other tasks. Training operations were especially difficult to conduct in the highly congested airspace over Kuwait.

The special operation forces had every technological means available in the assembled air forces. The USS *Constellation*'s F-18s, F-14s, and EA-6B's were assigned, along with British GR4 Harriers and USAF A-10 Thunderbolts, to hit twenty-eight targets. Intelligence sources had identified the targets, which included artillery pieces, bunkers, and military complexes on the island.

In the premission planning, O'Boyle was especially conscious of the need to avoid shooting if the Psyops packages had worked and the white flags of surrender were displayed. Had the Iraqis surrendered, the prestrike attacks would not have been made and the occupation troops would have been flown in without any preliminary bombing.

The attack began shortly after midnight. O'Boyle (whose call sign was Wooley 01) had more than sixty-four aircraft airborne, including the Predator on its first use in Operation Iraqi Freedom. There were more than twenty different types, ranging from the UAV to Navy P-3s. The Predator and the P-3s provided a high degree of situational awareness that made O'Boyle comfortable with his task. Northrop Grumman EA-6Bs carried on their jamming function.

The special operations forces anticipated, as always, the worst-case scenario. They had developed a plan in which A-10s would roll in immediately after the prestrike aircraft, moving from south to north and determining if there were any remaining antiaircraft threats that needed to be sanitized before the gunships were sent in.

In O'Boyle's words[1], "We wanted to be sure we used them [the gunships] judiciously; they are a national asset with a tremendous capability. All went pretty much according to plan except that bad weather made the fighters twenty minutes late off the *Constellation*. I made a decision to bump the time back for the helicopters to accommodate them because, on the basis of what we were seeing, I felt that the prestrike targets needed to be hit. This caused a ripple in everything, but I felt we had the time and the forces were prepared. Nothing ever goes according to plan. The main targets were numbered from one to nineteen, and from the rehearsals I'd learned to create a prioritized list, with pictures of each of the targets. Next to them I had the checklists, call signs, and the communication frequency pages all ready and available for me throughout the night.

"The delay caused aircraft to begin to stack up, so I would send them to various targets. The aircraft, because of their better situational awareness, would often call back in with a suggestion for an alternate target. We would have a fast negotiation on which ones needed to be hit first, and I kept a tally of them. There were A-10s, GR-4s, F-14s, F-18s, and F-16s available. I had their weapons capability associated with their call signs and assigned targets accordingly. All but a few of the bombs went off; one was a dud that gave us some concern because it landed near to an LZ [landing zone].

"The A-10s were exceptionally effective, providing a last-minute check to make sure that we were not surprised by the enemy. The A-10 pilots were very brave, flying low in bad weather to take out targets of opportunity. As they cleared the area, I moved our two gunships, Dodge 85 and 86, forward from the holding orbit to the area where the Quaker State and Pennzoil, the pipeline, outputs were. I was in Dodge 85 and went to the Al Faw metering and measuring (naturally nicknamed the M and M) facility.

"As the gunships approached the LZ, they saw targets that needed to be struck, lot of enemy activity in bunkers. Methodically and with great precision they started taking out targets—troops, artillery pieces, AAA, and vehicles around landing zones. The gunships were critical because bombing might have destroyed the very facilities we wanted to preserve.

"We had a force of eight Sikorsky MH-53M Pave Low helicopters orbiting. They came in as a seven-ship formation, and they took in a little over 100 Navy SEALs simultaneously to three different objectives: The seven-ship formation split off into a five-ship and two one-ships. One ship went to target Quaker State and the other to Pennzoil, where the LZs were called Maple and Spruce, respectively. The aircraft going to Maple and Spruce carried just assault troops, about eighteen each.

"The five-ship further split into two one-ships and a three-ship. The three-ship landed in LZ Pine, right on the metering station, one landing in LZ Dogwood and one in LZ Elm. Each of the MH-53s off-loaded Navy SEALs and some specialized vehicles that were going to take charge of northern and eastern gates and control ingress to compound and oil facilities.

"All of the helicopters (with one exception) took off immediately to return to the Forward Air Refueling Point staging area to pick up the lead contingent of Royal Marines. The idea was to get a lot of mass on the objective quickly. We used Pave Lows because the U.K. helicopters did not have the same night capability that we did.

"Then there came a delay because one of our Pave Low helicopters got stuck when a Navy SEAL vehicle rolled off and sank into a low spot in the oily ground. The front end of the vehicle was sunk well into the ground, while the rear end literally tied the helicopter to mud for fifteen minutes. We rolled gunships in on top of them because enemy vehicles were coming in to reinforce the compound. An A-10 took one out, while Dodge 85 took the other one. In the meantime, the SEALs came up with a plan to extricate the vehicle, and coolly proceeded to do so.

"We picked up the speed of the helicopter flow, and started to build combat power in the LZ. Six A-10s in three two-ship formations worked with gunships, cycling in to provide coverage over area [the] entire time. I was able to send them to areas a little farther north, where their capabilities were maximized. They killed anything moving down to where the gunships were working.

"The flow kept going throughout the night despite the low visibility and the delay from the vehicle being stuck. I had to find separate orbit points for the U.K. helicopters (Vader Flight) and the Pave Lows (Hasten Flight).

"One Pave Low helicopter in Hasten Flight took the first load onto the PPL site (Pennzoil). It landed directly on a bunker that had not been picked out by intelligence. However, the prestrike plan had made the enemy keep their heads down, the SEALs walked off the helicopter, and enemy surrendered.

"At the bunker, we found later that seven Iraqi officers had been executed by Fedayeen forces, presumably because they intended to surrender. Most the Iraqi force did fight, but many surrendered to teams on the ground. We even had the gunships warn some approaching vehicles by shooting around in front of them; it worked on a couple occasions; on a couple it did not and the gunships destroyed them.

"The ground teams had a Special Tactics Team [STS] controller from Air Force Special Operations Command. His call sign was Morgan Park (mine was Wooley One) and he was absolutely brilliant, organizing air support for teams on ground.

He was my main communication point with teams on the ground, telling us when we were to be called and when the LZs would be clear.

"The whole operation took six hours, from time we started until daybreak. A near constant flow of helicopters was needed to put in the force of over 1,000. Near the tail end of our operation, Navy SEALs and coalition forces were taking the gas and oil platforms in the Gulf."

In another action, Royal Marine Commandos were going in riverine craft up to Umm Kasr to take charge of the port. They saw an Iraqi PB 90 fast patrol craft that had not been depicted in any previous intelligence reports. It was a big threat and they called on O'Boyle for help. He made the necessary calls to get clearance to the area, working with both the Navy and the U.K. forces, got the airspace cleared, and moved in to attack. The Iraqi ship played hide-and-seek, taking refuge near a supertanker.

As time passed, the British forces became more and more concerned about the Iraqi ship, but Dodge 85 arrived, and its 105mm cannon sank the PB-90. This was the first heavy ship ever to be sunk by a gunship.

The entire operation proved to be an outstanding success, thanks to the rehearsals, the excellent weather forecasting, and the precision with which the mission was executed. One complication was that the mission had to be executed without penetrating the nearby Iranian airspace. Iranian air traffic controllers, speaking in good English, were friendly but firm in the warnings about maintaining a distance from their border.

No SOF mission is ever "typical," but the skill and expertise with which the Al Faw mission was executed are typical of special operation forces in all theaters.

NOTES

PREFACE

1. Author's interview with General Larry D. Welch, July 1, 2003.

CHAPTER 1: A CONTRAST IN VALUES

1. Robert Wall, "Rescue of a POW," *Aviation Week and Space Technology*, April 14, 2003, p. 29.
2. Walter J. Boyne, *Beyond the Wild Blue: A History of the U.S. Air Force* (New York: St. Martin's Press, 1997), pp. 292, 293.
3. Richard P. Hallion, *Storm over Iraq: Air Power and the Gulf War* (Washington, DC: Smithsonian Press, 1992), p. 163.
4. "Report to Congress on the Conduct of the Gulf War, Chapter VI, The Air Campaign," *American National Security Policy*, via http://www.fas.org/spp/starwars/docops/gw_ch6m.htm.
5. Charles D. Bright, ed., *Historical Dictionary of the U.S. Air Force* (New York: Greenwood Press, 1992), p. 304.
6. Hallion, *Storm over Iraq*, p. 174.
7. Author's interview with General McPeak, May 2, 2003.
8. Boyne, *Beyond the Wild Blue*, p. 298.
9. General Charles "Chuck" Horner in an interview with the author, May 16, 2003.
10. Bradley Graham, and Vernon Loeb, "An Air War of Might, Coordination and Risks," *Washington Post*, April 27, 2003.
11. Author's interview with General John P. Jumper, July 17, 2003.

CHAPTER 2: THE FORCES COMPARED

1. Author's interview with Lieutenant General Bernard E. Trainor, USMS, Ret., May 14, 2003.
2. Much of this information, including the speculative briefing by General Sultan, was derived in an interview with General Trainor by the author on May 14, 2003.
3. Author's interview with General Trainor, May 14, 2003.
4. Anthony H. Cordesman, *The Instant Lessons of the Iraq War* (Washington, DC: Center for Strategic and International Studies, 2003), p. 20.
5. John A. Tirpak "Desert Triumph," *Air Force*, May 2003, p. 10.
6. Chairman, Joint Chiefs of Staff, Gen. Richard B. Myers, Department of Defense News Briefing, March 21, 2003.
7. Robert Wall, "Attack on Iraq," *Aviation Week and Space Technology*, March 24, 2003, p. 24.
8. Author's interview with General John P. Jumper, June 17, 2003.
9. Congressional Research Services Report, *Iraq War: Defense Program Implications for Congress*, CRSe 46, June 5, 2003, p. 41.
10. Most of the information in this section was obtained in a May 23, 2003, interview with Robert Workman.
11. Jason Sherman, "Logistics Success Built on Sealift," *Defense News*, May 12, 2003, p. 32.
12. Gregg Easterbrook, "American Power Moves beyond Mere Super," *The New York Times*, April 4, 2003, via http://www.nytimes.com/2003/04/27/weekin review/27East.html.
13. John A. Tirpak, "The Space-Based Radar Plan," *Air Force*, August 2002, p. 63.
14. Craig Couvault, "Milstar Pivotal to War," *Aviation Week and Space Technology*, April 28, 2003, p. 50.
15. Peter Grier, "A Quarter Century of AWACS," *Air Force*, March 2002, p. 46.
16. Ibid, p. 46.

CHAPTER 3: "G" DAY BEFORE "A" DAY: SADDAM'S WORLD TURNED UPSIDE DOWN

1. John Pike, "Attacking Iraq," *Global Security*, p. 1, via http://www.global security.org/military/ops/iraqi_freedom_d3.htm.
2. Ibid, p. 2.
3. Anthony H. Cordesman, *The Instant Lessons of the Iraq War* (Washington, DC: Center for Strategic and International Studies, 2003), p. 4.
4. Pike, "Attacking Iraq," p. 1.
5. IRAQWAR.RU, based on Russian Military Intelligence (GRU) Reports, translated by Venik, provided to the author by George Mellinger.
6. http://www.iranexpert.com/2003/abzaid22february.htm.
7. Information provided by Major General Perry M. Smith, USAF (Ret.), in an interview with the author on May 14, 2003.
8. Author's interview with Vice Admiral Timothy J. Keating, June 4, 2003.
9. Lt. Gen. David D. McKiernan, "Operation Iraqi Freedom Briefing," April 23,

2003, via http://www.defenselink.mil/cgi-bin/dlprit.cgi? http://www.defenselink. mil/transcripts/20.

10. Author's interview with Colonel Timothy H. Hyde, May 16, 2003.

11. Lieutenant General Bernard E. Trainor, USMC, Ret., in an interview with the author on May 14, 2003.

12. Ibid.

13. General Accounting Office Report of February 4, 1992, to Howard Wolpe, Chairman of the Subcommittee on Investigations and Oversight Committee on Science, Space and Technology in the House of Representatives, via http://www.globalsecurity.org/space/library/report/gao/im92026.htm.

14. Elaine M. Grossman, "Patriot May Mistake Aircraft for Missile in Combat's Electronic Glut," *Inside the Pentagon*, April 24, 2001.

15. Pamela Hess, "The Patriot's Fratricide Record," *Washington Times*, April 24, 2003, via http://dynamic.washtimes.com/twt-print.cfm?articleID=20030424-42117=6399r.

16. Author's interview with Major General Donald Shepperd, April 28, 2003.

17. Author's interview with General Merrill A. McPeak, April 28, 2003.

CHAPTER 4: BAD NEWS (FOR SADDAM) BLOWING IN THE SANDY WIND

1. "Operation Iraqi Freedom—March 25, Day Six," via http://www.globalsecurity. org/military/ops/iraqi_freedom_d6.htm.

2. "CENTCOM Operation Iraqi Freedom Briefing, 27 March 2003," via http://www.centcom.mil/CENTCOMNews/transcripts/20030329.htm.

3. Mark Ayton, "Chronology, Operation Iraqi Freedom," *Air Forces Monthly*, May 2003, p. 52.

4. IRAQWAR.RU, based on Russian Military Intelligence (GRU) Reports, translated by Venik, provided to the author by George Mellinger.

5. Author's interview with General John P. Jumper, June 17, 2003.

6. Eric Schmitt, "6,300 Miles from Iraq, Experts Guide Raids," *New York Times*, June 24, 2003.

7. John Tirpak, "Find, Fix, Track, Target, Engage, Assess," *Air Force*, July 2000, pp. 24–29.

8. William B. Scott, "High Ground over Iraq," *Aviation Week and Space Technology*, June 9, 2003, p. 45.

9. Author's interview with General John Michael Loh, July 13, 2003.

10. Michael R. Rip and James M. Hasik, *The Precision Revolution, GPS and the Future of Aerial Warfare* (Annapolis, MD: Naval Institute Press, 2002, p. 69.

11. Susan H. H. Young, "Satellite Systems," *Air Force*, May 2003, p. 183.

12. Scott, "High Ground over Iraq," p. 45.

13. Author's interview with General Charles Homer, May 5, 2003.

14. Scott, "High Ground over Iraq," p. 46.

15. Tirpak, "Find, Fix, Track, Target, Engage, Assess," p. 26.

16. Rip and Hasik, *The Precision Revolution, GPS and the Future of Aerial Warfare*, p. 208.

17. Author's interview with General Jumper, June 17, 2003.

18. Author's interview with General Loh, July 13, 2003.
19. Ibid.
20. Walter J. Boyne, *Beyond the Horizons: The Lockheed Story* (New York: St. Martin's Press, 1998), p. 278.
21. "Common Ground Stations Provide Intel, Protection during Iraq Ops," *Inside the Army*, April 28, 2003, via Dr. Robert Mullins.
22. Scott, "High Ground over Iraq," p. 4.
23. "Global Hawk Used for First Time to Pass Data to F/A-18 for Attack on Iraqi Missile System," *Flight International*, via Dr. Robert Mullins.
24. David A. Fulghum and Robert Wall, "Baghdad Confidential," *Aviation Week and Space Technology*, April 28, 2003, p. 32.
25. Mark Ayton, "War Diary," *Air Forces Monthly*, May 2003, p. 56.

CHAPTER 5: COMBINED OPERATIONS AT THEIR BEST

1. Mark Ayton, "War Diary," *Air Forces Monthly*, May 2003, p. 53.
2. "The Advance on Baghdad," www.airforcesmonthly.com, via Lon Nordeen, p. 53.
3. "Operation Iraqi Freedom, March 28," via http://www.globalsecurity.org/military/ops/iraqi_freedom_d9.htm.
4. "The Advance on Baghdad," p. 54.
5. Ibid.
6. Mark Ayton, "Operation Iraqi Freedom Chronology," *Air Forces Monthly*, May 2003, p. 54.
7. "Operation Iraqi Freedom, March 29," via http://www.globalsecurity.org/military/ops/iraqi_freedom_d10.htm.
8. Anthony H. Cordesman, *The US–Iraqi Artillery Duel: Precision Artillery vs. Chemical Weapons?* (Washington, DC: Center for Strategic and International Studies, 2003), p. 2.
9. "Operation Iraqi Freedom, March 31."
10. "CENTCOM Operation Iraqi Freedom Briefing, 31 March 2003," via http://www.centcom.mil/CENTCOMNews/transcripts/20030335.htm.
11. IRAQWAR.RU, based on Russian Military Intelligence (GRU) Reports, translated by Venik, provided the author by George Mellinger.
12. "Naval Aviation: Few Major Lessons from Iraq," *Inside the Navy*, May 19, 2003, via Dr. Robert Mullins.
13. Robert Wall. "Old Field, New Client," *Aviation Week and Space Technology*, April 24, 2003, p. 78.
14. "AV-8B Harrier," via http://www.fas.org/man/dod-101/sys/ac/av-8.htm.
15. Alon Ben David, "Israeli-Made Decoy System Angers Baghdad," *Jane's Defence Weekly*, April 2, 2003.
16. Author's interview with General Michael Loh, July 13, 2003.
17. "Naval Aviation: Few Major Lessons Learned from Iraq."
18. Ibid.
19. Jason Sherman, "U.S. Super Hornet Proves Combat Reliability in Iraq," *Defense News*, June 2, 2003, interview with Commander Jeff Penfield, Commanding Officer of Strike Fighter Squadron 115, via Lon Nordeen.

20. Author's interview with vice Admiral Timothy J. Keating, June 4, 2003.
21. Author's interview with Robert Work, May 23, 2003.
22. Author's interview with General Loh, July 13, 2003.
23. Author's interview with General Merrill A. McPeak, April 30, 2003.
24. Author's interview with General John P. Jumper, June 17, 2003.

CHAPTER 6: AIR AND GROUND ACTIONS, WORKING TOGETHER

1. "CENTCOM Operation Iraqi Freedom Briefing, 01 April 2003," via http://www.centcom.mil/CENTCOMNews/transcripts/20030401.htm.
2. Mark Ayton, "War Diary," *Air Forces Monthly*, May 2003, p. 56.
3. Ibid.
4. Ayton, "War Diary," p. 56.
5. Scott Peterson and Peter Ford, "From Iraqi Officers, Three Tales of Shock and Defeat," *Christian Science Monitor*, April 18, 2003, via http://www.csmonitor.com/2003/0418/p01s03-woiq.html.
6. "Operation Iraqi Freedom, April 2, Day Fourteen," via http://www.globalsecurity.org/military/ops/iraqi_freedom_d14.htm.
7. Captains Benjamin W. Sammis and Travis A. Ford of HMLA-267 were the crew members.
8. IRAQWAR.RU, based on Russian Military Intelligence (GRU) Reports, translated by Venik, provided to the author by George Mellinger.
9. Author's interview with Vice Admiral Timothy J. Keating, June 4, 2003.
10. Paul J. Ryan, "Mine Countermeasures a Success," *Proceedings*, via http://imags.military.com/NewContent?file=NI_Mine_0503
11. Tim Butcher, "Dolphins Called In to Search for Harbour Mines," News.telegraph.co.uk via http://www.telegraph.co.uk/news/main.jhtml?xml-/news/2003/03/26/wdolph26.xml.
12. Tim Ripley, "Abrams Tank Showed 'Vulnerability' in Iraq," *Jane's Defence Weekly*, June 25, 2003.
13. David Hackworth, "Documented Coalition Losses in the II Persian Gulf War," *Military.com*, May 24, 2003, via http://orbat.com/site/agtwopen/iraq_equipment_losses.html.
14. "Laser Guided Bombs," via http://www.fas.org/man/dod-101/sys/smart/lgb.htm.

CHAPTER 7: A THUNDER RUN INTO BAGHDAD

1. Mark Ayton, "War Diary," *Air Forces Monthly*, May 2003, p. 58.
2. Mark Mazetti et al., "Pressing the Fight," *U.S. News and World Report*, April 7, 2003, via http://www.globalsecurity.org/org/news/2003/030407-iraq01.htm.
3. Ayton, "War Diary," p. 58.
4. "Operation Iraqi Freedom, April 7, Day Nineteen," via http://www.globalsecurity.org/military/ops/iraqi_freedom_d19.htm.
5. IRAQWAR.RU, based on Russian Military Intelligence (GRU) Reports, translated by Venik, provided to the author by George Mellinger.

6. Ibid.
7. Don Logan and Jay Miller, *Rockwell International B-1A/B* (Arlington, TX: Aerofax, 1986), pp. 1–5.
8. Author's interview with General John P. Jumper, June 17, 2003.
9. David Anthony Denny, "U.S. Air Force Uses New Tools to Minimize Civilian Casualties," *Issues in Focus*, via http://usinfo.state.gov/regional/nea/iraq/03031804.htm.
10. "Background Briefing on Targeting, March 5, 2003, via http://www.defense link.mil/cgi-bin/dlprint.cgi?, http://www.defenselink.mil/news/Mar200 . . . 04/21/2003.
11. Author's interview with Colonel Timothy H. Hyde, May 16, 2003.
12. Staff Sgt. A. J. Bosker, "Blue, Silver AEFs Get Rotations Back on Track," *Air Force News*, May 21, 2003, via http: //www.military. com/Content/Printer_Friendly_Version/1.1149..00.html@str_filename.
13. Peter Pae, "Friendly Fire Still a Problem," *Los Angeles Times*, via Lon Nordeen, Jr.
14. William Ayers III, "Fratricide, Can it Be Stopped?" via http://www.global security.org/military/library/report/1993/AWH.htm.
15. Timothy L. Rider, "Operation Iraqi Freedom Troops Receive Equipment and Training to Reduce Fratricide," via http://www.Monmouth.army.mil/monmessg/newsmonmsg/apr252003/m17frat.htm.
16. Kim Burger, "US Army Shares Radios to Avoid Gulf Fratricide," *Jane's Defence Weekly*, March 7, 2003, via http://www/janes/com/regional_news/europe/news/jdw/jdw030307_1_n.shtmal.
17. Author's interview with General Jumper, June 17, 2003.
18. Author's interview with Lieutenant General Bernard E. Trainor, USMC, Ret., May 14, 2003.
19. Author's interview with General David Grange, May 24, 2003.
20. Ibid.
21. Ibid.

CHAPTER 8: LESSONS LEARNED AND THE FIGHT TO WIN THE PEACE

1. "Operation Iraqi Freedom, April 10, Day Twenty-two," via http: //www.globalsecurity.org/military/ops/iraqi_freedom_d22.htm.
2. Dave Eberhart, "Iraqi V Corps: Mutiny or Surrender?" *NewsMax*, April 12, 2003, via http://www.newsmax.com/cgi-bin/printer_friendly.pl?page.
3. Bruce Rolfsen, "Air Power Unleashed," *Armed Forces Journal*, June 2003, p. 30.
4. Author's interview with Major General David A. Deptula, June 1, 2003.
5. Lt. Gen. T. Michael Moseley, *Operation IRAQI FREEDOM—by the Numbers*, Assessment and Analysis Division, USCENTAF, April 30, 2003.
6. Kim Burger, Nick Cook, Andrew Koch, and Michael Sirak, "What Went Right," *Jane's Defence Weekly*, April 28, 2003, via http://www/janes/com/defence/air_forces/news/jdw/jdw030428_1_n.shtmal.
7. Author's interview with General Charles "Chuck" Horner, May 14, 2003
8. Author's interview with General Michael E. Ryan, June 2, 2003.

9. Author's interview with Frank Hoffman, May 24, 2003.
10. Author's interview with General John Michael Loh, March 21, 2003.
11. Timothy L. Rider, "Robots Help with Battle in Iraq," Army News Service, April 22, 2003.
12. Commander James Paulsen, "Naval Aviation Delivered in Iraq," *Proceedings*, June 2003, p. 36.
13. Author's interview with General Homer, May 14, 2003.
14. Author's interview with General Loh, May 21, 2003.
15. Author's interview with Lieutenant General Bernard E. Trainor, USMC, Ret., May 14, 2003.
16. Courtesy of Colonel John Warden, provided electronically May 15, 2003.
17. My thanks to Major General David Deptula for his thoughts on these matters, via an electronic response to an interview conducted on June 3, 2003.

APPENDIX FOUR: APACHES AT ANACONDA

1. Rebecca Grant, "The Airpower of Anaconda," *Air Force Magazine*, September 2002, pp. 60–63.
2. Rebecca Grant, "The Airpower of Anaconda," *Air Force Magazine*, September 2002, p. 68.
3. Rebecca Grant, "The Airpower of Anaconda," *Air Force Magazine*, September 2002, p. 68.
4. Author's interview with General Merrill A. McPeak, April 30, 2003.

APPENDIX FIVE: "A PLATFORM OF LAST RESORT"—OVERVIEW OF THE NAVY'S F/A-18E/F PROCUREMENT PROGRAM

1. *"F/A-18E/F Super Hornet Milestones,"* via http://www.boeing.com/defense-space/military/fa18ef/fa18efmilestones.htm.
2. Loren B. Thompson, "Transformation vs. Tradition," *Sea Power*, June 2002, via http://www.navyleague.org/sea_power/june_02_05.php.
3. Bert H. Cooper, *"CBS Issue Brief 92035: F/A-18E/F Aircraft Program,"* December 6, 1996, via http://www.fas.org/man/crs/92-035.htm.
4. From *"F/A-18E/F" Super Hornet*, February 23, 2003, via http://www.global security.org/military/systems/aircraft/f-18ef.htm.
5. Chuck Spinney, "Howling Wilderness of Acquisition—Why the Super Hornet Is a Super Failure (II)," January 27, 2000, *Defense and the National Interest*, via http://www.d-n-i.net/fcs/comments/c341.htm.
6. From *"F/A-18E/F 'Super Hornet',"* February 23, 2003, via http://www.global security.org/military/systems/aircraft/f-18ef.htm.
7. From Wendy Karppi, ed., "Airscoop: Super Hornet Conducts Sea Trials," *Naval Aviation News*, March–April 1997, p. 4.

8. *"F/A-18E/F Super Hornet Milestones."*
9. Williamson Murray, "Hard Choices: Fighter Procurement in the Next Century," *Policy Analysis* 26 (February 1999), 12.

APPENDIX SIX: PERSONNEL RECOVERY IN OPERATION IRAQI FREEDOM

1. "A Piece of Iraq," *Air Force Times*, April 14, 2003, p. 14.
2. "Helicopter Squadrons Bring Rescue Skills to War Zone," *Navy Times*, April 7, 2003, p. 26.
3. Mary Beth Sheridan, "Raptors Hover on Edge of Battle, Ready to Save Downed Soldiers," *The Washington Post*, March 21, 2003, p. A6.
4. Mary Beth Sheridan, "Units Practice Key Search-and-Rescue Missions," *The Washington Post*, March 19, 2003, p. A1.
5. Lt. General T. Michael Moseley, Operation IRAQI FREEDOM—by the Numbers, Assessment and Analysis Division, USCENTAF, April 30, 2003, p. 9.
6. "Officials Search for Cause of Patriot Strikes on Coalition Aircraft," *Navy Times*, April 14, 2003, p. 13.
7. "Why Did They Die?" *Navy Times*, May 5, 2003, p. 21.
8. "Blackhawk Crash Kills Six in Afghanistan," AP, March 24, 2003.
9. "Suddenly, the War Turns Rough," *Navy Times*, April 14, 2003, p. 10.
10. "Tomcat Pilot Returns," *Navy Times*, April 21, 2003, p. 6.
11. Bradley Graham, "Patriot System Likely Downed U.S. Navy Jet," *The Washington Post*, April 4, 2003, p. A34; and "Patriot Missile Downed U.S. Jet," AP, April 14, 2003.
12. Bradley Graham, "Patriot System Likely Downed U.S. Navy Jet," *The Washington Post*, April 4, 2003, p. A34.
13. Eric Weiss, "Virginia Flier Confirmed Dead," *The Washington Post*, April 24, 2003, p. A14.
14. "Two A-10s Took Heavy Fire While Performing Unusual Mission," via InsideDefense.com, April 9, 2003.
15. William Arkin, "The Military Ain't Broke," *Los Angeles Times*, April 27, 2003, p. M1.
16. "Iraq Finds Allied Aircrew in Baghdad; Coalition Denies Reports," AP, March 23, 2003.
17. Anne Marie Squeo, "Drones Play Greater U.S. War Role," *The Wall Street Journal*, March 21, 2003.
18. Gordon Trowbridge, "Deep into Our Bag of Tricks," *Air Force Times*, April 7, 2003, p. 10.
19. Ibid.
20. "U.S. POW Rescued in Dramatic Raid," CNN, April 2, 2003; and Robert Wall, "Rescue of a POW," *Aviation Week and Space Technology*, April 14, 2003, p. 29.
21. Bill Gertz, "Team to Search for Pilot Lost Since the First Gulf War," *Washington Times*, March 22, 2003.
22. Jamie McIntyre, "Initials May Offer Clue to Missing Gulf War Pilot," CNN, April 24, 2003.

23. Bruce Rolfson, "Pave Low First Bird Lost in Iraq," *Air Force Times*, March 31, 2003, p. 11.
24. "Documented Coalition Losses in the II Persian Gulf War as of 11 Apr.," e-mail from Mr. Mike Sloniker, Lockheed-Martin (DCL).
25. "U.S.-Led Forces Strike at Iraq, Allies Unleash Ground Offensive," In *Wall Street Journal Europe*, March 21–23, 2003, p. A1.
26. CNN, March 25, 2003.
27. "Attrition," *Air Forces Monthly*, May 2003, p. 88.
28. Rowen Scarborough, "General Tells How Cell Phone Foiled U.S. Attack in Iraq," *Washington Times*, May 8, 2003.
29. Anthony H. Cordesman, *Instant Lessons of the Iraq War, Third Working Draft*, Center for Strategic and International Studies, Washington, D.C., April 14, 2003, p. 2.
30. "Attrition," *Air Forces Monthly*, May 2003, p. 88.
31. Ibid.
32. Cordesman, *Instant Lessons of the Iraq War*, p. 41.
33. Anthony H. Cordesman, *Instant Lessons of the Iraq War, Third Working Draft*, Center for Strategic and International Studies, Washington, D.C., April 19, 2003, p. 42.
34. "Documented Coalition Losses in the II Persian Gulf War as of April 11, 2003," e-mail from Mr. Mike Slomiker, Lockleed-Martin.
35. Peter Baker and Mary Beth Sheridan, "Marines Rescue Seven U.S. Prisoners," *The Washington Post*, April 14, 2003, p. 1.

Thanks to Darrel Whitcomb

APPENDIX EIGHT: SPECIAL OPERATIONS FORCES AT THE AL FAW PENINSULA

1. Author's interview with Col. Thomas O'Boyle, July 4, 2003.

INDEX